The PLO After the Lebanon War

Also of Interest

Galilee Divided: The Israel-Lebanon Frontier, 1916–1984, Frederic C. Hof, with a Foreword by Philip C. Habib

The Communist Movement in Palestine and Israel, 1919–1984, Sondra M. Rubenstein

The Middle East Military Balance 1984, Mark A. Heller, Dov Tamari, and Zeev Eytan

Security in the Middle East: Prospects and Problems in the 1980s, edited by Samuel F. Wells, Jr., and Mark A. Bruzonsky

†*The Middle East Since Camp David,* edited by Robert O. Freedman

†*The Republic of Lebanon: Nation in Jeopardy,* David C. Gordon

The Multinational Force and Observers in the Sinai: Organization, Structure, and Function, Mala Tabory, with an Introduction by Ruth Lapidoth

†*The Foreign Policies of Arab States,* Bahgat Korany and Ali E. Hillal Dessouki

†*Israel: Land of Tradition and Conflict,* Bernard Reich

Bibliography of Israeli Politics, Gregory Mahler

†*A Concise History of the Middle East,* Second Edition, Revised and Updated, Arthur Goldschmidt, Jr.

The Gulf and the Search for Strategic Stability: Saudi Arabia, the Military Balance in the Gulf, and Trends in the Arab-Israeli Military Balance, Anthony H. Cordesman

Peacekeeping on the Arab-Israeli Fronts: Lessons from the Sinai and Lebanon, Nathan A. Pelcovits

The Begin Era: Issues in Contemporary Israel, edited by Steven Heydemann

Deception, Consensus, and War: Israel in Lebanon, Shai Feldman and Heda Rechnitz-Kijner

†Available in hardcover and paperback.

About the Book and Author

This book investigates the developments within the PLO and its process of adjustment to a changed political environment in the aftermath of the Lebanon War. Dr. Sahliyeh probes the impact of the war on the PLO's political influence and bargaining power and examines the factors that determined Palestinian decision making after its troop withdrawal from Beirut. The Arab peace plan, reactions of the PLO's various factions to the Reagan initiative, and the PLO's attitudes toward Syria, Jordan, Egypt, and Israeli peace groups are also analyzed. The split within the PLO's main faction, Fatah, the conflict between the PLO and Syria, and the reconvening of the Jordanian parliament are among the significant issues affecting the PLO's political legitimacy and survival. The reconciliation with Egypt, the convening of the Palestine National Council in Amman, and the conclusion of an agreement for joint diplomatic action between Jordan and the PLO are also explored. Dr. Sahliyeh concludes by evaluating the PLO's ability to continue to exist as a viable political organization and speculates about various alternatives for its future.

The beginning of the book lays the groundwork for the evolution of the PLO's tactics and policies in the post-Beirut era. It seeks to offer possible answers to a number of questions: Why did Israel invade Lebanon? How did the Israeli public react to the war? Why was the reaction in the Arab world low key? How did the two superpowers manage the crisis in Lebanon and what were the constraints within which they operated?

Emile F. Sahliyeh received his Ph.D. from Georgetown University and is an associate professor of Middle Eastern studies at Birzeit University in the Israeli-occupied West Bank. He was also a Fellow at the Woodrow Wilson International Center for Scholars and is currently a Middle East Studies fellow at the Brookings Institution.

To my brother Hanna

The PLO After the Lebanon War

Emile F. Sahliyeh

Westview Press / Boulder and London

Westview Special Studies on the Middle East

All rights reserved. No part of this publication may be reproduced or transmitted in any form or by any means, electronic or mechanical, including photocopy, recording, or any information storage and retrieval system, without permission in writing from the publisher.

Copyright © 1986 by Westview Press, Inc.

Published in 1986 in the United States of America by Westview Press, Inc., Frederick A. Praeger, Publisher; 5500 Central Avenue, Boulder, Colorado 80301

Library of Congress Cataloging in Publication Data
Sahliyeh, Emile F.
  The PLO after the Lebanon war.
  (Westview special studies on the Middle East)
  Includes index.
  1. Lebanon—History—Israeli intervention, 1982- .
  2. Palestinian Arabs—Lebanon—Politics and government.
  3. Munazzamat al-Tahrir al-Filastiniyah. I. Title.
  II. Series.
  DS87.53.S25 1986   956.92′044   85-11469
  ISBN 0-8133-0116-5

Printed and bound in the United States of America

10   9   8   7   6   5   4   3   2   1

Contents

Preface xi

PART 1
THE WAR, ITS SETTING, MOTIVES, AND REACTIONS

1 Prelude to War 3

    Israel's Military Policy Toward the Palestinian Presence
      in Southern Lebanon 3
    The Arab World and Beyond 8
    The Second Begin Government 12
    Israel's War Goals 14
    Other Compelling Motives and Considerations 16
    Notes 22

2 Reaction to the Lebanon War 27

    Opposition in Israel to the War 27
    Opposition to the War in the Occupied Territories 33
    The Reaction of Arab Countries 36
    The Egyptian Attitude 43
    U.S. Policy During the War: Complicity or Incompetence? . 47
    The Soviet Policy of Inaction 54
    Sympathy in Western Europe 58
    Notes 64

3 Diplomatic Responses to the PLO Exodus from Beirut 71

    The Reagan Initiative 72
    Guiding Principles and Basic Positions 74
    Reaction to the Reagan Initiative 75
    The Arab Peace Plan of Fez 78
    Notes 83

PART 2
THE PALESTINE LIBERATION ORGANIZATION AFTER BEIRUT

4 Moderates and Rejectionists Within the PLO: Divisive Issues and a Search for National Unity 87

    A New Phase for the PLO 87
    The Views of the Moderates 91
    The Rejectionists' Alternative 101
    The Palestine National Council at Algiers:
       A Recipe for Inaction 108
    Notes 111

5 The Jordanian-PLO Dialogue 115

    Historical Background 115
    Jordanian Motives 121
    Palestinian Motives 125
    Problems for the Dialogue 127
    Notes 136

6 The Split Within Fatah and the Rift with Syria 139

    Prelude to Mutiny 139
    Grounds for the Rebellion 142
    The Syrian Connection 152
    Palestinian Reactions and Mediating Efforts 157
    Arab Reaction and Mediating Efforts 165
    The Exodus from Tripoli 168
    Notes 172

7 The Post-Tripoli Era: Toward a New Political Order 177

    Reconciliation with Egypt 178
    The Jordanian-PLO Dialogue Revisited 184
    In Search of an Elusive Goal: The Failure of
       Reconciliation Efforts Within the PLO 189
    The Seventeenth Session of the Palestine National
       Council in Amman and Beyond 196
    Notes 202

8 Epilogue: Arafat-Hussein Agreement for Joint Action 205

    The Future of the PLO 223
    A Divided PLO 226

Reconciliation Within the PLO 231
An Islamic PLO 236
Concluding Remarks 240
Notes 243

Afterword 245

Selected Bibliography 249
Index 257

Preface

Though the fallout of the Lebanon War has not yet settled, its implications for the PLO are well established. Not only has the PLO's military infrastructure in southern Lebanon and Beirut been shattered and its troops dispersed to several corners of the Arab world, but its influence and bargaining power in inter-Arab affairs have retracted. In addition, the tradition of preserving Palestinian national unity and the PLO's cohesion at all costs are no longer adhered to, allowing for more political flexibility and moderation. These developments are bound to influence the Palestinian nationalist movement, inter-Arab politics, and any future settlement of the Arab-Israeli dispute.

This study aims at examining the setting in which the Lebanon War took place and the motives that prompted the Israeli policy makers to invade Lebanon. The reaction of the concerned parties at the local, regional, and international levels are analyzed as well. The bulk of the study is devoted, however, to an investigation of the impact of the Lebanon War upon the cohesion, tactics, and policies of the PLO. It also deals with the means and the ways that the PLO utilized to cope with the exigencies of the post-Beirut era. The mutiny within Fatah, the PLO's main faction; its rift with Syria; the rapprochement with both Jordan and Egypt; and the resulting splits within the ranks of the Palestinian nationalist movement are also examined. The study concludes with a discussion of the Jordanian-Palestinian joint diplomatic initiative and speculates about the future of the PLO.

In addition to the published literature in the form of books and articles in scholarly journals, I have used a large number of interviews, press conferences, and speeches by various PLO and Arab leaders in newspapers, magazines, radio, and television from the summer of 1982 to the present for this study. These sources, particularly Radio Monte Carlo, provided ample opportunities for the various PLO leaders to express their political opinions and debate the several controversial issues concerning their organization in the post-Beirut era. I also dwelt heavily upon the various statements, pamphlets, and daily and weekly publications of the different PLO factions.

I am most grateful to Birzeit University's Research Center, which supported my research in 1983. My profound gratitude goes to Dr. Bakr Abu Kishk, the former director of the research center and currently the dean of the School of Business Administration at Birzeit University, for his encouragement and support. My colleagues, Saleh Abdul Jawad, Tomis Kapitan, and Tom Ricks, read several chapters of the manuscript and furnished me with the most valuable criticism and suggestions. I also benefited greatly from the comments of Dr. Mark Tessler during his several visits to my home in Ramallah.

Thanks are extended to Professor Michael Hudson, the director of Georgetown University's Center for Contemporary Arab Studies and Professor Harold Gortner, chairman of the Department of Public Affairs at George Mason University for providing me with office space and research facilities. My profound gratitude goes to Professor Larry Bowman, chairman of the Department of Political Science at the University of Connecticut, for his endless encouragement and moral support.

I was deeply touched by the continuous support from my students at Birzeit University and my friends and all of the volunteers who assisted me in collecting data, typing, editing, and reading. Without the generous help of these dedicated men and women, my book would not have been a reality. Finally, I am most grateful to my wife, Janet, who worked closely with me in typing and editing several drafts and compiling the bibliography since the inception of this study.

Emile F. Sahliyeh
Washington, D.C.

The PLO After the Lebanon War

Part 1

The War, Its Setting, Motives, and Reactions

1
Prelude to War

The 1982 war between Israel and the Palestine Liberation Organization (PLO) was not an accident, nor was it launched in response to a major military provocation or crisis: The war resulted from a deliberate, well-planned Israeli policy. The second government of Menachem Begin, which took office in August 1981, was dominated by people who firmly believed in finding military solutions to Israel's security concerns and strongly upheld the indivisibility of the "Land of Israel." They claimed that the PLO's military presence in Lebanon constituted a serious threat to Israel's security. Summer 1982 was a convenient time for waging the war because the Arab world was passing through a period of complete political disarray and the United States, Israel's main ally, was particularly sympathetic and supportive to Israel's security concerns.

**Israel's Military Policy
Toward the Palestinian Presence
in Southern Lebanon**

The two-decade period following the establishment of the state of Israel was characterized by relative calm and stability on the Israeli-Lebanese borders. The 1967 June War, however, altered this situation; the defeat of the Arab armies by the Israelis was accompanied by the rapid growth in the military power and popularity of the Palestinian resistance movement. In contrast to the conventional wisdom of the 1950s and 1960s, in which the regular Arab armies were expected to liberate all of Palestine, the new guerrilla movement advocated a Palestinian national struggle and a doctrine of popular warfare as the true means for emancipating Palestine.[1]

For purposes of carrying out guerrilla warfare tactics, Arab countries contiguous to the Jewish state assumed special significance to the PLO. After the bitter experience in the 1970 Jordanian civil war, however, Lebanon was expected to offer a safer haven for the Palestinian resistance movement. The political and military fragility of the Lebanese central government, the pervasiveness of socioeconomic cleavages within the Lebanese society, and the religious and ethnic sensitivities that continued to plague the Lebanese polity made the country an attractive base for launching Palestinian military operations against Israel.[2] Moreover, the presence of nearly a quarter of a million Palestinian refugees in Lebanon provided the PLO with a broad base of popular support and human resources.

In response to the PLO's operations, the Israeli government embarked on a policy of limited military reprisals to halt Palestinian strikes and provide stability for its northern borders with Lebanon. The crux of the Israeli policy was to hold the Lebanese government and various Lebanese groups accountable for the PLO's military activities. The Israeli government hoped to replicate its successful experiences with both Jordan and Syria in which it curbed guerrilla attacks. Because of Israel's punitive strikes, both Jordan and Syria had to cooperate with Israel to control the PLO-inspired military activities emanating from their territories. Israel hoped that by harming the interests of the Lebanese groups, including the Christians, Shi'ites, and Druze, it could compel them to work closely with the central Lebanese government to restrain the PLO's military operations and ultimately force them into a final military showdown with it. Similarly Israel aspired, through its policy of reprisal, to persuade the Lebanese government to dissociate itself from the 1969 Cairo Agreement with the PLO, which regulated the Palestinian military presence in Lebanon.[3] According to this agreement, the PLO was allowed to carry out military operations against Israeli targets from specific areas in Lebanon and have full control over the Palestinian civilians living in Lebanon.

With the outbreak of the Lebanese civil war in the mid-1970s, the collapse of the central Lebanese government, and the dismemberment of its army, the value of holding the Lebanese government responsible for Palestinian activities diminished.[4] From an Israeli perspective, the onset of the civil war in Lebanon was not overly distressing because PLO troops were tied down in the conflict and guerrilla raids upon northern Israel were deflected. In addition, Syrian intervention in the civil war, initially on the side of the Christian Maronites, tipped the local balance of power against the Palestinians and Lebanese leftists. This new situation forced the Israeli government to modify its tactics to meet the exigencies of the new order in Lebanon. In addition to continuing its policy of military reprisals against Palestinian positions, Israel initiated a policy of promoting local allies to fight the PLO's troops; this policy took the forms of overt military aid, training, and backing for some local Christians in southern Lebanon. At the same time, Israel began covertly to support the Christian Phalange party of

Pierre Gemayal and the National Liberals of former Lebanese president Camille Chamoun in the north.[5] Between 1975 and 1977, the Israeli Labor government invested $150 million in building up Maronite forces.

The overriding goal of Israel's new policy was to unify and strengthen the Christian troops vis-à-vis the PLO and its allies; however, Israel avoided direct military intervention on behalf of its Maronite friends. It hoped that its new alliance with the Maronites would further weaken the PLO and present vehement opposition to Syria's designs to establish hegemony over Lebanon. Israeli attempts to create local Christian militia allies in the south were further sustained by a decision to keep the Israeli-Lebanese borders open under the "Good Fence Policy" in which Lebanese Christians were encouraged to seek job opportunities and medical treatment in northern Israel.

With the coming to power of the Likud Coalition in May 1977, Israeli links with the Christian Maronites were further consolidated. At the same time, Syria's relations with the Christian Maronites began to deteriorate whereas relations with its former adversaries, the Palestinians and the Lebanese leftist forces, improved. As a result, the new Israeli prime minister, Menachem Begin, extended a moral commitment to protect the Christians in Lebanon against what he termed "the war of annihilation" and pledged to increase military support to them.[6] Israeli troops participated more actively in fighting against Palestinian forces in southern Lebanon and joined Christian militia forces in patrolling the area. In response, the Palestinians joined their troops with those of the Lebanese leftists, outnumbering the Christian forces. PLO fighters stepped up military activities against Israeli targets in the wake of the Begin government's intensification of settlement policies in the occupied territories and Begin's declaration that the West Bank and Gaza Strip were "liberated territories" and integral parts of Israel. Such military operations culminated in a guerrilla attack upon an Israeli bus on the coastal road between Haifa and Tel Aviv, in which thirty-four Israelis were killed.

Against this background, Israel launched its first massive invasion of Lebanon.[7] On March 14, 1978, the Israeli government ordered its armed forces to occupy a 10-kilometer strip in southern Lebanon to create a security belt free from PLO forces along its northern borders,[8] and by March 19, Israel expanded its military operation northward to the Litani River. The invasion was accompanied by heavy air strikes against PLO strongholds and its Lebanese sympathizers in the south. According to Ezer Weizman, the minister of defense, Israel had extended its military control all the way to the Litani River to define the zone that United Nations (UN) peace-keeping troops would monitor.[9] Both Israel and the PLO accepted UN Security Council Resolution 425, which called upon

Israel to withdraw its troops, demanded that the PLO cease its military operations, and proposed the introduction of UN peace-keeping forces.[10] By July Israel had withdrawn its troops and turned over the 10-kilometer security strip to its Christian allies led by Lebanese Major Sa'ad Haddad. The UN force was not allowed to enter Haddad's 10-kilometer Christian enclave, and Israel itself maintained a military presence in this buffer zone.

Israel's systematic and calculated bombardment of southern Lebanon during and after the invasion was intended to create a wedge between the Palestinians and the Lebanese civilians. Heavy bombing, in addition to vast destruction, led to the influx of tens of thousands of refugees to the crowded areas of Sidon, Tyre, and Beirut. Despite the presence of UN forces, Palestinian and Lebanese troops remained in southern Lebanon.

By early 1979, the Begin government proclaimed a new military policy toward the Palestinians in southern Lebanon—a policy predicated on the notion of preemptive strikes against PLO bases—whereby Israel would choose the time and place to launch attacks by land, air, or sea without waiting for PLO provocations. Israel and its Christian surrogates in the south continued shelling Lebanese civilians, particularly Shi'ite Muslims, to deepen the rift between the PLO and the local Lebanese.[11] In the radio broadcast of Haddad's Christian militia—"Voice of Hope"— statements were repeatedly made to the effect that if the PLO were not present in Shi'ite areas, no attacks would have been made upon civilian homes. This policy was stepped up in 1980: Israeli and Haddad's forces began to attack large civilian population centers, such as Sidon and Tyre, hoping to compel local Lebanese to evict Palestinians from their towns and villages. These methods began to pay off politically, particularly among the Shi'ite peasants who were unable to confront the Israelis; the Shi'ites formed their own militia, known as Amal, which on several occasions clashed with the Palestinian resistance forces.

In spring and summer 1981, the Begin government noticeably increased its military pressure against the PLO and stepped up military assistance to its Christian allies. In reaction to Syria's attempt to implement a limited program for national reconciliation inside Lebanon, which would allow more power for Lebanon's Muslim majority, Israel deployed some of its troops to preserve the privileged position of its Christian friends and to protect them from Syrian military moves initiated to end Phalange opposition. Begin's government did not welcome the Syrian moves and, as a warning, shot down two Syrian helicopters in the Bekaa Valley. In response, the Syrian government installed antiaircraft missiles in central Lebanon, increasing tensions between the two countries.[12] Meanwhile, the Israel government maintained its pressure upon the PLO in an attempt to force it out of southern Lebanon and launched a large ground assault in June. A month later, the Israeli air force waged a massive aerial bombardment against the PLO's headquarters in West Beirut. In return, the PLO began shelling Israel's northern settlements in the Galilee region. Israel's air raid resulted in hundreds of civilian casualties, prompting the administration of Ronald Reagan to dispatch Philip Habib as a presidential envoy to mediate a cease-fire agreement. Although it accepted the cease-fire agreement, the Israeli government never abandoned its goal of evicting the Palestinians from southern Lebanon.

Throughout the 1977–1981 period, several forces combined to restrain Israel's military behavior toward the Palestinians in southern Lebanon and check Begin's extremism. Despite providing massive aid to Israel, the Jimmy Carter administration exerted a moderating influence upon Israeli military operations inside Lebanon. Although the U.S. government supported the aims of Israel's invasion of Lebanon in 1978, such support was not unqualified.[13] The United States opposed an indefinite Israeli presence in southern Lebanon, which became explicit in the UN Security Council's swift endorsement of Resolution 425. The Carter administration was critical of Israel's use of antipersonnel weapons, such as cluster-bombs, against civilians; such weapons are prohibited by U.S. military sales agreements.[14] Carter also repeatedly criticized Israel's settlement policy in the West Bank and Gaza Strip, considering it illegal and an obstacle to peace; he was the first U.S. president to advocate the creation of a "homeland" for the Palestinians.

U.S. qualified support to Israel from 1977 through 1981 was also motivated by U.S. interests to "move forward in the peace process." The momentum generated by Anwar al-Sadat's trip to Jerusalem in November 1977 and by the signing of the Camp David accords in 1978 further restrained Israel's military behavior toward the Palestinians in southern Lebanon. In this context, Israel might have wanted to avoid jeopardizing its relations with both Cairo and Washington.

Another restraining factor was Israel's desire not to ignite an all-out war with Syria over Lebanon. In response to Egypt's unilateral moves with Israel, a coalition—the Front of Steadfastness and Confrontation States—was created and an alliance was in the making between Syria and Iraq.[15] Finally, Begin's first administration was more restrained in its behavior because three ministers in his cabinet—Minister of Defense Ezer Weizman; Minister of Foreign Affairs Moshe Dayan; Yigael Yadin, deputy prime minister—served as checks on his extremism.[16]

By 1981 these constraints were no longer present. The Arab world had become bitterly divided, and the momentum for peace did not survive Sadat's assassination. The new Egyptian president, Husni Mubarak, although adhering to his country's peace treaty with Israel, was also concerned about rectifying his relationship with the other Arab states. Moreover, the new Republican administration in the United States did not treat the Arab-Israeli dispute and the Palestinian problem with any sense of urgency. These developments coincided with the formation of the most militant and hawkish government in Israel's history; a government that resolved never to relinquish its control over the West Bank and Gaza Strip and harbored no illusions about its implacable hostility toward the PLO and Palestinian nationalism. These developments formed the immediate background against which the Lebanon War was planned and orchestrated.

The Arab World and Beyond

At the time Israel initiated the war in Lebanon, the Arab state system was feeble and fragmented.[17] Egypt's foreign policy in the wake of Sadat's trip to Jerusalem effectively excluded Egypt from any military part in the Arab-Israeli conflict and set it on a collision course with most Arab states. Several Arab governments, including those of Syria, Libya, Algeria, South Yemen, and the PLO, formed the Front of Steadfastness and Confrontation States in December 1977 to resist Egypt's policy of reconciliation with Israel. The rest of the Arab world was divided over Egypt's actions: Sudan, Oman, and Somalia supported Sadat's peace offensive whereas the others maintained a quiet posture and confined themselves to half-hearted opposition to Sadat's policy. Many of these countries dissociated themselves from Egypt when the Egyptian president concluded the two Camp David agreements and signed a peace treaty with Israel.

The Arab summit conference in Baghdad in fall 1978 witnessed the advent of a short-lived Arab consensus against Egypt. During this period of Egyptian ostracism, Iraqi President Saddam Hussein played a crucial role in orchestrating Arab opposition.[18] This consensus, however, lasted for a limited time; by 1979–1980 political developments had caused its breakdown. Besides the continuing conflict between Algeria and Morocco over the western Sahara and the existing Arab divisions over Lebanon between supporters and opponents of the Syrian and Palestinian presence in Lebanon, the Syrian-Iraqi hostility flared up again. The downfall of the Shah Reza Pahlavi regime and the advent of the Islamic revolution in Iran further contributed to fragmentation in the Arab world. Although the Islamic revolution in Iran was warmly welcomed by members of the Front of Steadfastness and Confrontation States, it was disheartening and disquieting to others:[19] Countries such as Iraq, Saudi Arabia, and the Gulf states feared an Islamic resurgence in their own societies.

Prelude to War   9

This situation was further complicated by the Soviet invasion of Afghanistan: Some Arab states supported and others opposed the Soviet military move.[20] The outbreak of the Iraq-Iran War in September 1980 further exacerbated tension in the Arab world.[21] Syria and Libya supported the Iranian war efforts, and early in the war they were reported to have extended military aid to Iran.[22] In contrast, Jordan, Saudi Arabia, the Gulf states, and Egypt sided with Iraq against Iran because of the Islamic revolution's challenge to the moderate Arab political order.

The discrepancy in the attitudes of Arab countries was so wide by the time the eleventh Arab summit conference was convened in Jordan in November 1980 that seven Arab countries, mostly members of the Front of Steadfastness and Confrontation States, boycotted the session.[23] Syria itself mounted a show of force on its borders with Jordan to display its displeasure about the convening of the conference. Less than a year later Crown Prince Fahd of Saudi Arabia put forth his peace plan as a comprehensive solution to the Arab-Israeli dispute. Fahd's peace plan, which implied recognition of Israel, only deepened the differences in the Arab world and led to the total collapse of the twelfth Arab summit conference in November 1981. Indeed, by the time Israel invaded Lebanon in early June 1982, the Arab world was politically divided, militarily weak, and plagued by hostilities and animosities. This situation may partly explain the Arab failure to respond to repeated Israeli provocations between 1981 and 1982, including the bombing of the Iraqi nuclear reactor and the annexation of the Golan Heights. Thus, the prevailing conditions in the Arab world directly or indirectly seemed to favor Israel's planned war against the PLO.

Outside the Middle East region, world leaders were occupied with two pressing international crises in the months preceding the outbreak of war. Martial law was imposed in Poland in an attempt to arrest the growth of the Solidarity movement, leading to heightened tensions between the two superpowers. Great Britain's dispatch of a naval task force to restore its sovereignty over the Falkland Islands was contested by the invading Argentinian troops. World leaders were also preoccupied with another threatened political conflict: Reports were circulating with increasing frequency that a major Iranian military offensive was planned against Iraq for late spring or early summer to conclude decisively the ongoing Gulf war in Iran's favor.

Aside from these crises, administrations with strong pro-Israeli sympathies came to power in France and the United States. The advent of the socialist government brought significant changes in France's Middle Eastern policy.[24] In contrast to the previous administration's policy, President François Mitterrand's government supported the Camp David accords and denounced Arab boycott measures against French firms that dealt with Israel. The new policy toward the Jewish state reached a climax when Mitterrand visited Israel in spring 1982. The reactivation of the Israeli-French Economic and Cultural Committee, suspended in 1967, was one of the main outcomes of his visit.

Just as the victory of the socialists led to the warming of relations between Israel and France, the election of Ronald Reagan brought to the White House an administration that, in the words of Israeli Foreign Minister Yitzhak Shamir, was "friendlier than any other American administration." Like Begin, President Reagan held an antisocialist worldview and projected a hostile attitude toward the Soviet Union. Both men believed in the centrality of military force in foreign policy. Though U.S. Middle Eastern policy did not shift abruptly with the advent of the Reagan government—because the Carter administration had laid the groundwork by advocating the formation of a U.S. rapid deployment force—the increasing militarization of U.S. foreign policy received a big boost by the new Republican administration.[25] The primacy of military force in foreign policy and the lack of urgency to find a solution to the Arab-Israeli conflict in general and the Palestinian problem in particular were two main features of Reagan's Middle Eastern policy prior to the Israeli invasion.[26]

According to the new U.S. administration, the primary threat to the Middle East came from the Soviet Union. This Soviet menace could best be contained by establishing regional military pacts, forging a strategic consensus, and enhancing the military capabilities of U.S. strategic partners in the Middle East. The notion of strategic consensus was predicated on the assumption that Middle Eastern countries, including the Arab states, would subordinate their mutual rivalries, hostilities, and grievances to meet the needs of U.S. strategic calculations in arresting Soviet expansionism and hegemony. Joint military maneuvering of U.S. troops and those of Egypt, Oman, and Sudan, various arms deals concluded with several Middle Eastern countries, and the signing of the Memorandum of Strategic Understanding with Israel in November 1981 were examples of U.S. attempts at building strategic consensus and enlisting cooperation in the Middle East.

In line with U.S. strategic thinking, Israel was assigned a key role in U.S. military planning for the region.[27] During his presidential campaign, Reagan told the Jewish Press Association that "Israel is a strategic asset for the United States . . . and indeed we must have policies that give concrete expression to that position."[28] In his first press conference as president, Reagan asserted that Israel's superior military force would be used to advance U.S. interests in the region.[29]

In an attempt to express the new administration's views on Israel's strategic utility, U.S. Secretary of State Alexander Haig, architect of this new policy, was dispatched to Israel. Haig reportedly left the strong impression with his hosts that the United States was prepared to adopt a tough stand toward Syria and the PLO.[30] Shortly after his visit, Begin spoke of the congruity of Israeli and U.S. interests in the Middle East and proclaimed that the visit reconfirmed the alliance between the two states. Their views were reported in accord on Syria, the PLO, and the Soviet Union. Begin declared that Israel and the United States had concluded that the Syrian troops stationed in Lebanon no longer served the "cause of peace" and that the PLO was a Soviet proxy that should be actively opposed. Begin also pointed out that Haig's visit reconfirmed both countries' opposition to Soviet expansionism and hegemony in the region.

The signing of the Memorandum of Strategic Understanding and Cooperation indicated that Israel was occupying a central position in U.S.–Middle Eastern military calculations. The Israeli prime minister commented that the agreement of strategic cooperation would arrest "the Soviet expansionist drive in the Middle East."[31] Though the agreement was suspended a few weeks later in the wake of Israel's decision to annex the Golan Heights, the thrust of U.S. strategic thinking provided Israel with the ideological cover necessary to vindicate its invasion of Lebanon because this act would lead to the weakening of Soviet protégés in the region.

Another aspect of Reagan's Middle Eastern policy was U.S. insensitivity to the demands and aspirations of the Palestinian people in general and the PLO in particular. An early pronouncement of the Reagan government indicated that fighting "international terrorism will replace human rights" as a key determinant of U.S. foreign policy.[32] The PLO was characterized as a terrorist organization, and Israel was believed justified in its "hot pursuit" of "PLO terrorists." Commenting on such official U.S. pronouncements, the secretary general of the Israeli Foreign Ministry stated, "We think that we will have more understanding of our need to strike at terrorism."[33]

In contrast to the policy of the Carter government, the new administration altered the official U.S. attitude toward the Israeli settlements in the occupied territories; Reagan declared that the settlements were "not illegal."[34] Such a policy statement encouraged Israel's inflexible stands on the future of the occupied territories—increasing settlement and systematic crackdown on Palestinian nationalism in the West Bank and the Gaza Strip.

In brief, the conception of the Arab-Israeli conflict from a superpower perspective and its relegation to a secondary stage coincided with Israel's long-standing attitude that political turmoil in the Middle East does not stem from the unresolved Palestinian question. Similarly, the centrality of military force to U.S. foreign policy, coupled with U.S. strategic identification with Israel, was likely to have influenced Israeli policymakers' thinking toward waging a war against the PLO in summer 1982.

The Second Begin Government

The June 1981 Israeli parliamentary elections brought to power the most hawkish government since the establishment of the Jewish state.[35] Prime Minister Begin, Defense Minister Ariel Sharon, Foreign Minister Yitzhak Shamir, and Israeli Chief of Staff Rafael Eitan—the four men who determined Israel's foreign and security policies—strongly believed in finding military solutions to Israel's security problems. They shared an unyielding hostility toward the PLO, a propensity toward adopting extreme military solutions, a belligerent foreign policy, and distrust and hatred of the Arabs.[36] These four men were also convinced that a final military showdown with the PLO was inescapable and that the policy of limited retaliatory strikes, followed in the 1970s, was not a viable means to halt the PLO's military activities. In their view, continuation of this policy would perpetuate the PLO's ability to threaten northern Israel. From the viewpoint of Israel's military planners, the PLO's acquisition of long-range artillery and multiple-rocket launchers further compounded Israel's security problem: The PLO was perceived as becoming a conventional military force in its equipment, deployment, and organization.[37]

This militaristic orientation of the Israeli government was exemplified by the destruction of the Iraqi nuclear reactor in June 1981, the massive Israeli aerial bombardment of West Beirut a month later, and the annexation of the Syrian Golan Heights in the same year. Mild Arab and world reaction, particularly that of the United States, to these provocations encouraged Israeli policymakers to go ahead with their decision to wage a war against the PLO. Israel's intentions to launch a war against PLO bases were known long before the actual outbreak of hostilities on June 6, 1982, as the debate over the military operation was conducted in the open.[38] Indeed, Ariel Sharon declared that he had been planning the operation since he took office in summer 1981.[39] In addition, the need to destroy the PLO's political and military infrastructure was advanced by senior Israeli military officers who wanted to establish a strong central Maronite government that would closely cooperate with Israel to expel the PLO and the Syrians from Lebanon.[40]

On December 2, 1981, Sharon was reported to have discussed his plans to destroy the PLO in Lebanon with Philip Habib, but the State Department in Washington did not take Sharon seriously. A month later, Sharon secretly visited Beirut where he discussed with his Christian allies his plan for the forthcoming war against the PLO.[41] Shortly after Sharon's trip, Chief of Israeli Military Intelligence Yehoshua Saguy visited the United States and met with senior military and civilian officials in the Reagan administration, including Secretary Haig. The aim of the meeting was to inform U.S. officials about a possible military operation against the Palestinians in Lebanon and to define what constituted a breach of the July 1981 cease-fire agreement between Israel and the PLO. Saguy also hoped to convince the U.S. officials that the cease-fire agreement should not only be applied to the Israeli-Lebanese borders. Around the same time, Israel's former ambassador to the United States, Moshe Arens, announced that the Israeli invasion was "a matter of time."[42] In spring 1982, journalists used various scenarios, maps, and commentaries in the U.S. media to speculate about the scope, nature, and intensity of the inevitable Israeli military operation in Lebanon.[43]

The timing for the invasion caused controversy inside Israeli ruling circles. Before April 25, 1982, the date for the final Israeli pullback from Sinai, a group of Israeli policymakers led by Sharon and Israeli Chief of Staff Rafael Eitan wanted to send the Israeli army into Lebanon.[44] In their view a large-scale military operation against the PLO in Lebanon would probably trigger a hostile reaction in Egypt that would countervene the peace treaty. Israel could then use this reaction as a pretext to perpetuate its control of Sinai. Sharon did not want to delay implementation of his war plans or wait for clear PLO violations of the cease-fire. From his perspective, any provocation emanating from Palestinian sources anywhere would suffice. Another group of Israeli policymakers, led by Prime Minister Begin, was more cautious about the timing of the war and favored returning Sinai on time because the war against the PLO could be waged at a later date to compensate Israel for the "national trauma" that it experienced as a result of its evacuation from Sinai.[45]

On several occasions, Israel tried to provoke the Palestinians in Lebanon into a breach of the 1981 cease-fire agreement by striking at Palestinian positions. On April 21, 1982, the Israeli air force bombed PLO bases in response to a land mine explosion in southern Lebanon, which resulted in the death of an Israeli soldier. A similar bombing raid took place on May 9. In both cases, the PLO exercised considerable restraint so it would not provide the advocates of the war in the Begin government with the pretext to implement their military plans. Through different channels, PLO leaders were well aware of the details of Israel's plan to invade Lebanon and instructed their forces in the front to refrain from responding to Israel's provocations. When the PLO failed to clearly breach the agreement, senior Israeli officials insisted that the cease-fire agreement should not be confined to Israeli-Lebanese borders but should include Israel proper, the occupied territories, and the world at large. This loose interpretation widened the opportunities for Israel to strike back at the Palestinian movement, as this arrangement was bound to be violated by any radical group within or outside the PLO that was dissatisfied with the agreement.

The assassination attempt on the Israeli ambassador in London on June 3 by an outside PLO splinter group furnished Israel with the necessary pretext to dispense with the "PLO menace" once and for all. For two days the Israeli air force carried out massive aerial bombing against PLO positions in southern Lebanon and Beirut, and in response, PLO fighters unleashed their long-range artillery at settlements in northern Israel, thus furnishing Israel with the immediate rationale for initiating the war.

Israel's War Goals

After its weekly session on June 6, 1982, the Israeli cabinet declared war against the PLO and announced that the military aim of its operation in Lebanon was to create a 25-mile security zone in southern Lebanon free from PLO men and artillery. The cabinet justified this goal on the grounds that it would provide safety and security to the civilian population of the towns and villages in northern Israel.[46] The declared limited objective of the war was ostensibly evinced by the name given to the Israeli military operation—"Peace for Galilee." The cabinet statement spelled out the limitations of the war: It was not intended to strike at Syrian troops stationed in Lebanon and it would be completed within forty-eight to seventy-two hours.

These limitations were reiterated by the Israeli prime minister in his speech to the Knesset (the Israeli parliament) two days after the beginning of the war. Begin declared, "Israel does not want any square millimeter of Lebanese territory." He added that the Israeli army would not attack the Syrian forces in Lebanon unless attacked itself and that the fighting would cease once the army secured the 25-mile security belt. "All that we want," Begin commented, "is that our citizens in Galilee shall no longer have to suffocate in bomb shelters day and night and shall be free from terror of sudden death by Katyuchas."[47]

The initial presentation of limited war objectives was intended to forge a national consensus inside Israel to back the government, prevent the war from becoming controversial, and generate sympathy and tolerance within the international community. Some of the real aims behind Israel's military thrust into Lebanon, however, began to unfold by the end of the first week of the invasion. The Israeli forces did not stop at the 25-mile security zone but continued northward to encircle the western sector of the Lebanese capital. Simultaneously, the Israeli air force launched a preemptive strike against Syrian antiaircraft missile bases in the Bekaa Valley and in the process engaged and destroyed a large number of Syrian war planes. The attack on Syrian troops was completely counter to earlier pronouncements by Israeli officials that they would not attack Syrians. Nevertheless, the destruction of the missile bases was fulfillment of the prewar Israeli objective of dismantling Syrian air defenses on Lebanese territory. At the same time the strike was intended to neutralize the Syrian force stationed in Lebanon to deter the Syrians from rendering any military assistance to the Palestinians. Israel also hoped to discredit Soviet-supplied weapons in the battlefield and preclude any possible Soviet military assistance to Syrian and Palestinian allies.

Meanwhile, Israel began to implement its plans to destroy the PLO's political and military infrastructure. The three-month siege of Beirut and the heavy bombardment of Palestinian positions from land, air, and sea, coupled with frequent interruption of the food, electricity, water, and medical supply lines to the besieged city, were indisputable signs of Israel's resolve to obliterate the PLO. Commenting on the expansion of the war objectives, Ariel Sharon stated, "We went into war to eliminate Palestinian terrorism in Lebanon. The goal was to push them twenty-five miles away from our northern borders in order to establish an area which will prevent any further terrorist activities." Israel did not give any guarantee to the Palestinians beyond this line; Sharon added, "When we mentioned the security belt, we never said that we were to leave the terrorists beyond this line."[48]

As the total destruction of the PLO proved illusory in view of the high cost, the Israeli government began to demand the withdrawal of all foreign troops from Lebanon. In an interview Israeli Chief of Staff Rafael Eitan insisted that Israel must achieve its military goals of getting the PLO out of Beirut, "since otherwise, we have to repeat the entire Lebanese military operation which will be many times more difficult."[49] Begin stated in a speech to the United Jewish Appeal, "We have to make sure that all the terrorists leave Beirut and Lebanon. None of them will be left. I can assure you none of them, because this is the only guarantee that we shall have peace, not only in our time, but also for generations to come, and we will."[50]

Another aim of the war was to create a strong central Lebanese government, presumably dominated by Israel's long-time ally, the Christian Phalange.[51] This objective became more significant because the Lebanese presidential elections were due to be held in August 1982. Israeli policymakers contended that such a government would prevent PLO troops from returning to Lebanon. The centrality of this issue was underlined by Ariel Sharon when he remarked that Israeli interests would benefit from a strong central Lebanese government. He inquired,

> Can anyone say that it is not in our interest to know what kind of government will be Lebanon? Will it be a government that will support the terrorists? Or it will be a government that rejects the terrorists? Will it be a government that agrees with the Syrian presence? Or it will be a government that will be ready to resist the Syrian presence?[52]

The conclusion of a peace treaty between Lebanon and Israel was also proclaimed by Israeli officials as one of the main war aims.[53] In a speech to the Knesset on June 30, Israel's minister of defense declared, "We are at the threshold of a new stage for peace where Egypt, Lebanon and Israel will soon form a triangle for peace on the Mediterranean."[54] The Israeli prime minister reiterated this position in his address to the United Jewish Appeal: "We shall sign a peace treaty with Lebanon that will be the second peace treaty with an Arab country that Israel signs."[55]

Other Compelling Motives and Considerations

Besides its publicly declared war goals, the Israeli government initiated the war for a variety of reasons. The Likud administration waged its war against the Palestinians in Lebanon to avoid some risks and unwelcome regional and international developments and to create new realities and opportunities more congruent with Israel's political preferences.[56]

For purposes of analysis, the motives that were operative in determining the policy pursued by Israel in summer 1982 can be divided into four main sets. The first set arose from Israel's determination to control permanently the West Bank and Gaza Strip and to arrest Palestinian nationalism and the PLO's political moderation. A second set was strategic: It included a number of perceived risks and uncertainties to Israel's national security and its regional military preponderance. A third set of motives covered domestic political considerations whereas the fourth group was economic and territorial in nature, coupled with ideological and religious justifications.

The Likud government, which came to power in May 1977, significantly changed Israel's policy toward the occupied territories. In contrast to the Labor government and its declared policy of territorial compromise with Jordan in return for peace and security, the Likud administration considered the West Bank (renamed Judea and Samaria) liberated territory and, therefore, an integral part of "Eretz Israel," or the complete land of Israel. Despite the signing of the Camp David accords in September 1978, officials of Begin's government did not conceal their goal of asserting Israel's sovereignty over the occupied territories; on the contrary, they ruled out any possibility of territorial compromise over the West Bank and the Gaza Strip. Between 1977 and 1982 Israel's policy was geared toward realizing Begin's dream of permanently controlling the occupied territories; the pervasiveness of such beliefs accounted for Israel's subsequent behavior in spring and summer 1982, including the government's severe crackdown on Palestinian nationalism in the occupied territories, the intensification of settlements there, and the launching of the war against the PLO.

Various ministers in the cabinet militantly opposed any form of Palestinian nationalism and believed that by destroying the PLO in Lebanon, the national aspirations of the Palestinians in the West Bank and Gaza Strip would dissipate. Indeed, the groundwork for the war—which would wipe out Palestinian nationalism—was laid soon after the second Begin government came to power. As April 25 approached—the date when Israel was committed to return Sinai to Egypt according to the Camp David agreement—the Israeli government worried about the second phase of the Camp David accords: The occupied territories would have to be addressed. Israel wanted to implement the second phase of the agreement—to establish self-autonomy in the occupied territories—in a way that enforced its own interpretation. This implementation was vital to Israel to ensure its permanent control, if not the ultimate annexation, of the West Bank and Gaza Strip.

Sharon began by replacing the military government in the occupied territories with a civilian administration and appointed Menachem Milson, a Hebrew University professor of Arabic, as the new head of the civilian government on November 1, 1981. Sharon and Milson contended that no link should exist between the West Bank Palestinians and the PLO in Lebanon and actively worked to promote the Village Council Leagues, which were made up of a group of villagers who ostensibly wanted to initiate development in the rural areas of the West Bank and were willing to work with the Israeli government. Sharon found Milson's premise of a "silenced majority"—who were prevented from negotiating with Israel by "PLO intimidation"—quite palatable.[57]

The elected mayors in the West Bank and Gaza Strip were asked to cooperate closely with the new civilian administration; however, they collectively refused on the grounds that the administration was illegal because it changed the status of the occupied territories and was a clear step toward Israel's annexation of the West Bank and Gaza Strip. In response, the Israeli government removed several mayors and their town councils, including Ibrahim Tawil, mayor of al-Bireh; Karim Khalaf, mayor of Ramallah, and Bassam al-Shak'a, mayor of Nablus, who represented the three major towns in the West Bank.[58] This move triggered a wave of popular uprisings in the occupied territories, the most violent since the Israeli occupation began in 1967, and Israeli military authorities along with armed settlers brutally cracked down on the demonstrators, killing twenty-one and injuring scores.

Israeli officials repeatedly attributed the upsurge of Palestinian nationalism in the West Bank and Gaza Strip to "PLO incitement and intimidation."[59] The war was launched, therefore, to destroy the PLO as an organized nationalist movement, to deny the West Bank and Gaza Palestinians any external political and moral support, and to deprive them of any point of reference, belonging, or national pride. In this context, Israel's defense minister declared, "The bigger the blow is and the more we damage the PLO infrastructure the more the Arabs in Judea, Samaria and Gaza will be ready to negotiate with us." He added, "I'm convinced that the effect of this campaign is reaching the house of every Arab family in Judea, Samaria and Gaza."[60] A similar statement was made by Israeli Chief of Staff Rafael Eitan in which he considered the war in Lebanon as a means to consolidate Israel's firm control over the occupied territories: "Israel is fighting in Lebanon to win the struggle for Eretz Israel."[61]

In addition to its attempt to affect adversely the political standing of the PLO among the population of the occupied territories, Israel prompted its war in Lebanon in response to increasing signals of PLO political moderation.[62] The Israeli policymaking elite anticipated the political repercussions involved in the PLO leaderships' attempts to diverge from their traditional strategy of armed struggle in favor of diplomacy and political strife as more reasonable vehicles to create an independent state in the West Bank and the Gaza Strip alongside Israel. The PLO's moderation would greatly diminish Israel's relentless efforts to depict it as a "terrorist organization" bound upon the destruction of the Jewish state. Israel's military expedition into Lebanon was designed to destroy the PLO's image as a moderate and reasonable body and to force the PLO into more violence and terrorism, thus contributing to the erosion of its credibility and respect; in turn any suggestion that Israel should open a dialogue with the PLO would be dismissed.

The fact that more than 100 states extended recognition to the PLO increased the Israeli fear that influential members of the international community would pressure Israel to make territorial concessions to the Palestinians and to deal directly with the PLO. Such fears were underlined by Minister of Foreign Affairs Yitzhak Shamir in a speech to the Haddassah National Convention in which he called upon all states in the world to dissociate themselves from the PLO.[63] He urged Arab countries to withdraw their recognition of the PLO and to stop their financial and military backing of the guerrilla movement. He made similar appeals to Western countries to close down PLO offices in their capitals and expel PLO representatives from various international organizations.

Equally alarming to Israel's policymakers was the adherence of the various PLO factions to the 1981 Palestinian-Israeli cease-fire agreement. The implications of the PLO's compliance with the cease-fire for almost one year were discomforting on several accounts. First, as demonstrated by its observance of the cease-fire, any future political settlement with Israel on the Palestinian question would probably be approved immediately by the PLO. The 1981 cease-fire agreement accorded the PLO considerable political legitimacy by treating the organization as an equal partner. Further, adherence to the agreement clearly signaled that the PLO was using diplomacy rather than violence to promote its political goals.

Arab moderation and increasing realism served as additional sources of anxiety to Israeli policymakers.[64] The introduction of the Fahd peace plan in summer 1981 constituted a further step toward an eventual Arab recognition of Israel. Precursor to the Arab peace plan (endorsed in September 1982, after the war, by the twelfth Arab summit conference of Fez, Morocco), the Fahd peace plan signaled the willingness of some Arab states to accord recognition and legitimacy to the Jewish state in return for a just and lasting peace if Israel relinquished the territories it occupied in the 1967 June War. Needless to say, increasing signals from the Arab world to recognize Israel were damaging to the Begin government's designs for the West Bank and Gaza Strip. Such conciliatory gestures could in the long run increase Arab political influence in the West and the United States, forcing Israel to come to terms with the Palestinians—a price the Israeli government would be unwilling and unprepared to pay.

In the wake of the return of Sinai to Egypt, the war may have also been intended to show the Arabs that Israel would not concede any more territory and that the Sinai compromise would not be replicated on other fronts. By occupying considerable Lebanese territory, the Likud government wanted to ensure that any new negotiations would be conducted around the newly acquired territories. The Israelis were certain that negotiations would be exceedingly difficult and time consuming, and this delay would give them time to create a situation in the West Bank and Gaza Strip that no Israeli government, irrespective of its political persuasion or political composition, could reverse.

The prospect of Egypt's return to the Arab world following Sadat's assassination, Egypt's recovery of Sinai, and the growing regional influence of Saudi Arabia (in view of its economic wealth and the strategic significance it received from the Reagan administration) were certainly not in harmony with Israel's regional political preferences and security interests. The neutralization of such unwelcome political developments was therefore deemed indispensable in Israel, and Israel's qualitative military superiority made such an objective feasible. Through its military campaign, Israel wanted to reestablish the prerogative of its military might and technological superiority by dissipating once and for all any Arab hopes of military victory. The Israeli prime minister stated that the war against the PLO "healed the nation" after the inconclusive 1973 October War.[65] Israel's vast arsenal of highly sophisticated weaponry facilitated this task. The Israeli chief of staff was reported to have told an Israeli newspaper, "Since I have built an excellent machinery worth billions of dollars, I must make use of it."[66] The building up of the fighting experience of the Israeli army further reinforced this military rationale for the war. Sharon pointed out that the new generation of soldiers and officers in the Israeli army recruited in the post-1973 war period had little actual experience in the battlefield.[67]

Although the United States assigned a central role to Israel in its Middle Eastern policy, Israel was not pleased with the growing attention that the Reagan administration paid to moderate Arab countries.[68] From an Israeli standpoint, the consolidation of the strategic dialogue between the United States and its Arab partner would adversely affect Israel's military superiority, compromise its security, and degrade its strategic utility in several ways. First, a U.S. policy of transferring large quantities of advanced weaponry to the Arab world might, in the long run, shift the regional balance of power in favor of Israel's Arab adversaries. This shift could convince the Arabs that Israel could be defeated on the battlefield, particularly after the inconclusive outcome of the 1973 October War. Second, because of Arab demographic weight and economic wealth, U.S.-Arab strategic cooperation could eventually diminish Israel's strategic utility to the United States and loosen the United States' firm commitment to help secure Israel's post-1967 borders. Third, a sustained strategic U.S.-Arab dialogue would prepare the ground for increased U.S. pressure upon the Jewish state to relinquish considerable portions of the territories occupied in 1967. Fourth, the Begin government was dissatisfied with the Memorandum of Strategic Understanding and Cooperation because it fell short of Israel's expectations of deeper U.S. military cooperation.

The war, therefore, was intended to disrupt the evolving strategic relationship between the United States and its Arab friends and to communicate unequivocally to the U.S. government Israel's centrality, if not exclusivity, in any strategic prognosis in the Middle East. In brief, through its initiation of the war against the PLO, Israel hoped to dissociate the Arabs from the United States. The Arabs would then be compelled to embark upon a hostile policy toward the West in general and the United States in particular, or alternately, U.S. inability to constrain the Israelis would embarrass the United States in front of its Arab allies.

Although officials of the Israeli government repeatedly asserted that Israel had no territorial ambitions in Lebanon, economic and territorial considerations may not have been entirely absent in the calculations of Israeli policymakers. Professor Eval Ni'man, leader of the Tchiah party and a member of Begin's cabinet, stated:

> The IDF [Israel Defense Forces] must be prepared for a long stay in Lebanon. . . . [T]he Israeli army in Lebanon will preserve our security more faithfully than any other force. . . . In the interim, Israel will reach a stage of social-economic development in the nearby region which geographically and historically is an integral part of Eretz Israel. Israel could possibly reach an agreement on border rectification. . . . It's also possible that Israel could integrate a strip south of the Litani, with its friendly citizens, into Israel's development plan.[69]

Israel's control of southern Lebanon would give it access to the Litani River, which could be exploited to meet Israel's water needs.[70] Further, Lebanon could serve as a market for Israeli products and a bridge for economic penetration into the Arab world. Such economic and territorial ambitions were cast in an ideological-religious disguise. The Israeli military rabbinate characterized the war in Lebanon as "a holy war" and as "divinely ordained."[71] The army rabbinate also published maps of Lebanon with Jewish names for villages and towns.

Finally, domestic political considerations were also operative in the Israeli decision to go to war. The support given to Prime Minister Begin by the Israeli public following the Israeli strike against the Iraqi nuclear reactor and Begin's reelection in June 1981 emboldened the hawkish elements in the Likud administration to launch a campaign against the PLO, particularly as the overwhelming majority of the Israeli public harbored no sympathy toward the Palestinian nationalist movement.

Notes

1. William B. Quandt, Fuad Jabber, and Ann Mosley Lesch, *The Politics of Palestinian Nationalism* (Berkeley: University of California Press, 1973).
2. For background information about Lebanese politics, see Michael C. Hudson, *The Precarious Republic: Political Modernization in Lebanon* (New York: Random House, 1968); and Kamal S. Salibi, *The Modern History of Lebanon* (London: Weidenfeld and Nicolson, 1965).
3. For the text of the Cairo Agreement concluded between the Lebanese government and the PLO, see Walid Khadouri, ed., *International Documents on Palestine: 1969* (Beirut: Institute of Palestine Studies, 1972).
4. For a useful study of Israel's military policy between 1975 and 1978, see Lewis W. Snider, P. Edward Haley, Abraham R. Wagner, and Nicki J. Cohen, "Israel," in P. Edward Haley and Lewis W. Snider, eds., *Lebanon in Crisis* (Syracuse, N.Y.: Syracuse University Press, 1979), pp. 91-112.
5. For further information, see Ze'ev Schiff and Ehud Ya'ari, *Israel's Lebanon War* (New York: Simon and Schuster, 1984), pp. 11-30.
6. Snider et al., "Israel," pp. 95-96; and Schiff and Ya'ari, *Israel's Lebanon War,* pp. 22-26.
7. Snider et al., "Israel," pp. 98-104. See also Walid Khalidi, *Conflict and Violence in Lebanon* (Cambridge: Harvard University Press, 1979), pp. 123-144.
8. *Jerusalem Post,* March 15, 1978.
9. In this context see the comments of Israel's Minister of Defense, Ezer Weizman, in *New York Times,* May 7, 1978; and his interview in *Ma'ariv,* March 24, 1978.
10. The Israeli withdrawal, among other considerations, was brought about by the following: the peace momentum, generated by Sadat's trip to Jerusalem, accompanied by an intense U.S. pressure upon Israel; the implicit Syrian acceptance to exercise control over PLO activities; and PLO readiness to cooperate with the UN peace-keeping forces.
11. For further information concerning the 1979-1981 Israeli military policy in Lebanon, see James A. Reilly, "Israel in Lebanon, 1975-1982," *Merip Reports* 12, nos. 6-7 (September-October 1982):19-20.
12. For a discussion of the Syrian intervention in Lebanon and its development, see Nigel Disney, "Why Syria Invaded Lebanon," *Merip Reports* 51, no. 6-8 (October 1976):3-10.
13. *New York Times,* March 17, 1978. For an official U.S. statement on the Israeli invasion of Lebanon, see also *New York Times,* March 25, 1978.
14. *Washington Post,* March 17, 1978.
15. The Steadfastness and Confrontation Front States consisted of Syria, Libya, Algeria, South Yemen, and the PLO.
16. For further information, see Amos Perlmutter, "Begin's Strategy and Dayan's Tactics: The Conduct of Israeli Foreign Policy," *Foreign Affairs* 56, no.

2 (January 1978):357–372. Compare this article with Amos Perlmutter, "Begin's Rhetoric and Sharon's Tactics," *Foreign Affairs* 61, no. 1 (fall 1982):67–83. Also, for a useful analysis of the impact of Israeli domestic politics upon cabinet formation and the resulting foreign policy, see Avi Shlaim and Avner Yaniv, "Domestic Politics and Foreign Policy in Israel," *International Affairs* 56, no. 2 (winter 1980):242–261.

17. For an assessment of the prevailing state of affairs in the Arab world prior to the war, see Allen Taylor, *The Arab Balance of Power* (Syracuse, N.Y.: Syracuse University Press, 1982). See also Allen Taylor, "The PLO and Inter-Arab Politics," *Journal of Palestine Studies* 11, no. 2 (winter 1982); Bruce Matti Weitzman, "The Fragmentation of Arab Politics: Inter-Arab Affairs Since the Afghanistan Invasion," *Orbis* 25, no. 2 (summer 1981); William B. Quandt, "The Middle East Crisis," *Foreign Affairs* 58, nos. 3–5 (1979–80); and J. C. Hurewitz, "The Middle East: A Year of Turmoil," *Foreign Affairs* 59, nos. 3–4 (summer 1980–1981).

18. For Iraq's evolving role during this period, see Claudia Wright, "Iraq— New Power in the Middle East," *Foreign Affairs* 58, no. 2 (winter 1979-1980).

19. John Cooley, "Iran, the Palestinians and the Gulf," *Foreign Affairs* 57, no. 5 (summer 1979).

20. Bruce Matti Weitzman, "The Fragmentation of Arab Politics."

21. Claudia Wright, "The Implications of the Iraq-Iran War," *Foreign Affairs* 59, no. 2 (winter 1980-1981).

22. *Washington Post,* October 8, 1980.

23. *Washington Post,* November 26, 1980.

24. Dominique Moisi, "Mitterrand's Foreign Policy: The Limits of Continuity," *Foreign Affairs* 60, no. 2 (winter 1981-1982).

25. Fred Halliday, "The Arc of Crisis and the New Cold War," *Merip Reports* 11, nos. 8–9 (October-December 1981).

26. For a detailed treatment of Reagan's Middle Eastern policy prior to the outbreak of the war, the reader is referred to Joe Stork, "Israel as a Strategic Asset," *Merip Reports* 12, no. 4 (May 1982). See also Amos Perlmutter, "Reagan's Middle East Policy," *Orbis* 26, no. 1 (spring 1982); Michael C. Hudson, "The U.S. Decline in the Middle East," *Orbis* 26, no. 1 (spring 1982); Walid Khalidi, "Regiopolitic: Toward a U.S. Policy on the Palestine Problems," *Foreign Affairs* 59, no. 5 (summer 1981); and Christopher Van Hollen, "Don't Engulf the Gulf," *Foreign Affairs,* 59, no. 5 (summer 1981).

27. Stork, "Israel as a Strategic Asset," pp. 3–12. Israel's strategic utility to the United States was partly influenced by the experience of the 1967 June War when Israel was perceived to have rescued pro-Western moderate Arab countries from Nasser's hegemonistic tendencies. It was also affected by the strategic cooperation between the United States and Israel during the 1970 civil war in Jordan when Israel was assigned the task of intervening on behalf of King Hussein. See William B. Quandt, *Decade of Decisions: American Policy Toward the Arab-Israeli Conflict, 1967–1976* (Berkeley: University of California Press, 1979); and Marvin Kalb and Bernard Kalb, *Kissinger* (New York: Dell Press, 1974).

24   Prelude to War

28. Jewish Telegraph Agency, June 16, 1980, quoted in Stork, "Israel as a Strategic Asset," p. 3.
29. *Middle East Observer,* February 15, 1981.
30. Schiff and Ya'ari, *Israel's Lebanon War,* p. 31; and *Jerusalem Post,* May 11, 1981.
31. *New York Times,* September 15, 1981.
32. See the comments of Alexander Haig in the *New York Times,* January 29, 1981.
33. *Washington Post,* March 16, 1981.
34. *Middle East Observer,* February 15, 1981.
35. Perlmutter, "Begin's Rhetoric and Sharon's Tactics," pp. 67–83.
36. Schiff and Ya'ari, *Israel's Lebanon War,* pp. 39–40.
37. The validity of this argument is highly questionable since the transformation of the PLO into a conventional force would make it vulnerable to Israel's sophisticated war machinery. This was evidenced in the Palestinian-Israeli war of 1982. See Yazid Sayegh, "The PLO's Military Performance in the 1982 War," *Journal of Palestine Studies* 12, no. 4 (summer 1983):8–23.
38. In this context, see *New York Times,* April 18, 1982; *Ha'aretz,* April 10, 1982; and *The Statesman,* April 12, 1982. See also Sheila Ryan, "Israel's Invasion of Lebanon: Background to the Crisis," *Journal of Palestine Studies* 11, no. 4/12, no. 1 (summer/fall 1982):22–35. For a revealing discussion, see also Ze'ev Schiff, "Green Light Lebanon," *Foreign Policy,* no. 50 (spring 1983), pp. 73–85. See also, Michael Jansen, *The Battle of Beirut* (London: Zed Press, 1982), pp. 1–5.
39. *Yediot Ahronot,* June 18, 1982; and *Jerusalem Post,* July 9, 1982.
40. *Davar,* April 17, 1982.
41. The trip to Lebanon was revealed by Sharon himself in a speech to the Knesset on August 12, 1982. See *Jerusalem Post,* August 13, 1982.
42. *Wall Street Journal,* February 23, 1982.
43. See *Christian Science Monitor,* March 18, 1982; *New York Times,* March 29, 1982. On April 8, 1982, an NBC news commentary detailed Israel's war plans, the size of the military operation, the equipment to be used, and the targets to be attacked. In Schiff, "Green Light Lebanon," p. 80.
44. *Jerusalem Post,* February 9, 1982; and Ryan, "Israel's Invasion," pp. 28–31.
45. In this context see the revealing comments by Israel's Minister of Foreign Affairs, Yitzhak Shamir, "Israel's Role in a Changing Middle East," *Foreign Affairs* 60, no. 4 (spring 1982):791.
46. See the statement of the Israeli cabinet in the *Jerusalem Post,* June 7, 1982.
47. *Jerusalem Post,* June 9, 1982.
48. *Times,* London, July 15, 1982.
49. *Ma'ariv,* July 2, 1982.
50. Israel Radio (English service), July 21, 1982.
51. Israel almost achieved this goal when on August 23, 1982, two-thirds of the members of the Lebanese Parliament were coercively assembled by the

Phalange militia to elect Bashir Gemayal, the leader of the Phalange party. Three weeks later Gemayal was killed by a bomb planted in the Phalange party headquarters in East Beirut, and his brother Amin Gemayal was elected in his place.

52. Israel Radio (English service), July 22, 1982.

53. According to the *Jerusalem Post,* June 10, 1982, the formation of a strong central Lebanese government that would conclude a peace treaty with Israel was included in Sharon's calculations before Israel invaded Lebanon.

54. Israel Radio (English service), June 30, 1982.

55. Israel Radio (English service), July 21, 1982.

56. For a very useful analysis of Israel's war motives, see Fuad Ajami, "The Crusade in Lebanon, Shadows of Hell," *Foreign Policy,* no. 48 (fall 1982):93–115. See also Jansen, *The Battle of Beirut.*

57. Michael Oren, "A Horse Shoe in the Glove: Milson's Year on the West Bank," *Middle East Review* 16, no. 4 (fall 1983):21–23.

58. The three mayors mentioned here, known for their pro-PLO stands, were also the victims of assassination attempts in summer 1980 by an extremist Israeli group called Terror Against Terror. Bassam al-Shak'a lost two legs when his car blew up, Karim Khalaf lost a foot in a similar incident, and on the same day Ibrahim Tawil discovered a bomb near his garage but escaped injury when police dismantled it.

59. In this context, see the views of the former civilian governor of the West Bank, Menachem Milson, in "How to Make Peace with the Palestinians," *Commentary,* May 1981.

60. *Times,* London, August 5, 1982; and *Time,* June 21, 1982.

61. *Jerusalem Post,* July 11, 1982.

62. For a more detailed treatment, see Y. Porath in *Ha'aretz,* June 25, 1982; and David Bernstein in the *Jerusalem Post,* June 15, 1982.

63. Israel Radio (English service), August 29, 1982.

64. Ajami, "The Crusade in Lebanon," pp. 94–96.

65. *Ha'aretz,* June 23, 1982.

66. *Yediot Ahronot,* May 14, 1982.

67. *Ha'aretz,* June 23, 1982.

68. For more information see the useful analysis by Adam M. Garfinkle, "U.S.-Israeli Relations: The Wolf This Time?" *Orbis* 26, no. 1 (spring 1982):11–18.

69. *Jerusalem Post,* June 24, 1982.

70. For an historical background of Israel's interest in the Litani River, see Shukri Najar, "Miah Nahr al-Litani Tutheer Shahawat Israel," *Shu'un Filistiniya,* nos. 129–131 (1982):106–112.

71. For more information see *Ha'aretz,* July 7, July 15, and July 26, 1982. See also *al-Hamishmar,* July 23, 1982.

2
Reaction to the Lebanon War

The overall reaction to the Lebanon War by the concerned actors at the local, regional, and international levels was incommensurate with the size of the invasion, the level of destruction, and the heavy casualties inflicted on Lebanese and Palestinian civilians. In Israel a small minority began to articulate arguments against its country's invasion of Lebanon whereas in the West Bank and Gaza Strip the war served as an added reminder to the Palestinians of the Likud government's uncompromising attitudes toward the future of the occupied territories. The prevailing anarchy in the Arab political system precluded any collective political or military action by the Arabs to salvage the embattled PLO. Western response, particularly that of the United States, the Soviet Union, and West European countries (the main actors directly and significantly involved in Middle Eastern politics), was also mild. Although the United States was tolerant of the wide range of Israeli war objectives, because they were congruent with the Reagan administration's strategic thinking, the Soviet policy response was notable for its low-level involvement to rescue its battered clients. In contrast, West European countries demonstrated a degree of sympathy with the Palestinian cause and expressed some willingness to restrain the Israelis in Lebanon. Their nonsuperpower status, however, did not allow them to translate their anger into tangible political actions that could limit the policies of the Begin government.

Opposition in Israel to the War

Although only a small portion of Israeli society expressed opposition to the war, the Lebanon War of 1982 was the first war in Israel's history in which considerable dissent was expressed. From the outset, a national consensus was forged concerning the initial war aims. During this period opposition to the war was extremely limited, particularly since the government proclaimed the immediate goal of establishing a 25-mile security belt in southern Lebanon free from PLO military presence. A few days after the war began, a small but articulate domestic opposition surfaced as Israel expanded its war objectives to include the siege of West Beirut and the military entanglement with Syrian troops. Some Israelis questioned the real motives behind the war, particularly as no major PLO military provocation necessitated a military operation of such magnitude and intensity. To many of these protesters, this war was the first in which Israel's existence was not directly threatened. The main dissenters at this early stage of the war were leftist groups. On June 8 the Israeli Communist party introduced a motion of no confidence in the Knesset against the Likud government's policy in Lebanon, but the move was defeated by an overwhelming majority of 94 to 3.

With the intensification of the government's military activities in Lebanon, dissent in Israel grew as opposition to the war disseminated through a broader spectrum of Israeli society.[1] Israeli public opinion began to cast doubt on the credibility of the army's communiqués and its war conduct. Criticism of the war came from six different sources. First, opposition emanated from the peace groups in Israel, including the Front for Democracy and Equality, the Israeli Communist party, the Sheli party, the Committee of Solidarity with Birzeit University, and the Peace Now movement. On June 26 many of these groups organized a public rally in Tel Aviv attended by 20,000 Israelis who called for a dialogue between Israel and the Palestinians.[2] A week later a second political rally, which attracted 100,000 Israelis, took place in Tel Aviv at which the immediate cessation of hostilities and the resignation of Ariel Sharon were demanded.[3] The demonstrators expressed support for the formation of an independent Palestinian state in the West Bank and the Gaza Strip alongside Israel and reiterated their call for a dialogue with the PLO. These demonstrations prompted progovernment groups to organize a large-scale demonstration of 250,000 Israelis on July 17 in support of the government's policy in Lebanon.

Second, protest was voiced by the relatives and parents of Israeli soldiers killed in the war. They staged demonstrations and published letters of protest in daily newspapers that denounced the war and urged its immediate termination. Third, Israel's academic and intellectual community questioned the real motives of Israel's military thrust into Lebanon and the feasibility of a military solution to the Palestinian problem.[4]

Fourth, members of the Israeli army who were involved in the actual fighting and had lost comrades provided opposition to the war. Some of these soldiers criticized the government's handling of the war and its insistence on solving the Palestinian problem through military means. They protested what they termed "the irresponsible use of the army and its military machinery by the government to promote political goals."[5] A group of Israeli reserve soldiers on leave from their duties in Lebanon demonstrated in front of the prime minister's office, denouncing the government's heavy bombardment of civilian centers in Lebanon.[6] In a letter to the Israeli prime minister, ninety soldiers charged that Begin was "spilling our blood and the blood of others on the behalf of the Phalangists."[7] In early August more than 2,000 reserve soldiers sent a petition to Begin demanding the resignation of his minister of defense.[8]

Dissent within the army reached a climax toward the end of July when Colonel Eli Geva, a commander of an Israeli brigade in Lebanon, resigned in protest of the army's heavy shelling of civilian centers.[9] The heavy casualties inflicted upon Palestinian and Lebanese civilians, the casualties and losses suffered by the Israeli army, and the disparity between the government's official pronouncements and the realities on the battlefield were sources of discontent among the Israeli soldiers. Prospects that the Israeli army might be stationed in Lebanon for a lengthy period and the government's compulsory military service caused added dismay. Again, some soldiers and retired generals of the Israeli army expressed the opinion that the Palestinian problem could not be solved militarily.[10] Such dissent within the army, however, should not be exaggerated; protesting soldiers and officers were in the minority. Discontent came mainly from reserve soldiers who were mobilized for limited periods (it is illegal for soldiers on active duty to voice their opinions).

Fifth, opposition arose from the principal Zionist political parties, mainly the ruling Likud party coalition and the Labor Alignment. Some members of the Likud party criticized the style with which Sharon managed the war; they were concerned about the government's reputation and prestige abroad. Such criticism also might have been caused by the power struggle and competition among the Likud party senior officials along with their fear that the war would enhance the prestige of Ariel Sharon and put him next in line to become prime minister. Criticism from within the government flared up on August 12 when Israel Radio announced that sharp protest was voiced against Sharon's handling of the war, particularly his order to the Israeli air force to bomb extensively the city of Beirut. Deputy Prime Minister and Minister of Housing David Levy, a contender for the office of the prime minister at that time, announced that the military operations ordered by Sharon on August 11 and 12 contradicted previous cabinet decisions. He also charged that members of the cabinet learned about the bombing only from the media—a very embarrassing development for the prime minister and the cabinet. Other ministers also opposed the army's occupation of Beirut. Mordichai Tzwpuri, the minister of communication, argued that the invasion of West Beirut would lead to heavy casualties among

Lebanese civilians and the Israeli army and also damage Israel's international standing. He further argued that the cost of a prolonged invasion would be prohibitive.[11]

The stand of Israel's main opposition party, the Labor Alignment, was ambivalent. Initially, the party supported the early aim of creating a security belt in southern Lebanon, which was clarified by the party's chairman, Shimon Perez, after his meeting with the Israeli prime minister on the first day of the war.[12] After a few weeks of vacillation, the political bureau of the party and the party's senior politicians talked openly of their opposition to the expanded goals of the war. They protested the army's occupation of West Beirut or any military activity geared to facilitate such an option.[13] In a radio interview former Minister of Foreign Affairs Abba Eban, while expressing his concern about the eroding image of Israel abroad and the deterioration of its international prestige, pronounced his opposition to the expansion of the original war aims. He called the siege of Beirut a "dark page in the moral history of the Jewish people."[14]

Senior Labor party members of the Knesset Committee on Foreign Affairs and Defense charged that government-supplied information was "misleading and deceiving."[15] They were equally critical of the means that the government employed to accomplish the wide-ranging objectives of the war. In a radio interview Shimon Perez spelled out the points of divergence between the Labor Alignment party and the Likud Coalition; he stated that his party supported the original war aims to bring peace to Galilee. In reaching the additional goals of the war, however, the Labor party preferred to use diplomacy. Perez was also skeptical about Israel's goal of creating a strong central Lebanese government once the Israeli army left Lebanon.[16]

Sixth, opposition to the war came from the Arab sector of the Jewish state, particularly from those Israeli Palestinians living in Galilee who protested the death of their fellow Palestinians in refugee camps in southern Lebanon. Many of these people had fled Galilee in the wake of the 1948 war. Memorial services and political rallies were held throughout Arab towns and villages in northern Israel.[17] Following the general meeting of the heads of local town councils, a communiqué was issued denouncing the war in Lebanon and calling for an unconditional Israeli withdrawal. Some participants characterized the conflict as "a war of annihilation against the Palestinian people and the Lebanese national forces."[18] A larger political rally called for by the Committee for the Defense of Arab Land and the League of Heads of Arab Town Councils was convened in Nazareth on July 10 and was accompanied by three antiwar demonstrations. In addition to their demands for an immediate Israeli withdrawal from Lebanon, the participants advocated

Israel's recognition of the PLO as the sole legitimate representative of the Palestinian people. They also called for the establishment of two separate states in Palestine for both Palestinians and Jews.[19]

The opposition in Israel articulated a number of arguments in support of its stands against the war. It argued that the Israeli government had misled the people by claiming that the primary aim of the war was to bring peace to Galilee through the expulsion of the PLO 25 miles from Israel's northern borders and that such a task would be completed within two to three days. They further argued that the war was waged principally for political goals and not for the defense and security of the country. The dissenters stated that the government also attempted to subvert the democratic process in Israel by arguing that wartime was not a time for political discussion. The opposition further contended that the PLO never constituted a credible threat to the security and survival of the state that necessitated a military response of such magnitude; accordingly, it suggested that the war was not defensive in nature—unlike Israel's previous wars. The heavy casualties among Israeli soldiers and the civilians in Lebanon and Israel's use of antipersonnel weapons, particularly the cluster-bomb, were additional sources of complaint for war opponents.[20] The cost of the war served as another argument in view of Israel's ailing economy, and still others worried that Israel was evolving into an expansionist, imperialist power in the Middle East.[21]

The government and its supporters responded to the opposition within Israel with a number of counterarguments. They pointed out that antiwar demonstrations were masterminded by the "enemy" and motivated by "self-hatred." In their view the opposition was aiding the enemy and undermining the morale of the people at home and the army on the front. Political discussion during wartime, they argued, was permissible only under one condition: that it did not assist the enemy. Concerning the expansion of the war aims, they contended that military objectives change in accordance with the realities in the battlefield and opportunities that arise throughout the course of the war. The government further argued that the goal of destroying the PLO's political and military infrastructure was debated publicly for some time. In addition, the destruction of the PLO was a worthy enterprise as it could lead to a solution of the Palestinian problem and the Arab-Israeli conflict and eradicate international terrorism. Proponents of the war argued that the often-criticized heavy civilian casualties came about because the PLO placed its forces and equipment among the civilians.

The influence and size of the opposition to the war inside Israel should not be overestimated; it was only a small portion of Israeli society. In addition, the leaders of the dissenting groups, including the Peace Now movement, were not in accord about the degree and intensity of their opposition. Despite their protests, the peace camp leaders were not hostile to the notion of creating a 25-mile security belt to ensure the safety of northern Israel but warned the government against going too far in its expanded war goals. At any rate, their influence was weak, and the lack of a firm stand by the U.S. government and its overall mild reaction to the war were crucial in minimizing the effectiveness of the opposition inside Israel. In this context, a member of the Israeli cabinet was reported to have stated, "I cannot show myself to be less of a patriot than the Americans."[22] The apparent indifference on the part of the Reagan administration led to a feeling inside Israel that the United States and Israel were coordinating their military moves and that the objectives and interests of both governments were compatible concerning Lebanon. Senior Israeli officials have on numerous occasions underlined the commonality of U.S. and Israeli objectives.[23]

On the whole, therefore, Israel's policy in Lebanon received widespread support inside the country. According to a public opinion poll conducted in early August 1982, 75 percent of those interviewed supported the government's policy in Lebanon whereas the war was opposed by only 19 percent.[24] Despite this overwhelming support, the poll further indicated that 76 percent of the Israelis believed that the war had failed to eradicate "PLO terrorism"; only 20 percent did not share this belief. Moreover, the poll delineated the divisions within Israeli society concerning the future of the occupied territories in the wake of the "military defeat" of the PLO. In response to a question about the preferred future status of the occupied territories, 16 percent of the respondents favored recognizing the legitimate rights of the Palestinian people, including their right to form an independent Palestinian state. In contrast, the return of the occupied territories to Jordanian sovereignty was favored by 37 percent whereas 33 percent advocated the annexation of the territories by Israel. The remaining 14 percent gave no answer.

Concurrently, the war enhanced the popularity of the Israeli prime minister and his minister of defense. Begin's popularity reached the level of 47.4 percent, 11 percent more than it had been at the beginning of the war.[25] Begin also enjoyed a fourfold lead over his nearest rival in the Labor opposition party, former prime minister Yitzhak Rabin, as the public choice for prime minister; the popularity of the Labor Alignment party declined by 7 percent. Similarly, the war enhanced the popularity of the defense minister, Ariel Sharon, by 15 percent. Sharon enjoyed a tenfold lead over his nearest rival in the opposition Labor Alignment party.

Despite these figures, the 1982 Lebanon War was the most controversial in the history of the Jewish state. Dissent of this magnitude during wartime was almost unprecedented. Unlike Israel's previous wars, this conflict was so prolonged and indecisive that it increased the prospects of casualties, which intensified the opposition in Israel to the war. Though the influence of this opposition was marginal during the war, it grew considerably in the wake of the massacres in the Sabra and Shatilla refugee camps and as a result of the continuing casualties among Israeli soldiers from Lebanese commando activities.

Opposition to the War
in the Occupied Territories

To the Palestinians living in the occupied territories, the news of the Israeli war against the PLO in Lebanon was shocking, as the war came after nearly a year of relative quiet on the Israeli-Lebanese borders. Equally shocking was the fact that the war broke out at a time when the PLO leadership was increasingly sending signals of political moderation. Moreover, the nature and the size of the invading forces left them with a deep sense of helplessness and frustration because of their inability to offer any credible assistance to their embattled brothers in Lebanon. Feelings of uncertainty and anxiety about what might happen after the war dominated West Bank and Gaza thinking. Such feelings were produced by the severity of Israel's military operation against the PLO and the ominous repercussions for the Palestine nationalist movement implied in this operation.

Despite these pessimistic feelings, West Bank and Gaza Palestinians resorted to any available means to demonstrate their support for and solidarity with the PLO. They issued statements denouncing the Israeli invasion of Lebanon and asserting the principle of the exclusive legitimate representational character of the PLO to the Palestinian people. On June 8 leading Palestinian personalities condemned the invasion and reiterated their support for the PLO. A joint statement was issued in mid-August on behalf of 150 national institutions including labor unions, professional associations, universities, municipalities, youth and women's organizations, and political and religious leaders.[26] A two-day strike was also proclaimed throughout the occupied territories on July 4 and 5 in support of the PLO, and spontaneous demonstrations, though limited, broke out in major towns. Throughout the war street demonstrations were staged relatively infrequently, in comparison with previous popular uprisings, because schools were closed for summer vacation[27] and because the war was preceded by a severe crackdown upon the Palestinian nationalist movement and its leaders inside the occupied territories a few months earlier. This crackdown included the arrest of demonstrators, the closure of universities, and the extension of town arrests of various nationalist figures.[28] Israeli military authorities also increased their censorship of local Arab press and banned it from circulation in the West Bank and Gaza. At the same time, the military government dissolved many of the remaining municipal councils in the occupied territories; the most noticeable action was the removal from office of the moderate mayor of Gaza, Rashad al-Shawa.

The shock of the Palestinians in the occupied territories over the magnitude and intensity of Israel's military operation against the PLO was tempered by a sense of pride toward the PLO whose forces had fought for weeks against sophisticated Israeli war machinery whereas in previous wars with Israel, Arab armies did not last more than a few days. Palestinian newspapers published in East Jerusalem highly praised the firm resistance displayed by PLO fighters throughout the war. *Al-Quds,* a daily paper known for its pro-Jordanian sentiments, commented, "Our young Palestinian men who stand alone to fight the massive Israeli war machinery repelling Israeli land, air and sea attacks have set a superior example for sacrifice, determination and clinging to every inch of the land." The paper continued, "Though Israel may realize some of its immediate goals, it will certainly not realize its long-term objecives of destroying the PLO and breaking the Palestinian will."[29] The pro-PLO Arabic daily, *al-Fajr,* spoke of its admiration for the PLO fighters: "The biggest surprise of this invasion was the heroic steadfastness of the Lebanese and Palestinian people, whose firm and determined resistance frustrated all of the aims of the Israeli military invasion and reversed all of its calculations." The paper added, "But the biggest surprise of all is the 'one common destiny' stand of the Palestinian people everywhere, symbolized by the PLO. The PLO is in the conscience of every Palestinian and cannot be destroyed or uprooted irrespective of the means of suppression."[30]

Aside from its deep sympathies with the PLO, the Palestinian press in East Jerusalem exhibited contempt, frustration, and anger at Arab countries for their failure to aid the PLO during the siege of Beirut. Arab attitudes were characterized as being incompetent, militarily inept, complacent, conspiring, and silent. *Al-Quds* complained that the tragic events in Lebanon were "treated by Arab officials with excessive negligence and cold nerves that drew the attention and surprise of all the strangers in the world."[31] After denouncing the Israeli invasion and Arab complacency, the pro-PLO newspaper, *al-Sha'ab,* referred to the Arab rulers as "a group of puppets moved by White House officials."[32] Criticism was launched against moderate and radical Arab countries alike. Members of the Front of Steadfastness and Confrontation States were denounced for their call upon the PLO to stay in West Beirut although they failed to provide any military assistance. Likewise, the Arab oil-producing states were condemned for their refusal to use oil and their financial assets in the West as political weapons in support of the Palestinian cause.[33]

The PLO's decision to evacuate its troops from West Beirut was met by widespread support and understanding in the occupied territories. Interviews with twenty-one leading West Bank and Gaza Strip personalities representing the professional, business, religious, and municipal leadership (expressing varying viewpoints on local politics), revealed that the PLO's decision to withdraw from West Beirut was unanimously hailed as wise, courageous, and rational.[34] In their view the decision was motivated by humanitarian considerations and concern for the protection of the West Beirut civilian population from intensified and indiscriminate Israeli military attacks. To some the PLO's decision resulted from a realistic assessment of the prevailing political and military realities stemming from Arab and international indifference to the fate of the Palestinians and their Lebanese allies.

Others believed that the decision to withdraw was made from a position of strength: PLO troops had bravely fought "the enemy" for a long time, thus frustrating Israel's attempts to obliterate the PLO and occupy West Beirut. These leaders also believed that after the evacuation the Palestinians would still feel like a unified and cohesive group, and they would firmly back the PLO as the sole legitimate representative of the Palestinian people. They argued that the PLO would keep the full confidence and trust of the Palestinians, and they did not regard the PLO's departure from West Beirut as a military or political setback. To some the dispersion of PLO forces would not end the Palestinian national struggle since the realization of their legitimate national rights should not be confined to one place or capital. Still others viewed the PLO's departure from Beirut as a sign of the organization's desire to pursue diplomacy as the main vehicle for accomplishing its political objectives. They contended that the PLO's decision would enhance its international prestige, respectability, and legitimacy, which in turn would improve the chances of realizing Palestinian national aspirations. Finally, those interviewed held that the PLO's decision to withdraw from Beirut was a sign of its autonomy and ability to make independent decisions.

In brief, reactions of the people in the West Bank and Gaza Strip to the war were directed at reasserting their loyalty and allegiance to the PLO—their sole legitimate representative. Expressions of such nationalistic sentiments by the Palestinians in the occupied territories throughout the war completely negated Israel's intended aim of dissociating the local population from the PLO.

The Reaction of Arab Countries

Arab states, individually or collectively, did not go much beyond verbal condemnation of the Israeli invasion of Lebanon and overall U.S. support for Israel's war aims. With the exception of Syria's short-lived military engagement with the Israelis early in the war, neither radical nor conservative Arab states offered the PLO any military assistance partly because of the overwhelming sense of helplessness and weakness among Arab monarchs and presidents in the face of Israel's massive qualitative military superiority and partly because of the bitter divisions and rivalries that plagued the Arab world prior to the outbreak of the war, leaving these countries too divided to act in concert against Israel. A collective Arab military response was further precluded by the fact that two out of the three confrontation states—Egypt and Jordan—had ceased to act as confrontation countries toward Israel. The signing of the Egyptian-Israeli peace treaty in 1979 neutralized Egypt, which had been the largest and most powerful of these Arab states. Since the 1967 June War Jordan had established a policy of avoiding direct military entanglement with Israel; this policy was clearly demonstrated in King Hussein's decision not to engage his army in the 1973 October War.

Although King Hussein was alarmed at the outbreak of the 1982 Lebanon War, he adopted a neutral stand. From a Jordanian standpoint, the expansion of the war engaging Syrian troops stationed in Lebanon could have led to an Israeli penetration into Jordanian territory to attack the Syrians—a development that would certainly have put King Hussein in an embarrassing situation. Hussein might also have feared that Israel's war in Lebanon and stated goal of destroying the PLO constituted a first step in implementing Sharon's plan to set up a Palestinian state in Jordan. Because 60 percent of Jordan's population is Palestinian, the Jordanian monarch feared that a PLO military defeat in Lebanon would lead to the radicalization of the Palestinian nationalist movement, which could have serious repercussions for the stability of his country. Thus, in a seeming attempt to placate the Palestinian population in Jordan, King Hussein expressed his sympathy with the PLO fighters and bitterly criticized U.S. backing for Israel during the war.[35] Although Jordanian Prime Minister Mudar Badran announced that his government would assist those Jordanians who wished to volunteer to fight alongside the PLO and that a ministerial committee would collect funds to assist Palestinian and Lebanese civilians, no official active encouragement existed for the Palestinians in Jordan to join the PLO troops. This inertia sharply contrasted to governmental pressures and inducements to its citizens to sustain Iraqi war efforts against Iran since the onset of the Iran-Iraq War.

Syria, the only remaining active confrontation country and a member of the Front of Steadfastness and Confrontation States, acted with considerable constraint throughout the war. Despite the strategic alliance agreement concluded between Syria and the PLO in April 1981, Syria's participation in the war was for a limited time.[36] Syrian President Hafez al-Assad ordered his troops stationed in Lebanon to observe the June 11 cease-fire agreement mediated by U.S. envoy Philip Habib only four days after the outbreak of the war. This action was consistent with Assad's post-1973 war policy of restraining the Syrian army from engaging in a full-scale war with Israel.

Several domestic and external constraints under which the Syrian regime was operating explained Syria's restrained behavior.[37] Mounting opposition within Syria by Moslem brothers and other discontented groups—culminating in the popular uprisings in Hamah in early 1982 and the consequent ruthless crackdown by the Syrian army against the opposition groups—led to the erosion of Assad's popularity. Syria also was becoming increasingly alienated from the Arab world because it backed Iran against Iraq. Strategic and military calculations compelled officials in Damascus to behave cautiously throughout the war. Israel's massive qualitative and quantitative military superiority, coupled with Syria's uncertainty about the reaction in the Soviet Union to a full-scale war, had persuaded Syria's decision-makers to refrain from tangling with the Israelis. Moreover, the fact that Israel was waging its war on Lebanese and not Syrian territory diminished Syria's incentives to confront the Israelis, particularly since the Assad regime was anxious to maintain its special status and privileged position in Lebanon. Any serious challenge to Israeli war aims in Lebanon could have resulted in a large-scale war between the two states, leading to the eviction of Syrian troops from Lebanon. Although Syria's policymakers were keen to avoid such an outcome, Assad was equally concerned not to pay an intolerable price for joining the war in terms of casualties and losses in military equipment that would further demoralize his army.[38]

Libya, Syria's main partner in the Front of Steadfastness and Confrontation States and the most vocal Arab country, did not go beyond verbal bellicosity, condemnation of the Israeli invasion, and harsh criticism of Arab incompetence in responding to Israeli provocation. Libya also sharply denounced the United States, the main supporter of Israel's war efforts. Toward the end of June, Mu'ammar al-Qaddafi, the Libyan leader, called upon Arab heads of state to dispatch ten military divisions and 500 war planes to Lebanon to fight alongside the Palestinians and the Lebanese nationalists. He also urged Arab countries to reject U.S. mediation, expel Philip Habib, and impose economic sanctions upon Western countries, including an oil embargo and the withdrawal of assets from Western banks.[39] In response to reports of the PLO's intentions to leave West Beirut, the Libyan leader sent an urgent appeal to the PLO leadership to "commit suicide" rather than withdraw, an act that would "immortalize the Palestinian cause."[40] In reaction, Yasir Arafat bitterly attacked such empty slogans and unfulfilled military pledges, which in his opinion accounted for the tragic conditions in Lebanon. Arafat also reminded Qaddafi that no support was forthcoming from any Arab country to the besieged PLO and expressed his astonishment at Qaddafi's pessimism.[41]

The Arab's policy of inaction was not confined to the military level: Arab oil-producing states were reluctant to use economic sanctions against the West. On June 16, 1982, Arab members of the Organization of Petroleum Exporting Countries (OPEC) rejected a Libyan demand to impose an oil embargo against the West. Saudi Arabia, the most influential member of OPEC, was opposed throughout the war to any imposition of economic sanctions. During the Arab League emergency session of foreign ministers, convened in Tunis on June 26, 1982, Prince Saud al-Faisal of Saudi Arabia stated that his country would not consider an oil embargo or economic sanctions against the West.[42] The reluctance of the Arab oil-producing states to use their economic power possibly resulted from the oil glut in the world market, which diminished the effectiveness of using oil as a political weapon and led to a reciprocal decline in the power of OPEC members.[43] The United States, the main target of an oil embargo, was reported to have a strategic two-year supply of oil in case a ban was imposed on the flow of oil from the Arab world. Arab countries felt further constrained by the fact that Saudi Arabia and the Gulf states were tied to the Western economic system, thus depriving Arab countries of any real alternative to withdrawing their financial assets. Similarly, the military reliance of these countries upon the United States and perceived security threats emanating from the Iran-Iraq War diminished the rationale to use Arab economic leverage against the West.

Despite repeated calls by several Arab countries for a summit conference of Arab heads of state to discuss how to cope with the Israeli invasion of Lebanon, the necessary two-thirds majority of the Arab League members was not forthcoming.[44] Arab rulers' failure to meet during the war was predictable. The mere fact of convening a summit for Arab monarchs and presidents during the crisis would have obligated the rulers to make decisive resolutions and implement them. Shying away from attempting such a task was partly caused by the military weakness of the Arab states in the face of Israel's military superiority. In addition, for Arab actions to be effective, they had to be collectively presented to the West and in particular to the United States—Israel's main custodian—in the form of threats or inducements. The lack of an Arab consensus precluded that from happening. Similarly, because of their bitter divisions and mutual hostilities, Arab states were unable to decide on a unified policy on how to manage the Israeli invasion. Some Arab countries probably were not happy about the prospect of a summit conference failing, particularly at a time when Israel was pounding an Arab capital and was firm in its drive to obliterate the PLO.

Arab reluctance to attend a summit conference also was caused by a disagreement over the agenda of the proposed conference. From a Palestinian perspective, the agenda of a summit meeting should naturally focus on the various options to repel the Israeli invasion whereas for the Lebanese government the priority of an Arab conference should be to preserve Lebanese territorial integrity and national unity and to demand the withdrawal of foreign forces from Lebanon, including those of Syria, Israel, and the PLO. In contrast, Saudi Arabia preferred to resume the postponed 1981 summit conference in Morocco that would have entailed the examination of the Fahd peace plan. Other Arab countries, such as Jordan and Iraq, made their participation in the summit conference contingent upon discussing the Iraq-Iran War, Syrian aid to Iran, and the role of the Syrian forces in Lebanon.

The possibility cannot be entirely dismissed, however, that some moderate Arab countries were not too displeased with Israel's war against the PLO. A militarily weak PLO would be easier to deal with than a viable PLO with an independent base of operation. A humiliated PLO might be forced into a more conciliatory posture for peaceful accommodation with Israel, and a crippled PLO would diminish its ability to stir up violence in the region. To Arab radicals like Libya Israel's war against the PLO reconfirmed Libyan convictions of "no compromise with Israel and the United States." Radicals hoped that Israeli occupation of Lebanon would increase the support for forces of rejectionism in the region, slow down Egyptian attempts to rejoin the Arab fold, and direct the PLO leadership toward a more amiable posture in line with Qaddafi's thinking.[45]

On the other hand, total destruction of the PLO by the Israelis would be disquieting to Arab rulers on four main accounts. First, the massive bombing by Israel of an Arab capital and its siege were the strongest confirmation to the Arab masses of the military weakness or indifference of their leaders. Second, the dismemberment of the PLO would probably change the Palestinian question into an Arab issue, as happened between 1948 and 1967. Such an eventuality would necessarily require that Arab countries and their armies once again "liberate Palestine" on behalf of the Palestinians, particularly if a diplomatic solution was not forthcoming.

Third, it is unlikely that Arab leaders would be willing to assume the onus of presiding over the territorial concessions that would be requisite for a political settlement with Israel—a role they would prefer the PLO to play. Fourth, complete destruction of the PLO's political and military infrastructure in Lebanon could force the Palestinians into radicalism and violence out of desperation. From an Arab perspective, this development would adversely affect the stability of Arab regimes, erode the PLO's international legitimacy, and dissipate any hopes of a settlement to the Arab-Israeli conflict.

Arab leaders used several approaches to preserve the relative viability of the PLO and to quiet public criticism. The emergency meeting of the Arab foreign ministers in Tunis toward the end of June 1982 set up an ad hoc six-member committee that dispatched delegations to the permanent members of the UN Security Council to rally support for the "Arab cause."[46] Individual Arab countries, particularly Jordan, Saudi Arabia and Egypt, sent their own diplomatic envoys to various Arab and Western capitals for consultation. Letters and cables were forwarded to world leaders, particularly those of the two superpowers and Western European countries. The immediate concern of these diplomatic efforts was to disengage the fighting forces and lift the siege of Beirut in order to ensure the physical survival of the Palestinian leadership and its fighters against a final imminent Israeli assault. After the failure to separate the fighting forces, Arab diplomatic efforts aimed at securing a safe conduct for the PLO's leadership out of Beirut. This goal was behind the meeting of the foreign ministers of Saudi Arabia and Syria with President Reagan on July 20, 1982. Beyond these immediate concerns, Arab diplomatic endeavors were intended to enlist support for long-term solutions to the Lebanese crisis and the Palestinian problem.

Denouncing the Israeli invasion into Lebanon and U.S. support to Israel was another avenue used by Arabs to deflect public criticism. Members of the Gulf Cooperation Council in their final communiqué warned the United States that Israel's occupation of West Beirut would "threaten regional and international stability."[47] In a similar move, a Saudi official statement broadcast by Radio Riyad on July 20, 1982, called upon the various members of the UN Security Council to impose economic and military sanctions upon Israel to force the Begin government to withdraw its troops from Lebanon. The Arab countries also resorted to the UN General Assembly as a forum from which to enlist support for the PLO. The Arab bloc countries called for a special emergency session of the General Assembly to condemn the Israeli invasion of Lebanon and demand the imposition of sanctions upon the Jewish state.[48] They further asked for the implementation of previous UN resolutions on the Palestinian question, particularly those calling for the Palestinian right to self-determination and the creation of an independent Palestinian state in the West Bank and Gaza Strip.

The Arab media, particularly the press, served as an additional outlet for Arab anger. Irrespective of its political orientation, the Arab press charged the United States with collaboration and partnership in the war, though the degree of U.S. involvement was perceived differently by Arab moderates and radicals. The outbreak of the war was met with severe hostile reaction in the press of the radical Arab countries, including Syria, Libya, South Yemen, and Algeria.[49] In their view, the war was intended to impose "imperialist and Zionist hegemony" in the Middle East and bring the region under the U.S. umbrella. The media in these countries criticized pro-Western moderate Arab states for failing to develop a counterstrategy to repel the Israeli invasion and accused them of being silent partners in the war.[50]

The press in the moderate Arab countries exhibited a similar degree of hostility toward the West and in particular toward the United States.[51] It held the U.S. government responsible for Israel's continued violations of the cease-fire, charging that Washington supplied Israel with advanced weapons that enabled the Israeli government to launch its "aggressive war" into Lebanon. Mild U.S. reaction to the war and the Reagan government's frequent use of its veto power to defeat UN Security Council resolutions that denounced the Israeli invasion furnished additional grounds for bitter criticism. The moderate Arab press called for solidarity and reconciliation to meet the challenges of Israel's massive military operation in Lebanon and urged the Arabs to "shy away from the devastating effects of their disunity" and the "futility of their divisions and rivalries."

The decision of the PLO leadership to withdraw its troops from West Beirut to areas outside Lebanon was seen by most Arab countries as a mixed blessing. Although the decision meant an end to the siege of the city and diffusion of tensions, the withdrawal was a source of great embarrassment to the Arab countries. It also meant that the Arab world would have to accommodate the departing Palestinian troops. Though ultimately Jordan, Iraq, Syria, North Yemen, South Yemen, Algeria, Tunisia, and Sudan expressed their willingness to give sanctuary to PLO forces, none of the Arab countries wanted to have a large concentration of PLO fighters stationed in its territory. This reserve was partly a response to fears of adverse domestic repercussions and political instability that would accompany a Palestinian military presence. The possible exploitation of these armed Palestinians in a recipient country by a rival Arab regime served as a disincentive to accommodate large numbers of Palestinian fighters. Thus individual Arab countries that indicated willingness to absorb evacuated PLO troops demanded that the PLO fighters be returned to their countries of origin; for example, a Palestinian fighter with an Iraqi connection should be returned to Iraq or a Palestinian fighter with ties to Syria should be returned to Syria. Political and ideological affinities of the departing PLO troops also played a part in their admission into Arab countries. Many Arab states stipulated that the evacuated Palestinians should be placed in camps far from urban centers.

Other Arab countries demanded that their territories should not be used for initiating military operations or military planning against Israel. In response to Arafat's desire to make Tunis a new political headquarters, the Tunisian prime minister indicated that the city would only serve as a political base for the PLO and could not be used as a center for military planning.[52] In a complete reversal of his post-1970 civil war policy, King Hussein agreed to accept 1,000 PLO soldiers in Jordan. During an interview with a U.S. television network, the Jordanian ambassador to the United States stated that this shift in policy was an attempt to terminate the Lebanese conflict and deny Israel any pretext of prolonging its occupation of Lebanon.[53] He added that this shift was made possible after an understanding had been reached with the PLO leadership that Jordanian territory would not be used for military activities against Israel. This policy, he argued, was in line with Jordan's desire to reach a peaceful settlement to the Arab-Israeli dispute, and he expressed the hope that the PLO would join Jordan in that endeavor.

In a letter to the PLO chairman, the Jordanian government spelled out three conditions for receiving PLO troops.[54] First, Jordan agreed to readmit the Palestine Liberation Army unit that was stationed in Jordan before the outbreak of hostilities. Second, PLO soldiers carrying valid or expired Jordanian passports were allowed to return to Jordan provided that Jordan would be notified in advance of their names and that they had not been convicted by Jordanian courts. Third, the government statement stressed that those PLO elements wishing to come back to Jordan should give up their military struggle and live as normal law-abiding citizens.[55]

The position of the Syrian government on the question of admitting PLO soldiers was more complex. Initially, President Assad rejected the whole notion of the PLO troops' withdrawal from West Beirut and declined to grant sanctuary to PLO fighters.[56] Syrian officials repeatedly argued that the diplomatic mission of Philip Habib should concentrate on the withdrawal of the "Israeli invading army" from Lebanon and not the withdrawal of the Palestinian troops.[57] The Syrian government justified its opposition to the evacuation of PLO forces on the grounds that Syria was greatly concerned with keeping the Palestinian question alive. Syrian Foreign Minister Abd al-Halim Khaddom stated that Syria would not receive any PLO troops because this action would mean "a liquidation of the Palestinian cause and revolution." He added that the Palestinians should stay where they were, awaiting the realization of their national aspirations.[58]

Shortly before the actual departure of the PLO from West Beirut, however, the Syrian government altered its posture. A government statement announced that Damascus would be willing to admit as many PLO soldiers as wished to go there. According to official Syrian accounts, this decision was only taken in the wake of formal, direct requests by the PLO leadership to evacuate some troops to Syria. "When the Palestinians see it in their best interests to leave West Beirut," commented the Syrian ambassador to the United States, "we are bound to receive them."[59] Despite this official Syrian rationale, the shift in the government's position on the PLO's withdrawal was certainly caused by more serious considerations. One cannot exclude the possibility that the shift was brought about by increasing Arab pressures, especially that of Saudi Arabia. The shift could have also been generated by Syria's increasing recognition of Israel's military determination to wipe out West Beirut— a development that would further undermine and embarrass the "pan-Arab regime" in Damascus. The fact that Syria was still maintaining one army unit inside the besieged city was also critical in the Syrian decision.

Alternatively, the switch in Syria's posture emanated from its desire to preserve its leverage and influence over the Palestinian resistance movement. The readiness of Iraq and Jordan (Syria's implacable adversaries) to admit some PLO fighters aroused anxieties in Damascus that Syria might be losing its control over the PLO in favor of Jordan and Iraq. The Soviet Union, which earlier opposed the PLO's departure as part of its policy to undermine U.S. diplomacy, eventually allowed Syria, its main client in the region, to participate in determining what kind of Lebanon would emerge from the crisis. Finally, Syrian willingness to receive the PLO fighters was designed to show the U.S. government a degree of flexibility and readiness to collaborate in any future U.S. diplomatic moves provided that Syrian interests and concerns were taken into account.

The Egyptian Attitude

Egypt was the only Arab country to establish formal diplomatic relations with Israel, for which it had to pay a price: Its membership in the Arab League was suspended and the majority of Arab states severed diplomatic and economic relations with it. The Israeli invasion of Lebanon came as a mixed blessing to the Egyptian government. On one hand, Israel's war against the PLO was an embarrassment to the Egyptians because the peace treaty with Israel had excluded Egypt from the Arab-Israeli military equation and was perceived by the Arabs as having facilitated the Israeli invasion. On the other hand, the war allowed Egypt to accelerate its reentry into the Arab fold because it could assume a pan-Arab, pro-Palestinian posture and exploit its diplomatic leverage with Israel, Western Europe, and the United States to promote the Palestinian cause. Egypt's political stands, therefore, were dictated throughout the war by these two compelling, though opposing, motivations: upholding its treaty commitments to Israel and attaining readmittance into the Arab arena.

Israel's massive military operation in Lebanon led to widespread criticism in Egypt at both popular and official levels. The war produced the worst crisis in Egyptian-Israeli relations since Sadat's visit to Jerusalem in fall 1977. On several occasions Egyptian opposition parties called for a break in diplomatic relations with Israel and the renunciation of the Camp David agreements.[60] Egyptian opposition newspapers called upon the government to reevaluate Cairo's relations with the United States and to cancel U.S. military facilities in Egypt.

Despite these calls, the Egyptian government asserted that it would not abrogate its treaty with Israel, though ultimately the government recalled its ambassador from Tel Aviv and kept contact with the Jewish state at a low level. However, it stopped short of severing diplomatic relations. Egyptian governmental officials argued that the Israeli invasion of Lebanon was a serious setback to the peace process. They contended that talks on autonomy for the West Bank and Gaza Strip would not be resumed until Israel pulled back its troops from Lebanon, broadened its interpretation of self-autonomy, and relaxed its tough policy in the occupied territories.[61]

Egyptian diplomacy was directed toward achieving several immediate and long-term objectives. The Egyptian government was keen on preventing any final Israeli military assault upon the western sector of the Lebanese capital. The government called for the disengagement of the combatants through the withdrawal of Israeli forces south of Beirut to enable the Palestinians to withdraw from their positions and establish a dialogue with the Lebanese government to regulate the PLO presence in Lebanon.[62] Moreover, Cairo repeatedly asserted that U.S. diplomatic efforts should not be confined to finding a solution to the siege of Beirut but should also be directed toward a comprehensive settlement of the Palestinian problem.[63] During his meeting with the U.S. presidential envoy to the Middle East, President Mubarak underlined this point when he announced that Egypt rejected U.S. plans that suggested that the Beirut crisis should assume primacy and urgency. Mubarak stressed that the future of the Palestinians and their right to self-determination should constitute the bases for a comprehensive settlement and pointed out that Egypt could not receive the Palestinian fighters without laying the foundation for a general political settlement.[64] The Egyptian government tried to link the evacuation with a U.S. commitment to solve the Palestinian question and initiate a dialogue with the PLO. Egyptian diplomatic efforts were also directed at loosening U.S.-Israeli ties.[65] Finally, Egypt called on both the PLO and Israel to exchange simultaneous and mutual recognition.

For the first time since Sadat's initiative in November 1977, official contacts between the PLO and Egypt were renewed, and Egypt worked actively to defend the PLO despite their continuing differences. On June 21, 1982, President Mubarak urged the PLO leadership to form a Palestinian government in exile and offered Cairo as the seat for that government. However, his offer was contingent upon the requirement that such a government should use only political and diplomatic means to advance Palestinian national rights. The Egyptian government welcomed the statement that Arafat signed before a U.S.-congressional delegation on July 26, 1982, in which he recognized UN resolutions pertaining to the Palestinian question. Two days later the Egyptian Foreign Ministry issued a statement urging the Reagan administration to take advantage of Arafat's peaceful gesture by opening a dialogue with the PLO.

Though the Egyptian government based its refusal to admit PLO soldiers on the ground that Israel's military and psychological pressures upon the PLO were unacceptable, the terms of the Israeli-Egyptian peace treaty would not allow Egypt to embrace PLO fighters or to encourage PLO activities from Egyptian territory. President Mubarak's call upon the PLO leadership to form a government in exile could be seen as a way out of this political dilemma. Probably the Egyptian refusal to receive the PLO was intended to generate pressure upon Western Europe and the United States to search actively for a just solution to the Palestinian problem. In the opinion of the Egyptian government, the issue was not the evacuation of PLO troops from West Beirut but the massive bombing of the city and the evacuation of Israeli troops from Lebanon. In a speech to the Egyptian People's Assembly on the thirtieth anniversary of the Egyptian revolution, President Mubarak pointed out that the evacuation of PLO troops from Beirut should be discussed with the "legitimate Lebanese government" and the PLO leadership, or through an "Arab framework."[66]

To implement the broad outlines of its policy, the Egyptian government embarked upon an active diplomatic offensive with numerous regional and international actors. Despite his isolation in the Arab world, Mubarak called for the convening of an Arab summit conference and dispatched emissaries to Jordan, Iraq, Saudi Arabia, and Lebanon. In a press conference the Egyptian president expressed his disappointment with the U.S. attitude toward the Israeli invasion of Lebanon. He warned that such a U.S. position "will not only effect the Egyptian-American relations but it will also have an impact upon American-Arab relations. . . . I told every American official that I met in Egypt that the situation in Lebanon will create more problems and troubles and that America will lose more of its credibility."[67] Cairo's frustrations with U.S. policy stands remained verbal; the nature of Egypt's military and economic ties with the United States limited Cairo's freedom of action. In addition, Egypt's political leadership was convinced that the United States would be needed to bring about a comprehensive settlement of the Arab-Israeli conflict.

Dissatisfaction with U.S. policy during the war, particularly the reluctance of the Reagan administration to exert sufficient pressure upon Israel to end the siege of Beirut, forced the Egyptian government to look toward Western Europe for support. Egypt tried to coordinate its political stands with the European Economic Community by sending senior Egyptian foreign diplomats to several European capitals. Egypt also joined France in submitting a joint draft resolution on July 29, 1982, to the UN Security Council that called for the disengagement of the fighting troops and the preservation of the cease-fire in Lebanon. The Franco-Egyptian draft resolution was predicated upon the European Economic Community communiqué of June 30, 1982, which asserted the right of self-determination for the Palestinians and the "association" of the PLO with the peace process. It was also based on UN Security Council Resolution 242, which called upon the states in the region to recognize each other within secured and defensible borders. The draft resolution, however, went beyond Resolution 242 by urging Israel and the PLO to exchange mutual and simultaneous recognition.[68] Egypt's submission of the draft resolution with France aimed at extracting political gains for the PLO in return for the evacuation of Beirut. Egypt's goal for the inclusion of the PLO in the political settlement and the recognition of the Palestinians' right for self-determination went beyond the diplomatic efforts launched jointly by Saudi Arabia and Syria which resulted in the launching of the Reagan initiative. Such positive diplomatic moves by the Egyptian government were mainly behind the decision of the PLO's leadership to reconcile with Cairo following the Palestinians' exodus from Beirut.

The political fragmentation of the Arab countries and their mutual hostilities and bitter rivalries, coupled with the intensity of the Israeli military operation in Lebanon, diminished Arab capacities and propensities to respond effectively to the Israeli challenge. More significantly, the war demonstrated the bankruptcy of the pan-Arab ideology, for both the ruling elite and the masses, and the fallacy of the Arab nationalists' argument that the Palestinian issue constituted the core of all Arab concern. During the war no spontaneous mass demonstrations took place in Arab capitals, in which protesters demanded intervention on behalf of the Palestinian cause. Moreover, the war displayed the futility of the moderate and radical Arab states' diplomacy with their respective patrons, whether in the East or the West. Superpowers' indifference to, if not tolerance of, Israel's devastating offensive in Lebanon testifies to the lack of credibility and respectability that Arab kings and presidents enjoyed with their custodians.

U.S. Policy During the War: Complicity or Incompetence?

In the months preceding the outbreak of war the Reagan administration tacitly accepted Israel's need to strike at PLO troops in Lebanon to provide Israel's northern borders with stability and security. Israel's planned military operation in Lebanon was consistent with Reagan's policy of containing the Soviet Union and its protégés in the Middle Eastern region. Although President Reagan in a press conference[69] denied that his administration possessed any advanced information about the timing or details of the war, some influential members of Reagan's government knew and tacitly approved the operational plans of Israel's invasion.[70] Commenting on this issue, Egyptian Minister of State for Foreign Affairs Boutros Ghali argued that although President Reagan denied any prior knowledge of the war Secretary of State Alexander Haig knew about it. Ghali further contended that Secretary Haig gave Israel the green light to invade Lebanon in exchange for an Israeli promise to support his candidacy for the 1984 U.S. presidential election.[71]

Statements by senior Israeli cabinet ministers also indicated advanced U.S. knowledge of the war. During a visit to Washington shortly before the outbreak of the war, Ariel Sharon was reported to have told Alexander Haig that an Israeli military operation in Lebanon was "likely to start at any moment."[72] In a later interview Sharon revealed that he had communicated to his U.S. hosts, "We cannot live under the threat of Palestinian terrorism from Beirut. We don't see any alternative except to go there and clean up. We don't want you to be surprised. We don't know when it will happen."[73]

Even without the comments of Egyptian and Israeli ministers, it is highly unlikely that the United States had not observed the widely visible concentration of Israeli troops along the Lebanese borders, particularly because Washington possesses the world's most sophisticated surveillance system. The news of the invasion was not kept secret, and U.S. press and media speculated about the nature and intensity of Israel's planned military operation in Lebanon. The deployment of U.S. Navy war ships in the Eastern Mediterranean shortly before and after the outbreak of the war further indicated Washington's advanced knowledge of Israeli designs against the PLO. Apparently the U.S. naval deployment was initiated to provide military protection for the Israeli invading force and to serve as a deterrent against any possible Soviet military intervention on behalf of the Palestinians and Syrians.[74]

Once the war broke out, official U.S. government response was mild and tolerant. This posture was manifested by the reluctance of the Reagan administration to use its leverage over the Israelis to limit the expansion of their initial war goals. Moreover, during most of the war the U.S. government refrained from publicly criticizing Israeli military objectives and frequently used its veto power in the UN Security Council to obstruct the endorsement of draft resolutions. These draft resolutions called upon Israel to abide by the cease-fire and withdraw from Lebanon and proposed the imposition of sanctions should Israel not comply. The U.S. ambassador to the United Nations justified the frequent use of veto power on the basis that such draft resolutions were "sufficiently unbalanced" and "one-sided" and did not aim at "ending the cycle of violence."[75]

Furthermore, the Reagan administration supported the Israeli position that the Middle East could not return to the situation that existed prior to the outbreak of hostilities.[76] A few days after the outbreak of the war, Haig called for the withdrawal of all foreign forces from Lebanon.[77] Later, a State Department spokesperson clarified Haig's statement by demanding that Syrian forces withdraw from Lebanon and that the Palestinian presence be regulated by the Lebanese government.[78] After his meeting with President Reagan in the third week of June, the Israeli prime minister reconfirmed that both countries shared common interests in Lebanon, such as the withdrawal of foreign troops, the restoration of Lebanese national independence through the creation of a strong central Lebanese government, and the preservation of stability and security to northern Israel.[79]

The resignation of Alexander Haig and his replacement by George Schultz as U.S. secretary of state did not substantially alter U.S.-Middle Eastern foreign policy. Schultz's appointment led to speculation that the United States would pursue a more balanced policy in handling the Arab-Israeli dispute and would be tougher on Israel.[80] Contrary to these expectations, the new secretary of state maintained continuity of policy toward the Lebanon crisis and proceeded with U.S. endeavors to resolve the Beirut crisis through the evacuation of PLO forces. Like Haig, he did not favor any public confrontation with the Begin government.[81] Moreover, Schultz preserved traditional U.S. policy concerning the recognition of the PLO,[82] despite the PLO's apparent attempts throughout July to open a dialogue with Washington.[83] The United States also continued pressuring the Arab states to persuade the PLO to leave West Beirut as soon as possible on the grounds that the PLO's postponed departure would contribute to hardening the position of the hawkish elements in the Begin government. Finally, Schultz reiterated the U.S. policy of absolute commitment to Israel's security, survival, and well-being.

Despite these policy continuities, Secretary Schultz used language not spoken during Haig's tenure in the State Department. During his Senate confirmation hearing on July 13, 1982, Schultz spoke of the "legitimate needs of the Palestinian people" and underlined the importance of solving "the Palestinian problem in all of its dimensions." In his opinion, self-autonomy talks could not be successful without the participation of representatives of the Palestinian people. Differences also began to evolve between Israel and the United States over the means that the Begin government was employing to implement its war objectives. Although Washington favored diplomatic settlement to the Beirut crisis through the "good offices" of U.S. mediator Philip Habib, Israel kept up its military pressure against West Beirut. On July 6, the U.S. president announced that his government was prepared to dispatch marines to Lebanon to facilitate and supervise the withdrawal of the PLO forces and help the Lebanese government restore sovereignty over its entire capital.

The Israeli government did not respond by abandoning its policy of military escalation and massive bombardment from land, air, and sea of the western sector of the Lebanese capital. The Begin government frequently prevented water, electricity, food, and medical supplies from reaching the besieged civilians. Moreover, reports increasingly spoke of Israel's use of antipersonnel weapons, such as cluster-bomb shells, against civilian targets. Such actions were in violation of the 1978 U.S.-Israeli military sales agreement,[84] which prohibited the deployment of such weapons against civilian targets and confined their use to strictly military sites and only to occasions when Israel was attacked by more than one hostile state.[85] In reaction, the Reagan administration suspended the shipment of 4,000 cluster-bomb artillery shells but did not aggressively pursue its investigation to determine the validity of reports of Israeli violations of the 1978 agreement.[86]

The repeated heavy bombardment of West Beirut in the first week and a half of August prompted the United States to warn Israel that the Begin government's continual assaults jeopardized the "special relationship" between the two countries. Washington further threatened to withdraw from the diplomatic negotiations and suspend the mission of Ambassador Habib if Israel did not abide by the cease-fire.[87] An emergency session of the National Security Council was called by President Reagan to discuss the options available to force observance of the cease-fire. Following Israel's massive bombing of West Beirut on August 12, U.S. media spoke of the anger and the outrage of the president. This occasion was the first time that Reagan publicly expressed his outrage over the bombing of West Beirut; this restrained Israel's military activities, thereby allowing the PLO to evacuate.

Though the formulation of U.S. foreign policy is complex because it involves a variety of domestic, political, and bureaucratic variables, U.S. policy response to the war in Lebanon was heavily influenced by global and military considerations. Israel's war in Lebanon served a number of U.S. foreign-policy objectives. The military operation was consistent with the Reagan administration's obsession to check the Soviet influence and military presence in the Middle East and to weaken its protégés in that region. By advancing its security and strength, the Begin government was seen as enhancing the security of the pro-Western moderate Arab countries against the Soviet-backed Arab radicals.

The war was also perceived to have opened new opportunities for U.S. diplomacy in the region. The PLO's military defeat was envisioned as creating new conditions for a lasting peace whereby Jordan would be encouraged to join Egypt in the peace talks. Moreover, the war provided the opportunity to revise Lebanon's political map through the reinstatement of a pro-Western central government in Beirut and the removal of Syrian and Palestinian forces from Lebanon.[88]

The deployment by Israel of its military force to advance its national security goals was not alien to Reagan's political philosophy in which military power assumed a pivotal role. Equally significant, the war presented an opportunity to test the quality and the effectiveness of U.S.-supplied weapons in the battlefield and at the same time to discredit the Soviet-supplied Syrian arms as inferior to their U.S. counterparts. The destruction of the Syrian antiaircraft missile bases in Lebanon by the Israeli air force was a severe blow to the Soviet air defense systems, and the shooting down of more than eighty Syrian war planes was seen as a clear sign of the qualitative superiority of U.S. weapons. A group of U.S. generals visited the war zone toward the end of July and reported that the Israeli military had acquired a vast amount of technical information and military experience that would be valuable to U.S. strategic planners.[89] About the same time an Israeli military delegation visited Washington to discuss terms for sharing intelligence gathered in the war.[90]

Occasional U.S. moves to restrain Israel's military behavior were dictated by strategic considerations. The United States was unwilling to risk a superpower nuclear confrontation over the local conflict in Lebanon, though it was prepared to back any efforts to contain the Soviet Union in the region. U.S. diplomatic initiatives to rescue the Syrian troops stationed in the Bekaa Valley following the destruction of their missile bases were dictated by a desire not to entangle the Soviet Union directly. This goal was achieved by arranging the June 11, 1982, cease-fire agreement between Israel and Syria. The decision of the Reagan administration a few days later to delay the sale of seventy-six F-16 war planes was intended to limit Israel's action against Syria and to avoid any showdown with the Soviet Union, which was bound to Syria through the 1980 Treaty of Friendship and Cooperation.

President Reagan's offer to dispatch U.S. marines to help evacuate PLO troops from Lebanon, coupled with his public outrage over the massive Israeli bombardment of West Beirut in August, was also determined by U.S. national interests in the region. The Israeli defense minister's goal of achieving a visible and resounding military victory that would put him safely on the road to succeed Begin clashed sharply with overall U.S. regional interests, particularly because the U.S. government was preparing a diplomatic offensive following the PLO's evacuation from Beirut. Israel's policy of continual military escalation against West Beirut was also perceived as a threat to U.S. interests. Israeli military activities were extremely embarrassing to the pro-Western, moderate Arab countries because of their inability to furnish any tangible support to the Palestinians. From this perspective, U.S. moves to rescue the PLO were mainly intended to preserve the prestige of their moderate Arab clients. The United States was also concerned about alienating such friends and pushing them closer to the Soviet Union.

A final military solution to the Palestinian presence in West Beirut might have appeared to have endangered U.S. postwar diplomacy as it would further damage the prestige and credibility of the United States. The destruction of the western segment of the Lebanese capital would certainly diminish whatever legitimacy was left to the Lebanese national government, which the United States was certainly hoping to avoid, and would block the road for future efforts toward national reconciliation among the various Lebanese factions. The destruction of an Arab capital and the PLO would undermine the broader U.S. objective of Arab and Palestinian participation in any future peace talks. A contingency of this sort would certainly impede U.S. efforts to settle the Middle East conflict. The United States was keen to avoid the image that its diplomacy had failed: By providing safe conduct for the PLO, it hoped that its image would be preserved and improved as a country that "rescued" the Palestinians from total destruction at a time when the Soviet Union, the PLO's long-term and natural ally, did almost nothing to help.

Despite the fact that global, strategic, and national interests occupied a primary position in determining U.S. policy toward the 1982 Lebanon War, domestic politics cannot be dismissed as entirely irrelevant. Traditional U.S. policy toward the Arab-Israeli conflict has been dictated by domestic politics; the government's pro-Israeli policy was heavily influenced by the U.S. public's sympathies, the strong Israeli lobby, the media, and the significance of the Jewish vote in congressional elections. One could argue that because the war broke out a few months before midterm congressional elections, President Reagan might have been tempted to pursue a pro-Israeli posture to enlist more Jewish votes in support of his Republican party.

Although domestic politics may have entered the calculations of senior U.S. officials, strategic rationale outweighed internal considerations in molding the U.S. response to the war. A significant degree of deviation can be seen in the impact of internal politics upon the making of U.S. foreign policy. Exposure via the U.S. media to descriptions of the heavy damage and casualties inflicted upon Lebanon and its population aroused some anti-Israeli sentiment within the U.S. public. An opinion poll[91] conducted in early August revealed that 60 percent of the U.S. public believed that Israel went too far in its invasion of Lebanon. In contrast, only 16 percent approved Israel's war aims. Forty-three percent of those questioned favored the imposition of sanctions against Israel, including the suspension of military aid. The poll further indicated that about 50 percent of the respondents supported the opening of a dialogue with the PLO; 42 percent expressed their opposition to such an initiative.

Equally significant dissent began to surface in the U.S. Jewish community,[92] which at the outset of the war supported Israel's initial war aim of creating a 25-mile security belt in southern Lebanon. When the violence, bloodshed, and destruction increased, prominent U.S. Jewish leaders publicly criticized the expanded war aims, denying that they were necessary for the defense of Israel and blaming the Begin government for the hardships inflicted by the war. They expressed their grief for the heavy casualties among the Palestinian and Lebanese civilians and denounced the use of antipersonnel weapons.

Other opposition to the war was voiced by members of the U.S. Congress concerned about the massive destruction to West Beirut's infrastructure, the heavy casualties among the civilian population, and the use of U.S.-made cluster-bombs. In a June 21 Senate hearing, Israel's use of cluster-bombs was questioned, and by mid-July some criticism was heard on Capitol Hill about the Reagan administration's report for Congress that did not conclusively determine whether Israel's use of U.S.-supplied weapons was offensive or defensive.[93] The report stated that Israel may have violated U.S. arms agreements in its invasion of Lebanon. Democratic Chairman of the House Foreign Affairs Committee Clement J. Zablocki commented that the report was "not responsive" and added that "it reaches no judgment on whether Israel used cluster-bombs, and there is no doubt in my mind that they did."[94] Such congressional concerns were possibly behind the reported cool reception accorded the Israeli prime minister during his U.S. visit in the third week of June and to Israeli Foreign Minister Yitzhak Shamir in early August. Begin's meeting with the Senate Foreign Relations Committee was characterized by sharp exchanges; one senator called the meeting a "total disaster for Begin and not much better for Israel."[95]

The Reagan government was reported to have been concerned about the growing erosion in U.S. public support for Israel.[96] More disturbing to the administration was the image that the United States was unable to restrain Israeli moves. Viewed from this perspective the U.S. decision to delay the shipment of 4,000 cluster-bombs to Israel and President Reagan's warnings in early August might appear to have been prompted by mounting U.S. criticism toward Israel's excessive military policy. These moves were also motivated by the Reagan administration's desire to project itself as being "in control of the situation."[97] Thus, criticism of Israel within the United States forced the Reagan administration to diverge on several occasions from its supportive policy toward Israel's war aims, which were basically congruent with Washington's strategic interests in the Middle East.

Finally, bureaucratic and personal rivalries played a part in determining U.S. policy toward the war. In the third week of the war, some reports suggested that senior officials in the Reagan administration did not enjoy a unified position on how to respond to Israel's expanded war aims.[98] These reports spoke of two competing groups. The first group, led by Alexander Haig and Jeane Kirkpatrick, U.S. ambassador to the United Nations, was not opposed to the expanded war aims and preferred to abstain from publicly criticizing Israel on the grounds that any confrontation would be counterproductive because it could lead to more inflexibility on the part of the Likud. In view of his pro-Israel sympathies, Reagan was more inclined to endorse Haig's recommendations. For Haig, the war provided the opportunity to strengthen his position in the White House against his main rival, Secretary of Defense Caspar Weinberger.

The second group, led by Caspar Weinberger and supported by William Clark, the national security advisor, publicly expressed its preference for decreasing U.S. aid to Israel, denouncing the Israeli invasion of Lebanon, and favoring a public rebuke of the Begin government in view of Israel's military escalation. The differences between the groups resulted more from personal and bureaucratic rivalries than differences concerning major policy issues. With the resignation of Alexander Haig and his replacement by George Schultz, a former business associate of Caspar Weinberger, a qualitative shift in U.S. Middle Eastern policy and a hardened stand toward Israel were not forthcoming.

The Soviet Policy of Inaction

In contrast to previous Arab-Israeli conflicts, the involvement of the Soviet Union in the 1982 war was limited and insignificant.[99] Soviet policy responses were confined mainly to verbal criticism and denunciation of the Israeli invasion, as well as statements of moral support for the PLO and of admiration for the steadfastness of the Palestinian and Lebanese people. The Soviet leadership also promised diplomatic cooperation with the group of Arab states at the United Nations.[100] From the beginning of the war, the Kremlin gave no sign that it intended to intervene directly on behalf of the PLO and its Lebanese allies; the PLO representative in Moscow announced early in the war that the Soviet Union did not want to get involved.[101] A few weeks later during a visit to Moscow as part of an Arab delegation, Farouq al-Qadoumi, head of the PLO political department, demanded that the Soviet Union demonstrate a show of force in support of the Palestinians. Soviet Foreign Minister André Gromyko was reported to have responded that Qadoumi's request was "out of the question" and that the Soviet Union would confine its activities to diplomacy.[102]

Moscow's unwillingness to intervene directly was motivated by an overriding objective of averting a full-scale war between Syria and Israel. Such war was perceived to involve high risks for Moscow and Damascus as it could erode the stability of the Assad regime and necessitate direct Soviet military intervention, which would carry the risk of transforming a local conflict into a confrontation between the two superpowers.[103] Soviet reluctance to become directly involved in the war generated a great deal of disappointment and frustration among PLO leaders. Salah Khalaf, commonly known as Abu Iyad, the second man in Fatah (the main faction of the PLO), complained in a radio interview about Soviet hesitation and indecisiveness: "From the first hour we wanted the Soviet position to be more radical but our Soviet brothers have their own way of acting."[104] In another statement the chairman of the pro-Moscow Democratic Front for the Liberation of Palestine, Nayef Hawatmeh, pointed out, "The Soviet Union cannot secure its solidarity with us and with the people of Lebanon by confining its support to political and diplomatic pressures." He urged the Soviet leaders to "use all the possible means including military force" to assist the PLO.[105] PLO Chairman Yasir Arafat sent a number of messages to the Soviets appealing for help to put an end to "Israel's aggression."

In an attempt to counter Palestinian and Arab criticism and dissatisfaction with its inconsequential involvement in the war, the Soviet Union reasserted its support for the PLO and the Arabs in their "just struggle" and held the United States responsible for the outbreak of hostilities. On June 14, the Soviet government issued a statement expressing its concern over the Israeli military operation in Lebanon. The statement assured the Arabs of Soviet support to encounter "Israeli aggression" but did not contain any serious threat to halt Israel's advance against West Beirut and enforce the cease-fire.[106] In an interview with Pravda on July 20, Soviet President Leonid Brezhnev reiterated his government's support for the PLO as the sole legitimate representative of the Palestinian people and called for the lifting of the siege of West Beirut and the immediate withdrawal of the Israeli army from Lebanon. Brezhnev repeated his call for convening an international peace conference in which all concerned parties would participate, including Israel, the Soviet Union, the United States, and the PLO, to find a solution to the Middle East conflict.

Through its press, Moscow attributed the ease with which Israel initiated the war to the Arab states' lack of unity and their bitter rivalries.[107] Moscow was also unhappy about the Arab countries' inability to convene a summit conference to discuss the crisis. This inertia supported the Soviet argument that the absence of Arab solidarity had facilitated the Israeli invasion of Lebanon. The Soviet media criticized the Arab countries' opposition to using their economic wealth as a political weapon against the West. In addition to its criticism of Arab states, the Soviet Union held the United States accountable for the eruption of hostilities. Moscow repeatedly charged that the Reagan administration gave Israel the green light to invade Lebanon and that the war would not have been possible without massive U.S. economic and military aid.

President Reagan's announcement in early July that his administration would be willing to send U.S. marines to Lebanon to supervise the PLO evacuation was disturbing to Soviet leadership. In a letter to his U.S. counterpart, Brezhnev warned that any move by the United States to land its troops in Lebanon would compel the Soviet Union to "build its policy in the region with due consideration of this fact."[108] The Soviet leader, however, explained in a Pravda interview on July 20, 1982, that his government was not opposed to the stationing of UN forces in Lebanon to preserve the cease-fire and supervise the departure of PLO troops from West Beirut, provided U.S. troops would not be included in the force.

The Soviet Union's warning did not amount to an ultimatum; it was sufficiently vague to allow the country the option of doing nothing. The message was possibly a rhetorical gesture by the Soviet Union, intended to be heard in the Arab world and to improve Moscow's image. The Soviet leaders probably felt that they could not afford to remain quiet concerning the landing of U.S. troops in Lebanon and the deployment of the U.S. navy close to Lebanese territorial waters at a time when the Soviet navy was hardly visible in the region. Seen from this perspective, Brezhnev's letter to Reagan was designed to voice Soviet concerns over U.S. moves, and in view of the low-level Soviet involvement in the war, the letter aimed at averting the further alienation of the Kremlin's Arab and Palestinian clients. Moscow was also determined to preclude any possible U.S. political or military gains that would result from the introduction of U.S. troops in Lebanon.

The U.S. offer to dispatch marines to Lebanon was directly connected to the evacuation of PLO forces from Beirut; U.S. participation in the evacuation process would enhance the image of the United States in the Arab world as the country that spared West Beirut from destruction and provided an "honorable departure" for the Palestinian fighters. Prospects of this sort were extremely discomforting to the Soviets. Brezhnev's letter to Reagan aimed at projecting the Soviet Union as the country that exerted pressure upon the West to find a quick solution to the Beirut crisis. One could also argue that the initial Syrian decision to refuse the admission of PLO fighters was in response to Soviet desires to abort U.S.-mediated efforts that aimed at a PLO withdrawal from Beirut.

Aside from its gestures of diplomatic support for the PLO, Soviet policy responses remained insubstantial throughout the war. Traditional Soviet policy toward the Arab-Israeli conflict centered around two main aspects: a call for a negotiated diplomatic settlement of the conflict and an active military engagement including arms sales, replacement of war losses, and threats of direct military intervention on behalf of its Arab clients. Why did the Soviet Union exhibit a high degree of restraint and a low-level involvement in the 1982 Lebanon War? Why did it fail to extend to the Arabs the same kind of military backing that it had almost a decade earlier in the 1973 October War?

Restrained Soviet behavior was in line with Moscow's Middle Eastern policy of the post-1973 October War period. According to this policy, the Soviet Union was willing to give diplomatic aid and support to its clients in the Middle East and was very cautious not to sanction war or to intervene in local conflicts to avoid superpower confrontation. This policy was reinforced by the fact that, despite heavy military, political, and economic Soviet investment in several Arab countries since the late 1950s, Moscow failed to create reliable Arab allies. Several Arab countries, including Egypt and Iraq, went to Western Europe and the United States for support and aid and began to believe that the main menace to regional and political stability emanated from the Soviet Union.

With the decline in anticolonial and anti-Western sentiments and the concomitant growth in the wealth and influence of the pro-Western moderate Arab countries, Soviet ability to wield influence over regional affairs in the Middle East diminished.[109] In contrast to the 1950s and 1960s when the Arab political system was dominated by feelings of hostility toward the West and the Arab leaders looked to Moscow for economic, political, and military aid, the 1970s and 1980s witnessed a shift in Arab politics. Anti-Western sentiments were replaced by feelings of friendship and cooperation with the West. The wealthy Arab oil states and the Western countries became the new source of influence and economic and military aid. Moscow's influence had been declining since 1972 when Sadat expelled Soviet military advisors and technicians from Egypt.[110] The U.S. policy of excluding the Soviet Union from the peace process contributed further to the decline of the Kremlin's power in the region.

Other factors and considerations were crucial to the Kremlin's decision to remain inactive for most of the war period. Moscow's hesitation to intervene directly on behalf of its Arab clients was the result of a realistic assessment of Arab military capabilities, which precluded the chances of winning a full-scale war with Israel. The poor military performance of the Arab armies in the various Arab-Israeli wars and Israel's capture of modern Soviet military equipment and its handing over of such weapons to the United States perhaps convinced the Soviet leadership of the diminishing utility of the policy of further military investment and active engagement in the Middle Eastern conflict. Israel's vast military arsenal was another serious consideration for the Soviet military leaders; to restrain the Israelis, a large-scale Soviet troop deployment would be needed to counterbalance the qualitative military superiority of the Israeli army. The Soviet Union was unwilling to undertake a contingency of this sort, not only for logistic and tactical reasons but also because it entailed a high risk of a superpower confrontation. The value of the PLO to Soviet interests in the region was not thought to be commensurate with the risks involved. Soviet backing of the Palestinian guerrilla movement over the years was expedient: The PLO was seen as a mechanism by which to advance

Soviet interests in the Middle East and to counterbalance U.S. political gains.[111] Differences also existed between the PLO and the Soviet Union on policy issues such as the Soviet invasion of Afghanistan.

The aging leadership in the Kremlin and the deterioration in the health of President Brezhnev did not favor any risk taking. Continued Soviet military involvement in Afghanistan and the precarious situation in Poland further compounded the problems for the Soviet leadership. Finally, Soviet diplomats were engaged in normalizing relations with the People's Republic of China and attempting to manage already deteriorating relationships with Western countries, particularly the United States.

Sympathy in Western Europe

In West European countries the Israeli invasion of Lebanon was met with condemnation of the attackers and sympathy for the civilian war victims.[112] Two days after the outbreak of the war the ten members of the European Economic Community (EEC) issued a statement condemning the Israeli invasion and the aerial bombardment that preceded it.[113] The statement characterized the invasion as an outright violation of the rules of international law and morality, warned that it undermined the prospects of settling the Arab-Israeli conflict through peaceful means, and called upon Israel to withdraw its troops from Lebanon.[114]

A combination of factors were behind the disquieting effect the Israeli invasion of Lebanon had on Western Europe. West European countries were afraid that the Israeli war against the PLO and its occupation of Lebanon would undermine and endanger Western economic interests in the Middle East as the Arab states might impose economic sanctions against the West because they supported Israel. The war could threaten the stability of the pro-Western moderate Arab countries, particularly the oil-producing states. An additional source of anxiety to the Europeans was the fact that Israel's military operation in Lebanon could have widened the conflict by engaging the two superpowers. From a West European perspective the invasion heightened the differences between the United States and its European allies because of the divergence between their approaches to the Middle Eastern crisis. In the latter's view, the war in Lebanon demonstrated how little influence the U.S. administration could exert upon the Israeli government despite the enormous economic and military aid it gave to Israel.

In spite of their denunciation of the Israeli invasion, the European capitals had few options to effect developments in the Middle East, and therefore they confined their activities to the political level. Toward the end of June, in Brussels the EEC heads of state formalized their attitudes toward the Lebanon War.[115] Their final communiqué called upon the concerned fighting parties to observe the cease-fire, advocated the immediate and simultaneous withdrawal of Israeli and Palestinian troops from in and around Beirut, and demanded the prompt withdrawal of all foreign troops from Lebanon. An exception to the last demand concerned those forces authorized by the central government in Beirut. The Europeans expressed the hope that through the implementation of their recommendations, "stability and peace" would be restored to Lebanon and the central government could extend its sovereignty over the country as a whole.

In line with the broad outlines of their Middle Eastern policy, established by the Venice declaration of June 1980, members of the EEC adjured that negotiations should commence among the Arabs and Israelis based on the premise of providing security for all countries in the Middle East and justice for all the peoples in the region. The Brussels communiqué warned that Israel's resort to military force would not contribute to the preservation of its security in the long run; on the contrary, the realization of the legitimate rights of the Palestinian people would ensure long-term security and stability for the Jewish state. The communiqué further supported the Palestinians' right to self-determination, called for their representation in any future peace talks, and reiterated the European position that the PLO should be associated with the peace talks. EEC members, however, did not advocate recognizing the PLO as the sole legitimate representative of the Palestinian people or express public support for the imposition of mandatory sanctions against Israel.

The Brussels communiqué contained a number of points significant for the Palestinian problem and the Arab-Israeli conflict. The call by the EEC countries for the PLO to withdraw its troops from Lebanon (which was included in the general call for foreign troop withdrawal) meant the dismantling of the PLO's most important military base. It also expressed a European preference that the PLO and the Palestinian people pursue diplomacy to achieve their national goals and abandon their strategy of armed struggle as an avenue to restore Palestinian rights. In addition, the European call was necessitated by the desire of these countries to end the Israeli siege of West Beirut in return for the evacuation of Palestinian troops from the city.

To demonstrate their concern over the war, EEC members dispatched diplomatic envoys to the Middle East to confer with Israeli and Arab officials. In early July the prime minister of Holland (then chairman of the EEC) toured the region to explain EEC attitudes toward the war and explore possibilities for separating the fighting forces to sustain the cease-fire. In an interview in *al-Ahram,* a semiofficial Egyptian daily, the Dutch prime minister stated that the Brussels declaration constituted the proper ground for the solution of the Palestinian and Lebanese problems and underlined the call of the EEC members for mutual and simultaneous recognition between the PLO and Israel. He further remarked that, in the opinion of Western European countries, the PLO evacuation from Beirut should be completed without the imposition of humiliating conditions upon the Palestinian fighters.[116] In their meeting of July 19, 1982, the EEC foreign ministers expressed their concern about the deteriorating situation in the Middle East, repeated Israeli violations of the cease-fire, and rising anti-Western sentiments in the region. A decision was taken to suspend the foreign aid agreement with Israel in the amount of $40 million. This move had a limited effect, however, as Israel relies almost exclusively upon the United States for its economic and military aid.[117]

Despite the consensus reached at Brussels, the ten members of the EEC were divided into two main camps.[118] Their division revolved around a number of issues, including the European attitude toward the U.S. handling of the Arab-Israeli dispute, the type of sanctions to be used against Israel in case of its refusal to withdraw from Lebanon, the formation of a multinational peace-keeping force, and the role the PLO would play in the peace talks. The first group of states, led by West Germany and Holland, opposed the emergence of any independent European Middle Eastern policy and called for closer cooperation and coordination with the United States on matters related to the Arab-Israeli dispute. In this regard, the foreign minister of West Germany during a visit to Jordan in mid-July 1982 declared that European initiative and diplomatic moves on the Palestinian issue and the Arab-Israeli conflict would not contradict or conflict with those of the United States. Moreover, from the early days of the Israeli invasion West Germany insisted that a return to the situation that existed before the war would not lead to positive results. At the insistence of this group of states the Brussels declaration called for the withdrawal of all foreign troops from Lebanon and the restoration of the authority of the central Lebanese government. Similarly, West Germany and Holland opposed the imposition of any sanctions upon Israel because of its invasion of Lebanon. They also did not favor referring directly to the PLO in their June 30 communiqué. Finally, they insisted that the proposed international peace-keeping force should supervise the withdrawal of all foreign troops from Lebanon, including those of the PLO.

In contrast to these attitudes, the second group of states, led by France and Greece, favored endorsing a more balanced policy toward the Arab-Israeli conflict, which would take into account Europe's interests in the Arab world. These states advocated the differentiation of European

Middle Eastern policy from that of the United States and urged that the EEC countries should explicitly define their attitude toward the Arab-Israeli conflict. At the insistence of these states the Brussels declaration referred directly to the PLO and called for its inclusion in the peace process. Both Greece and France supported the imposition of sanctions against Israel for its failure to withdraw from Lebanon. On the question of forming an international peace-keeping force, France wanted the mission of such a force to be confined to the disengagement of the fighting troops in and around Beirut.

In addition to their collective stand, the ten members of the EEC embarked upon individual diplomatic moves. Representatives were sent to the Middle East, including the foreign ministers of Italy, West Germany, and Great Britain and senior officials from the French Ministry of External Affairs. Greece received some PLO fighters for medical treatment in its hospitals, and the Greek prime minister was the first head of state to receive Arafat following his departure from Beirut. In addition, France, Italy, and Great Britain agreed to send troops to participate in the international peace-keeping force in Lebanon.

Among EEC countries France played the most active role throughout the war and was the most concerned to distinguish its Middle Eastern policy from that of the United States. The Begin government hoped that France would serve as Israel's advocate in the EEC. Within one year of its coming to power, however, the French government changed its policy: It sharply condemned the Israeli invasion of Lebanon and demanded the preservation of the political integrity of the PLO and Lebanon's unity and territorial integrity. This shift in French Middle Eastern policy was dictated by several compelling factors. The Israeli bombing of the French-sponsored Iraqi nuclear reactor in mid-1981 was embarrassing to the French government because it came shortly after the visit of the French president to Israel. Israel's invasion of Lebanon in early summer 1982 was particularly irritating to France in view of the historical and cultural links between Lebanon and France.[119]

Preserving its economic interests and business and military contracts in the Middle East was an additional factor in determining the French response to the war. The Arab oil-producing states, particularly Saudi Arabia, enjoyed considerable leverage in their dealings with France that could be used to hurt the French economy if a deliberate leaning by France toward Israel was perceived during the crisis. Closely linked to these economic considerations, the diplomatic pressures exerted by some Arab countries, like Egypt, affected the way in which the French government managed the crisis. French diplomatic moves were made in response to Arab expectations of an assertive French diplomatic posture to counterbalance U.S. biases toward Israel. Paris was also concerned that a decisive Israeli military victory backed by the United States could trigger Arab economic sanctions against the West. Finally, personal and psychological considerations were behind the modification of François Mitterrand's policy toward Israel. Despite his pro-Israeli stand and his friendship with the Jewish people that dated from World War II, Mitterrand seems to have resented being taken for granted by the Israeli government. To the French government, the needless destruction and heavy casualties caused by the expansion of Israel's war efforts could not be justified on the grounds of providing security for northern Israel.

For these and other reasons the French government embarked upon an active diplomatic campaign to restrain Israel's war aims and preserve the PLO as a significant factor in a solution to the Arab-Israeli dispute. France supported the imposition of sanctions upon Israel in the EEC Brussels meeting, and on June 26, 1982, submitted a draft resolution to the UN Security Council proposing the disengagement of the fighting forces in and around Beirut. France also opposed Israeli attempts to obliterate completely the PLO because such an action would lead to the disappearance of an institution that represented the Palestinian interests. In joint collaboration with Egypt, France submitted another draft resolution on July 29 calling for the commencement of negotiations among all concerned parties that would guarantee the existence, security, and rights of all states and peoples in the Middle East. Mitterrand's government sent troops to Beirut as part of the multinational force to supervise the evacuation of PLO fighters from West Beirut, and in July the French president and his minister of external affairs met with the head of the PLO political department.[120]

Such policy stands led to a cooling of relations between Israel and France. The Israeli Foreign Ministry sent an official memorandum to its French counterpart criticizing Mitterrand's Middle Eastern policy and charging that the French president was not a friend of Israel. The Israeli government was opposed to the participation of French troops in the multinational force and only accepted it after Mitterrand sent a letter to Begin pledging that his troops would withdraw immediately if the PLO refused to leave Beirut. In a Knesset speech on August 12, Begin declared that Israel accepted the participation of the French troops in facilitating the expulsion of the PLO fighters.

The broad outlines of French Middle Eastern policy were spelled out by the French president in a television and radio address to his nation in which he contended that his government's policy rested upon three cardinal principles: presence, evenhandedness, and peace.[121] Mitterrand argued that the French presence in the Middle East, and in Lebanon in particular, was predicated upon the historical and cultural links that

France shared with Lebanon and stemmed from France's status as a permanent member of the UN Security Council. By the principle of evenhandedness, the French president meant a balanced approach in handling the Arab-Israeli conflict and the Palestinian problem. This policy emanated from the French government's firm belief in the right of the Israeli people to live in peace behind secured and recognized borders and equally stipulated the right of the Palestinian people to have their own homeland and to establish the institutions that they chose. The French evenhanded policy was also based on the right of the Lebanese people to establish their national unity and territorial integrity. Mitterrand further elaborated that France's policy toward Israel would not be conducted at the expense of the Arabs and that French-Arab policy would not be carried out at the expense of Israel. Concerning the third principle, Mitterrand contended that peace could only be achieved through a comprehensive settlement to the Arab-Israeli conflict and the Palestinian problem and should be pursued through political means, diplomacy, and negotiations. In this context, Mitterrand called for simultaneous and mutual recognition between the Israeli and Palestinian peoples.

Despite the French government's acceptance of the principle that the Palestinian's political aspirations must be accounted for and despite the official contacts that the French government kept with PLO officials, President Mitterrand's policy throughout the war refrained from recognizing the PLO as the sole legitimate representative of the Palestinian people.[122] Although France regarded the PLO as the faction most representative of Palestinian views, it believed that the PLO could not and should not monopolize the concept of representation.

In conclusion, the overall mild reactions to the Lebanon War at the local, regional, and international levels, coupled with the dismantling of the PLO's political and military infrastructure in southern Lebanon and Beirut had a significant direct bearing upon the PLO's postwar diplomacy and tactics. Not only did the PLO's leaders have to draw a new strategy to replace the old strategy that was predicated upon the political and the military presence in Lebanon, but they were also compeled to enter into new diplomatic alliances and a reorientation of past policies. The unfolding of certain political developments immediately after the exodus from Beirut reconfirmed to the Palestinian leaders the lessons that they had learned during their siege in West Beirut. The new rules of the game in the postwar era would revolve around diplomacy and the forging of close ties with the moderate Arab countries, particularly Jordan. It was to these political developments that attention would now have to be drawn.

Notes

1. For more information about Israeli opposition to the war, see Michael Jansen, *The Battle of Beirut* (London: Zed Press, 1982), pp. 65-75; Zachary Lockman, "The Israeli Opposition," *Merip Reports* 12, nos. 6-7 (September-October 1982):25-32; Emanuel Farjoun, "A Dier Yassin Policy for the 80's," *Merip Reports* 12, nos. 6-7 (September-October 1982); "Itlala 'ala al-Rai' al-A'm al-Mu'ared Lilharb fi Israel," *Filistin al-Thawra* no. 460 (June 4, 1983):68-71; *Sunday Times*, August 1, 1982; *New York Times*, June 28, 1982; and *al-Hamishmar*, July 2, 1982.
2. *Davar*, June 28, 1982.
3. *Jerusalem Post*, July 5, 1982.
4. See, for instance, *Yediot Ahronot*, June 21, 1982; and *al-Hamishmar*, June 22, 1982.
5. *Davar*, June 28, 1982.
6. *Al-Hamishmar*, June 28, 1982; and *Yediot Ahronot*, July 5, 1982.
7. *Ha'aretz* (weekly edition), July 4-9, 1982.
8. Jewish Telegraph Agency, August 10, 1982.
9. For more information on the Geva case, see *Ha'aretz*, July 28, 1982.
10. *Ha'aretz*, July 2, 1982; *The Observer*, London, July 4, 1982; and *International Herald Tribune*, July 12, 1982.
11. *Davar*, July 17, 1982.
12. *Jerusalem Post*, June 7, 1982.
13. *Ha'aretz*, July 30, 1982.
14. Israel Radio (English service), August 5, 1982.
15. *Davar*, July 17, 1982.
16. Israel Radio (English service), July 10, 1982.
17. Joan Mandell and Salim Tamari, "The 100 Year War: Report from the West Bank and Gaza," *Merip Reports* 12, nos. 6-7 (September-October 1982):43.
18. Ibid.
19. *Al-Tali'a* (Jerusalem Arabic daily), July 11, 1982.
20. *Al-Hamishmar*, August 11, 1982; *Yediot Ahronot*, July 16, 1982; and *Ha'olem Hazae*, June 16 and August 4, 1982.
21. *Ha'aretz*, August 20, 1982; and *al-Hamishmar*, August 5, 1982.
22. Ze'ev Schiff, "Green Light Lebanon," *Foreign Policy*, no. 50 (spring 1983):83.
23. In this context, see the comments of Prime Minister Begin, *New York Times*, June 22, 1982; and Yitzhak Shamir, *Ha'aretz*, August 5, 1982.
24. *Yediot Ahronot*, August 9 and 16, 1982. The poll included 1,194 Israelis.
25. *Ha'aretz*, July 30, 1982.
26. *Ha'aretz*, August 18, 1982. See also the statement of West Bank and Gaza mayors on July 6, 1982, sent to Western leaders, condemning the Israeli invasion and U.S. military complicity in the war (*al-Fajr* [Jerusalem daily], July 6, 1982).
27. Since the mid-1970s the student movement in the occupied territories has been largely responsible for the demonstrations and strikes against the Israeli

occupation. For more information about opposition in the occupied territories to the war, see Mandell and Tamari, "The 100 Year War," pp. 42-43.

28. Extensions of town arrests included, among others, the mayor of Ramallah, Karim Khalaf; the mayor of al-Bireh, Ibrahim Tawil; the mayor of Nablus, Bassam al-Shak'a; the mayor of Anabta, Wahid al-Hamdallah; the president of the Engineers Association, Ibrahim Dakkak; the editor of *al-Sha'ab* (Jerusalem daily), Akram Haniya; and the president of In'ash al-Usra (women's association), Samiha Khalil.

29. *Al-Quds* (Jerusalem daily), June 9, 1982.

30. *Al-Fajr,* July 21, 1982. For similar comments, see *al-Fajr,* June 25 and 27, 1982.

31. *Al-Quds,* July 31, 1982.

32. *Al-Sha'ab* (Jerusalem daily), July 28, 1982. See also *al-Sha'ab,* July 26 and August 2, 1982.

33. *Al-Sha'ab,* June 30, 1982; *al-Quds,* July 14, 1982.

34. The interview appeared in *al-Bayader al-Siyassi* (biweekly Arabic magazine published in East Jerusalem), no. 25, September 1, 1982. Those interviewed include seven mayors, two deputy mayors, four lawyers, three medical doctors, two leaders of professional unions, two businesspeople, and an Islamic religious leader. These twenty-one leading figures in the occupied territories represent the various current political forces in the West Bank and Gaza Strip, including communists, supporters of the various factions of the PLO, pro-Jordanians, and leaders of the Islamic movement.

35. *Al-Dustur* (Jordanian daily), June 17 and July 7, 1982.

36. Amos Perlmutter, "Begin's Rhetoric and Sharon's Tactics," *Foreign Affairs* 61, no. 1 (Fall 1982):78-81.

37. For more information, see Alasdair Drysdale, "The Asad Regime and its Troubles," *Merip Reports* 12, no. 9 (November-December 1982); Hanna Batatu, "Syria's Muslim Brethren," *Merip Reports* 12, no. 9 (November-December 1982); and Fred Lawson, "Social Bases for the Hamah Revolt," *Merip Reports* 12, no. 9 (November-December 1982).

38. Within the first week of the war Syria lost some ninety war planes and its antiaircraft missile bases in the Bekaa Valley. These losses resulted from the limited military confrontation between Israel and Syria, as Syria intended to preserve its prestige in the Arab world and fulfill its pan-Arab obligations as the only Arab country to support the Palestinians.

39. "Sawt al-Watan al-Arabi al-Kabeer" (Libyan Radio), June 28, 1982.

40. "Sawt al-Watan al-Arabi al-Kabeer," July 4, 1982.

41. See Arafat's letter to Qaddafi on July 4, 1982, in *Rasa'il min Qalb al-Hsar* (Jerusalem: Abu Arafa Agency for Publication and Press, July 1983), p. 161. This book contains all letters, cables, and directives from Yasir Arafat during the war period (in Arabic).

42. *New York Times,* June 27, 1982.

43. For an opposing view of the feasibility of imposing an oil embargo, see Claudia Wright, "The Turn of the Screw—The Lebanon War and American Policy," *Journal of Palestine Studies* 11, no. 4/12, no. 1 (summer/fall 1982):3-22.

44. Calls for the conference came from Lebanon, the PLO, Libya, Tunisia, North and South Yemen, and Egypt.
45. *Middle East International,* July 3, 1982, pp. 6–7.
46. The committee consisted of the foreign ministers of Algeria, Saudi Arabia, Kuwait, Syria, Lebanon, and the PLO.
47. See the final communiqué of the Gulf Cooperation Council in *al-Watan* (Kuwaiti daily), July 14, 1982. The Gulf Cooperation Council consists of Saudi Arabia, Kuwait, Bahrain, Qatar, United Arab Emirates, and Oman.
48. United Nations, *Weekly News Summary,* July 17–23, 1982.
49. See, for instance, *al-Sha'ab* (Algerian daily), July 23–24, 1982, translated in *Journal of Palestine Studies* 11, no. 4/12, no. 1 (summer/fall 1982):193–194.
50. "Sawt al-Watan al-Arabi al-Kabeer," June 28, 1982.
51. See, for instance, an editorial in *Arab News* (Saudi Arabia), July 20, 1982; *al-Dustur* (Jordanian Arabic daily), June 17 and July 7, 1982; and an editorial in *al-Ra'i* (Amman), July 28, 1982, translated in *Journal of Palestine Studies* 11, no. 4/12, no. 1 (summer/fall 1982):194–207.
52. Radio Monte Carlo (Arabic service), August 21, 1982.
53. Ambassador Majali was interviewed by the American Broadcasting Corporation's (ABC's) "Nightline" program, August 11, 1982.
54. *Al-Dustur,* August 8, 1982.
55. *Al-Ra'i* (Jordanian daily), August 8, 1982.
56. *Time,* July 26, 1982.
57. SANA (Syrian Arab news agency), July 8, 1982.
58. *Al-Ba'ath* (Syrian daily), July 18, 1982.
59. Syrian Ambassador Jawadati (ambassador to the United States) was interviewed on ABC's "Nightline" program, August 11, 1982.
60. See *al-Ahram,* July 12, 1982, and *Al-Ahali* (Egyptian opposition paper), August 4, 1982, translated in *Journal of Palestine Studies* 11, no. 4/12, no. 1 (summer/fall 1982):196–201; Bahgat Korany, "The Cold Peace, the Sixth Arab-Israeli War, and Egypt's Public," *International Journal,* Summer 1983; and Wahid Abd al-Majid, "Mawquf Masr al-ghazu al-Isra'ili li al-Lubnan," *al-Siyassa al-Dawliya,* no. 70 (October 1982):160–162.
61. See the interview with Kamal Hassan Ali, deputy prime minister and minister of foreign affairs in Egypt, in *Rose al-Yusuf* (Egyptian weekly), July 18, 1982. See also interview with Boutros Ghali, Egypt's minister of state for Foreign Affairs in *al-Musawer* (Egyptian weekly), July 1, 1982.
62. Ibid.
63. For the contents of the messages sent by President Mubarak and his foreign minister to their U.S. counterparts, see *al-Ahram,* (Egyptian daily), July 20, 1982.
64. *Al-Ahram,* July 26, 1982.
65. Interview with Boutros Ghali in *al-Musawer,* July 1, 1982.
66. President Mubarak's speech was broadcast on Cairo Radio (Arabic service), July 26, 1982.
67. *Al-Ahram,* June 23, 1982.
68. United Nations, *Weekly News Summary,* July 24–30, 1982.

69. *New York Times*, June 30, 1982.
70. Schiff, "Green Light Lebanon," pp. 73-85.
71. Boutros Ghali discussed the Haig connection in *al-Musawer* (Egyptian weekly), July 1, 1982.
72. Schiff, "Green Light Lebanon," p. 80.
73. *Jerusalem Post*, June 30, 1982.
74. For further information about U.S. naval movement, see Claudia Wright's article in *New Statesman*, June 18, 1982. See also, *In These Times*, September 8-14, 1982.
75. For instance, on June 9, 1982, the United States vetoed a Spanish draft resolution in the UN Security Council, and on June 25, 1982, the United States vetoed a French draft resolution. See *New York Times*, June 10 and 26, 1982.
76. *New York Times*, June 12, 1982.
77. *Wall Street Journal*, June 14, 1982.
78. *Washington Post*, June 15, 1982.
79. *Jerusalem Post*, June 22, 1982. For additional statements on the commonality of interests between the United States and Israel, see *Washington Post*, July 7, 1982; *Jerusalem Post*, July 1, 1982; and *Ha'aretz*, August 5, 1982.
80. Such speculations were made because of Schultz's connections with the Bechtel Corporation, which enjoys economic interests and close links with the Arab countries. For more information, see Wright, "The Turn of the Screw—The Lebanon War and American Policy," pp. 8-14. Schultz was expected to have a more balanced approach toward the Arab-Israeli dispute when during a foreign relations Senate hearing he spoke of the significance of the Palestinian problem to peace efforts. He declared that "the legitimate needs of the Palestinian people must be addressed" and that a solution to the Palestine question "in all of its dimensions" must be attempted (Voice of America [English service], July 13, 1982).
81. *Sunday Times* (London), August 8, 1982.
82. During the Ford administration the United States committed itself, through former Secretary of State Henry Kissinger, not to recognize the PLO until the PLO recognized Israel and accepted UN Resolutions 242 and 338.
83. Such diplomatic moves included Arafat's meeting with Israeli journalist Uri Avneri, the speech of the late Issam Sartawi at the French Institute of International Relations in which he declared that "the PLO recognizes Israel's right to exist," and Arafat's signing of a statement before an American congressional delegation in Beirut in which he accepted all UN resolutions pertaining to the Palestinian question.
84. For articles on Israel's use of cluster-bombs, see *Washington Post*, June 12, 14, 21, 22, and 29, 1982; *New York Times*, June 22, 1982; and for a detailed treatment of Israel's use of antipersonnel weapons, see Kevin Danaher, "Israel's Use of Cluster Bombs in Lebanon," *Journal of Palestine Studies* 11, no. 4/12, no. 1 (summer/fall 1982).
85. *Washington Post*, April 13, 1978.
86. *Washington Post*, July 20, 1982.

87. For U.S. reaction to the continued Israeli bombing of West Beirut, see *Washington Post*, August 2, 5, and 13, 1982; and *New York Times*, August 2, 5, 10, and 13, 1982.

88. In this context, see the comments of former Secretary of State Henry Kissinger in *Washington Post*, June 16, 1982. See also *New York Times*, June 9, 1982; *Times*, London, June 23, 1982; and *International Herald Tribune*, July 6 and 8, 1982.

89. *Washington Post*, August 9, 1982.

90. *Wall Street Journal*, August 5, 1982.

91. The public opinion poll is found in *Newsweek*, August 16, 1982.

92. See Larry Davidson, "Lebanon and the Jewish Conscience," *Journal of Palestine Studies* 12, no. 2 (winter 1983); *Newsweek*, July 12, 1982; *San Francisco Chronicle*, June 23, 1982; and *In These Times*, July 28–August 10, 1982.

93. *New York Times*, July 1, 1982.

94. *Washington Post*, July 17, 1982, quoted in Danaher, "Use of Cluster Bombs," p. 56.

95. Quoted in *Newsweek*, July 5, 1982.

96. See *Washington Post*, June 11, 1982; *U.S. News and World Report*, July 19, 1982; Joe Stork and Jim Paul, "The War in Lebanon," *Merip Reports* 12, nos. 6–7 (September-October 1982):59–60; and *Newsweek*, August 23, 1982.

97. Stork and Paul, "The War in Lebanon," p. 60.

98. See *New York Times*, June 21, 1982; *Jerusalem Post*, June 27, 1982; and Barry Rubin, "The Reagan Administration and the Middle East," in Kenneth A. Oye, Robert Lieber, and Donald Rothchild, eds., *Eagle Defiant: U.S. Foreign Policy in the 1980s* (Boston: Little, Brown and Co., 1983).

99. For a useful analysis of Soviet reactions to the war, the reader is referred to Karen Dawisha, "The U.S.S.R. and the Middle East: A Superpower in Eclipse," *Foreign Affairs* 61, no. 2 (winter 1982/1983); and Galia Golan, "The Soviet Union and the Israeli Action in Lebanon," *International Affairs* (London) 59, no. 1 (winter 1982/1983). Compare these two articles with William B. Quandt, "Soviet Policy in the October Middle East War I," *International Affairs* (London) 53, no. 3 (July 1977); William B. Quandt, "Soviet Policy in the October Middle East War II," *International Affairs* (London) 53, no. 4 (October 1977); and Muhammad al-Said Salim, "al-Itihad al-Sovieli wa al-harb al-filistiniya," *al-Siyassa al-Dawliya*, no. 70 (October 1982), pp. 151–153.

100. Partial exceptions to the low-level Soviet involvement in the war were signals sent by the Kremlin leaders warning Israel not to extend its military operation beyond the Lebanese borders. These signals included the placement on alert of a number of Soviet air-borne divisions, the Soviet request for flight rights over Turkey, the reinforcement of the Soviet naval fleet in the Mediterranean, the replacement of Syria's war plane losses, and the visits of Soviet military experts to Syria to assess the reasons for the poor military performance of the Syrian troops. For more information, see Dawisha, "The U.S.S.R. and the Middle East," pp. 438–441.

101. WAFA (Palestinian news agency), June 7, 1982, reported by Golan, "Soviet Union and Israeli Action," p. 11.

102. *International Herald Tribune,* July 7, 1982, and *Jerusalem Post,* July 7, 1982.

103. Golan, "Soviet Union and Israeli Action," pp. 7–9.

104. Abu Iyad was interviewed on Radio Monte Carlo (Arabic service), "Hadatha Ghadan" (news analysis program), June 11, 1982. Henceforth referred to as Radio Monte Carlo.

105. *Sunday Times,* July 4, 1982. See also Golan, "Soviet Union and Israeli Action," p. 12.

106. Pravda, June 14, 1982, reported by Radio Monte Carlo.

107. Tass, June 24, 25, July 1, 2, and August 10, 1982; and Pravda, July 6, 1982, as reported by regional broadcasts.

108. Pravda, July 8, 1982, reported by BBC.

109. Dawisha, "The U.S.S.R. and the Middle East," pp. 445–449.

110. For more information, see Robert O. Freedman, *Soviet Policy Toward the Middle East Since 1970* (New York: Praeger, 1975).

111. Golan, "Soviet Union and Israel Action," pp. 9–16. See also Galia Golan, *The Soviet Union and the Palestine Liberation Organization: An Uneasy Alliance* (New York: Praeger, 1980).

112. For background information on Western European Middle East policy, see Allen Taylor, "The Euro-Arab Dialogue: A Quest for Inter-Regional Partnership," *Middle East Journal* 32, no. 4 (fall 1978); Steven J. Artner, "The Middle East: A Chance for Europe?" *International Affairs* (London) 56, no. 3 (summer 1980); and Harvey Sicherman, "Politics of Dependence: Western Europe and the Arab-Israeli Conflict," *Orbis* 23, no. 4 (winter 1980).

113. For an overall assessment of the European reaction to the war, see Pamela Ann Smith, "The European Reaction to Israel's Invasion," *Journal of Palestine Studies* 11, no. 4/12, no. 1 (summer/fall 1982):37–47.

114. *International Herald Tribune,* June 10, 1982. For more information about European reaction, see also *Times* (London), June 10, 1982; *Guardian,* June 7, 1982; and *Le Monde,* July 4, 1982.

115. For the text of the communiqué, see *Journal of Palestine Studies* 11, no. 4/12, no. 1 (summer/fall 1982), p. 343.

116. *Al-Ahram,* July 4, 1982.

117. *International Herald Tribune,* July 20, 1982.

118. Jamal Abdul Jawad, "al-Siyassa al-Urobiya nahwa al-ghazu al-Isra'ili il al-Lubnan," *al-Siyassa al-Dawliya,* no. 70, October 1982.

119. For a historical background of French-Lebanese relations, see John P. Spagnolo, *France and Ottoman Lebanon, 1861–1914* (London: Ithaca Press for the Middle East Center, St. Anthony's College, Oxford, 1977).

120. *Le Monde,* July 14, 1982.

121. President Mitterrand's speech was broadcast over Radio Monte Carlo, July 17, 1982.

122. For further elaboration, see the comments attributed to the director general of the French Ministry in *al-Ahram,* July 4, 1982.

3
Diplomatic Responses to the PLO Exodus from Beirut

Immediately after the departure of PLO troops from West Beirut, the Palestinian problem and the Arab-Israeli conflict were treated with a sense of urgency. For the first time an Arab peace plan was collectively endorsed, the Reagan administration spelled out its position concerning the resolution of the Palestinian problem, and the PLO chief, Yasir Arafat, was received in some Western European capitals. One aim was common among these diplomatic moves: to make use of the new political realities after the war. With the military defeat of the PLO in Lebanon and the physical dispersion of its troops to several Arab countries, the Palestinian political leadership would pursue less ambitious and more realistic goals. The launching of these diplomatic initiatives had disquieting effects upon the unity and cohesion of the Palestinian nationalist movement in the postwar period.

Despite this long-term negative impact, the PLO appeared to be emerging from the crisis politically triumphant. As a sign of sympathy and of increasing understanding of the Palestinian question, some European capitals accorded the PLO new grounds for international respectability and legitimacy—a boost that the PLO sorely needed after its exodus from Beirut. The Greek prime minister was the first head of state to receive Yasir Arafat; two weeks later the Palestinian leader was invited to Rome to address a worldwide interparliamentary conference at which he received a standing ovation from most delegates. During his visit to Rome, Arafat met with the Italian president and his foreign minister. More significant, however, was Arafat's meeting with Pope John Paul II. A spokesperson for the Pope announced that Arafat's papal audience was intended to demonstrate the Vatican's concern for "the suffering endured by the Palestinian people," but added that Arafat's visit to the Pope did not imply formal recognition of the PLO.[1] Irrespective of this reservation, Arafat's reception at the Vatican had the effect of recognition, since it indicated an understanding of the

Palestinian cause and the PLO's role in representing the interests and the rights of the Palestinians.

The Reagan Initiative

On September 1, 1982, President Reagan outlined a plan for the resolution of the Palestinian problem and the Arab-Israeli dispute, which came to be known as the Reagan initiative. In this plan, Reagan noted that, with the departure of the PLO from West Beirut, "We have an opportunity for more far-reaching peace efforts in the region" and that "the Lebanon war, tragic as it was, has left us with a new opportunity for Middle East peace. . . . We must seize it now and bring peace to this troubled area." Reagan asserted that his initiative was in line with traditional U.S. Middle Eastern foreign policy, manifested in the U.S. commitment to bring peace to the region. The initiative was also undertaken to advance the notion of strategic consensus since settlement of the Arab-Israeli dispute would buttress U.S. efforts to contain the Soviet Union and increase U.S. influence in the region.

A configuration of factors determined the timing and the nature of the Reagan initiative. The decline in the political influence of the PLO when it lost its independent base of operation in Lebanon allowed the Reagan administration to advocate the "Jordanian option" and treat Jordan as a principal partner in the peace talks. The Reagan initiative also was intended to avert inflexible stands and unilateral actions by Israel, which could include the annexation of the West Bank and Gaza in the wake of its massive military assault of Lebanon. The timing of the initiative—a few days before the convening of the twelfth Arab summit conference—was designed as a gesture toward those moderate Arab countries that closely cooperated with the United States during the war to bring about the withdrawal of the PLO troops from Beirut. It also aimed at dismissing criticism by radical Arab countries of U.S. complicity during the war and at heading off any expected Arab sanctions against the United States. Further, the United States wanted to give the Arabs the opportunity to discuss Reagan's plan and to come up with a positive response, particularly as the initiative furnished the Arabs with the hope that they might regain the occupied territories.[2]

The Reagan initiative also probably was embarked upon in reaction to the repeated calls by the Arab countries and those in Western Europe that the United States be more assertive and evenhanded in its Middle Eastern policy. One cannot rule out the possibility that the Reagan administration undertook its peace plan in response to the mounting criticism inside the United States concerning the heavy casualties and destruction inflicted by the Israeli invading army upon Lebanon and to the growing impatience with the tendency of the Israeli prime minister to act unilaterally and on some occasions in defiance of U.S. interests in the Middle East. In addition, expectation was widespread that after the war the United States should come out with a peace settlement that would break the deadlock in the peace talks. William Quandt, an advisor on Middle Eastern politics to the Carter administration, argued that the Reagan initiative "was long overdue."[3] A criticism of the Reagan administration's mismangement of the Arab-Israeli conflict also came from former President Jimmy Carter. In an article in the *Washington Post* on September 1, 1982, Carter criticized the Reagan administration's lack of interest in fulfilling its role as a "full partner in the peace talks." He urged that the future of the Palestinian people should constitute the focal point in the search for a comprehensive settlement of the conflict and warned that the physical dispersion of the PLO troops to several Arab countries would not lead to a resolution of the Palestinian problem. In his view the time was appropriate to try to resolve the dispute, especially as the threat to Israel's security decreased with the evacuation of PLO troops from southern Lebanon.

Although the Reagan administration did not anticipate that Begin's government would alter its inflexible stands, the initiative was intended to stimulate a debate inside Israel and promote positive responses among the Israeli opposition parties, particularly as the Reagan initiative resembled the Allon plan, which represented the official standpoint of the Labor party.[4] However, senior officials of the Reagan administration asserted on several occasions that the United States had no plans to apply sanctions to compel the concerned parties to come to the negotiating table. Commenting on this issue, Caspar Weinberger stated, "I do not think it is time to talk about sanctions or pressures or actions. I think it is time to see the degree of general support throughout the area." He expressed the hope that Israel would ultimately change its position as it would find out that "this is the best way for them."[5] Similar views were also expressed by Secretary Schultz. In his opinion, pressure upon Israel could come from the opportunities afforded by achieving peace:

> Peace prospects are prospects of tremendous importance, not only to the security of Israel and its neighbors but also to the development of their economic, social and cultural well being. . . . We do not have any plan to try to maneuver people in peace negotiations by talking about withholding aid. . . . We will hold up the objective of peace for everybody. The more positive response that is given to it, the more important the reality of that peace will be.[6]

U.S. determination not to use sanctions against Israel to bring it to the negotiating table was also confirmed by Yitzhak Shamir when he declared after a trip to the United States that the Reagan administration did not even hint at applying sanctions against his country.[7]

Guiding Principles and Basic Positions

In contrast to the Camp David approach, in which the United States confined itself to the role of mediator and refrained from publicly putting forward its own ideas on key issues, the Reagan initiative promised more active U.S. involvement in the peace process. The Reagan peace plan also spelled out the positions of the United States concerning the meaning of peace, its parameters, and its components. These positions, nevertheless, did not amount to preconditions for the commencement of negotiations. The U.S. plan assumed that diplomacy and negotiations constituted the only avenue for the resolution of the Arab-Israeli conflict and pointed out that "only through the process of negotiations can all the nations of the Middle East achieve a secured peace."

The Reagan initiative invited the states in the region to acknowledge three political realities. One reality was that military force by itself had proved to be incapable of providing Israel with a durable peace despite its regional qualitative and quantitative military superiority. The initiative also acknowledged that despite the PLO's military defeat, "the yearning of the Palestinian people for a just solution of their claims" did not diminish. Finally, the Arab countries were called upon to recognize Israel's right to exist behind "secured and defensible borders" and to abandon the use of force in favor of diplomacy to settle their grievances against Israel.

The success of the U.S. peace plan was heavily contingent upon the nature and the extent of Jordan's willingness to participate in the anticipated negotiations. The PLO was not assigned a role, and no serious considerations were attached to a PLO option in view of its weakened position after the war and because an option of this sort had few advocates among the members of the U.S. foreign policy apparatus. Yet some State Department officials, including the secretary of state, spoke subsequently of the relevance of the PLO in the negotiations. George Schultz described the PLO as "part of the Palestinian issue" and "standing for it to a certain extent" and advised the PLO to urge King Hussein to come to the peace talks.[8] A few weeks later Assistant Secretary of State Nicholas Veliotis declared that the United States acknowledged that "the PLO is considered by the Arabs as a legitimate spokesman for the Palestinians and it enjoys significant support throughout the Arab world and inside the Palestinian community."[9]

The Reagan initiative also spelled out specific ideas concerning a comprehensive settlement to the Arab-Israeli conflict. In line with the

Camp David accords, the initiative declared a five-year transition period for the West Bank and the Gaza Strip during which "a peaceful and orderly transfer of authority from Israel to the Palestinians" would take place. The purpose of this transition period was twofold: to prove that the Palestinians would be capable of governing themselves and to show that self-autonomy would not pose a threat to Israel's security. Following this five-year period, the initiative promised to grant the Palestinians in the occupied territories full autonomy in association with Jordan. The U.S. peace plan explicitly ruled out the formation of an independent Palestinian state or Israel's permanent control or annexation of these territories. Concerning the delineation of borders between Israel and Jordan, the initiative stated that the degree of the Israeli withdrawal would depend upon "the extent of true peace and normalization and the security arrangements offered in return." The initiative also demanded that Israel immediately freeze the construction of new settlements in the occupied territories and announced that the United States would oppose the expropriation of additional land for settlement activities. Finally, the Reagan plan contended that Jerusalem should not be divided again, that its final status should be determined through negotiations, and that the Palestinian inhabitants of the city should have the right to vote in the proposed elections of the "autonomy council."

Reaction to the Reagan Initiative

The announcement of the Reagan peace plan was received favorably in Congress and among the U.S. media and public. Skepticism was voiced, however, concerning the administration's ability to implement its initiative and the style of diplomacy that the president assumed in dealing with the Arab-Israeli conflict. Zbigniew Brzezinski, former national security advisor for the Carter administration, argued that the Reagan initiative was important as it attested to the U.S. involvement in the search for a settlement.[10] He added, however, that the success of the initiative would be contingent upon what the U.S. government would do in the coming months. Brzezinski contended that a follow-up strategy by top U.S. officials was needed for the success of the initiative and anticipated that, in view of Israel's settlement activities and the categorical rejection of the initiative by the Begin government, the Reagan administration would back down from its initiative. A similar cautionary note was made by Talcott Seelye, former U.S. ambassador to Syria, who claimed that the lack of continuity in applying pressure on Israel in the past convinced the Israeli government that the United States was not serious about its initiative.[11] He therefore advised that determination and consistency on the part of the U.S. government would convince

Israel not to accelerate its settlement activities in the occupied territories. Reagan's style of diplomacy was also criticized by Saul Linowitz, Carter's envoy to self-autonomy talks, who expressed his disagreement with "publicly putting forward" a plan for the Middle East. In his view, quiet, private diplomacy was more likely to produce positive results.[12]

The Israeli reaction to the Reagan initiative was not unpredictable.[13] The U.S. peace plan threatened a core Israeli interest—permanently retaining control, if not actual annexation, of the occupied territories. The launching of the initiative immediately after the PLO's departure from West Beirut was extremely irritating to Israel as it appeared to deny the Likud government the political fruits of its military victory. Any success for the Reagan initiative could, therefore, erode the political power of the Likud government.

Soon after its announcement, the Israeli cabinet sharply denounced the Reagan initiative and accused the United States of interference in internal Israeli affairs. In an apparent challenge to the U.S. initiative, the Israeli government announced the establishment of eight new settlements in the West Bank and Gaza Strip.[14] In a Knesset debate held in early September 1982, the Israeli prime minister rallied majority support to reject the Reagan initiative.[15] According to the official communiqué of the Israeli cabinet emergency session, the categorical rejection of the initiative was made on the basis that it contradicted the letter and the spirit of the Camp David accords on a number of issues, including the meaning of self-autonomy, the status of East Jerusalem, the freeze on settlements, the linkage of the occupied territories with Jordan, and the questions of security and sovereignty over the occupied territories. The government's communiqué asserted that Israel would not enter any negotiations on the basis of the U.S. peace plan.[16]

In addition to the outright rejection by the Israeli government as a collective body, individual members of the ruling coalition expressed vehement opposition to the terms of the Reagan initiative. The call for a freeze on Israel's settlement activities and the ruling out of a permanent control or annexation of the territories by Israel constituted the core of their criticism. In a Knesset speech on February 1, 1983, the Israeli prime minster declared, "The freezing of settlements is not possible. It would be similar to freezing of life. . . . Israel will never abandon this policy. . . . It is the right of the Jews to spread in safety and peace in all of their forefathers' land."[17] In a similar statement Sharon contended, "No one would stop us from settling the strategic areas of the land of Israel. Israel is alone responsible for its security. We will not rely on any guarantee of anybody including that of our best friend the United States."[18] While attending the inauguration of a Jewish settlement south of Jerusalem, Deputy Foreign Minister Yahuda Ben Meir declared that

Israel's answer to the Reagan initiative should be the establishment of more Jewish settlements in the occupied territories "as this is the best proof that no force will be able to uproot us from our homeland from the land of Israel."[19] Rabbi Chaim Druckman, a Likud Knesset member, went to the extent of advocating: "The government should prove by action that it rejects the Reagan plan by annexing the territories."[20]

The call by the Reagan initiative to link the occupied territories with Jordan furnished Israel with another reason to reject the initiative. Eliahu Ben Alisar, chairman of the Knesset committee on defense and foreign relations, explicitly ruled out any association of this sort. In a speech to the Haddassah National Convention, he declared, "Jordan has no right to these provinces of western Eretz Israel. . . . Jordan has occupied these lands in 1948, kept them until 1967 and this does not give it any more right than the right of an occupier, not recognized by anybody in the international community except Britain and Pakistan. . . . so what right does Jordan have today to these provinces? None."[21] Similarly, in his letter replying to the Reagan initiative, Begin categorically rejected any return of the West Bank and Gaza to Jordan. He said, "Judea and Samaria will never again be the West Bank of the Hashemite Kingdom of Jordan."[22]

In contrast to the vehement opposition of the Likud government, the Labor Alignment quickly endorsed the Reagan initiative, considering it "reasonable grounds" for negotiations. The initiative was in line with the Allon plan, the official stand of the Labor party for settling the Arab-Israeli conflict. For this reason Shimon Perez, chairman of the Labor Alignment, welcomed the initiative as a basis for "serious dialogue" with Jordan.[23] The Mapam party, the other main partner in the Labor Alignment, also gave a warm reception to the Reagan initiative. The secretary general of the party, Victor Shintov, acknowledged that the Reagan plan contained "positive elements" and that it should be examined "seriously."[24] The Labor Alignment was displeased with Begin's outright rejection of the U.S. peace plan. In its view, this categorical rejection could trigger U.S. pressure upon Israel. If Israel refused to reach a settlement with Jordan on the basis of territorial compromise, it could find itself at a later stage compelled to negotiate with the PLO.[25] Labor party officials also warned that the insistence of the Likud government that eventually it would annex the occupied territories with their 1.2 million Palestinians would certainly threaten the Jewish demographic nature of the state of Israel.

Israel's leading newspapers expressed mixed feelings concerning their government's flat rejection of the Reagan plan. The independent Hebrew daily, *Ha'aretz,* argued that the Reagan proposal was not inconsistent with the Camp David accords and charged that the Israeli prime minister was making "a big mistake" by rejecting the U.S. plan entirely.[26] *The Jerusalem Post* (English daily) cautioned that Begin's outright rejection would further isolate Israel in the international community.[27] In a similar tone, *Davar* considered the total rejection of the initiative "unrealistic."[28] *Ma'ariv*, a progovernment daily, voiced disagreement with the Reagan initiative, particularly the call for a freeze on the construction of additional Jewish settlements in the West Bank and Gaza.[29]

The Arab Peace Plan of Fez

The Reagan initiative was received with mixed reactions in the West Bank and the Gaza Strip. Moderate forces in the occupied territories spoke favorably of the initiative and thought that it constituted a serious attempt on the part of the Reagan administration to resolve the Palestinian problem. They urged PLO chief Yasir Arafat to coordinate closely with King Hussein and to reach an accord as soon as possible so that negotiations could begin before the Reagan administration became preoccupied with the 1984 presidential elections. Toward the end of November 1982, approximately 200 leading personalities in the West Bank and Gaza signed a document supporting the Jordanian-PLO dialogue and Palestinian national rights. In contrast, supporters of PLO hard-line groups opposed the Reagan initiative on the grounds that it ruled out the formation of a Palestinian state and did not assign any role for the PLO. In particular, this opposition did not welcome the idea of associating the occupied territories with Jordan.

The reaction of the Arab countries directly concerned with the U.S. peace proposals came in line with their foreign policy orientations. Countries known for their moderate political stands, such as Jordan and Egypt, welcomed the positive aspects of the Reagan initiative and urged the Arab countries to study them carefully. Reagan's demand for a freeze on Israeli settlements, his insistence upon full autonomy for the Palestinians, the linkage of the future of East Jerusalem to the occupied territories, and the opposition to Israel's permanent control or annexation of these territories were favorably received by the governments in Cairo and Amman.[30] Reagan's promise to restore Jordanian sovereignty not only to the West Bank but also to the Gaza Strip was favorably received by the Hashemite regime. In an interview with the British Broadcasting Corporation (BBC), King Hussein remarked, "The Reagan initiative is the most courageous stand taken by any American administration ever since 1956. I believe it to be a very constructive and a very positive move and I would certainly like to see it continue and evolve."[31]

The favorable reception of the Reagan initiative was not unqualified: It was criticized for its overemphasis on Israel's security needs and its opposition to the formation of an independent Palestinian state. In response to its reactiviation of the Jordanian option, a foreign ministry spokesperson in Amman reaffirmed Jordan's compliance with the 1974 Arab summit resolution that acknowledged the PLO as the sole legitimate representative of the Palestinian people.[32] Jordan's cautious acceptance of the initiative was prompted by the need for a Palestinian and Arab legitimization to join the peace talks.

In contrast to the Egyptian and Jordanian attitudes, the Syrian government-controlled press rejected the Reagan initiative, considering it a continuation of the Camp David accords. The initiative was envisaged as a clear indication that no U.S. Middle Eastern policy existed except an Israeli one, and this situation was insulting to the Arabs since the initiative only took into account Israel's security interests.[33] President Assad's opposition to the U.S. peace plan was a byproduct of a number of considerations.[34] The failure of the U.S. plan to account directly for Syria's grievances against Israel was partly responsible for the hostile Syrian attitude as it did not address itself directly to the Syrian Golan Heights occupied in 1967. Syria was also irritated when the United States excluded its ambassador from the consultations with the ambassadors of Jordan, Israel, and Saudi Arabia in the process of preparing for the president's initiative. A Syrian acceptance of the Reagan initiative would necessarily entail a recognition of Israel, which the Assad regime was not yet prepared to do. Moreover, the Syrians could not welcome the fact that the Reagan initiative ignored the Palestinians' rights for self-determination, as the Ba'ath ruling party, being a pan-Arabist regime and a proponent of the Palestinian cause, could not accept the role of Jordan as the main representative for the Palestinians. In addition, the Assad regime wanted to avoid the image of military weakness and desperation through its acceptance of the Reagan plan, particularly after its poor and brief military performance in the first days of the war. Nor can one dismiss the possibility that the Syrian government's opposition was tactical in nature: it could have been hoping to extract more concessions from the United States. Finally, President Assad's decision to oppose the Reagan plan probably was prompted by the fact that the initiative excluded the Soviet Union, Syria's main patron, from the peace process.

The announcement of the Reagan initiative just a few days before the convening of the twelfth Arab summit conference in Fez, Morocco, gave the Arab kings and presidents the opportunity to deliberate upon it. Though the initiative was not formally endorsed, the Arab countries attached considerable significance to it, attested to by the emergence of the Palestinian-Jordanian dialogue intended to lay the foundation for a confederation between the occupied territories and Jordan. Further, the initiative served as an impetus for the Arabs to come up with an alternative peace plan.

During their conference, Arab states were concerned about formulating a common policy that would make up for their loss of prestige and credibility throughout the war period, which resulted from their failure to defend the embattled Palestinians and their inability to exert tangible influence upon Western countries, especially the United States. The rulers succeeded in producing for the first time a joint Arab peace plan, despite their rivalries and mutual hostilities. Unlike the Reagan initiative, the Arab peace plan advocated the creation of an independent Palestinian state in the West Bank and Gaza Strip with East Jerusalem as its capital. Moreover, the Arab initiative called for the withdrawal of the Israeli army from all the territories it occupied in 1967, including East Jerusalem, the Golan Heights, and the West Bank and Gaza Strip. In addition, the Arab plan demanded the dismantling of all Jewish settlements constructed after the 1967 war. In sharp conflict with the Reagan initiative, the conferees at Fez reconfirmed that the PLO was the sole legitimate representative of the Palestinian people and insisted that it should play a central role in any future negotiations.

In line with the Reagan initiative, the Arab peace plan advocated placing the occupied territories under UN supervision but specified a few months' transitional period and invited the UN Security Council to ensure the peace and security of the states in the region, including a Palestinian state. Finally, the Arab peace proposals spoke of guarantees for freedom of worship and the religious rights of all people in the holy places in Jerusalem.

Immediately after the termination of the conference, King Hassan of Morocco, spokesman for the summit conference, declared that the Arab peace plan constituted a first step toward nonbelligerency and that it would be followed later by normalization of relations and the establishment of diplomatic ties with Israel.[35] A few days later King Hussein of Jordan in a television interview described the Arab peace plan as "a major milestone" where an Arab consensus was reached concerning the basis for a just and lasting solution to the Arab-Israeli conflict. The king cautioned, however, that the endorsement of the peace plan did not mean that peace was imminent, though he asserted, "It is certainly the foundation in my view towards the establishment of a just and durable peace."[36]

A number of considerations were functional in determining the nature of the Arab peace plan. As noted earlier, the launching of the Reagan initiative served as an incentive for the Arabs to come up with an alternative peace strategy. The military defeat of the PLO in Lebanon and the expulsion of its leadership and troops from Beirut facilitated such a task, as the PLO's ability to stir up violence for Arab moderates was reduced. In addition to the decline in the political influence of the PLO, the moderate Arab countries, who were mainly behind the peace plan, felt less inhibited by radical Arab states who a year earlier thwarted the endorsement of the Saudi Fahd peace plan. The military inaction of these radical Arab states during the siege of Beirut undermined their credibility and deprived them of a moral claim to be the main custodian of the Palestinian cause and revolution.

Nevertheless, the Arab diplomatic initiative tried to strike a balance between the views of moderates and radicals and to account for Palestinian interests and the dictates of political realities. First, Arab reconfirmation of the PLO as the sole legitimate representative of the Palestinians and its insistence that it should play a central role were designed to strengthen and promote moderation within the Palestinian nationalist movement and confine the PLO's activities to the diplomatic scene away from radicalism and violence. At the same time, the Arab peace plan aimed at limiting the maneuverability of King Hussein, particularly since the Reagan initiative specified that Jordan play a pivotal role and reestablish its soveriegnty over the occupied territories. The apparent limitation upon King Hussein's freedom of action was intended to keep the PLO within the main stream of Arab moderates and to appease Syria, Jordan's main adversary, by arresting its fears that the king would unilaterally embark upon a policy of reconciliation with Israel. Similarly, the call by the Arab summit upon Israel to withdraw from all occupied territories was meant to address Syrian grievances and interests of regaining the Golan Heights. The summit attempt to enlist the Syrian endorsement of the peace plan was made, not only to ensure Syrian support, but also to guarantee that the Assad regime would grant the acquiescence if not the consent of the PLO's radical factions to the peace plan, particularly since the leaders of these factions live either in Syria or in Syrian-controlled territories in Lebanon.

By inviting the various members of the UN Security Council to oversee the implementation of the Fez peace plan, Arab countries were hoping to directly involve the Soviet Union. A step of this sort was thought to enhance the chances of success for the Arab peace plan since otherwise the Soviet Union could obstruct political moves that would fail to account for its interests in the Middle East. Moreover, the involvement of the Soviet Union might also be seen as a sign of Arab displeasure toward the United States' indecisive and biased handling of the Arab-Israeli dispute.

Article 7 of the Arab plan implied an indirect recognition of Israel that was intended to communicate to the Western countries, Israel, and the United States Arab willingness to eventually grant the Jewish state full recognition in return for the recovery of the occupied territories. An explicit recognition of Israel was not feasible at the time since it would have certainly been opposed by the radical Arab states in the conference and by the PLO. Even Arab moderates harbored some doubts about the rationality of such a step, as they were uncertain about the ability and willingness of the United States to exert and sustain pressure upon Israel to soften its uncompromising attitude over the occupied territories. Arab countries made concerted efforts to appear positive, and their unanimous adoption of a peace plan was an indication of the triumph of diplomacy and reason over rhetoric and rejectionism. Despite the fact that the seven member Arab League delegation, led alternatively by King Hussein and King Hassan, visited the capitals of the five permanent members of the Security Council to explain and enlist support for the Arab peace plan, the plan remained inoperative. The Arab peace plan gave the Reagan initiative the bare minimum of support needed if the United States decided to press against the defiant Israeli government.

Although it seemed for some time that the United States was serious in its endeavors to solve the Palestinian problem, fateful events that followed in Lebanon once again obscured the Palestinian issue. The assassination of Bashir Gemayal, Israel's occupation of West Beirut, and the massacre of several hundred Palestinian civilians in the refugee camps of Sabra and Shatilla made Lebanon again the pivotal point of U.S. Middle Eastern policy. Amid Lebanon's political and military turmoil and anarchy, the political credibility of the United States as a reliable mediator in Middle Eastern problems incurred a major blow.[37] A quick withdrawal of the Israeli army from Lebanon and a freeze of Israeli settlement activities in the occupied territories came to be recognized by the Arabs as the new yardstick for the reestablishment of U.S. credibility. The United States failed on both accounts, and the Palestinian question was once again left behind in favor of what were perceived to be more urgent and pressing problems in Lebanon. In spite of this, the resounding echo of the Reagan initiative continued to be widely heard in inter-Palestinian and inter-Arab affairs and proved to be a dividing factor inside the PLO. Despite its shortcomings and Israel's unyielding hostility to it, the main value of the Reagan initiative was to give rise to Arab and Palestinian hopes and expectations that with the help of the United States they would be able to restore Arab sovereignty over the occupied territories. The prevelance of such hopes has indeed unleashed the reconciliation efforts between Jordan and the

PLO and has led to the concomitant rupture in the inter-Palestinian relations and Palestinian-Syrian ties.

Notes

1. *International Herald Tribune,* September 15, 1982.
2. William Quandt, in an interview on BBC's "World Today," September 2, 1982.
3. Ibid.
4. For the Labor party's stand on a political settlement, see Yigal Allon, "Israel, the Case for Defensible Borders," *Foreign Affairs* 55, no. 1 (October 1976):38–53.
5. Weinberger made these remarks in an interview with BBC's program, "Twenty-Four Hours," September 7, 1982.
6. Schultz was interviewed on CBS's "Face the Nation," September 5, 1982.
7. *Ma'ariv,* October 29, 1982.
8. Schultz, interview on CBS, September 5, 1982.
9. Nicholas Veliotis was interviewed on NBC's "Meet the Press," September 26, 1982.
10. Brzezinski was interviewed on ABC, September 2, 1982.
11. Voice of America (Arabic service), September 4, 1982.
12. Linowitz was interviewed on BBC's "World Today," September 2, 1982.
13. Khalil Nakhleh and Clifford Wright, *After the Palestine-Israel War: Limits to U.S. and Israeli Policy* (Belmont, Mass.: Institute of Arab Studies, 1983), pp. 43–51.
14. *Jerusalem Post,* September 6, 1982.
15. The vote was 50–36 and can be found in *New York Times,* September 9, 1982.
16. For the text of the communiqué, see *Jerusalem Post,* September 3, 1982.
17. *Ma'ariv,* February 2, 1983.
18. *Ma'ariv,* December 15, 1982.
19. Ben Meir's comments were broadcast by Israel Radio (English service), September 2, 1982.
20. Ibid.
21. Excerpts from Ben Alisar's speech were broadcast by Israel Radio (English service), September 1, 1982.
22. For the text of the letter, see *Jerusalem Post,* September 6, 1982.
23. *Washington Post,* September 4, 1982.
24. *Al-Hamishmar,* September 3, 1982.
25. Nakhleh and Wright, *After the Palestine-Israel War,* p. 48.
26. *Ha'aretz,* September 6, 1982.
27. *Jerusalem Post,* September 6, 1982.
28. *Davar,* October 21, 1982.
29. *Ma'ariv,* September 6, 1982.
30. See *al-Dustur,* September 4 and 5, 1982, and *al-Ahram,* September 5 and 6, 1982.

31. King Hussein was interviewed on a BBC television program, "Panorama," September 13, 1982.
32. *Al-Dustur,* September 4, 1982.
33. *Al-Ba'ath,* September 4, 1982.
34. Sa'ad al-Din Ibrahim, "Mubadarat al'Ra'is Reagan," *al-Siyassa al-Dawliya,* no. 70 (October 1982):149–50.
35. *New York Times,* September 11, 1982.
36. King Hussein interview (BBC), September 13, 1982.
37. John Sigler, "United States Policy in the Aftermath of Lebanon: The Perils of Unilateralism," *International Journal* 38, no. 4, 1983.

Part 2

The Palestine Liberation Organization After Beirut

4
Moderates and Rejectionists Within the PLO: Divisive Issues and a Search for National Unity

The Israeli invasion of Lebanon in summer 1982 placed the PLO at a critical juncture in its history. The Palestinian resistance movement's loss of its independent base of political and military operations in Lebanon adversely affected its cohesion, unity, and viability.[1] During the post-Beirut era the PLO was confronted with a variety of challenges and risks that required it to make definitive choices. The attitudes toward the Reagan initiative and the Arab peace plan of Fez; the nature of the PLO's relations with Jordan, Egypt, Syria, and Israeli peace groups; and the type of political and military strategy that the PLO should pursue—all were crucial issues that required clear approaches and united Palestinian stands. The unfolding of these issues, however, deepened the already existing political cleavages among PLO factions. During the first nine months following the PLO's evacuation from Beirut, the instinct of political survival and the desire to preserve Palestinian national unity prevailed. During this period, the leadership of the different Palestinian factions worked to deemphasize their conflicting views, culminating in the Palestine National Council (PNC) meeting in Algiers in February 1983. Despite these attempts, the PLO moderates and rejectionists remained apart, and their deep-seated divisions persisted. By May 1983, the PLO's organizational viability and cohesion began to seriously erode when a mutiny took place inside Fatah, the PLO's main faction, leading to a polarization of the Palestinian nationalist movement between supporters and opponents of Arafat.

A New Phase for the PLO

It is not an overstatement to say that the degree of political and military freedom that the PLO enjoyed in Lebanon could not be replicated anywhere else in the Arab world (as it is hard to imagine that any of the countries hosting PLO troops would allow them to develop a strong military infrastructure or to pursue their own political objectives as freely as they did in Lebanon). Indeed, the Lebanese political climate, including the absence of an effective central government and the deep-seated divisions within Lebanese society allowed the PLO to operate as a state within a state. The fact that the PLO was dispersed throughout the Arab world denied the organization its main and easily accessible source for human resources and recruitment in the Palestinian refugee camps of Lebanon.[2] Furthermore, because Palestinian troops were dispersed to several Arab countries, the PLO could not pursue its long-held strategy of carrying out an armed struggle against Israel. Though it is too early to determine whether the Palestinian resistance could still launch its military operations against Israel from Lebanon, the 1982 war appears to have ended the PLO's ability to engage the Israelis from a contiguous Arab country. Like the other Arab bordering states (Egypt, Syria, and Jordan), Lebanon will in all probability no longer allow its territory to be used for waging guerrilla attacks against Israel.

The PLO's ability to exploit Lebanon for military purposes was further constrained by the fact that after the withdrawal of the bulk of its troops, the Palestinian presence in Lebanon was reduced largely to an unarmed civilian population. Moreover, with the dispersal of PLO troops it would be inconceivable for Palestinian fighters to practice their guerrilla tactics from their remote sanctuaries in North and South Yemen, Algeria, and Sudan. In addition, the PLO's loss of Lebanon as a military base reduced to a large extent the significance of traditional external supplies of military equipment and diminished the relevance of the PLO's possession of conventional arms, including tanks and heavy artillery. These new realities were bound to affect the PLO's ability to preserve itself as a national liberation movement.

Equally significant, the losses of the PLO's military infrastructure in southern Lebanon and its political headquarters in West Beirut were associated with a visible reduction in its capacity to exploit the political potential of its military force and its translation into tangible political influence and bargaining power. This decline was attested to by a number of developments—which could hardly be imagined prior to the Israeli invasion of Lebanon—that began to unfold soon after the Palestinians' departure from West Beirut. To begin with, the Reagan initiative designated a central role for Jordan in the process of solving the Palestinian question. This decision was concomitant with denying the PLO any place in the "peace process" and ruling out the formation of an independent Palestinian state. The willingness of the Jordanian monarch to explore the opportunities provided by the Reagan initiative also signaled the diminishing influence of the commando groups. The reconvening of the Jordanian parliament with 50 percent of its representatives coming from the West Bank, in January 1984 (after a ten-year suspension), would not have been possible if the PLO had continued to enjoy the same power and influence it did prior to the war. A crippling blow to the prestige and credibility of the PLO came from inside the Palestinian movement itself with the open split in the PLO's main faction, Fatah. This split culminated in fierce battles between Arafat's supporters and his Libyan- and Syrian-backed opponents in the Bekaa Valley in central Lebanon and spread northward to Tripoli toward the end of 1983, leading to the evacuation of the remainder of the PLO troops loyal to Arafat.

The Lebanon War also compounded the PLO's standing problem of dependency upon a divided Arab world: The dislocation of the PLO's military force made it more vulnerable to Arab pressures and interference in internal Palestinian affairs to the extent of fomenting dissent and rebellion. At the same time, the PLO was caught between the bitter rivalries and divisions of the Arab countries; the various PLO factions maintained special relationships with their respective Arab custodians and adhered strictly to the policies dictated by these countries. For instance, the pro-Libyan and pro-Syrian hard-line groups inside the PLO worked against Arafat's diplomatic moves that included his dialogue with Jordan and his attempts to reconcile with Egypt. Similarly, the close relationship that Arafat enjoyed with Saudi Arabia partly prompted him to accept the Saudi-sponsored Arab peace plan of Fez.

The uprooting of the PLO from Lebanon further undermined the already precarious organizational unity of the Palestinian resistance movement.[3] Although the PLO was expected to serve as an umbrella organization with its institutions as forums for political debates, its component groups did not hesitate to act independently and outside the PLO political councils. The fact that many of these groups have been in existence for nearly two decades contributed to the development of autonomous institutional interests, power bases, and particularistic identities and ideological affinities.[4] In addition, their political allegiances to different external patrons impeded these PLO groups from forming united political stands. The disperson of PLO fighters also created new problems of coordination, communication, command, distribution of funds, and control of smaller factions within the PLO.

Though differences of opinion among the Palestinians concerning a political settlement of their future had existed since the mid-1960s, such differences in the post-Beirut era were transformed into open cleavages and actual military confrontations. The question of strategies and options to be pursued led to acrimonious debates between the PLO's moderates and radicals. The main area of controversy was what attitude the PLO should endorse in regard to the Reagan initiative: Some argued that the initiative should be given a chance whereas others ruled out any dealings with the "imperialists." The United States was unwilling to open a dialogue with the PLO until the latter recognized Israel's right to exist and until it accepted UN Security Council Resolution 242. This policy, coupled with Israel's unyielding stand over the future of the occupied territories, reinforced the rejectionists' quest for maximalist demands at the expense of moderation and realism. The massacres at the refugee camps of Sabra and Shatilla shortly after the exodus of the PLO from West Beirut further exacerbated the tension inside the guerrilla movement. Heated debates about which attitudes to adopt toward Jordan and Egypt, whether or not to maintain contacts with Israeli peace groups, and what type of relationship to have with Syria also were generated inside and outside the PLO's councils.

At the heart of the controversy was an underlying struggle between those who wanted to pursue diplomacy and negotiations as realistic tools for advancing Palestinian national aspirations and those who continued to harbor many illusions about the utility and the relevance of military struggle to liberate Palestine. The PLO moderates were inclined to coordinate their moves with the foreign policies of Saudi Arabia, Egypt, and Jordan—a step vehemently opposed by the hardline groups who wanted to establish preferential relationships with both Syria and Libya. The outbreak of these differences inside the PLO was associated with the rapid erosion of its central decision-making apparatus. This erosion was manifested by the fact that different voices were speaking for the PLO, complicating the official position of the organization and making it more ambiguous.[5] The multiplicity of spokesmen was in contradiction to the Palestine Central Council resolution of December 1981, which stipulated that all PLO factions would conform to the official statements and declarations approved and initialed by the PLO Executive Committee.[6] Moreover, as a result of these controversies, the PLO's political institutions failed to perform their assigned role effectively. For instance, the Palestine Central Council (PCC) and the Palestine National Council (PNC) met only after several delays. The PCC, which was convened toward the end of November 1982, also failed to resolve the internal divisions within its ranks over cardinal issues, such as the attitudes toward the Arab peace plan and the relationship with Jordan. Similarly, the PNC meeting was delayed several times before it was finally convened toward the middle of February 1983. Because of the ineffectiveness of the PLO's political councils, calls were made for the convening of a popular Palestinian congress to discuss the future of the Palestinian question.

The variety of viewpoints inside the PLO did not conform precisely to its organizational divisions; differences of opinion were discernible within individual PLO factions, particularly within Fatah. Arafat's political stands varied to an extent from those of Salah Khalaf (Abu Iyad) and Nimr Saleh (Abu Saleh), both of whom belong to Fatah's Central Committee.[7] Similarly, ideological considerations and affinities did not always serve as the guiding principles that delineated the political positions of the various groups inside the Palestinian nationalist movement. Despite their hostilities to "Arab reactionary regimes," the Popular Front for the Liberation of Palestine and the Democratic Front for the Liberation of Palestine—the two hard-line, Marxist-oriented PLO groups—accepted at the PNC meeting at Algiers the Arab peace plan of Fez and the notion of confederation with Jordan following the creation of an independent Palestinian state.

Despite the pervasiveness of the divisive issues inside the PLO, the instinct for political survival and the desire to preserve the PLO as a representative organization prevailed. During the first six months after the Palestinians' departure from West Beirut, PLO leaders agreed that their policy differences should not lead to the breakup of the Palestinian resistance movement. They argued that any split in PLO ranks could seriously undermine the exclusive representational character of the organization and allow Jordan to reestablish a claim of sovereignty over the occupied territories. Arafat's personal prestige, his diplomatic skills and maneuvering, and the political weight of his organization, Fatah, allowed him to a certain extent to impose his political preferences upon the rest of the organization during the six-month period that followed the evacuation from Beirut.

The Views of the Moderates

In contemporary Palestinian political thinking, the concept of "moderation" refers to the mainstream political stands prevailing inside the PLO in the last decade. Moderation was manifested in the increasing signals toward political and diplomatic flexibility and the acceptance of a Palestinian state in the West Bank and Gaza Strip alongside Israel. This stream of thinking has been represented by Arafat and his close associates inside Fatah. Fatah has been considered the backbone of the Palestinian nationalist movement and has traditionally enjoyed considerable political influence in the PLO Executive Committee, the PCC, and the PNC. This influence has enabled Fatah to control and shape the most critical decisions in these three councils.

The centrality of Fatah inside the PLO has been derived over the years through the interplay of a number of factors. About 80 percent of the PLO's fighting force and 90 percent of the political positions inside the PLO have been filled by Fatah people. In view of Fatah's political and military preponderance, two-thirds of the large sums of money allocated annually by the Arab states to the PLO go directly to its own account.[8] Arafat's personal charisma, popular appeal, and skills as a mediator in inter-Palestinian fighting constitute an added asset to Fatah's influence. With few exceptions—most notably the split in Fatah's ranks in early summer 1983—the core of Fatah's leadership has remained in control of organizational affairs since the early 1960s.

The focus by Fatah upon Palestinian national unity, independence, consciousness, and identity, together with the absence of dogmatism in its political thinking and its propensity toward flexibility and pragmatism, accounted for the widespread civilian support that Fatah commanded within the Palestinian community, inside and outside the occupied territories. Fatah's moderate stands also enabled its leaders to be admitted in inter-Arab councils. Its doctrine of noninterference in internal Arab affairs was received well by Arab heads of state, prompting many of them to extend economic, political, and military backing to the main PLO faction. Because of the moderation of Fatah's leadership the Arab rulers granted the PLO the status of the sole legitimate representative of the Palestinian people. Likewise, the pragmatism and flexibility of the views of Fatah's leadership broadened the PLO's international support: More than 100 states recognized the organization, and the UN General Assembly granted it observer status.

Despite these assets, Fatah did not enjoy a free hand in managing PLO internal affairs and foreign policy; its policymaking power was limited by a variety of constraints. The need to preserve Palestinian national unity and maintain the PLO as a representative organization figured prominently in Arafat's calculations and decisions.[9] Moreover, the fact that Fatah is not a homogeneous and doctrinaire organization but rather a loose coalition of varying political tendencies forced its leadership to weigh its moves carefully and rally support behind such moves. Similarly, the presence of hard-line groups inside the PLO, with strong and determined leadership and ties with radical Arab countries, further constrained the freedom to maneuver of the PLO moderates. Radical Arab countries such as Syria and Libya were determined to stop what they termed "Fatah's slipping in the liquidationist solutions."

Regardless of these constraints, a growing number inside the PLO began to believe that the Lebanon War had demonstrated the limitations of the strategy of armed struggle and that the Arab countries were unwilling and unprepared to fight on behalf of the Palestinians. Advocates of this moderate trend wanted to utilize the favorable diplomatic climate toward the Palestinian cause created by the war and called for intensifying contacts with the West in an attempt to underline their peaceful intentions. They also expressed interest in granting some form of recognition to Israel's right to exist. The aim of such a move was to facilitate efforts to exert pressure upon Israel to make meaningful concessions to the Palestinians.

The constraints under which Fatah was operating inhibited the PLO moderates from fully pursuing their diplomatic efforts. The United States and Israel continued to harbor bitter hostility toward PLO and Palestinian political aspirations. These constraints explained why Fatah's political stands were indecisive, confusing and not sufficiently bold and imaginative, though far from being completely negative and rejectionist. Although Fatah's moderate leadership demonstrated some willingness to give the floating peace plans a chance, it simultaneously continued to pay lip service to the relevance of the strategy of military struggle. The moderate leadership was unwilling to gamble with too many odds working against it. With such mixed feelings and sentiments, the leadership of the PLO moderates approached the Reagan initiative, coordination with Jordan, and contact with Egypt, Syria, and Israeli peace groups.[10]

Moderates inside the PLO acknowledged that U.S. participation in a settlement to the Palestinian problem was indispensable in view of its massive economic, military, and political support to the Jewish state. One of the main preoccupations of the PLO's moderate leadership was to initiate a dialogue with the United States without any precondition in an attempt to avoid U.S. insistence upon prior Palestinian recognition of Israel and the acceptance of UN Resolution 242. However, the announcement of the Reagan initiative fell short of Palestinian expectations. Although the initiative was perceived by some moderate leaders as a step forward, they thought that it did not go far enough in addressing Palestinian national grievances. Commenting on the announcement of the Reagan peace plan, Farouq al-Qadoumi, head of the PLO's political department, announced that the PLO believed that the initiative encompassed "some positive elements," including U.S. opposition to Israel's annexation of the occupied territories and a call for a freeze to Israel's settlement activities. He argued that these two aspects provided grounds for discussion inside the PLO.[11]

The positive though cautious early pronouncements by PLO moderate officials concerning the Reagan initiative may have been intended to signal that the PLO's attitude was no longer absolute negativism and rejectionism. On the contrary, it aimed at indicating the PLO's willingness to welcome the positive aspects of any peace plan and work on improving its negative aspects. These positive aspects of the Reagan initiative, however, did not constitute strong incentives for the PLO's leadership to extend an explicit endorsement. To start with, the PLO's moderate leadership found it difficult to accord formal acceptance to the initiative because it did not address the realization of Palestinian national rights and aspirations, including the right of forming an independent Palestinian state.[12] The failure of the initiative to assign any role for the PLO in the peace process furnished another reason for Palestinian dissatisfaction.

Moreover, the chances for the moderates to deal with the Reagan initiative were hampered by the vehement opposition voiced by PLO hard-line groups and by certain elements inside Fatah itself.[13] The advocates of Palestinian moderation were also uncertain about how serious U.S. Middle Eastern policy was this time, particularly as the U.S. government declined to pressure Israel to stop its settlement activities and was unable to persuade the Israelis to withdraw their troops from Lebanon. This mood of uncertainty was reinforced by the already existing feelings of distrust and suspicion among the Palestinians toward U.S. management of the conflict. U.S. support for Israel's war aims and diplomatic efforts directed at evicting the PLO troops from Beirut were too fresh in the minds of PLO leaders. The massacres at Sabra and Shatilla refugee camps further increased anti-U.S. sentiments among the Palestinians. In a Radio Monte Carlo intereview on November 12, 1982, Arafat himself attributed the moral responsibility for the massacres to the failure of the U.S. government to honor its pledges and commitments to provide protection and safety to the Palestinian civilians in Lebanon.

These considerations and reservations were ultimately responsible for the PLO moderates' cautious rejection of the Reagan initiative, regarding it as an inadequate tool to furnish a sound basis for "a just and lasting settlement." The initiation of the Palestinian-Jordanian dialogue could be seen as an attempt by Arafat and his colleagues to explore the potentialities of the Reagan initiative. The key issues for the dialogue—the formation of a confederation between the West Bank and Jordan and the setting up of a joint negotiating team—were in line with the spirit of the Reagan peace plan.[14]

In contrast to the cautious rejection of the Reagan initiative, the moderates inside the PLO accepted the peace plan submitted by Saudi Arabia to the twelfth Arab summit conference of Fez. According to Arafat, the Palestinian delegation to the conference contributed significantly to the formulation of the Fez peace plan. A PLO representative was included in the Arab League's seven-member delegation, which was entrusted with visiting the capitals of the five permanent members of the Security Council to enlist support for the "Arab cause." Though Arafat's close association to the Saudi royal family partly induced him to accept the Fez peace plan, the plan itself, particularly the call for the creation of an independent Palestinian state, was consistent with

Fatah's position in the post-1973 war era. Seen from this perspective, the acceptance of the plan was an additional sign of the PLO's diplomatic flexibility and its willingness to opt for a political settlement to the Palestinian problem.

The moderates' endorsement of the Arab peace plan was not received with overwhelming support: Article 7, which contained an implicit recognition of Israel, caused much controversy within the movement. While the summit was still going on, Abu Saleh, along with the representatives of the Popular Front for the Liberation of Palestine and Popular Front for the Palestine General Command, held a press conference in which he denounced Article 7, labeling it a major concession by the Palestinians to "the zionist enemy." On January 27, 1983, Abu Musa, a member of Fatah's Revolutionary Council, criticized Arafat's endorsement of the Arab peace plan and called for its renunciation. This lack of agreement accounted for the PCC's failure to formalize a united Palestinian stand toward the Arab peace plan, as its final communiqué on November 26, 1982, refrained from accepting or rejecting the Fez plan. This issue was only settled after Arafat and his supporters used heavy pressure and persuasion, and the Palestine National Council endorsed the Arab peace plan as the minimum acceptable plan for the Palestinians.

The renewal of contacts with the Egyptian government in summer 1982 was another signal of the moderates' flexibility and willingness to reconsider their alliances in the Arab world. In their view, the Lebanon War demonstrated clearly that the exclusion of Egypt from the Arab fold weakened the Arab's military position. They further argued that setting aside Egypt's military preponderance and political weight would only serve Israel's long-term interests. They concluded that the Arab countries should help Egypt resume its proper place in inter-Arab politics and councils.[15] Some PLO officials, including Sa'id Kamal, the PLO representative in Cairo, and Ahmed Sudki al-Dajani, a PLO Executive Committee member, reestablished contact with the Egyptian government in summer 1982 after a five-year absence of public diplomacy. The pro-PLO stands of the government of President Mubarak, manifested in opposition to Israel's war objectives, paved the road for the resumption of dialogue with the Egyptian regime.

The Camp David accords and the peace treaty with Israel proved to be stumbling blocks in the way to full normalization with Egypt. Fatah's hard-line elements and the rejectionist groups within the PLO continally warned against any rapprochement with the Egyptian government. This attitude explains why contacts with Egypt were kept at a low profile during this phase, despite the desire of the moderates to strengthen such relationships. Subject to the pressure of the hard-line groups, the moderates made the improvement of ties with Egypt contingent upon the extent to which the government would dissociate itself from the Camp David agreement. The PLO leaders took a different approach with regard to the Egyptian people; they steadily increased and improved their dealings with Egypt's opposition groups.[16] The presence of a large nongovernmental Egyptian delegation at the PNC meeting in Algiers attested to the significance that the PLO gave to the Egyptian opposition groups.

Attitudes toward Israel and Israeli peace groups were additional areas of concern for the moderates in the PLO. The dovish elements among the moderates openly called for the recognition of Israel and the enhancement of contacts with the Israeli peace groups. The main advocate of this approach was the late Issam Sartawi, a leading political advisor to the PLO chairman, who was assassinated by the splinter PLO group of Abu Nidal in April 1983. Sartawi argued that the time had come for the PLO to embark upon a peace offensive particularly because the strategy of armed struggle was increasingly irrelevant in the wake of the destruction of the PLO's military infrastructure in Lebanon.[17] To broaden the support for Palestinian national rights, Sartawi underlined the significance of increasing contacts with the Israeli peace groups and argued that the aim of such Palestinian-Israeli dialogues was to convince the Israeli public of the PLO's peaceful intentions and its readiness to settle the Palestinian question through political means. Contacts of this sort were also expected to enhance the PLO's international legitimacy and pave the road for Western and U.S. recognition of the PLO. In the long run, Sartawi contended, the Palestinian-Israeli dialogue would lead to the emergence of a third political force inside Israeli society that would oppose the "bellicosity and the expansionist" tendencies of Israel's two main political parties. Earlier Arafat himself, in an interview with the Italian daily *Republica* on September 15, 1982, indicated his willingness to meet with representatives of Israeli peace groups and those Israeli civilians and military personnel who opposed their government's policy in Lebanon and were willing to support Palestinian national rights. Upon the advice of Sartawi, Arafat met with three representatives of Israel's peace groups in Tunis toward the middle of January 1983. This meeting came as a tangible translation for the conciliatory mood among PLO moderates.

Along with the notion of promoting ties with Israel's peace groups, the PLO chairman and some of his aides expressed interest in the concept of mutual and simultaneous recognition between the Israelis and Palestinians. On July 25, 1982, while besieged in Beirut, Arafat signed a statement before a U.S. congressional delegation in which he recognized all UN resolutions that dealt with the Palestinian problem.

The recognition of Israel was implied in this statement despite the denial by a PLO spokesperson of such an implication. In response to the fury in Palestinian circles generated by Arafat's signature on the statement, the spokesperson added that the PLO would not recognize Israel unless the latter complied with UN resolutions. A few weeks earlier, Arafat had declared in an interview with Israeli journalist Uri Avneri that peaceful coexistence between a Palestinian state and Israel was possible and that the PLO was ready to establish a Palestinian state in any part of Palestine from which Israeli troops would withdraw.[18] A few months later, Khaled al-Hassan reiterated the significance of the concepts of peaceful coexistence and mutual recognition between the PLO and Israel, provided that the U.S. government would ensure the implementation of Palestinian national rights.[19]

Signs of political pragmatism were also discernible in the attitude of Fatah's leadership toward the Palestinian presence in Lebanon. With the departure of the PLO's troops from Beirut, the overriding goal of the moderate leadership was to coordinate with the Lebanese government to ensure the safety and protection of the Palestinian civilians. This issue became more acute with the massacre at the refugee camps of Sabra and Shatilla. Khalil al-Wazir, commonly known as Abu Jihad, stated that the protection of Palestinian civilians and their property in the camps was the responsiblity of the Lebanese government and asserted that these refugees were subject to the authority of the central government in Beirut. He also acknowledged the right of the Lebanese government to restore its sovereignty over the entire country.[20]

Unlike the hard-line groups in the PLO that insisted on retaining their troops on Lebanese territory, the moderates indicated their willingness to discuss the future of the remaining PLO forces inside Lebanon. Commenting on this issue, Abu Jihad declared, "In such discussions the interests and unity of the Lebanese people will be taken into consideration."[21] Likewise, Arafat was not opposed in principle to the evacuation of the remainder of Fatah's troops from Lebanon, although he stated that he would be reluctant to do so before a complete Israeli withdrawal.

Attitudes toward Syria during and after the war were both complex and problematic. Irrespective of their political and ideological orientations, the PLO leaders, particularly those in Fatah, expressed their bitter disappointment and lack of understanding toward the Assad regime's reluctance to engage its army in defense of the Palestinians. In a January 21, 1983, interview with Radio Monte Carlo, Abu Jihad summarized the main sticking points in the relationship between Syria and the PLO. He pointed out that the determination of the PLO to retain its independence and Palestinian national identity angered the

Syrians who viewed such attitudes as provincial and regionalistic. He stated, "We are not regional, but it is our right to take the path that we believe in and the decisions that we want, as it is Syria's right to take decisions in line with its vision, environment and interest. . . . The PLO wants to maneuver in any form it sees fit to defend the Palestinian cause. . . . Our judgments and basis of calculations as a revolution and as an organization differ from those of Syria, the state and the party, with its territory, army, politics, and style of diplomacy." Earlier Arafat underlined the same point when he stated in a November 12, 1982, Radio Monte Carlo interview, "I'm not a carbon copy of anyone."

The absence of Syria's military cooperation and coordination during the Israeli invasion was cited as another source of tension between Fatah and the Syrian regime. Abu Jihad blamed Syria for its failure to engage its army in the war. In an attempt to reduce Israeli military pressure upon the PLO, Fatah leaders had preferred to widen the zone of military operations through Syrian military participation in the war. The Palestinians complained that Syria's military calculations were not in harmony with those of the PLO during the siege of Beirut, as the Assad regime insisted that it alone would determine the place and the timing for a military offensive. Fatah leadership argued that though it had sent messages to Syria urging Assad to keep the borders open for individual Arab fighters willing to fight alongside the PLO the government remained reluctant to do so. Damascus denied this accusation and contended that no Arab fighters had rushed to the defense of the Palestinians.

Differences also broke out between Syria and the Palestinian moderates concerning Arafat's political moves during the siege, particularly his acceptance of the principle of evacuating the Palestinian fighters from West Beirut. This policy conflicted with Syria's advice to the PLO to exhibit a greater degree of "steadfastness and resistance." Commenting on this issue, Abu Jihad argued that "resistance cannot be pursued for the sake of resistance," particularly as there were no expectations of military support forthcoming to rescue the Palestinian fighters. Abu Iyad as well condemned the "apathy" of Syria and the other members of the Steadfastness and Confrontation States and characterized them as "the front of talk and nothing but talk." The absence of Syrian military support necessitated embarking upon a political solution that could ease the suffering of the civilians in West Beirut. Abu Jihad also rejected the Assad regime's criticism of Arafat's decision to disperse the PLO fighters to several Arab countries and contended that Syria did not want to accommodate a large number of these fighters.

These bad feelings between the Syrian regime and Fatah's leadership were further extenuated after the PLO evacuation from Beirut. Arafat's selection of Tunis rather than Damascus as the new PLO headquarters, followed by Assad's decline to be in the delegation of Arab kings and presidents welcoming Arafat to Morocco in September 1982, constituted additional signs of the deterioration in the relationship between Syria and the PLO. Arafat's search to improve relations with both Egypt and Jordan conflicted also with Syria's political preferences, despite his repeated assertions that the PLO did not intend to join the Iraqi-Jordanian-Egyptian axis against Syria. In an attempt to diminish the tension of the relationship, some PLO officials depicted the rift between Syria and Fatah as a struggle for power, a personal rivalry, and a misunderstanding between Arafat and Assad. Though a personality conflict may have accounted to an extent for some of the problems between the PLO and Syria, its significance should not be overexaggerated to blur the discrepancy in their political perceptions, preferences, and interests.

Despite the severity of these criticisms, the Fatah leadership was careful not to alienate the Assad regime. Its common interests with Syria compelled it to search for compromises with Damascus. Syria and the PLO needed each other to check the expansionist tendencies of Israel. From a Palestinian perspective, Damascus was the only Arab capital to assert repeatedly its determination to confront Israel. Moreover, Syria was logistically important to the PLO because the Syrian-controlled Lebanese areas were the only remaining sites from which the Palestinian commandos could launch their military operations. Also the PLO received and hoped to continue to receive many of its arms from the outside through Syrian ports. Uncertainty about the political outcome of U.S. and Arab peace plans and the lack of trust in U.S. Middle Eastern policy in general reduced the incentives of the Palestinian moderates to risk an open confrontation with the Syrians. Needless to say, Syria's military dominance and the influence it wielded in inter-Arab politics and over Palestinian hard-line groups made Fatah's leadership aware of the capacity of the Assad regime to seriously complicate matters for the PLO, particularly since the Syrian government had not in the past shied away from intervening directly against the PLO when it was perceived to be in Syria's interests. The possibility could not be excluded that pressure from the Soviet Union was exerted upon the PLO to be more accommodating and more forthcoming in its coordination and cooperation with Damascus. Such considerations were certainly behind the repeated calls of Fatah's top people to ameliorate relations with Syria, and although points of tension and conflict still existed, appeals continued to be made for a reconciliation. Even after his humiliating expulsion from Damascus toward the end of June 1983, Arafat expressed his desire to go back to Syria, "I say to you, if Syria threw me out of the door, I would try to come back through the window. If the window were locked, I would dig a tunnel to get back to Syria. I have equal rights in Damascus like every Syrian."[22] Even though he complained repeatedly about Syrian behavior, Abu Jihad asserted that despite the problems besetting their relationship, both "have no choice except to remain in one front and to unite in the face of common dangers and threats."[23] Abu Iyad underlined the significance of maintaining sound relations with Damascus when he stated, "Syria remains the lungs through which the Palestinian revolution breathes."[24] He asserted that the conflict between Syria and the PLO was exaggerated. Fatah's appeals to improve relations with Damascus included an insistence that such a relationship be constructed on the basis of equality, trust, and respect for the autonomy and independence of each other. Fatah's suspicion of Syria was substantiated in the early summer of 1983 when the Assad regime supported the rebellion against Arafat leadership. It is in this context that the conciliatory statements by some of Fatah's leaders in the initial phase after the war should be understood.

To sum up, the broad objective of the PLO moderates in the first phase of the post-Beirut era was to proceed cautiously to appropriate for themselves a role in any political settlement that would realize the national rights of the Palestinian people. This necessitated the search for a new strategy to meet the exigencies of the post-Beirut era. The PLO's concern to preserve the national unity in the initial phase after withdrawal from Beirut slowed down the efforts of breaking away from past policies. Such a departure came in late 1984 and early 1985. In the initial phase this approach was implemented through cautious rejection of the Reagan initiative, endorsement of the Arab peace plan, initiation of a dialogue with Jordan, gradual opening toward Egypt and Israeli peace groups, and deliberate distancing of the PLO from Syrian control. The uncertainty about whether a political settlement would ever be reached compelled the moderate leadership to acknowledge the relevance of the strategy of armed struggle as an avenue to achieve Palestinian national aspirations. In this regard, the chairman of the PLO stated, "Dropping the military struggle will lead to surrender." He qualified his statement by asserting, "The PLO does not speak of the military option in an absolute manner." The implementation of such an option in Arafat's view would depend on the outcome of political and diplomatic negotiations.[25] Fatah's leadership did not want to be outbid by the PLO rejectionists' repeated assertion of the need to preserve an armed struggle. Moreover, the frequent reference to military struggle was deemed necessary to maintain the PLO as a national liberation movement, particularly after its dispersal to several Arab countries. The occupied territories were singled out as a theatre for Palestinian military operations; however, it was hard to imagine how such a policy could be implemented in view of the dispersal of Fatah's troops to remote areas of the Arab world and the immense obstacles in the way of PLO fighters who attempted to carry out military activities from any Arab country adjacent to Israel. It is also exceedingly difficult to imagine that the people in the occupied West Bank and Gaza Strip could carry on a military struggle in view of Israel's tight military security and the fact that the Palestinians in the occupied territories are unarmed and do not have easy access to weapons.

The Rejectionists' Alternative

The rejectionist elements inside the PLO differed with the moderates on most issues that preoccupied the Palestinian nationalist movement in the post-Beirut era. The Reagan initiative was vehemently opposed by the rejectionists, particularly its notion of authorizing Jordan to speak for the Palestinians. Some even opposed any talk about a confederation with the Jordanian regime prior to the creation of an independent Palestinian state. They were also determined not to withdraw their troops from Lebanon or establish contacts with the Egyptian regime and Israeli peace groups. Unlike the moderates, they advocated the consolidation of ties with both Syria and Libya and stressed the reliance upon the strategy of military struggle as the principal means of realizing Palestinian rights.

During the first nine months after the withdrawal of the PLO forces from Beirut, the rejectionist camp consisted of five factions: the Popular Front for the Liberation of Palestine (Popular Front), the Democratic Front for the Liberation of Palestine (Democratic Front), the Popular Front for the Liberation of Palestine General Command (General Command), the Palestine Popular Struggle Front (Popular Struggle Front), and the pro-Syrian faction, al-Sa'iqa. The five groups together served as a system of checks and balances inside the PLO's political institutions, limiting Fatah's range of policy options.[26]

Despite the factions' overall agreement on many issues, two trends can be distinguished within the rejectionist camp. One trend, espoused by the General Command, Popular Struggle Front, and al-Sa'iqa, opposed any political settlement to the Palestinian question and attacked Arafat's diplomatic moves after the war. The three groups offered military support to the rebellion inside Fatah in early summer 1983 and demanded the removal of Arafat from office following his trip to Egypt.

In contrast, the Popular Front and the Democratic Front, although differing with Arafat's diplomatic moves and his optimism about the possibility of a political settlement, continued to acknowledge his leadership of the PLO and were willing to compromise with him. Both groups maintained a neutral stand concerning the split inside Fatah, and, despite their condemnation of Arafat's trip to Cairo, they continued their dialogue with Fatah to reach a national reconciliation. Their break with Fatah came after the convening of the Palestine National Council's seventeenth session in Amman in November 1984 and the signing of an agreement for joint diplomatic action between Arafat and Hussein in February 1985. The two groups together are the most influential among the hard-line groups; their influence was derived from the support of certain radical Arab countries and from the charismatic leadership of George Habash, secretary general of the Popular Front, and Nayef Hawatmeh, secretary general of the Democratic Front. Both organizations also enjoyed a fairly wide base of civilian support, especially in refugee camps. Their Marxist orientation was partly responsible for the popularity of the two groups among the poorer classes, student movements, and some intellectual groups in Palestinian society. Furthermore, the Popular Front's origins in the Arab nationalist movement of the 1950s broadened its sources of support among Arab nationalist circles. For these and other reasons, the two organizations wielded influence inside the Palestinian nationalist movement incommensurate with their representation, enabling them to modify and even obstruct the endorsement of undesirable policies by the PLO's political institutions.

The rejectionist camp identified six dangers that threatened the continued viablity and survival of the PLO. These were defined in a joint statement issued by the five groups on January 16, 1983, following their meeting in Tripoli, Libya. The six dangers were the initiation of the Reagan plan, Jordan's willingness to participate in the "peace process," the launching of the Arab peace plan at Fez, Palestinian contacts with the Egyptian government, the dialogue with Israeli peace groups, and the willingness of the Lebanese government to sign a normalization agreement with Israel. In the opinion of the radical groups, the launching of the Reagan initiative was the most ominous danger to the Palestinian revolution.

Soon after the initiative was announced, spokesmen for the Popular Front and the Democratic Front sharply denounced the U.S. proposal on the grounds that it did not address the national interests of the Palestinian people and aimed at solving the Arab-Israeli dispute at the expense of the Palestinians and their representative, the PLO.[27] The Reagan initiative was seen as an extension of the Camp David accords since it was designed to advance the prestige and credibility of the

United States in the region and to incorporate the Middle East into the "imperialist camp." The rejectionists further argued that through its invitation to Jordan to represent Palestinian interests and its avoidance of appropriating any role for the PLO, the Reagan initiative aimed at "liquidating the Palestinian revolution." Unlike the PLO moderates, the rejectionist groups entirely dismissed any positive aspect to the plan. In this context, the leader of the Popular Front, while inquiring about the wisdom and rationale of accepting the Reagan plan, pointed out a number of serious flaws and shortcomings, and commented, "Will it realize our rights of return, self-determination and the formation of an independent Palestinian state? The answer is clear. The acceptance of the Reagan plan will not realize these goals." He added, "If we accept the Reagan plan will the land come back to us? Will settlements stop? Why don't we then learn from the history and the truth behind the Zionist movement. . . . The land will never be restored except through armed struggle." Habash concluded, "It is wrong to separate between the land and the revolution and between the land and the Palestine Liberation Organization."[28]

The consistently pro-Israel stands of the U.S. government reinforced the anti-U.S. posture of the hard-line groups. Moreover, the exclusion by the Reagan initiative of both Syria and the Soviet Union (the traditional allies of PLO hard-liners) furnished the rejectionists with an added reason to oppose the U.S. plan. The initiative's invitation to Jordan to join the peace talks was alarming to the rejectionists, particularly in view of King Hussein's expressed desire to enter into a political settlement on the basis of the Reagan initiative. The rejectionists also viewed talks between Arafat and Hussein concerning a confederation between the Palestinians and the Jordanians as premature and urged that such talks be deferred until after the formation of an independent Palestinian state. The rejectionists found it difficult to reconcile with the Jordanian monarch, who between 1970 and 1971 liquidated the Palestinian military and political elements in Jordan. The rejectionists also vehemently opposed King Hussein's attempt to form a joint Palestinian-Jordanian negotiating team and were equally resentful of any West Bank participation in such negotiations. In their view, delegations of this type would diminish the exclusive representative character of the PLO.

The endorsement of the Arab peace plan of Fez was envisaged by the rejectionists as constituting another danger to the survival of the Palestinian revolution. They believed that the adoption of such a plan demonstrated the military weakness of the Arab countries, their willingness to recognize the "Zionist entity," and their abandonment of the military option. Leaders of the hard-line PLO factions argued that "Arab reactionary governments" were hoping to establish a link between the Fez plan and the Reagan initiative.[29] Article 7 of the Arab peace plan, which implicitly recognized Israel, was especially abhorrent to the rejectionists. Commenting on this issue, Habash stated, "This article will make it easier for Arab reactionary regimes to embark upon negotiations with the Zionist enemy."[30] The representatives of the Popular Front and Ahmed Jibril's General Command issued a statement on the last day of the Arab summit meeting at Fez, criticizing Article 7. They argued that it was in complete contradiction with the various resolutions of the PNC and PLO's charter and contended that its endorsement constituted a major concession by Palestinians and Arabs in return for "imaginary hopes."[31] Two weeks later, four of the hard-line groups issued a joint statement rejecting among other things Article 7 on the grounds that it legitimized "the Zionist enemy's usurpation of our land."[32]

The rejectionists' suspicion of the Arab peace plan was further deepened by the fact that the summit was convened only after the PLO's withdrawal from West Beirut. The rejectionist leaders recalled that the Arab countries' repeated intervention in Palestinian internal affairs left a negative impact upon the course of the "Palestinian national struggle" and warned against Arab attempts to create a wedge between the PLO and the Palestinians in the occupied territories. They urged the Palestinian nationalist movement to safeguard itself against such encroachment.

In the opinion of the rejectionists, contacts with the Egyptian regime furnished an added threat to the Palestinian revolution. Unlike the moderate groups, the rejectionists opposed establishing any contacts with the government of President Mubarak before it altered decisively its attitude toward the Camp David accords and its peace treaty with Israel. They contended that a Palestinian rapprochement with Egypt should be commensurate with how far Egypt was willing to distance itself from Israel. The cancellation of the Camp David accords was the price demanded by the rejectionists to normalize their relationship with the Egyptian government. This policy explained their opposition to the moderates' attempts to work for the readmission of Egypt into the Arab fold. The hard-line groups wanted to deny Egypt the opportunity to use its political and demographic weight in the Arab world to implement the "imperialists' plans." Like the moderate forces, the rejectionists drew a distinction between the Egyptian regime and what were termed the "progressive democratic forces" inside Egypt.[33] Contacts with such groups were expected to be strengthened.

The Israeli-Lebanese talks on foreign troop withdrawal were also perceived as seriously challenging the PLO. The rejectionists insisted that the PLO support the Lebanese nationalist forces and promote their resistance to the Israeli occupation of Lebanon. They were also determined to mobilize the Lebanese masses against any concessions the Gemayal government might make to the Israelis. Unlike the PLO moderates, the hard-line groups insisted upon the continued presence of their troops in Lebanon. In line with their pan-Arabist ideological orientations, the leaders of the rejectionist camp argued that resistance to the Israeli occupation of south Lebanon was an Arab responsibility and that Israel's military presence had undermined Lebanese sovereignty and its Arab allegiance.[34] The aim of such tough stands was to ensure for the rejectionists the freedom of military activities against the Israeli occupying forces on Lebanese territory.

Arafat's meeting with representatives of Israeli peace groups in January 1983 at his headquarters in Tunis triggered a wave of bitter criticism in the rejectionist camp. In Damascus the hard-line groups issued statements sharply denouncing Arafat's move and characterizing it as "national treason." The pro-Syrian group, al-Sa'iqa, published a warning against "all those who gamble with the Palestinian cause." The rejectionists' condemnation of Arafat was not unanimous, however; Hawatmeh's Democratic Front did not participate in the anti-Arafat campaign and declined officially to denounce Arafat's meeting with Israeli peace groups. In an interview with the French news agency on January 25, 1983, Hawatmeh minimized the political significance of such a meeting, characterized it as being "mainly ceremonial," and argued that the meeting would have no influence upon the political decisions inside Israel. It should be noted that contacts with progressive Israelis and Jews were not unusual in Hawatmeh's front. The Democratic Front traditionally stressed its willingness to open a dialogue with any Jew that would recognize Palestinian national rights, including the rights of return, self-determination, and the formation of an independent Palestinian state. Indeed, a few weeks after the PLO's withdrawal from Beirut, it was reported that Hawatmeh intended to submit a proposal to the Palestine national council calling for a mutual and simultaneous recognition between Israel and the PLO.[35]

Despite the perceived seriousness of these dangers, the PLO hardline groups were convinced that their revolution would continue to victory. In their view, the Palestinian resistance movement possessed the capabilities and resources to overcome the hurdles of the post-Beirut era. In a lengthy interview in *al-Hurriya* (Democratic Front publication) on February 22, 1983, Hawatmeh pointed out, "The road for liberation is a long one and there are no magic solutions for the problem." He further underlined the significance of the continuation of the Palestinian struggle and a change in the regional balance of power in favor of the Palestinian cause. Hawatmeh cautioned that the survival of the Palestinian revolution required the strengthening of Palestinian national unity among PLO factions. A strict adherence to the principle that the PLO is the sole legitimate representative of the Palestinians and the preservation of its autonomous decision-making were also deemed necessary for the continued viability of the PLO.

In the opinion of the rejectionists, military struggle was the only guarantee for the survival of the Palestinian revolution.[36] The relatively heavy casualties incurred by the Israeli army in Lebanon and the long duration of the war led the rejectionists to believe that there was a true possibility of defeating the "Zionist enemy." Despite the difficult circumstances in which the PLO found itself after the dispersal of its troops, the rejectionist leaders pledged that they would continue the strategy of armed struggle. Such a strategy, they contended, would frustrate the Reagan initiative and other "liquidationist solutions," including the proposed Palestinian-Jordanian delegation for peace talks. They also argued that the Lebanon War had reconfirmed the impossibility of peaceful coexistence between Palestinians and Israelis.

The rejectionists gave special attention to the occupied territories, and they repeatedly expressed their determination to set up military operations inside Israel. An appeal was made to the Palestinians in the West Bank and the Gaza Strip to reactivate the Palestine National Front to include all Palestinian nationalist forces and institutions.[37] The task of such a front would be to coordinate Palestinian activities against the Israeli military authorities and Jewish settlements, fight the Reagan initiative and the Camp David accords, and resist the formation of an alternative leadership to the PLO, particularly the Israeli-sponsored village leagues and the pro-Jordanian group.

Concerning the Arab world, the rejectionists urged that PLO support be widened to include the Arab arena and socialist countries. In line with the pan-Arabist orientations of some of the rejectionists, the Palestinian nationalist movement was envisioned as an integral part of the Arab world, and the attainment of Arab unity was seen as a prerequisite for the liberation of Palestine. The rejectionists contended that the relationship of the PLO with the Arab countries should be structured around the commitment of these countries to the promotion of the Palestinian cause.[38] They divided the Arab world into two rival camps: the reactionary camp and the non-reactionary nationalist camp. The reactionary camp, led by Egypt, Saudi Arabia and Jordan, wanted to incorporate the Middle East in the imperialist sphere at the expense of dropping the military struggle, the PLO, and Palestinian national rights. In contrast, the non-reactionary nationalist group of states, led by Syria, Libya, Algeria and South Yemen, opposed U.S. "imperialist designs" and "liquidationist solutions" for the region.

The leaning of the PLO's hard-line groups toward the non-reactionary Arab countries did not prevent some of them from criticizing the failure of such countries to extend military aid to the PLO during the siege of Beirut. In this context, Nayef Hawatmeh expressed the disappointment of his organization concerning Syria's policy of military inaction during the war when he stated, "We originally thought that we were fighting the war with the Syrians side-by-side. Unfortunately, this was not applied in practice. The Syrian participation in the war came too late and too sporadically."[39] Assad's strict supervision of the PLO's military activities inside Syria and in the Syrian-controlled territories of Lebanon furnished additional grounds for Palestinian complaints but did not provide incentives for the leaders of the hard-line groups to break away from the Damascus government.[40] On the contrary, the post-Beirut era was marked by the rejectionist leaders' repeated calls to upgrade Palestinian-Syrian relations to the level of a strategic alliance.

Despite the perceived shortcomings of Syria's policy, Damascus was considered a natural ally to the Palestinians by the rejectionists. At least two reasons accounted for the close ties between Syria and the hard-line groups. First, the bulk of the rejectionist forces and their leadership was based in Syria or in the Syrian-controlled portions of Lebanon. This dependence compelled the rejectionist leadership to cooperate with the Assad regime and even be subservient to the policies and interests of the Syrian government. Second, and equally important, the Syrian political stands concerning the rejection of the Reagan initiative, the Arafat-Hussein talks, and the Israeli-Lebanese troop-withdrawal talks were congruent with rejectionists' political attitudes. It was therefore in the interest of both to frustrate the Jordanian-PLO dialogue and any other plan that would not take into account their grievances and particular concerns.

Despite the fact that the Assad regime has not allowed Palestinian military operations to be launched from Syria proper since the signing of the Syrian-Israeli troop disengagement agreement in 1974 and that Syria has abstained from openly encouraging the PLO's military activities from Syrian-controlled Lebanese territory, geopolitical and military considerations figured prominently in the rejectionists' rationale for the advancement of Palestinian-Syrian relations. The proximity of the Syrian territories to Israel was envisaged as vital for the continuation of the strategy of military struggle. In view of the dispersal of the PLO troops, Habash argued, "The Palestinian revolution cannot afford to become a refugee revolution."[41] For this reason the rejectionists urged that special efforts be made to overcome the obstacles in the way of improving relations with Damascus. Such an improvement of relations, however, should be sought in a framework of mutual confidence, respect, and understanding of the specific circumstances of each party and the freedom of each to make its independent judgments and decisions.[42]

The Palestine National Council at Algiers: A Recipe for Inaction

When the Palestine National Council was convened at Algiers in the middle of February 1982, widely divergent political attitudes concerning the problems that engulfed the PLO continued to characterize the relationship between Palestinian moderates and hard-liners. The PLO moderates were alarmed by the pace of Israeli settlement activities in the occupied territories and were conscious of their military weakness and the concomitant drop in their political influence and bargaining power. These considerations prompted them to favor the pursuit of diplomacy to salvage the occupied territories and cope with the exigencies of the post-Beirut era. The moderates were also inclined to open a dialogue with the United States despite the perceived limitations of the Reagan initiative, and they wished to improve relations with Egypt and expressed an interest in confederating with Jordan.

In contrast, the rejectionists did not view the question of Israel's settlement activities with the same sense of urgency and immediacy, though they recognized its seriousness. In their opinion, a settlement of the Palestinian question on the grounds of the Reagan initiative and the Arab peace plan of Fez in the context of regional Arab military inferiority would not realize Palestinian political aspirations. The hard-line groups, therefore, categorically rejected the Reagan initiative and argued against any close relationship with Egypt and Jordan and instead called for the forging of an alliance with Syria.

Amid this background of opposing views and conflicting political tactics and priorities, the Palestinians went to Algeria to attend the sixteenth session of the Palestine National Council. Because of this diversification in their political attitudes, the PNC communiqué was deliberately vague, allowing each contender to claim that its own political preferences and views pervaded the discussions. Vagueness and compromise therefore characterized the resolutions that the conferees at Algiers endorsed to avoid further divisions within the PLO's ranks.[43]

Concerning the nature of the relationship between the Palestinians and the Jordanians, the PNC, in line with the wishes of the moderates, accepted the concept of confederation and agreed to upgrade its relationship with the Hashemite Kingdom of Jordan to a special level. At the insistence of the rejectionists, however, the PNC ruled that such a state of affairs would only come about after the formation of an independent Palestinian state. Moreover, subject to the wishes of the rejectionists, the communiqué precluded any authorization to Jordan or any Palestinian group outside the PLO to negotiate on behalf of the Palestinians, on the grounds that the PLO alone has the exclusive right of representation. Although the PNC resolution kept the door open for Arafat to continue his dialogue with King Hussein, such a decision fell short of Jordanian expectations: It failed to come up with a clear statement allowing Jordan and non-PLO Palestinians to participate in the "peace process." In addition, the PNC insistence that confederation would only take place between two sovereign states clashed sharply with the Reagan initiative.

Another compromise resolution was reached with regard to the Reagan initiative. Contrary to the demands of the rejectionist groups to reject flatly the initiative, the moderate forces managed to persuade members of the PNC to characterize it as an unsuitable tool to bring about a just settlement of the Palestinian problem and the Arab-Israeli dispute. This qualified rejection was designed to permit Arafat some freedom to try to improve the Reagan initiative and to keep the door open for a dialogue with the United States. A more favorable reception was accorded the Arab peace plan because the conferees at Algiers considered it the absolute minimum to be accepted for the Palestinian people. In an apparent concession to the hard-line elements, the PNC stipulated that the Arab peace plan be complemented by military action and preparations so as to alter the regional balance of power in favor of the PLO. The PNC reiterated its endorsement of President Brezhnev's 1980 plan, which called for Palestinian and Arab recognition of Israel in return for the formation of an independent Palestinian state and the recognition of the PLO as the sole legitimate representative of the Palestinian people.

Other compromises were also reached concerning Palestinian relations with Egypt and contacts with Israeli peace groups. In line with the wishes of rejectionists and moderates alike, the PNC once again denounced the Camp David accords and the self-autonomy plan. The Mubarak regime, however, was not denounced, raising the speculation that Palestinian contacts with the Egyptian regime should be cautiously pursued. The PNC called for the consolidation of ties with what it termed "Egypt's progressive and democratic forces," which proved to be provocative and irritating to the Egyptian government. A few days after the conclusion of the PNC meeting, President Mubarak, in a speech to the Egyptian parliament, rejected the PNC resolution—considering it an interference in Egyptian internal affairs—and reaffirmed his country's commitment to the Camp David accords and the peace treaty with Israel.[44] On the question of contacts with Israeli peace groups, the PNC retained the PLO's traditional policy of establishing ties with

Jewish groups and individuals as long as such contacts would serve Palestinian national interests. The PNC, however, failed to address the question of recognizing Israel.

In line with the wishes of the hard-line groups, the PNC passed a resolution calling for the consolidation of ties with "brotherly Syria" and the reactivation of the Front of Steadfastness and Confrontation States. This political stand was tempered by the moderates' insistence to strengthen Palestinian ties with all Arab countries. In a further concession to the hard-line groups, the political communiqué underlined the need to promote and escalate the strategy of military struggle from all Arab fronts against Israel. To facilitate such a task, the communiqué called for regrouping the PLO's dispersed fighters and strengthening ties with the Lebanese nationalist forces. The communiqué also pledged not to attack Israeli civilians and expressed a desire to confine the PLO's military activities inside Israel and the occupied territories. Finally, the PNC heavily emphasized the need to preserve Palestinian national unity and the autonomy of Palestinian decision-making. It also urged Palestinians in the West Bank and Gaza Strip to form a national front in order to advance the cause of Palestinian national unity and to frustrate the Reagan initiative and the Camp David accords.

Despite the pressing problems that the PLO faced in the post-Beirut era and the urgent need to find solutions, the PNC failed to come up with an imaginative political strategy that would allow the PLO to participate effectively in a political settlement of the Palestinian question. The inconclusive nature of the PNC communiqué resulted from the interplay of several factors. The democratic tradition that governs the discussions inside the PLO's political councils and the insistence of the PLO's leadership upon consensus building and applying unanimity rule in making decisions in an atmosphere of political diversities and competing ideologies narrowed the range of imaginative political choices. Complicating this situation were the hard-line groups, supported and sustained by radical Arab countries, which deprived the PNC of the ability to make a well-defined political strategy. Moreover, the fact that the West Bank and the Gaza Strip Palestinians were not represented in the PNC, because of Israel's opposition to their participation in PLO meetings, deprived the moderates of additional weight, since those Palestinians were the most anxious to end occupation.

Despite these constraints upon the PLO's ability to produce a well-defined policy, the prevailing political and military conditions in the Middle East were not favorable for the Palestinians and therefore precluded any bold initiatives. In addition to the physical dispersal of Palestinian troops and leadership, Israel remained as hostile as ever toward the achievement of Palestinian national rights and stepped up its settlement activities in the occupied territories in contradiction to the Reagan initiative. The United States itself did not deviate from its policy of not recognizing the PLO, and it neither succeeded in getting the Israelis out of Lebanon nor in bringing about an agreement that could lead to such an eventuality. Moreover, the Arab countries themselves showed no sign of willingness or readiness to fight on behalf of the Palestinians, and despite their collective endorsement of the Fez peace plan, they failed to make it operational. In view of this overall situation, it was hard to imagine that the PNC could have come out with a different policy. To the conferees at Algiers the overreaching goal for the PLO after Beirut was to survive in the new, unfavorable environment, surrounded by formidable challenges and copious external expectations of Palestinian political magnanimity and foresight. Participants in the PNC were under immense psychological pressure to project a unified position and a sense of viability in the face of these challenges. The PLO leadership was aware of the need to preserve Palestinian national unity so as to remain a representative organization and maintain its organizational respectability, legitimacy, and recognition. This awareness explains the pervasiveness of the slogans of national unity, cohesion, and independence heard throughout the PNC sessions and the repeated assertions by PLO leaders that their differences were healthy signs and points of strength attesting to the PLO's democratic tradition.

The tone of moderation reflected in some PNC resolutions did not impress those awaiting the results of the PNC meeting. From a U.S. perspective, for instance, these gestures were not generous enough to constitute sufficient grounds for opening a dialogue with the PLO—a step that the United States prefers to avoid indefinitely. Similarly, the inconclusive nature of the PNC political communiqué failed to persuade King Hussein to move forward in the peace process and ultimately prompted him to break off his six-month-old dialogue with Yasir Arafat. Finally, despite the feelings of self-confidence and national unity that prevailed in the PNC meetings, political cleavages among the various PLO factions did not vanish; soon after the termination of the Algiers conference, differences between moderates and rejectionists again surfaced, and in less than three months, they developed into a mutiny inside Fatah.

Notes

1. For an assessment of the impact of the Lebanon War upon the PLO, see Aaron David Miller, "The PLO: What Next?" *Washington Quarterly* 6, no. 1 (winter 1983):116–125; Helena Cobban, "The PLO in the mid-1980's: Between the Gun and the Olive Branch," *International Journal* 38, no. 4 (1983):635–651;

Dan Schueftan, "The PLO After Lebanon," *Jerusalem Quarterly*, no. 28 (summer 1983):3–24; Kenneth Stein, "The PLO After Beirut," *Middle East Review* 15, nos. 3–4 (spring-summer 1983):11–17; Usamah al-Ghazali Harb, "Howla Mustaqbal al-Muqawama al-Filistiniya Ba'ad al-Harb al-Sadissa," *al-Siyassa al-Dawliya*, no. 70 (October 1982):131–136; and Eric Rouleau, "The Future of the PLO," *Foreign Affairs* 62, no. 1 (fall 1983):138–156.

2. For background information on the PLO's recruitment in the refugee camps of Lebanon, see John Cooley, "The Palestinians," in P. Edward Haley and Lewis W. Snider, eds., *Lebanon in Crisis* (Syracuse, N.Y.: Syracuse University Press, 1979), pp. 23–29.

3. For a useful treatment of the PLO's composition, see William B. Quandt, "Political and Military Dimensions of Contemporary Palestinian Nationalism," in William B. Quandt, Fuad Jabber, and Ann Mosely Lesch, *The Politics of Palestinian Nationalism* (Berkeley: University of California Press, 1973), pp. 79–91. See also Helena Cobban, *The PLO: People, Power and Politics* (Cambridge: Cambridge University Press, 1984).

4. Muhammad Y. Muslih, "Moderates and Rejectionists Within the Palestine Liberation Organization," *Middle East Journal* 30, no. 2 (spring 1976):127–140.

5. Dia' Rashwan, "Athar Qadaya al-Taswia al-Siyasiya 'ala al-Tamasok al-Dakhili fi Munadamat al-Tahrir al-Filistiniya," *al-Siyassa al-Dawliya*, no. 71 (January 1983):59–63.

6. The Palestine Central Council consists of around eighty members representing the eight PLO factions, independent Palestinian personalities, and Palestinian unions and associations. It serves as an intermediary body between the PLO's Executive Committee and the Palestine National Council. For a detailed treatment of the PLO's political institutions, see Rashid Hamid, "What is the PLO?" *Journal of Palestine Studies* 2, no. 4 (summer 1973).

7. See the interviews with Abu Iyad in *al-Tali'a* (Kuwaiti biweekly), September 22, 1982; and in *al-Musawer* (Egyptian weekly), October 29, 1982. See also the interview with Abu Saleh in *al-Tali'a*, October 6, 1982.

8. Miller, "The PLO: What Next?" pp. 118–119; Cobban, "The PLO in the mid-1980's," pp. 636–644; and John W. Amos II, *Palestinian Resistance: Organization of a Nationalist Movement* (New York: Pergamon Press, 1980).

9. In this context, see the comments of Khaled al-Hassan (Fatah Central Committee member) in *New York Times*, February 3, 1982; and interview of Abu Jihad (Arafat's deputy commander-in-chief), Radio Monte Carlo, November 26, 1982.

10. For a discussion of the PLO's attitudes to these issues, see Hassan Abu Talib, "Qadaya al-Amal al-Filistini," *al-Siyassa al-Dawliya*, no. 74 (October 1983):5–25.

11. *Al-Safir* (Lebanese daily), September 3, 1982. Similar statements were made by Abu al-Za'im (senior political advisor for Arafat) in a Radio Monte Carlo interview, November 26, 1982.

12. See the interviews with Abu Jihad in *al-Anba'* (Kuwaiti daily), September 12, 1982, and *Filistin al-Thawra* (PLO weekly publication), January 15, 1983. Similar comments were made by Yasir Arafat in a Radio Monte Carlo interview,

November 12, 1982, and an interview with *Rose al-Yusuf* (Egyptian weekly), January 3, 1983. See also Abu Iyad's interview in *al-Musawer,* October 29, 1982.

13. See the interview with Abu Saleh (Fatah Central Committee member and later a principal leader of the rebellion) in *al-Tali'a,* October 6, 1982.

14. For a detailed treatment of the Palestinian-Jordanian dialogue, see Chapter 5 in this book.

15. These views were expressed by Arafat in his Radio Monte Carlo interview, November 12, 1982; and in *al-Musawer,* January 1, 1983. Abu al-Za'im (senior political aide to Arafat) was also interviewed by Radio Monte Carlo, November 26, 1982.

16. See the statement of Abu Jihad in *Filistin al-Thawra* (PLO Publication), January 15, 1982.

17. Sartawi expressed these views in a lengthy interview on Radio Monte Carlo, January 28, 1983.

18. For the text of Arafat's interview, see the Hebrew weekly, *Ha'olem Hazae,* July 5, 1982.

19. *Christian Science Monitor,* November 4, 1982.

20. *Al-Safir,* June 29, 1982.

21. Radio Monte Carlo, October 29, 1982.

22. Radio Monte Carlo, July 11, 1983.

23. Radio Monte Carlo, January 21, 1983.

24. *Le Temps* (Tunisian daily), February 17, 1983.

25. See Arafat's interview in *Rose al-Yusuf,* January 3, 1983.

26. For more information, see Aaron David Miller, *The PLO: The Politics of Survival* (New York: Praeger, 1983); and Amos, *Palestinian Resistance,* pp. 58–59 and 81–84. See also Muhammad Y. Muslih, "Moderates and Rejectionists," pp. 135–141; and Cheryl A. Rubenberg, "The PLO Response to the Reagan Initiative: The PNC at Algiers," *American-Arab Affairs,* no. 4 (February 1983):53–69.

27. *Al-Safir,* September 3, 1982.

28. Habash was interviewed on Radio Monte Carlo, April 8, 1983.

29. Habash interview on BBC's program "Twenty-Four Hours," February 16, 1983.

30. Ibid.

31. *Al-Safir,* September 10, 1982.

32. *Al-Safir,* September 24, 1982.

33. The progressive democratic forces inside Egypt include the leftist- and Marxist-oriented groups opposed to the Camp David accords and the establishment of diplomatic relations with Israel. For more information concerning the rejectionists' attitudes toward Egypt, see "Waduh al-Ru'iya," an official statement by the Popular Front for the Liberation of Palestine Central Committee, following its January 26, 1983, meeting in Damascus, February 3, 1983, pp. 22–25. See also the interview with Nayef Hawatmeh in *al-Hurriya* (Democratic Front for the Liberation of Palestine publication), February 22, 1983.

34. "Waduh al-Ru'iya," p. 29. See also the comments of Bassam Abu Sharif (official spokesman for the Popular Front) in *al-Safir,* January 5, 1983.

35. *Al-Ahram*, October 1, 1982.
36. "Waduh al-Ru'iya," pp. 16–17.
37. The Palestine National Front was launched in August 1973 by pro-PLO figures in the occupied territories to rally support for the PLO.
38. These views were expressed by Habash and Hawatmeh in an interview with Radio Monte Carlo, February 18, 1983.
39. *Al-Ahram*, July 19, 1982.
40. *Al-Ahram*, October 12, 1982.
41. Radio Monte Carlo, February 18, 1983.
42. "Waduh al-Ru'iya," p. 28. See also Nayef Hawatmeh's interview in *al-Hurriya*, p. 16.
43. For an assessment of the PNC political communiqué, see Patrick Seale, "PLO Strategies: Algiers and After," *World Today* 39, no. 4 (April 1983):137–143; Ibrahim Abu-Lughod, "Flexible Militancy: Report on the Sixteenth Palestine National Council," *Journal of Palestine Studies* 12, no. 4 (summer 1983):25–40; Rubenberg, "The PLO Response."
44. *Al-Ahram*, March 6, 1983.

5
The Jordanian-PLO Dialogue

With the loss of its independent base for political and military operations in Lebanon and the reluctance of the Arab countries to defend Palestinian interests, the PLO's leadership was left with only one realistic option after the war—diplomacy. For this political option to be meaningful, however, a reconciliation with Jordan seemed to be inescapable; and to facilitate this, the leadership of the mainstream PLO made the historic move of ending the Palestinian-Hashemite enmity. The shift of the PLO's primary constituency from Lebanon toward the Palestinians in the occupied territories and Jordan made the reconciliation with Jordan an urgent task.

To forge a diplomatic accord with Jordan in order to bring about a negotiated settlement to the Palestinian problem was premature within the context of preserving Palestinian national unity. Nevertheless, the beginning of the Jordanian-Palestinian dialogue, immediately after the exodus from Beirut, was indispensable for the full diplomatic coordination that was eventually reached in February 1985.

Historical Background

Following the advent of the state of Israel in 1948 and until the June War of 1967, Jordan was the strongest claimant to represent Palestinian interests. Palestinian leadership during this period was not forthcoming as the physical dispersion of the Palestinian people was accompanied by a division of their political loyalties among various Arab regimes and political ideologies. Throughout this period, King Hussein emphasized that the West Bank was an integral part of the Hashemite Kingdom of Jordan and that the Palestinian and Jordanian peoples were inseparable. Jordan also defined the Palestinian problem as its top priority and took upon itself the "sacred task" of liberating Palestine.[1]

In the mid-1960s a gradual erosion began to take place in Jordan's claim to be the exclusive representative of the Palestinians. In January 1964, the first Arab summit conference convening in Cairo called for the establishment of a separate Palestinian entity and the formation of the Palestine Liberation Organization. A year later, Fatah, which had been in the making since the late 1950s, launched its first military operation against Israel. The Ba'ath regime in Syria, a bitter rival of Gamal Abd al-Nasser's government, extended political, economic, and military support to Fatah in response to Nasser's sponsorship of the PLO. Both Fatah and the PLO became serious contenders with Jordan for guardianship and representation of Palestinian national interests. Reacting to these developments, the Jordanian government firmly opposed any Palestinian commando infiltration into Israel and frustrated the attempts of the PLO and Fatah to recruit, mobilize, or organize the Palestinians inside Jordan's refugee camps.

The outbreak of the 1967 June War dealt a major blow to Jordan's claim to represent Palestinian interests. Not only was the West Bank lost to Israel, but the credibility and the prestige of the Arab regimes and their conventional armies were severely undermined. The war gave preeminence to the Palestinian resistance movement, with its slogan of armed struggle and popular warfare, and laid the ground for the PLO to play a pivotal role in inter-Arab politics and to claim that it exclusively represented the Palestinian people.[2] The launching of the notion of a separate Palestinian national identity by the commando groups shook the very foundations of the Jordanian regime's political legitimacy since it presented itself as an alternate source of political allegiance and identification among Jordan's Palestinian population (who make up the majority of the population of Jordan).

Jordan's fears were further compounded by the increasing popularity of the Palestinian resistance movement among Arabs and Palestinians alike. Jordan was also worried that the ascendancy of the commando groups would undermine its chances to represent Palestinian interests and eventually erode its political legitimacy in the West Bank. In addition, the attempt of the resistance groups to consolidate themselves politically and militarily among the Palestinians in East Jordan endangered the political stability of the regime. Furthermore, the commando groups' military operations against Israel multiplied Jordan's internal political stability problems, particularly since Israel initiated a policy of punitive strikes against Jordanian population and economic centers to induce the regime to curtail Palestinian military activities. These factors and others were behind the repeated military confrontations between the Jordanian army and the Palestinians, culminating in the 1970 September civil war and the termination of the Palestinian military presence in Jordan by July 1971.

With the eviction of the resistance movement a new phase in the Palestinian-Jordanian relationship began. This was characterized by political rivalry between Jordanians and Palestinians over their respective roles in representing the Palestinians.[3] Partly as a result of this struggle in March 1972 King Hussein proposed the formation of a United Arab Kingdom, consisting of the East Bank and West Bank of Jordan. According to his plan, both regions would be granted self-autonomy, and a central government, headed by the king himself, would be in charge of foreign and defense policy. This federation project was sharply denounced by the PLO, which viewed it as an encroachment upon Palestinian national rights and its role to represent such rights. In view of Jordan's political isolation following the eviction of the Palestinians in 1971, King Hussein's plan did not draw any official Arab backing.

Between 1973 and 1976, the rivalry between Jordan and the Palestinian resistance movement was settled in favor of the PLO. A combination of factors and political developments in those years made the PLO's victory possible. The 1973 October War between Israel and both Syria and Egypt discredited the Hussein regime's claims over the West Bank since the king decided not to engage his army directly along the Jordanian-Israeli border. Jordan's position was further weakened by the postwar diplomacy of U.S. Secretary of State Henry Kissinger. Kissinger's step-by-step approach to disengage the fighting armies on the Syrian–Egyptian and Israeli borders excluded Jordan from such a political arrangement. Moreover, the political realities emerging from the war, manifested in the Israeli and Arab desire to diffuse the crisis, had an impact on the PLO's thinking. A moderate trend, advocated by Fatah, al-Sa'iqa, and the Democratic Front, began to emerge inside the Palestinian nationalist movement. This trend favored the adaptation of the PLO tactic in order to allow Palestinian participation in the proposed Geneva conference. As a result of this trend, in 1974 the Palestine National Council in its twelfth session endorsed the concept of establishing a "national authority" in the occupied territories. The resolution also aimed at enhancing the PLO's standing among Arab moderate countries.

A major blow was dealt to Jordan's quest to represent Palestinian interests when Arab heads of state convening in Rabat, Morocco, in 1974, designated the PLO as the sole representative of the Palestinian people. Around the same time, the UN General Assembly extended observer status to the PLO. Developments in the West Bank and the Gaza Strip during this period also favored the PLO at the expense of Jordan.

Between 1973 and 1976, Palestinian national consciousness accelerated in the occupied territories and increased the political gains of the PLO, culminating in the overwhelming victory of the pro-PLO mayors in the 1976 municipal elections.[4] The rising influence of the PLO in the occupied territories was made possible through the interplay of a number of factors. The radicalization of the student movement and the expansion of the student body (as a result of opening new universities) rapidly advanced the position of the PLO in the West Bank and the Gaza Strip. In addition, the continuation of Israel's policy of land expropriation, the construction of more Jewish settlements, and the periodic religious tensions between Palestinians and Israelis in the Jerusalem-Hebron region further strengthened Palestinian nationalistic feelings. Another problem for King Hussein arose from the reluctance of the Israeli Labor government to give political concessions to the pro-Jordanian elite of the West Bank and Gaza Strip, thus diminishing its influence and position. The fact that Jordan did not enjoy direct supervision over the West Bank's internal affairs allowed the process of "de-Jordanization" to continue. It came as no surprise that more than 180 West Bank and Gaza Strip politicians, representatives of municipalities, professional associations, and societies, sent a petition to the Arab summit conference at Rabat, pronouncing the PLO to be their sole legitimate spokesman.

The reassessment by the PLO of its political strategy vis-à-vis the occupied territories also affected its standing. The Palestine National Council in January 1973 called upon the Palestinians on the West Bank and Gaza Strip to form a Palestine National Front (PNF) and urged them to be more vocal and active in their support for the PLO. By August 1973, the PNF was formed, consisting of a coalition of political groups including followers of Fatah, the Democratic Front, representatives of local communists, independent politicians, and representatives of municipalities and various associations. Pro-Jordanian figures were excluded from the PNF. In its first manifesto the PNF described itself as "the political arm of the PLO in the occupied territories" and asserted the Palestinian national rights to self-determination and the formation of an independent Palestinian state.

Despite Jordan's accession to the Rabat Resolution, tension and suspicion remained the main features of Jordanian-Palestinian relations. This state of affairs began to change with the improvement in Syrian-Jordanian relations by the mid-1970s. The government of President Assad began to exert pressure upon the PLO to normalize its relations with Jordan. As a result of Syria's efforts, the first round of public talks since 1971 between Jordanians and Palestinians took place in February 1977. This round was followed by a meeting between Arafat and Hussein a few weeks later. Moderates inside the PLO justified the renewal of their contacts with Jordan on the grounds that Jordan was a confrontation state and that it continued to assume a central position in the Arab-Israeli conflict. The proximity of Jordan to occupied territories was also cited as one reason for the rapprochement because it would allow the PLO direct access to the West Bank.

The improvement in their relationship did not keep Jordan and the PLO from competing to control political affairs inside the occupied territories. They remained at odds concerning the Palestinian political and military presence inside Jordan because Amman continued to adhere to the post-1970 war policy of not allowing Palestinian military and political activities on Jordanian territory.

The political developments between 1977 and 1979 further accelerated the process of normalization between Jordanians and Palestinians. Sadat's trip to Jerusalem in November 1977, the signing of the Camp David agreement in September 1978, and the conclusion of the Israeli-Egyptian peace treaty in March 1979 brought Jordan and the PLO closer together. Jordan's public opposition to the Camp David accords and the severing of its diplomatic relations with Cairo facilitated this process. Recommendations from the Arab summit conference at Baghdad in fall 1978 urged Jordan and the PLO to continue their dialogue and to deepen their cooperation. In a move geared to underline the significance of such cooperation, Baghdad summit conferees decided that the $150 million paid annually by Arab countries to advance the steadfastness of the people in the occupied territories should be jointly distributed by Jordan and the PLO. This move resulted in the formation of a Palestinian-Jordanian joint economic committee.

The newly assigned economic role for Jordan and its indecisive attitude toward the Camp David accords deepened existing differences between the moderates and the rejectionists inside the PLO. Though the Baghdad resolution was economic in nature, the rejectionists were convinced that it had serious political implications that could not be easily ignored. They argued that the resolution could be interpreted as a green light for the Jordanian monarch to try at an appropriate moment to share with the PLO the right of representing Palestinian interests. The decision was also seen as a partial deviation from the 1974 Rabat summit resolution. The rejectionists were unimpressed with Jordan's declared opposition to the Camp David agreements; they argued that though the official communiqué of the Jordanian government rejected the agreement, it failed to refer to the PLO as the sole legitimate representative of the Palestinian people.[5] The communiqué also underlined the readiness of the government to enter a political settlement under more favorable conditions. The rejectionists' suspicion was further increased when Jordan submitted a number of inquiries to the Carter administration concerning the meanings and potentialities of the Camp David agreements.

The Palestine National Council in its fourteenth session in January 1979 debated the question of what type of relationship the PLO should have with Jordan.[6] The proponents of the dialogue declared that the normalization of ties with Jordan would keep the regime away from the Israeli-Egyptian peace talks and would preserve the country's anti–Camp David posture.[7] In contrast, the opponents of the dialogue insisted that Jordan give clear concessions to the PLO before the commencement of the talks. In particular, they wanted Jordan to allow the PLO to resume its political and military activities. They also demanded that Jordan drop its newly acquired right of participation in the distribution of Arab financial assistance.

After long deliberation, a compromise resolution was reached. To improve the PLO ties with Jordan, Hussein's government should fulfill three conditions: recognize the PLO as sole legitimate representative, continue to oppose the Camp David agreements, and allow the PLO to exercise "all types of struggle" from Jordanian territory. In its turn, the Jordanian government insisted that cooperation with the PLO be confined to the diplomatic level and to the rendering of economic aid to the West Bank and the Gaza Strip; in no way should the cooperation entail allowing the PLO to exercise political and military activities inside the country. At any rate, the Jordanian-Palestinian relationship between 1979–1982 was mainly confined to the work and activities of the joint economic committee. Strong incentives did not exist to induce the PLO to search for closer ties with Jordan, particularly since the PLO enjoyed its statelike status in Lebanon. Likewise, the deadlock in the self-autonomy talks between Egypt and Israel and the low priority given by the Reagan administration to the resolution of the Arab-Israeli dispute in 1981–1982 decreased King Hussein's interest in pursuing a dialogue with Arafat.

The Israeli invasion of Lebanon in summer 1982 radically altered the situation. The unfolding of new political realities as the result of the war affected the nature and the content of the Palestinian-Jordanian dialogue. To begin with, the dispersal of the PLO troops to several Arab countries deprived it of a significant portion of its military effectiveness, resulting in noticeable decline in its bargaining power and political influence. In an attempt to enhance its chances of political survival, the militarily weakened PLO began to look for closer partnership with Jordan.

Second, the Lebanon War had the immediate effect of diminishing the political influence of the radical Arab countries in view of their embarrassing policy of military inaction during the siege of Beirut, despite their militant rhetoric of defending the Palestinian revolution and checking Israel's expansionist policy. The brief psychological vulnerability of both Syria and Libya gave way for a while to a rise in the influence of moderate Arab countries, evinced in the endorsement of the Saudi-sponsored Arab peace plan of Fez that called implicitly for the recognition of Israel. Third, the launching of the Egyptian-French peace plan, the Reagan initiative, and the Arab peace plan of Fez, although pointing out that diplomacy rather than military force could be the appropriate tool to resolve the Arab-Israeli dispute in the post-Beirut era, referred in varying degrees to the significance of Jordan's role in any political settlement and the importance of Palestinian-Jordanian close cooperation.

Against the background of PLO military weakness, Jordan's enhanced status, radical Arab countries' psychological vulnerability, and the increasing tendency among Arab moderates to support a political settlement to the Palestinian problem, the Jordanian-PLO dialogue flourished. Both King Hussein and Arafat were aware of the need to move swiftly and avail themselves of the new political opportunities presented by the various peace plans, particularly the Reagan initiative. They hoped to achieve some progress before the commencement of the 1984 presidential elections in the United States, since during a presidential campaign consideration of domestic politics would prevail, compelling the U.S. administration to pursue a strong pro-Israeli posture.

Jordanian Motives

Despite Jordan's acceptance of the PLO's role in representing Palestinian national interests, King Hussein's interest in recovering the occupied territories never waned. As noted earlier, the low-key policy pursued by Jordan prior to 1982 was dictated by the political gains of the PLO in the 1970s and the overwhelming support it derived from the Palestinians inside and outside the occupied territories. Nevertheless, the political and military decline of the PLO and the pivotal role assigned to Jordan by the United States in the resolution of the Palestinian question revived Jordanian interests in pursuing its drive to recover the West Bank.

The absence of any serious alternative for the restoration of the occupied territories induced the king to accept the Reagan initiative. The convening of an international conference to resolve the Arab-Israeli dispute did not seem likely because of U.S. and Israeli opposition to such a conference, and the cold war climate that governed the relationship between Moscow and Washington.[8] Likewise, the Arab peace plan of Fez did not seem to have a better chance of success. Moreover, the fact that no Arab military option existed to recover the occupied territories made the situation more dismal. In contrast, it was contended that the Reagan initiative offered reasonable grounds to recover such territories. Jordan by itself, however, was incapable of representing the Palestinians because, despite the military defeat of the PLO, the organization continued to possess widespread political legitimacy inside and outside the occupied territory. The PLO could also mobilize the Palestinians of the West Bank and Gaza Strip to frustrate any Jordanian unilateral move to recover the territories. Moreover, Hussein was certain that, in case of a final political settlement, some kind of territorial concessions would have to be made to Israel. By including the PLO in such negotiations, the king would thus not be the only one making such concessions. An agreement, therefore, between Hussein and Arafat on the basis of the Reagan initiative and UN Security Council Resolutions 242 and 338 was deemed essential to enable the king to explore the prospects for a political settlement.

In addition to these considerations, Jordan's relevance to the political settlement was dictated by a number of other factors. In an article in *Foreign Affairs Magazine*, Jordan's Crown Prince Hassan discussed several reasons why his country was significant in any settlement for the Arab-Israeli conflict.[9] First, Jordan continued to possess a legal claim to the West Bank, and such a status was acknowledged by UN Security Council Resolutions 242 and 338. Both resolutions called for the return of the territories to Jordanian sovereignty. Second, Jordan's rules and regulations had been enforced in the West Bank after the Israeli occupation in 1967, and the West Bank was still represented in Jordan's legislative process. Fifty percent of Jordan's Parliament members are still drawn from that area. Third, Jordan was in charge along with the PLO of distributing economic aid throughout the occupied territories, and salaries of government officials were still paid by the Jordanian treasury. Fourth, Jordan's pertinence to any political settlement was also attested to by the fact that the majority of the Jordanian population is Palestinian and that many of those who live in the occupied territories carry Jordanian citizenship. A fifth consideration referred to Jordan's historical linkage to the Palestinian problem: The government had devoted time and energy over the years for the "defense" of Palestinian rights. Finally, the prince cited the presence of common economic interests between his country and Israel, including the development of the waters of the Jordan River and tourism.

Along with these six reasons, considerations of national security also figured prominently in the calculation of Jordan's policymakers. Jordan was genuinely concerned about its security and internal political stability in the wake of the Lebanon War. Government officials were afraid that with the termination of the Palestinian military presence in southern Lebanon and Beirut, the Begin government might attempt to resolve the Palestinian question at the expense of Jordan's royal family. Senior members in the Israeli cabinet, including Shamir and Sharon, asserted repeatedly that there was no need for a "second Palestinian state" since

Jordan is a Palestinian state. The seriousness of such declarations to the Hashemite regime emanated from the fact that two-thirds of its population are Palestinians. Jordan was also convinced that Israel's policy of continual land expropriation and construction of additional Jewish settlements on the West Bank and the Gaza Strip were parts of the Israeli government's drive to resolve the Palestinian problem. Adnan Abu Awdeh, Jordan's minister of information, declared that Israel's settlement activities and the continual influx of Palestinians from the occupied territories posed a serious threat to his country's national security, and he added, "Israel conceives of the West Bank Palestinians as a demographic extension population in east Jordan. And this raises the fear in Jordan that Israel will ultimately push these Palestinians across the bridge."[10] The Jordanian official communiqué of April 10, 1983, which announced the breakdown of the Hussein-Arafat talks, also underlined the significance of this problem: "Jordan was and still is a target for Israeli aggression and expansionist policy which threaten Jordanian national identity."[11]

Such security fears compelled the Jordanian government to seek a political accord with the PLO. This political move was hoped to diminish any incentive by the PLO to stir up violence and internal political instability in the wake of its loss of Lebanon and the dispersal of its troops to several Arab countries. Similarly, Jordan's favorable reception of the Reagan initiative was viewed as advancing the country's national security. By accepting the Reagan initiative, Jordan would ensure that Washington would stand by its side against any Israeli threats. Moreover, the king began to widen Jordan's security environment by expanding the role of the Jordanian army to include the protection of the oil fields in the Gulf region. By doing so, Jordan hoped to demonstrate its strategic significance and relevance to the military policy of the United States toward the Middle East. Jordan also hoped to acquire new and sophisticated U.S. arms to augment the strategic capabilities of its army and to deepen U.S. military commitment to Jordan's national security.

Considerations of inter-Arab rivalries also played a role in Jordan's desire to forge a close political alliance with the PLO. Jordan did not want to allow the PLO to be under the hegemony of radical Arab countries, particularly Syria. The king pointed out that "the choice for Jordan was whether to leave room for any Arab party the right to interfere in the Palestinian problem, or to draw a future formula that would satisfy the aspirations of every Palestinian and every Jordanian, and which would preserve for each side its separate identity and personality."[12] Moreover, one could argue that Jordan's interest in the dialogue with the PLO for the return of the occupied territories aimed at precluding forever the possibility of forming an independent Palestinian state in these territories since Jordan feared that such a state could in the future make claims to the East Bank by fomenting political instability among the Palestinians.

In addition to the security rationale, considerations of prestige, historical mission, and personal commitment to the Palestinian problem were behind the king's attempt to form a political alliance with Arafat on the basis of the Reagan initiative.[13] Hussein was concerned not to be portrayed by history as the one who lost the West Bank and East Jerusalem to Israel. He was further convinced that unless diplomatic moves were quickly made toward a political settlement, new realities caused by Israeli settlement policy would be created in the occupied territories making things exceedingly difficult to reverse. In an address to a group of Jordanian politicians in January 1983, the king stressed the significance of such an issue:

> If the PLO is capable of establishing a sovereign independent Palestinian state on its national soil, then honestly there is no need to discuss the future relationship between the Palestinians and the Jordanians because the relationship had developed in the past and is still developing and will continue into the future. But if the establishment of a Palestinian state is hampered in one way or another and there is still another way that would lead to the restoration and the salvation of the land before it is too late, if we can formulate a position based upon the present realities and the belief in the necessity of the ultimate victory of justice and a commitment to reach our goals, let us then work for such an agreement and abide ourselves by it.[14]

Moreover, the social, economic, cultural, and human ties between Palestinians and Jordanians over the years reinforced the King's resolve to search for a political settlement through coordination with the PLO. In his speeches, the king frequently referred to the Palestinians and Jordanians as members of one people and one family.

To create the appropriate climate for coordination with the PLO, the Jordanian government, in sharp contrast to its policy during the 1970 postwar period, allowed those PLO fighters with Jordanian citizenship into the country. The king himself received some evacuated PLO troops in August 1982 after their departure from West Beirut. Moreover, soon after the arrival of Arafat in Athens, King Hussein dispatched two high ranking officials to convey Jordan's desire to coordinate closely with the PLO. This move was followed by a public invitation for Arafat to come to Jordan to start discussions concerning the future of the relationship between Palestinians and Jordanians. In an interview with the British Broadcasting Corporation (BBC) on September 13, 1982, the king declared that the aim of such talks was to discuss the formation of a federal union on the two banks of the river and to formulate a joint Palestinian-Jordanian diplomatic approach. Hussein reiterated his invitation to Arafat during a speech a week later to Jordanian politicians.[15]

Palestinian Motives

Although Jordan's political ascendancy and enhanced political credentials stood behind its interests in reaching a common diplomatic approach with the Palestinians, the instinct for political survival and the need to strengthen PLO bargaining power and to preserve it as a representative organization served as powerful incentives for the moderate leadership of the PLO to coordinate with Jordan. As stated earlier, the Lebanon War and the Reagan initiative left the PLO with no real alternative for political action. Yet the Palestinian leadership was keen on avoiding the relegation of its organization to a secondary status and on not endangering its political achievements over the years. Despite its shortcomings, the Reagan initiative was not entirely rejected but was seen as a positive starting point that could be enlarged to account for Palestinian national grievances. From the Palestinian leadership's viewpoint, categorical rejection of the Reagan initiative would be seen as a sign of indifference to a peaceful settlement of the Palestinian problem. It was concerned not to give Jordan the opportunity to advance its legitimacy and increase its chances of being accepted as a claimant to the occupied territories. The fear of Jordan's unilateral participation in a peaceful settlement prompted the PLO leadership to search for closer ties with the Jordanian monarch, similar to the dialogue initiated following the signing of the Camp David accords in September 1978.

In addition to the political survival considerations, an increasing sense of realism and pragmatism was behind the PLO's search for closer ties with Jordan. One could argue that the Lebanon War had convinced many PLO leaders that effective Arab military and political support of the Palestinians was unlikely to be forthcoming and that the strategy of military struggle in the post-Beirut era was being rendered increasingly irrelevant to the realization of Palestinian national aspirations. Instead, they thought that diplomacy and political negotiations would be more useful tools to achieve some of these goals and that coordination with Jordan was an essential step.[16]

Aside from these political considerations, the initiation of the dialogue with Jordan was seen to result in several other political payoffs. To begin with, a common Palestinian-Jordanian diplomatic approach would help decelerate the gradual Israeli annexation of the occupied territories because the dialogue was anticipated to generate international pressure upon Israel. Second, by embarking upon the dialogue, the PLO would avert an unnecessary, bitter struggle for power and would instead gain the time needed for rebuilding the social, economic, political, and cultural institutions and for the reorganization and regrouping of its dispersed troops. Third, the dialogue with Jordan would reinforce the widespread support for the PLO inside the occupied territories. Fourth, such talks also could afford the PLO the opportunity to contact the Palestinian masses inside Jordan and could open prospects that the PLO might eventually be able to reestablish its political and military presence and resume its military activities against Israel, should the diplomatic option fail. Commenting on some of these payoffs, *Filistin al-Thawra*, a PLO publication, described Arafat's contacts with the Jordanian monarch as a "service to the Palestinian cause as this would increase the steadfastness of our people in the occupied territories and will help to preserve the relationship with our people inside Jordan. Such talks should also improve Jordan's stand towards the Palestinian problem."[17]

The presence of strong ties between Palestinians and Jordanians furnished a congenial climate for the initiation of the dialogue. Moderates and rejectionists alike inside the PLO spoke of the special relationship between the Palestinian and Jordanian people.[18] In their view, such close ties transcended the points of difference that the PLO continued to have with the Jordanian regime.[19] Moreover, the steps taken by King Hussein during and after the siege of Beirut, including the granting of a sanctuary for some of the PLO's fighters, left a positive image upon moderate Palestinian leaders. Finally, following the dispersal of his troops, the PLO chairman felt less inhibited by radical Arab countries, particularly Syria, to pursue his pro-Jordanian policy.

Arafat's first visit to Amman in October 1982 provided an opportunity for him to reconcile fully with the king, allowing the dialogue that they started five years earlier to continue. The two sides agreed to get two committees to supervise the PLO troops stationed in Jordan and to study the economic conditions of the Palestinians inside the occupied territories. Moreover, the leaders defined two main problems for their future discussions: the type of relationship between Palestinians and Jordanians in the future and the nature of the PLO's participation in the peace talks, including some degree of authorization to Jordan to represent the Palestinians.[20] Aside from these, Arafat's first trip to Jordan did not yield tangible results in view of the complexities of the issues discussed and the limitations imposed upon Arafat's freedom of action by PLO institutions.

Following Arafat's third visit to Jordan in early December 1982, Jordan and the PLO agreed to establish a higher committee headed by Arafat and the Jordanian prime minister to discuss the questions of confederation and the formation of a joint Palestinian-Jordanian negotiating team to enter the peace talks. Undoubtedly the setting up of such a committee attested to Arafat's recognition of Jordan's enhanced political position and his desire to explore jointly with the king various political options to resolve the Palestinian question. Commenting on such an issue, the PLO chairman told *al-Mustaqbal* magazine on December 3, 1982, that the commitment of his organization to the Arab peace plan "allowed it also to discuss the other political initiatives." He further revealed that the aim of his talks with King Hussein was also to discuss the framework for the future relationship between the occupied territories and Jordan and to make the necessary arrangements in advance. Arafat asserted that the formation of an independent Palestinian state did not constitute a condition for his talks with the king.

The December talks also dealt with the PLO's participation in the expected peace negotiations. It was reported that the PLO's role in any political settlement could be accomplished in one or more of the following three forms: the formation of a joint PLO-Jordanian delegation, the formation of a delegation of non-PLO Palestinians who would clearly reflect the PLO's political preferences and who would be selected by the PLO itself, or the setting up of an Arab League delegation that would include a PLO representative.[21]

Problems for the Dialogue

Despite the achievements of the Jordanians and Palestinians in the first few months of their dialogue, their talks confronted obstacles from the outset. The final breakdown of the dialogue in April 1983 resulted from a combination of six obstacles: Palestinian disunity and Arafat's indecisiveness, Jordan's feelings of insecurity, Israel's intransigence, the lack of Arab backing for the dialogue, the failure of U.S. Middle Eastern diplomacy, particularly in Lebanon, and Soviet determination to frustrate U.S. Middle Eastern diplomacy and to reassert its presence in the region. Perhaps with the exception of the Palestinians in the occupied territories, Arafat was unlikely to carry the rest of the PLO with him toward a political settlement on the basis of the Reagan initiative. Arafat's Jordan policy enjoyed solid backing from the Palestinians in the West Bank and the Gaza Strip. Shortly after his visit to Jordan in October 1982, twenty leading personalities in the occupied territories issued a statement endorsing Arafat's policy of opening a dialogue with Jordan and protesting the Syrian criticism of Arafat's trip to Amman. The mayor of Gaza, Rashad al-Shawa, stated, "I believe that the chairman of the PLO has the right to talk to King Hussein in Amman to pave the road for cooperation with Jordan."[22] A few days later a number of politicians, including the mayors of Bethlehem, Gaza, and Jericho and the former governor of Jerusalem, signed a petition urging the PLO to continue its dialogue with Jordan. Some even called upon the PLO to recognize UN Security Council Resolutions 242 and 338, to openly accept the Reagan initiative, and to engage in simultaneous and mutual recognition between the PLO and Israel.[23]

According to a public opinion poll conducted in early February 1983, a few days before the convening of the Palestine National Council in Algiers, 80 percent of the respondents supported the continuation of the dialogue between Jordan and the PLO, and only 15 percent opposed it. *Al-Bayader al-Siyassi* added that 89 percent of the 750 respondents interviewed expressed their complete support for Arafat's leadership of the PLO.[24] Leading political figures in the occupied territories also urged both King Hussein and Arafat to reach an agreement as soon as possible concerning the federation between the West Bank and the East Bank and to form a joint delegation to enter the peace talks. They further wanted both Jordan and the PLO to use the positive aspects of the Reagan initiative.[25]

The widespread support that Arafat's Jordan policy generated throughout the occupied territories did not tip the balance of power in favor of the moderates inside the PLO; opposition to the dialogue was mounting. The two main issues of the dialogue—the future relationship of the occupied territories with Jordan and PLO participation in the political settlement—generated acrimonious debates among the various factions.[26] The rejectionists had serious reservations about Arafat's talks with Jordan and argued that a successful conclusion of the dialogue on the basis of the Reagan initiative would negate Palestinian national rights. The five groups expressed their vehement opposition to giving any authorization to Jordan and equally rejected the concept of confederation before the formation of an independent Palestinian state.

In the opinion of the Popular Front, it was incomprehensible to talk about confederation with Jordan after the PLO's military setbacks in Lebanon and the dispersal of its troops to several Arab countries. According to Habash, the immediate task of the Palestinians should be to continue their struggle until they created their own state. In its publication *al-Thawra Mustamirra,* the Popular Front charged that King Hussein's federation plan aimed at "liquidating the Palestinian revolution, breaking up Palestinian national unity and creating further tension between Syria and the PLO." It further alleged that the Jordanian monarch wanted to use his repeated meetings with Arafat to open a dialogue with Israel in an attempt to restore Jordanian sovereignty over the West Bank.[27] Similar opposition was expressed by the Popular Front

General Command and the Popular Struggle Front. Both organizations warned Arafat not to fall into King Hussein's trap and not to give him any mandate to speak in the name of the Palestinians; both were also critical of Arafat's failure to consult with the PLO's political councils to get their prior approval for his talks with the king. Commenting on Arafat's talks, Samir Abu Goshe, secretary general of the Popular Struggle Front, stated that "we are for Arab unity, but not for confederation with Jordan."[28]

A slightly different attitude toward the dialogue was held by the secretary general of the Democratic Front. Nayef Hawatmeh, a Jordanian himself, pointed out that the relationship between Palestinians and Jordanians had always been a special one. The special nature of their relationship was made possible by the high degree of social, economic, cultural, and historical integration between the two communities. In Hawatmeh's view, this fact would have to be taken into account in the Palestinian-Jordanian discussion. The Democratic Front insisted that the bilateral talks be conducted within the limits of the Palestine National Council's sixteenth session resolutions and the 1974 Rabat Arab summit decisions. The front also asserted that the nature of the relationship between Palestinians and Jordanians should be determined "through the free choice of both peoples."[29]

Under the influence of the hard-line groups, the PLO's political councils were reluctant to extend sufficient political support to Arafat's dialogue with Hussein. For instance, the Palestine Central Council convening in Damascus toward the end of November 1982 did not address the question of the dialogue in its final communiqué. This omission may have been deliberate to avert further friction among the proponents and opponents of the dialogue. One could also argue that the convening of the Central Council in Damascus, which is known for its hostility toward the Jordanian-Palestinian rapprochement, was the motivating factor for omitting the dialogue in the council's final communiqué. The conferees were concerned about preventing further deterioration of Palestinian-Syrian relations.[30]

Similarly, the final communiqué of the Palestine National Council three months later did not come out in favor of an open Jordanian-PLO dialogue. The council tried to regulate and control Arafat's talks with Jordan. Though the communiqué gave Arafat the green light to continue his dialogue, it ruled out any attempt to authorize Jordan to represent Palestinian interests. It asserted instead that only the PLO could do so. The council also dismissed any possibility of the formation of a joint Palestinian-Jordanian negotiating team. In addition, it underlined the need to form an independent state.

To reduce the anxiety generated by the talks, advocates of the dialogue were careful to emphasize that their talks with Jordan did not aim at giving a mandate. They asserted that there was no departure by Jordan from the 1974 Rabat resolutions.[31] In this regard, Arafat announced that the final authority for determining the nature and the type of relationship between Palestinians and Jordanians was vested in the PLO's leadership and the Palestine National Council. He asserted that he would have to seek their approval and guidance for any agreement that he might reach with the king.[32] Proponents of the dialogue tried to dismiss the fears of the rejectionists by emphasizing that a confederation with Jordan would come about after the formation of an independent Palestinian state. In underlining the significance of this issue, Issam Sartawi argued that the creation of an independent state in the occupied territories "is not only necessary to meet Palestinian national needs, but it is also imperative for Jordanian national security."[33]

The inconclusive nature of U.S.–Middle East diplomacy and the United States' continual refusal to open a dialogue with the PLO weakened Arafat's position vis-à-vis his critics. Throughout the dialogue, PLO officials were skeptical about U.S. ability to push for a political settlement. "Our own experiences tell us not to trust American pledges and promises," Arafat told Radio Monte Carlo on February 3, 1983. One could argue that a more assertive U.S. diplomatic effort and a firmer commitment to implement its initiative could have saved the Palestinian-Jordanian dialogue and strengthened the forces of moderation inside the PLO. Referring to the Palestinian frustration with the U.S. posture, Arafat's deputy Abu Jihad pointed out that "what we want are new factors and new developments that will give us confidence and trust in the American attitude. We do not want to be confronted with deadlines and we should not put ourselves at this critical position of agreeing or disagreeing or rushing into decisions without signs of improvement in American policy stands."[34]

Because PLO hard-line groups and their Arab guardians were continuing to pressure Arafat not to go too far in his dialogue with Jordan and because U.S.–Middle East diplomacy was deadlocked, the proponents of the dialogue began to express their doubts about the practicality of continuing their talks with Jordan. In addition, King Hussein's repeated public statements that a political settlement to the Arab-Israeli conflict and the Palestinian problem could only take place on the basis of the Reagan initiative and UN Security Council Resolutions 242 and 338 were a source of embarrassment to Arafat and his colleagues. They concluded that in view of the prevailing situation the signing of an agreement with the king would be very risky for Arafat and could produce further dissent among the Palestinians. One could also argue that the PLO chairman found it extremely difficult to break away from the tradition of Palestinian national unity, something that he had advocated over the years and worked consistently to preserve.

In light of these considerations, Arafat repeatedly postponed his trips to Jordan following the conclusion of the Palestine National Council session in February 1983. At Jordan's insistence that the dialogue be brought to a successful conclusion, the proponents of rapprochement began to call for the convening of an Arab summit to discuss the status of Jordanian-Palestinian relations. They were certain that a resolution at an Arab forum would probably favor the PLO. Moreover, they called upon the king to negotiate on the basis of the Arab peace plan of Fez and to drop the Reagan initiative.[35]

In early April 1983 during Arafat's last trip to Jordan prior to the breakdown of the talks, Hussein and Arafat were reported to have reached a draft agreement for a joint diplomatic approach on the basis of the Reagan initiative. To sign the agreement, Arafat needed the endorsement of the Executive Committee of the PLO. The PLO Executive Committee and the Fatah Central Committee met in emergency session in Kuwait between April 5 and 8 and refused to extend their support to the proposed agreement. The conferees instead drafted a new set of proposals and sent them with two PLO emissaries to Jordan for consideration. According to the new proposals, Palestinian-Jordanian diplomatic efforts should be based on international peace initiatives other than those sponsored by the United States and by UN Security Council Resolutions 242 and 338. They wanted in particular to substitute the Arab peace plan of Fez for the Reagan initiative. They insisted that the PLO participate in any political settlement and that prominent PLO figures represent the Palestinians. They also demanded in advance a U.S. guarantee of a freeze on Israeli settlement activities and restoration of Arab sovereignty to the occupied territories. Finally, they insisted that the new agreement clearly reflect Palestinian national rights of self-determination and statehood.

The new proposals were totally unacceptable to the Jordanian government: They showed the PLO's unwillingness to demonstrate the needed political flexibility and returned the Palestinian-Jordanian talks to the point from which they started in October 1982. The government issued a communiqué on April 10, 1983, formally ending its public dialogue with the PLO.[36] Jordan announced that it would not unilaterally join any negotiations and absolved itself from the responsibility of liberating the West Bank and the Gaza Strip. The communiqué left the PLO the task of finding "the appropriate ways and means through which they can save themselves and their land and the realization of their declared goals in the manner they see fit." It further asserted

Jordan's commitment to the 1974 Rabat resolution and pledged that it would work through the Arab League to support the PLO. The statement concluded by asserting that the government would take certain measures to enhance its national security and internal political stability through the introduction of restrictions upon the immigration of Palestinians from the occupied territories.

The decision to terminate the dialogue with the PLO was not surprising. By early 1983, Jordan was convinced that the risks involved in continuing the dialogue surpassed any possible political payoffs.[37] The failure of U.S. diplomatic efforts to bring about an Israeli troop withdrawal from Lebanon made it exceedingly difficult for Jordan to believe that the United States would be able to convince the Likud government to withdraw from the West Bank and the Gaza Strip without an open U.S.-Israeli confrontation—an option the Reagan administration was unwilling to undertake. The king was cautioned by Chinese, British, and Soviet leaders not to trust U.S. pledges and promises during a presidential election year.

Israel's rigid posture and inflexible political stands contributed heavily to Jordan's decision to halt the dialogue. The Begin-Shamir government continued to stall talks on a troop withdrawal agreement from Lebanon so as to avoid addressing the crucial issue of the future of the occupied territories. This attitude aroused Jordan's uncertainty about the utility of conducting negotiations with Israel. Jordan was also unwilling to engage in a cumbersome and lengthy negotiating process similar to the one Egypt experienced over withdrawal from Sinai. Time and time again, Israeli policymakers continued to pronounce their categorical rejection of the Reagan initiative and their determination to continue building settlements in the occupied territories. The Israeli government did not view with equanimity the rise of the Jordanian-PLO dialogue, seeing it as a direct challenge to Israel's national security. A spokesman for the government warned Jordan that his country would act swiftly in the event of any military activity emanating from inside Jordan.[38]

Because of Israel's intransigence and the incompetence of U.S. Middle Eastern diplomacy Jordan insisted upon the fulfillment of a number of conditions prior to its entry to any peace talks.[39] According to Jordan's minister of foreign affairs, such conditions included an early agreement on a timetable for the withdrawal of Israeli troops from Lebanon and Israeli commitment to freeze its settlement activities of placing more Jews in the occupied territories. In an attempt to dismiss Syria's suspicion, the minister also insisted that the Palestinians participate in any political settlement and that their participation be endorsed and approved by the PLO.

Jordan's diminishing enthusiasm for the dialogue may have also stemmed from the opposition of certain royal family figures, the army, and some tribal chieftains. Such forces did not favor the return of the West Bank to Jordan on the grounds that West Bank Palestinians could be a destabilizing factor and that they would be hard to control after more than a decade and a half of resisting Israeli military occupation. They also were perhaps unhappy about the prospects of adding more people to the Palestinian majority in eastern Jordan.

The absence of genuine Arab support for the Jordanian-PLO dialogue contributed to the ultimate collapse of the talks, despite the king's optimistic remarks that the overwhelming majority of Arab heads of state would support any agreement reached between Arafat and himself. In truth Arab countries confined their role to statements of encouragement. Algeria, Iraq, the Gulf states, Egypt, and Saudi Arabia declared on different occasions that they would go along with any agreement reached between the Palestinians and Jordanians. A typical example of this verbal support was a statement of the Saudi Prince Sultan, when he told a correspondent that his country "welcomes and blesses any Jordanian-Palestinian accord."[40] The Egyptian government for its part pointed out that the dialogue would enhance the chances of creating a Palestinian state, advance the Palestinian cause, and increase the pressures upon Israel to join the peace talks. Egypt was also anxious for Hussein and Arafat to make progress in their talks before the beginning of the U.S. presidential elections.[41]

Aside from these encouraging remarks, the Arab states did not do much to bring the Hussein-Arafat talks to a successful conclusion. Their reluctance perhaps resulted from their adherence to the 1974 resolution that upheld the PLO as the exclusive representative of the Palestinian people and from their collective endorsement of the Fez plan, which committed them to the formation of an independent Palestinian state and to the PLO's centrality in any political settlement. For its own reasons, Saudi Arabia, the main financier of the PLO, did not use its financial leverage to persuade Arafat to be more forthcoming in his dialogue with the king.[42] Saudi Arabia also declined to use sufficient leverage to modify Syria's opposition to the dialogue. The country's hesitation was not hard to understand at the time as the Saudi rulers did not want to provoke the Syrians into giving further aid to Iran against Iraq in the Gulf war and move it closer to the Soviet Union. Moreover, the failure of U.S. diplomacy in Lebanon did not provide the Saudi Arabians with sufficient reasons for working to neutralize Syria's opposition to the dialogue. Finally, it is wrong to assume that because it assisted Syria financially Saudi Arabia enjoyed diplomatic control over Syria's policymaking apparatus. Instead, one could argue that the Saudi tolerance to the Syrian policy stance on Lebanon and Jordan resulted from its desire to appease Syrian rulers and keep them as a barrier to Israeli expansionist policy in the region.

The indecisiveness of the moderate Arab countries was complemented by the hostility of both Syria and Libya to the Palestinian-Jordanian dialogue. Soon after Arafat's trip to Jordan in October 1982, Ahmad Skandar, Syria's minister of information, questioned Arafat's authority and political legitimacy to speak in the name of the Palestinians and the PLO: "We do not believe that there is only one person who enjoys the right to speak about the Palestinian problem. Mr. Arafat is the Chairman of the PLO's Executive Committee and therefore he cannot speak in its name without mandate or authorization."[43] On January 23, 1983, the Syrian government hosted a meeting for the foreign ministers of both Libya and Iran. The three ministers issued a joint statement condemning the Camp David accords and what were termed "attempts that aimed at extracting concessions from the PLO" and "American imperialist plans in the region." They pledged to support the continuation of the Palestinian military struggle and to work for the reactivation of the Front of Steadfastness and Confrontation States and the inclusion of Iran in that front.[44] As noted earlier, Libya, with Syrian blessing and encouragement, hosted a conference for PLO rejectionist groups to pronounce their firm opposition to the Hussein-Arafat talks. In addition, Syria gave refuge to Arafat's critics and allowed its capital to be used as a forum for directing all types of criticism and condemnation of Arafat's policies. In its drive to impede the Hussein-Arafat talks, the Syrian regime felt emboldened by its superior military force and its control of the rest of the PLO factions including hosting the political leadership and military troops of the various hard-line groups. These served as powerful instruments in the hands of the Syrian government, which eventually deterred Hussein and Arafat from bringing their talks to a successful conclusion.

Undoubtedly, Arafat's leaning toward moderate Arab countries and his willingness to search for a political settlement of the Palestinian problem, as well as his determination to free the PLO from Syrian hegemony, conflicted sharply with Syria's desire not to loosen its control over the Palestinian card. Syria's tight grip on the PLO could be used at the appropriate moment to help it recover the Golan Heights. Moreover, the adverse reaction of the Syrian government to the Arafat-Hussein rapprochement came in response to the deterioration in relations between Damascus and Amman and the growing hostility between Arafat and Assad. The PLO chairman's political accord with the Jordanian monarch conflicted with Syria's perception of itself as a custodian of the Palestinian cause and the only Arab country qualified to speak in the name of the

Palestinians. Finally, Syria held Jordan partly responsible for the regime's domestic problems and was angered by King Hussein's criticism of Syria's military intervention in Lebanon and the close ties that Jordan was forging with Iraq, Syria's implacable adversary.

The attitude of the two superpowers was also partly responsible for the breakdown of the talks. Despite the repeated assertions by various U.S. officials of their country's commitment to the Reagan initiative, the White House failed to take the steps necessary to back up its peace plan, and the president did not devote the energy and the single-mindedness needed to tackle the complexities of the Arab-Israeli dispute. Arab hopes and expectations of a new U.S. resolve to solve the Palestinian problem were dissipated soon after the announcement of the Reagan initiative. The unfolding of political developments in Lebanon shifted the focus of U.S. policy concerns from the occupied territories to Lebanon.[45] As mentioned earlier, U.S. policy objectives of establishing political stability in Lebanon and effecting the withdrawal of all foreign troops from the country were considered by Palestinians and Jordanians to be tests of the seriousness and credibility of the United States and the extent of its leverage over Israel. When Washington failed to accomplish these objectives, both Jordan and the PLO found it difficult to imagine how the United States could get Israel out of the West Bank and the Gaza Strip. U.S. credibility was further eroded when the White House did not even try to have Israel comply with the dictates of its peace initiative; instead, its economic aid to Israel continued unabated and the U.S. Congress boosted its foreign aid to Israel by $375 million. This weakness in U.S. Middle Eastern diplomacy and its leaning toward Israel ultimately undermined the Hussein-Arafat talks.

Instead of accepting partial blame for the breakdown in the talks, the Reagan administration chose a cold war explanation for the collapse of the dialogue:[46] It held Arab and Palestinian radicals and presumably the Soviet Union responsible for the inconclusive nature of the talks. Likewise the U.S. government did not assign any responsibility to Israel's inflexible political stands as one of the causes for the failure of the dialogue. Instead, the U.S. secretary of state went to the extent of calling upon Arab League members to withdraw diplomatic recognition of the PLO.

The U.S. exclusion of the Soviet Union from the peace process compelled Kremlin leaders to work to frustrate various aspects of U.S. Middle Eastern policy. The Soviet leaders advised the Jordanian monarch on several occasions not to trust U.S. pledges and not to join U.S.-sponsored political settlement projects.[47] Moscow worked also to advance its political and military presence in the region through substantially enhancing the military capabilities of its Syrian clients. In this regard, the Soviet Union supplied Damascus with new and sophisticated weapons including warplanes, tanks, surface-to-surface and surface-to-air missiles that could reach targets deep within Israel. It also increased the presence of its military personnel and experts to buttress Assad's opposition to the U.S.-sponsored Israeli-Lebanese agreement and the Jordanian-PLO dialogue. In addition to these military steps, the Soviets reassured the Syrian leaders that Moscow would stand by their side in the event of any Israeli attacks upon Syria through the invocation of the 1980 Treaty of Friendship and Cooperation. This reassurance came in a declaration by Soviet Foreign Minister Andrei Gromyko on April 5, 1983.

The combination of these factors at the local, regional, and international levels worked to frustrate the Jordanian-PLO dialogue. Though attempts were made by King Hassan of Morocco to bring Hussein and Arafat together, the two men did not meet until almost a year later. In the meantime, the stage was being set for a major upheaval inside the PLO when a split within Fatah took place one month after the collapse of the Hussein-Arafat talks.

Notes

1. For more information see Shaul Mishal, *West Bank/East Bank: The Palestinians in Jordan, 1949–1967* (New Haven, Conn.: Yale University Press, 1978).

2. William B. Quandt, Fuad Jabber, and Ann Mosely Lesch, *The Politics of Palestinian Nationalism* (Berkeley: University of California Press, 1973).

3. Wahid Abd al-Majid, "al-Filistiniyun wa al-Urdun beina al-Muwajaha wa al-Hiwar," *al-Siyassa al-Dawliya*, no. 57 (July 1979):78–81. See also Hassan Abu Taleb, "Tatawwer al-Hiwar al-Urduni al-Filistini," *al-Siyassa al-Dawliya*, no. 71 (January 1983):55–58.

4. For a useful study of political trends in the occupied territories and the rise of PLO support, see Ann Lesch, *Political Perceptions of the People in the Occupied Territories* (Washington, D.C.: Middle East Institute, 1980).

5. For the text of the communiqué, see *al-Dustur,* September 20, 1978.

6. For an English translation of the text of the PNC communiqué, see *Journal of Palestine Studies* 9, no. 2 (winter 1979).

7. A summary of these arguments can be found in Fakhri Jaber, "al-Ulaiqat al-Filistiniya al-Arabiya," *Shu'un Filistiniya,* no. 134 (November 1983):140–143.

8. See the king's interview in *al-Nahar,* May 1, 1983.

9. Hassan Ibn Talal, "Jordan's Quest for Peace," *Foreign Affairs* 60, no. 4 (spring 1982):804–807.

10. Abu Awdeh was interviewed by Radio Monte Carlo, November 26, 1982.

11. *Al-Dustur,* April 11, 1983.

12. *Al-Nahar,* May 1, 1983.

13. See the interview with King Hussein in *Wall Street Journal,* April 14, 1983.

14. Radio Jordan, January 10, 1983.
15. *Al-Dustur,* September 21, 1982.
16. These views were well expressed by Dr. Issam Sartawi, Arafat, and Abu Jihad.
17. *Filistin al-Thawra,* no. 428, October 16, 1982.
18. In this context see the comments of Farouq al-Qadoumi in *Filistin al-Thawra,* no. 442 (January 22, 1983), p. 35. Habash, Hawatmeh, and Abu Iyad made similar statements in their interview with Radio Monte Carlo, February 18, 1983.
19. For more information see *al-Dustur,* October 11–12, 1982. See also *Filistin al-Thawra,* nos. 428–429, October 16 and 23, 1982.
20. *Al-Mustaqbal,* December 4, 1982.
21. See interview with Nabil Sha'th, a political advisor to Arafat, in *Le Monde,* December 8, 1982. See also his interview in *Jordan Times,* December 4, 1982.
22. *Al-Quds,* October 13, 1982.
23. *Al-Quds,* November 19, 1982.
24. *Al-Bayader al-Siyassi,* no. 27, February 12, 1983.
25. These views and others were expressed in the lengthy interviews with more than 100 West Bank and Gaza Strip personalities conducted by *al-Bayader al-Siyassi,* November 19, 1982, pp. 25–46.
26. For a summary of the rejectionist views, see Suleiman Jaber, "Malameh Marhalat ma ba'd Beirut," *Shu'un Filistiniya,* nos. 132–133, pp. 133–136.
27. Quoted in *al-Safir,* October 17, 1982.
28. Jaber, "Malameh Marhalat ma ba'd Beirut," p. 136.
29. Ibid., p. 135.
30. Hassan Abu Taleb, "al-Hiwar al-Urduni al-Filistini ma bein al-Tawaquf wa al-Isstimrar," *al-Siyassa al-Dawliya,* no. 75 (January 1974):116–118.
31. Comments of this sort were made by Abu al-Za'im on November 26, 1982, in a Radio Monte Carlo interview, and by Abu Jihad in *Filistin al-Thawra,* no. 443 (January 29, 1983):4.
32. *Filistin al-Thawra,* no. 428 (October 16, 1982):9.
33. Interview with Radio Monte Carlo, January 28, 1983. See also in this context the interview with Yasir Abd Rabbo in *Jordan Times,* December 4, 1982.
34. Interview with Radio Monte Carlo, April 1, 1983.
35. Statements of this sort were made by Khaled al-Hassan, Radio Monte Carlo, April 8, 1983, and by Abu Iyad in *al-Watan* (Kuwaiti daily), March 21, 1983.
36. An English translation of the communiqué can be found in the *Jordan Times,* April 11, 1983.
37. For an explanation of the Jordanian reasons, see King Hussein's interview with *Wall Street Journal,* April 14–15, 1983, and his interview in *al-Nahar,* May 1, 1983.
38. *Ma'ariv* (Israeli daily), October 11, 1983.
39. *Al-Nahar,* February 20, 1983.

40. Radio Monte Carlo, December 3, 1982.

41. See interview with Kamal Hassan Ali (Egypt's minister of foreign affairs) in *Monday Morning* (Lebanese weekly), November 29, 1982. See also the comments of President Mubarak in *al-Ahram,* December 6, 1982, and April 8, 1983.

42. William R. Brown, "The Puzzles in Saudi Policy," *Christian Science Monitor,* May 11, 1983.

43. *Al-Nahar,* October 12, 1982.

44. Syrian Arab News Agency, January 23, 1983.

45. See John H. Sigler, "United States Policy in the Aftermath of Lebanon: The Perils of Unilateralism," *International Journal* 38, no. 4 (summer 1983).

46. For U.S. reaction, see *New York Times,* April 11–13, 1983.

47. See the king's interview in *Wall Street Journal,* April 14, 1983.

6
The Split Within Fatah and the Rift with Syria

Though differences in political opinions and attitudes among the various PLO factions increased after the withdrawal from Beirut, they did not lead to a split within the movement until nine months later. As noted earlier, the slogans of maintaining Palestinian national unity and preserving the PLO as a politically representative organization reinforced the centripetal tendencies inside the movement. Unity, however, was not expected to last forever. The loss of the PLO's independent base of operations in Lebanon, the dispersal of its leadership between Syria and the moderate Arab countries, and Arafat's diplomatic maneuvering were not likely to take place without any serious ramifications for the movement. On May 10, 1983, a group of Fatah military officers declared a mutiny and submitted a set of demands aimed at limiting the power of Arafat and subduing voices of political moderation inside the organization.

Prelude to Mutiny

Though divisions were not uncommon inside the PLO, this was the first time that Fatah was subjected to a major shake-up since its inception. Prior to the outbreak of the Lebanon War, a dissident movement of this magnitude in the PLO's main faction was hard to imagine, as was the extent of the undermining of Arafat's leadership in the organization. Fatah's viability in the past two decades resulted from the interplay of a variety of factors and considerations. First, the movement's internal political stability and the survival of its leadership were rooted in the high degree of political legitimacy that Fatah's Central Committee enjoyed inside the movement and among the Palestinian people. This wide base of political legitimacy stemmed from the popular appeal of Fatah's ideas, Arafat's own charisma, and his image to many as a symbol for the Palestinian cause. The presence of such a high degree of political legitimacy had certainly reduced the incentives for potential rebels to mount an attack upon Fatah's leaders since they knew that such a move would be widely condemned.

Second, the legitimacy of Fatah's leadership was not only confined to the Palestinian constituency, since Arafat's political flexibility and moderation had won him Arab and international acceptance and respectability. Arab kings and presidents accredited to the PLO the status of being the sole legitimate representative of the Palestinians, and the United Nations accorded the organization an observer status in the General Assembly. Throughout the years, most Arab rulers supported Arafat's leadership of the PLO and rendered political, economic, and military aid to his organization, which ultimately contributed to Fatah's political stability and the preeminence of its leadership. Arafat's stature was also enhanced by the fact that Arab kings and presidents treated him as a head of state and admitted him to their inner councils.

Third, the relatively liberal climate inside Fatah, which included toleration for a range of opinions and trends from Marxism-Leninism to Arab nationalism and Islamic revivalism, averted sudden political explosions within the movement. From the beginning, Fatah's leaders wanted their organization to serve as an umbrella institution allowing the coexistence of various trends, which through cooperation would realize Palestinian rights in accordance with the movement's political program.

Fourth, Fatah s large political and military apparatus and statelike status in Lebanon enabled Arafat and his colleagues in the Central Committee to extend political rewards and inducements, and, if need be, employ them for intimidation, reprisals, and coercion. This powerful instrument was reinforced by Arafat's political mediating skills and role as coordinator among the various trends. In addition, the fact that more than three-fourths of Arab financial backing went directly into Fatah's own account gave the movement's leaders another powerful device by which to wield political influence and to reap material benefits and led to the growth of vested interests in the survival of the organization and its leadership.

These factors among others permitted Arafat and his colleagues to wield political power and command political loyalty inside the movement over the years. When the PLO withdrew from Lebanon, however, many of these conditions changed and new elements were introduced, rendering the PLO's continuing viability an illusory goal. Before examining the political dynamics inside Fatah after the war, it should be noted that on occasion Fatah's political plurality resulted in minor dissident movements or attempts at rebellion.[1] The emergence of these centrifugal tendencies came as a reaction to major political developments and policy changes in the PLO.

Following the termination of the PLO's military presence in Jordan in July 1971, controversy broke out inside the Palestinian resistance movement, revolving around the questions: Who was responsible for the military confrontation with the Jordanian regime? What type of strategy for the future should the PLO adopt? As a result, the Abu Nidal group broke away from Fatah during the movement's third popular congress in September 1971. According to Fatah officials Abu Nidal's move was engineered by the Iraqi government to cover up for its complacency during the 1970 Palestinian-Jordanian civil war: Despite the presence of Iraqi troops inside Jordan, the Iraqi government did not heed the repeated appeals to intervene on behalf of the PLO.

Two years later, another controversy erupted inside the PLO concerning a political settlement to the Arab-Israeli conflict. As a result of the 1973 October War, a group within the PLO was determined to oppose any Western-sponsored political solutions and vowed to continue its commitment to the strategy of military struggle. In contrast, a second group expressed interest in exploring the potential for a political settlement on the basis of establishing an independent state in the occupied territories. It also expressed its desire to join an Arab League delegation at the proposed Geneva peace conference.

The pro-Chira Marxist elements inside Fatah, led by Khaled al-Amleh, commonly known as Abu Khaled, opposed diplomacy as a tool to resolve the Palestinian problem and refused to accept the PNC endorsement of the establishment of a national authority in the West Bank and the Gaza Strip. Instead, Fatah's Maoist elements sided with the Popular Front General Command, the Popular Front, and the pro-Iraqi Arab Liberation Front and expressed their opposition to the formation of an independent Palestinian state inside the occupied territories. Their opposition was based on the conviction that such a political entity would contradict the Palestine National Charter and would deviate from the strategy of armed struggle and the principle of liberating all Palestine. Abu Khaled and some of his followers entered a secret dialogue with what came to be known as the Rejectionist Front inside the PLO. Their move, however, was not successful as they did not enjoy a strong following inside Fatah. Separatist sentiments of this sort were subdued in the wake of the outbreak of the Lebanese civil war in the mid-1970s, when Syria initially intervened on the side of the Christian groups against the Palestinians and their Lebanese leftist allies. In response, the PLO's factions united to confront the Syrian Christian military alliance.

In the opinion of many PLO leaders, the 1974 political controversy constituted the origin of the mutiny that erupted inside Fatah almost ten years later.[2] According to Abu Iyad, differences inside Fatah began to take the form of political, military, and ideological blocks after 1976.[3] He asserted that Fatah's Central Committee did not take appropriate measures at the time to arrest the growth of such secessionist tendencies, though the two leaders, Abu Khaled and Abu Saleh, were reminded not to form a specific ideological and military group inside Fatah.

The first large Israeli invasion of southern Lebanon in early spring 1978 furnished the third occasion for an attempted rebellion against Fatah's leadership. A group of Fatah officers led by Naji Allush rejected Arafat's acceptance of UN Security Council Resolution 425, which called upon the Palestinians to cease their military operations against Israel from Lebanese territory. Allush and his followers also refused to cooperate with the UN emergency troops to be stationed in southern Lebanon. Their attempted rebellion was supported by the Iraqi government, which was not pleased with the introduction of UN troops in Lebanon or with Arafat's acceptance of the cease-fire. Iraq was also angered by the evolving political accord between Syria and the PLO in July 1977. Nevertheless, Allush's attempted rebellion failed, as Arafat was able to manage the crisis and to impose discipline and order inside his organization. At the same time, Arafat removed from office two discontented officers, Abu Khaled and Abu Musa, and appointed them to administrative posts.[4]

Grounds for the Rebellion

The unfolding of political developments after the war adversely affected many of the sources that had accounted for Arafat's influence and power over the years. To begin with, the destruction of the PLO's military structure in southern Lebanon and Beirut deprived him of a significant tool, which in the pre-Lebanon War phase had enabled him to impose organizational discipline and unity upon his followers. Arafat's control over the remainder of Fatah's troops was significantly weakened when he departed from Beirut. Without his leadership in Lebanon, ample opportunity was afforded the disenchanted, the discontented, and those seeking positions of power to plan their next moves. Despite the serious ramifications of the war to the PLO's future, no serious attempt was made to evaluate its experience in Lebanon, nor was the organization's military performance during the war investigated. The convening of the Palestine National Council in Algiers left many problems untackled, and its final communiqué did not yield a clear strategy for future Palestinian political moves.

Political uncertainties, confusions, and dissatisfactions among the Palestinians were further increased by the inconclusive nature of Arafat's postwar diplomacy of accepting the Arab peace plan, dialogue with Jordan, and contacts with the Egyptian government and Israeli peace groups, and his refusal to categorically reject the Reagan initiative. These aspects of Arafat's diplomacy were particularly antagonistic and provocative to the Syrian government, which was determined not to relinquish its control over the Palestinian cause. Finally, the massacres of the Palestinians at the refugee camps of Sabra and Shatilla dealt a heavy blow to Arafat's leadership and diplomacy as many of his critics held him morally responsible for the tragedy, arguing that had the PLO remained in Beirut, the massacres would not have taken place. These factors among others ultimately led to the undermining of Arafat's political authority and the outbreak of a mutiny against his leadership.[5]

Early signs of discontent and disapproval of Arafat's policies came soon after the evacuation of West Beirut, when Abu Saleh, a member of the PLO delegation to the Arab summit conference, denounced Arafat's acceptance of the Arab peace plan. A few months later, Abu Saleh, without authorization from Fatah's Central Committee, attended the conference of the five rejectionist groups in Tripoli, Libya. On January 27, Abu Musa, supported by Fatah Central Committee member Samih Quayk—commonly known as Qadri—and Abu Khaled, delivered a speech before a closed session of Fatah's Revolutionary Council in Aden in which he sharply attacked Arafat's postwar policy.[6] On April 10, 1983, Abu Nidal's group assassinated Issam Sartawi (Arafat's confidant and political advisor).

In a number of moves geared to assert his authority within Fatah and to check the influence of his critics, Arafat suspended Abu Saleh's membership in Fatah's Central Committee and the Palestine National Council. This move was followed by the demotion of Qadri from his post as the head of Fatah's Office of Mobilization and Recruitment. Arafat also abolished the Department of Jordanian Affairs that had been headed by Qadri in a goodwill gesture to King Hussein.

Toward the end of April 1983, the PLO chairman appointed fifty-one of his followers to military posts for Fatah's troops inside Lebanon. Of these, the appointments of Haj Isma'il to lead Fatah's troops in northern Lebanon and of Abu Hajem as a commander of Fatah's troops in central Lebanon replacing Abu Musa and Abu Khaled proved to be highly controversial. The two appointments served as the spark that ignited the rebellion against Arafat. Haj Isma'il and Abu Hajem were accused by their rivals inside Fatah of "defeatist, incompetent and cowardly" behavior during the Israeli invasion of southern Lebanon. The rivals charged that such military appointments constituted the first step in the withdrawal of PLO troops from Lebanon to facilitate the passage of U.S.-sponsored solutions.

Haj Isma'il denied the accusation that his appointment as the commander of Fatah's troops in northern Lebanon was anything more than an organizational matter, asserting that it was simply a routine transfer to a new post. He also dismissed the allegations that his troops left the war zone after the first day of the invasion, arguing that his unit fought with its "modest" military capability for six days after the outbreak of hostilities. "With the several hundred troops under my command, I was unable to stop an invasion of this magnitude. I fought within my capabilities. To repel such an invasion required the presence of a large Arab army which was beyond my responsibility."[7]

Irrespective of the validity and the relevance of the arguments used by Arafat's opponents, it was within the prerogative of the PLO chairman to make such military appointments. It was not unnatural in view of the disintegration of the PLO's military infrastructure in southern Lebanon and Beirut for Arafat to reorganize his troops and appoint people personally loyal to him in key posts to ensure political stability and his control over the remainder of Fatah's troops in Lebanon. Certainly Arafat's move should not have been surprising at a time of mounting tension in his relationship with Syria and increasing criticism of his diplomatic moves by pro-Syrian figures in his organization. The removal of people with dubious loyalty from positions of power therefore was a normal procedure.

In addition to their refusal to accept the military appointments, the leaders of the rebellion differed with Arafat on three other cardinal issues: Fatah's organizational affairs, Arafat's management of the Israeli invasion, and his postwar diplomacy. With regard to Fatah's internal problems, the dissidents argued that their movement was suffering from the absence of channels of open communication and feedback and Arafat's deliberate neglect of the resolutions and recommendations of Fatah's three institutions (the Central Committee, the Revolutionary Council, and the Popular Congress).[8] Abu Musa, the military leader of the rebellion, charged that few individuals within Fatah's Central Committee controlled the policymaking apparatus and that the majority of the members were uninformed about what was going on, though decisions were made in their name.[9]

It was also suggested that major decisions, such as the acceptance of the Arab peace plan of Fez, the dialogue with Jordan, and contacts with Egypt and Israeli peace groups, were made without collective approval of Fatah's leadership and institutions. In the dissidents' view, this situation came about because of Arafat's distrust of collective leadership, the growth of democratic trends inside Fatah, and Arafat's refusal to introduce organizational reforms. In the rebels' opinion, the presence of such organizational constraints compelled them to press their case outside Fatah's legal institutions.

Arafat's handling of the Israeli invasion of southern Lebanon furnished another ground for criticism from the opposition circles. The dissidents criticized the speed with which the Israeli army conquered the south and advanced northward toward Beirut.[10] Abu Musa argued that, in view of the arms stored in the south and the number of Palestinian troops stationed there, the PLO's military performance should have been qualitatively better and should have lasted longer. The opposition blamed Fatah's leadership for abandoning large quantities of weapons and ammunition in the south.

Abu Musa and his colleagues also attributed the defeat of the PLO in southern Lebanon to the fact that throughout the 1970s Arafat and Abu Jihad had transformed the commando groups into a semiconventional army and equipped it with moderate and heavy weaponry, making it vulnerable to Israeli ground and air strikes. Although one cannot discount the validity of such a statement, the influx of former Palestinian officers from the Jordanian army (such as Abu Musa and Abu Khaled) into the PLO after the 1970 September civil war resulted in the introduction of army discipline and heavy equipment into the ranks of the organization.[11] Furthermore, the semiconventional nature of the PLO forces was necessitated by the prevailing military and political conditions in Lebanon as the various Lebanese militias were equipped with medium and heavy arms. This situation forced the PLO leaders to match their weaponry with those of their enemies to protect themselves and the Palestinian refugees.

The leaders of the rebellion did not confine their criticism to the PLO's poor military performance during the Israeli invasion, but also lamented the fact that Arafat's leadership did not even try to draw the appropriate conclusions and lessons from the Lebanon experience. In their view, the Lebanon War had unveiled a number of significant lessons for the organization's future course of action.[12] To start with, they argued, the Beirut experience demonstrated that Palestinian, Lebanese, and Syrian fighters were not only capable of resisting the Israeli army but also of inflicting heavy casualties against its rank and file. Second, the Lebanon experience revealed that "long-term popular warfare" was an appropriate strategy for fighting the "Zionist enemy" and that time was working on the side of the Palestinian people. Third, in their opinion the long duration of the war disproved the myth about Israel's ability to launch a successful surprise attack upon its neighbors. Finally, the war demonstrated that the prolongation of the struggle with Israel would have disruptive effects upon the unity and the cohesion of Israeli society.

In the opinion of Fatah militants, the refusal by Arafat and his colleagues to draw the appropriate lessons from the Lebanon experience was rooted in their antirevolutionary stands and their concern to preserve their power, privileged positions, and material benefits inside the PLO. It also emanated from an adverse attitude to political change and underestimation of the fighting capabilities of the Palestinian people. The leaders of the opposition further argued that in an attempt to cover up the failure to bring about a well-defined strategy, Arafat and his associates exaggerated the immediate political gains of the PLO following its departure from Beirut.

The question of the PLO's withdrawal and the dispersal of its troops to several Arab countries constituted an additional grievance for the rebels.[13] In contrast to the aura of heroism and victory that accompanied the departure of the PLO troops from Beirut in August 1982, leaders of the rebellion regarded the withdrawal as a sign of surrender to Israeli military pressure and U.S. diplomatic maneuvering and a submission to the desire of "Arab reactionary regimes." They contended that Arafat prematurely pulled out from the city, since Israel certainly would not risk attempting to occupy West Beirut in view of the heavy casualties that would incur to its army. The rebels also contested Arafat's assertion that the dispersal of the PLO's troops was a sign of strength, arguing that "the true fighters and revolutionaries" opposed the notion of withdrawal on the grounds that they would lose an irreplaceable base for military and political operations. Arafat's opponents further claimed that he was opposed to the return of the dispersed PLO fighters to Lebanon and that he had suspended the salaries of those who insisted upon coming back.

A third area in which the leaders of the rebellion differed significantly from the PLO chief was related to Arafat's postwar diplomacy. Arafat's diplomatic moves sharply deviated from the PLO charter and the various resolutions of the Palestine National Council concerning such cardinal issues as the strategy of military struggle, liberation of all Palestine, and the nature of Zionism. With regard to the strategy of armed struggle, Arafat's opponents alleged that his policy was geared to dismiss the relevance and the usefulness of such a strategy.[14] By doing so, they claimed that Arafat was attaching a new meaning to the concept of the Palestinian national struggle; such a definition would restrict the struggle to the issues of the PLO's recognition as the sole legitimate representative of the Palestinian people by Western Europe and the United States and its acceptance as a negotiating partner in any political settlement.

Fatah militants argued that limiting the Palestinian national struggle to the question of extracting Western and Israeli recognition was a dangerous step since it would lead to a change in "the revolutionary national mission of the Palestinian people and their joint struggle with the Arab masses" and facilitate passage of "imperialist and Arab reactionary liquidationist solutions."[15] For these reasons the dissidents found it incomprehensible that the chairman of the PLO was seeking Western recognition. In their opinion, the struggle between Arab and Palestinian nationalism, on one hand, and Zionism and imperialism, on the other, was "an existentialist one" and should not therefore be reduced to the mere question of recognition. Commenting on this issue, Abu Musa pointed out that merely declaring one's intention of exchanging mutual and simultaneous recognition between the Israelis and the Palestinians would undermine the inevitability of the struggle between Israel and the Arabs. The dissidents further contended that drawing a distinction between the struggle against Israel and contacts with the West and United States was a dangerous move, as it would lead to an accommodation with the "hostile forces" and would "confuse the allies with the enemy."[16] They finally alleged that Arafat had deliberately produced this confusion to facilitate his contacts with the United States and Israeli peace groups and to create new problems with the "real supporters of the Palestinian revolution."

On the basis of such arguments Fatah militants vehemently opposed Arafat's repeated meetings with Israeli peace-camp figures. They rejected the distinction that Arafat and his political advisors made between "progressive Zionism" and "reactionary Zionism";[17] they declared that such a distinction was superficial and in violation of the Palestine national councils. In their opinion, Zionism is "racist, expansionist, and colonialist in its objectives, methods, and techniques." They also pointed out that the declarations by PLO officials of their readiness to recognize Israel would damage their organization's credibility and prestige in the world and that the contacts with the Israelis would encourage "reactionary Arab regimes" to enter into political settlement with the Jewish state.

According to Arafat's opponents, a second serious breach of the Palestine National Charter occurred with the abandonment of the goals of liberating all Palestine and establishing a secular democratic state to replace Israel. They charged that Arafat began to put aside this goal in 1974, when the Palestine National Council under heavy pressure from Arafat accepted the notion of forming a "national authority" in the occupied territories. Under Arafat's pressure, the National Council endorsed the creation of an independent Palestinian state on the West Bank and Gaza Strip in 1977. The Fatah dissidents further alleged that in 1982 Arafat permanently laid to rest the idea of establishing an independent state when he initiated his dialogue with King Hussein to federate the West Bank with the East Bank on the basis of the Reagan initiative.

A third major area of Arafat's "deviationist" policy was evinced in his readiness to form a government in exile and to abandon the PLO as a "national liberation organization." The notion of a government in exile was publicized after Arafat's meeting with a group of Palestinian businessmen and intellectuals toward the end of June 1983 in Tunis.[18] During the meeting, proposals were made to establish an independent Palestinian state in the West Bank and Gaza Strip and to form a provisional government to replace the PLO. These proposals were based on the UN Partition Resolution of November 29, 1947, which called for the creation of an Arab state and a Jewish state in Palestine. It was also suggested in the meeting that, in addition to its other functions, the PLO would undertake the supervision of this new body until the Palestine National Council convened in an emergency session to promulgate the constitution for such a state.

Arafat's deputy Abu Jihad dismissed any immediate plan to form a provisional government and insisted that the discussion of such a government was only a theoretical exercise. He also ruled out any plan to materialize such a project in the near future, since such a step would be premature without Palestinian national unity.[19] Despite Abu Jihad's denials, leaders of the rebellion were convinced that Arafat was planning to go along with such a project, particularly after his failure to crush their movement. In their opinion a government in exile would ensure that Arafat and his associates would continue to play a pivotal role in Palestinian affairs and would preserve their privileged positions and interests. The rebels also contended that this new political device would enable Arafat to present himself as acceptable to the United States and Arab moderate countries and would also facilitate the incorporation of Palestinian leadership in the "Arab reactionary camp."[20]

The government in exile was also opposed on the grounds that it was initiated outside the PLO's institutions and that prevailing regional conditions were not conducive for its formation. The PLO was still far from liberating Palestine, and the land for such a state was still under Israeli military occupation. Fatah militants felt that they must demonstrate the dangers of the government-in-exile plan to the Palestinian people and consolidate their ties with the rest of the PLO's hard-line groups and the "progressive Arab countries" (including Syria and Libya) to frustrate the plan's passage. In addition, they opposed the convening of an emergency session of the Palestine National Council because it would afford Arafat the opportunity to discuss his plans.

Arafat was also attacked for his endorsement of the Arab peace plan of Fez; his opponents charged that the adoption of the plan had not been sanctioned by Fatah's Central Committee or the other PLO councils.[21] They considered Arafat's acceptance of the plan as a sign of submission to Saudi Arabian pressures. Most of their criticism was directed against Article 7, which in their view proposed to "end the state of war between Israel and the PLO, drop the military option and extend recognition to the enemy." Commenting on this issue, Abu Saleh pointed out that "there is a wide Arab trend supported by a Palestinian minority that wants us to drop the gun and to rely upon diplomacy as a means to realize the goals of our people. But the Palestinian is a fighter and a revolutionary, and is not a refugee as the imperialists try to project him." He further dismissed any significant effectiveness of Arab diplomatic efforts to resolve the Palestinian question since "Arab diplomacy with all of its weight, failed even to let water supplies reach us when we were besieged in West Beirut."[22]

Arafat's policy of a gradual opening to Egypt was also severely criticized. The rebels were afraid that contacts with Egypt would diffuse its diplomatic isolationism in the Arab world and would open the door for other Arab countries to follow the Palestinian example. Moreover, contacts with the Egyptian regime conflicted with Fatah's political program, which demanded the elimination of the Camp David accords and the cancellation of the Egyptian-Israeli peace treaty as preconditions to the improvement of Palestinian-Egyptian relations.[23]

The choice of which attitude the PLO should take toward both Lebanon and Syria also stood behind the heated debate and the harsh charges and countercharges between Arafat and his opponents. Statements by some Fatah Central Committee members of their readiness to initiate a dialogue with the government of President Amin Gemayal drew criticism from opposition circles. Fatah officials also expressed their willingness to withdraw the remainder of their troops from Lebanon. Arafat appealed to the Lebanese president to start "a brotherly and quiet dialogue."[24] Earlier, Abu Jihad spelled out four conditions to bring about a PLO troop withdrawal from Lebanon, including the granting by the Lebanese government of a symbolic political and military presence for the PLO, a guarantee for the safety and security of the Palestinian refugee civilians, and the initiation of a dialogue between the PLO and the government.[25] Arafat and his associates also expressed their sympathy for the suffering of the Lebanese people and their need to live peacefully away from violence and counterviolence. To underline their concern for Lebanese national unity, integrity, and sovereignty, Fatah officials appealed to the Palestinians in Lebanon not to interfere in the country's internal affairs and to entrust the security and the safety of those Palestinians into the hands of the Lebanese army, which was described as "a responsible Arab army."[26]

In response to these conciliatory statements, leaders of the opposition sharply denounced the attempt to normalize relations with the Lebanese government, which in their view had committed crimes against the Palestinian people and cooperated with the Israelis during the 1982 summer invasion. They concluded that the improvement of the relationship between the PLO and the Lebanese government would encourage the latter to step up its "repressive policy" against the Palestinians. Fatah militants vehemently opposed the withdrawal of the rest of the PLO's troops from Lebanon for a number of reasons.[27] First, the withdrawal would serve only the interests of "reactionary regimes," would be an abandonment of the strategy of armed struggle, and would facilitate the "implementation of liquidationist solutions." Second, by withdrawing the PLO's troops, the organization would not only forego a "historical opportunity" to regroup its forces in Lebanon and resume its military operations against Israel but would also dissociate itself from the Arab nationalist movement by abandoning the Lebanese nationalist forces and the Syrian army. Finally, they argued that the withdrawal of the PLO's troops would serve Israel's security interests, prolong its occupation of Lebanon, reduce Israeli casualties, and diminish Israeli mass public opposition.

To avert such dangers, Fatah dissidents advocated the return of the dispersed Palestinian fighters to Lebanon and the resumption of military operations against Israel. In line with their Arab nationalist sentiments, they contended that Lebanon was the natural place for PLO fighters to encounter the Israelis and frustrate the Israeli-Lebanese agreement.[28] A Palestinian military presence would reinforce Lebanese national independence and sovereignty and provide protection for the Palestinians in their refugee camps. Finally, Fatah militants extended their support to the antigovernment forces represented by the Lebanese National Salvation Front, which consisted of Druze leader Walid Jumblatt, Nabih Berri, leader of the Shi'ite Amal, and former Christian Lebanese president Sulaiman Franjieh.

Though the rebels agreed with Arafat that Arab support was essential to sustain the Palestinian revolution, they differed on the source for that support. Support to the PLO should come from the progressive Arab countries led by Syria and Libya that, unlike other Arab states, were committed to the continuation of the Palestinian revolution and the strategy of armed struggle. Moreover, Syria was the only remaining confrontation state willing to check Israel's "expansionist drive" in Lebanon and elsewhere in the Middle East. In addition to this rationale, dictates of political realism were present in the minds of the leaders of the rebellion: The call to solidify ties with Syria was brought about by the fact that without Syrian support or acquiescence, the chances for success of their movement were negligible. The growing tension between Arafat and Assad created a commonality of interests between the two sides. Had Arafat's opponents adopted a critical attitude toward the Damascus government's poor military performance during the Lebanon War, the regime would have aborted the movement from the outset.

Despite the coincidence in interests between the rebels and Syria, a number of incongruities could be discerned in their basic positions. First, the militant overtone of Fatah's opposition and its emphasis on the strategy of military struggle against Israel contradicted the cautious policy that the Assad regime had pursued since its coming to power in 1970. Notwithstanding its public rhetoric, it was hard to imagine that the Syrian government would allow PLO radicals to resume military operations from Syria proper or to endorse openly their activities from Lebanese areas under Syrian control. The rulers in Damascus were concerned not to provide the Israelis with excuses to launch punitive strikes against Syrian forces. In fact, since the signing of the Syrian-Israeli troop disengagement agreement of 1974, the common borders had been quiet. The Syrian government also insisted, when it accepted the evacuated PLO fighters from Beirut, that they should be disarmed and stationed in areas remote from urban centers. In view of this restrictive policy, it was difficult to imagine how Fatah militants could pursue their strategy of armed struggle.

A second incongruity between the attitudes of Fatah dissidents and their Syrian backers pertained to their differences concerning a political settlement for the Arab-Israeli dispute. Although the Assad regime was not opposed to a political settlement that would address the Syrian national grievances (as manifested in the regime's acceptance of UN Security Council Resolutions 242 and 338 and its acceptance of the 1982 Fez peace plan), the rebels insisted that the only path for the liberation of Palestine was the pursuit of military struggle. Third, the two sides differed sharply concerning U.S. mediating efforts, and, although Syria had on several occasions accepted the United States as a diplomatic go-between, the rebels were adamant and uncompromising in their hostility to what they termed "American imperialism."

Finally, in view of these political differences, the negative image of the Syrian rulers following Arafat's expulsion from Damascus, and Arafat's repeated accusations that the dissidents were stooges in the hands of the Syrians, the leaders of the rebellion were careful to stress their autonomy and independence from Syrian control. They pointed out that Syria's present policy meshed well with their own political positions and accounted for the close ties that they enjoyed with the Syrian government. Abu Musa, military leader of the rebellion, declared that we will be with Syria as long as it will say no to the Reagan initiative and will continue its confrontation policy with Israel. Once it withdraws or retreats from such a policy, my attitude will then change. I align myself with the Syrian army because it is standing against the enemy and if Syria were to withdraw from Lebanon I would not withdraw.[29]

In summation, Arafat's opponents concluded that he no longer enjoyed political legitimacy because of his deviationist policies. In their opinion, he had broken away from the Palestinian national consensus that envisaged the PLO's existence as contingent upon the realization of Palestinian national rights and the liberation of all Palestine through the strategy of armed struggle. They contended that Arafat's policies sharply departed from those goals. This departure necessitated a new leadership since the preservation of the old leadership would impede accomplishing the "goals of the revolution." The leaders of the opposition presented themselves as a substitute for Arafat's leadership and later formed an alternative revolutionary council for Fatah. Their demands for reform were expected to bring back unity, legitimacy, and collective leadership in Fatah. They argued that the legitimacy and unity of the organization could be restored through strict adherence to their program and the Palestinian National Charter.[30]

The Syrian Connection

Initially Fatah officials assumed that the dissidents were a small and isolated group and that containing them would not be difficult. However, the opposition inside Fatah grew, and by early June the rebellion took on a new dimension when actual fighting broke out between Arafat supporters and opponents. The transformation of an apparent political protest movement into an armed rebellion could be explained in several ways. From the beginning, the dissidents were determined to oust Arafat and his associates with or without Syrian backing. Alternately, being uncertain of its ability to keep Arafat in line Syria sanctioned the escalation of violence to end Arafat's military presence in Lebanon. This move would reduce Arafat's credentials for leading the PLO, while giving his opponents the advantage of possessing military bases and the option of launching military operations against Israel. The resort to violence was probably deliberately pursued by Arafat to tarnish the image of his opponents and to depict the fighting as a Syrian-Palestinian conflict and not an inner Palestinian one. The increasing possibility that the fighting could eventually be settled in favor of his opponents— giving them some legitimacy in the eyes of the Palestinians—compelled Arafat to pursue the course of military confrontation.

Arafat and his colleagues in Fatah's Central Committee chose the second explanation, with some justification, to explain the outbreak of the fighting. Several Fatah senior officials began directly or indirectly to implicate Syria and Libya and their protégés inside the PLO in the mutiny.[31] The ostensible neutrality of the Syrian regime toward the mutiny within Fatah was perplexing to Fatah's Central Committee members. The facts that the mutiny took place in Lebanese areas under Syrian control and that it occurred only a few days after Arafat's meeting with Assad and their agreement to form joint committees to look into their political differences were behind Fatah's suspicion of Syrian complicity in the rebellion.

With the recurrence of military clashes and the takeover by the opposition groups of Fatah's storage facilities and supply offices in Damascus, senior Fatah leaders began openly to speak of Syria's involvement in the mutiny, accusing the government of facilitating the transfer of Libyan arms to the dissidents and claiming that the Syrian intelligence services were giving them guidance. Moreover, with the increase in the level of violence, the Arafat leadership became more and more convinced that the mutiny would not have taken place without Syrian advance knowledge and authorization. Abu Iyad inquired, "Isn't Syria capable of stopping this inter-Palestinian conflict? Even if we started the fighting, why didn't they stop us? And if Abu Musa is the one who did it, why didn't they stop him?"[32] By the third week of June, allegations of Syria's intervention in Fatah's internal affairs took a new turn when Arafat and some of his aides began to talk publicly about direct Syrian military participation in the fighting and contended that Syrian tanks were encircling Fatah troops in central Lebanon, obstructing their communication lines and supply routes.[33]

Allegations of Syrian intervention in the fighting were vehemently rejected by Syria and its protégés inside the Palestinian nationalist movement. The dissidents dismissed Arafat's charges as invalid and argued that they did not need any external assistance as their troops possessed sufficient human resources to defend their cause. They further contended that Syria and Libya and the three PLO factions (the Popular Front General Command, the Popular Struggle Front, and al-Sa'iqa) were completely neutral concerning Fatah's crises.

By implicating Syria and other PLO factions in Fatah's internal dispute, leaders of the opposition argued that Arafat was trying to achieve several objectives.[34] First, the notion of outside intervention was used to cover up Arafat's inability to suppress the uprising and to conceal that Arafat's own troops first resorted to arms to settle the dispute. Moreover, Arafat was concerned to arrest the popularity of the protest movement and to check shifting loyalties toward the opposition.

Second, Arafat's charges were an exercise in mass deception used to arouse Palestinian feeling and to propagate the idea that the protest movement was not genuine but rather engineered by Syria and Libya. Third, by implicating the two Arab countries in the fighting, Arafat was attempting to discredit the two regimes and generate intense Arab pressure upon Syria to alter its neutral stance vis-à-vis Fatah's uprising.

Denials of outside intervention in internal Fatah affairs came also from the Popular Front General Command, the Popular Struggle Front, and al-Sa'iqa. On June 21, 1983, the spokesman for the Popular Front General Command denied that his organization was providing any military support to the rebels, though he did not conceal his group's moral and political support. Ahmed Jibril, secretary general of the organization, underlined his movement's grievances, which were discernible in three main areas.[35] First, the general command opposed Arafat's autocracy and personal hegemony over the PLO and his resort to repressive measures to suppress "the true fighters and revolutionaries." Arafat's post-Beirut diplomacy constituted a second ground for the disagreement. The general command was particularly apprehensive of Arafat's acceptance of the Fez peace plan, the dialogue with Jordan, and his contacts with Egypt and Israeli peace groups. Finally, the general command was critical of the personal corruption and mismanagement of the organization's affairs.

These charges, countercharges, and denials by the representatives of the two Palestinian camps would not have been as serious if Damascus were not implicated in the fighting. Before discussing Syria's counterreaction to Arafat's charges, it should be pointed out that the Fatah-Syria relationship over the years was far from smooth, and the personal animosity between Arafat and Assad was not new.[36] As early as 1966, Assad in his capacity as minister of defense ordered Arafat imprisoned for a few months. Four years later, Assad opposed the engagement of the Syrian air force to assist commando groups during the 1970 September civil war in Jordan. The mid-1970s witnessed a bitter fight between the PLO and Syria in which the latter sided with the Christian forces against the Palestinians and their Lebanese leftist allies in Lebanon's civil war.

Throughout the remainder of the 1970s, the PLO was able to survive because of the backing that it was getting from both Egypt and Iraq, Syria's adversaries. But with the signing of the Egyptian-Israeli peace treaty in March 1979, and the outbreak of the Iraq-Iran War in September 1980, the PLO's ability to play one Arab country against another was severely curtailed, and its degree of autonomy was reduced as its dependency upon Syria increased. This greater dependency led to the conclusion of a strategic alliance agreement between Syria and the PLO in spring 1981.

With the outbreak of the Lebanon War, a number of political developments and considerations once again distanced Arafat and Assad from one another. Syria's national pride was injured by Arafat's choice of Tunis as the political headquarters of the PLO and of Algiers as a meeting ground for the Palestine National Council. In addition, Fatah officials' repeated references to Syria's military paralysis during the Israeli siege of Beirut angered the regime. Criticism of this sort would not have been possible if Arafat had been stationed in Damascus. The Syrian government was also unhappy about Arafat's equivocal attitude toward the Reagan initiative and his rapprochement with Jordan, Iraq, and Egypt.

These various aspects of Arafat's postwar diplomacy and his determination to free the PLO from Syria's control and to preserve his organization's freedom to maneuver would undermine the government's attempt to use the Palestinian question as a bargaining card in its quest to recover the Golan Heights. They were also not in line with the Syrian president's effort to appropriate for his country a pivotal role in the region and to gain U.S. respect and attention.[37] Viewed from this perspective, the mutiny was meant to signal Arafat to be attentive to Syria's policy concerns. No doubt the influx of modern Soviet weaponry and Soviet backing emboldened the Syrian government to pursue an assertive policy and an inflexible political stand toward Arafat.

Prior to the outbreak of the mutiny, the Syrian government tried to communicate its determination not to loosen its control over the PLO or to permit Arafat's postwar diplomacy to undermine its regional interest. In addition to the repeated public statements by Syrian officials critical of Arafat's diplomatic moves, Syrian intelligence officers were alleged to have provided Abu Musa and his colleagues with the names of 200 Fatah officers whose help could be solicited in the rebellion as early as October 1982.[38]

Around the same time, Abu al-Walid, commander of the PLO's troops, was assassinated in a part of central Lebanon under Syrian control. A month later, the Syrian government allowed the notorious group of Abu Nidal (which carried out several assassination attempts against leading Arafat supporters) to open offices in Damascus. In December 1982, senior Syrian army officers were reported to have contacted a number of Fatah people as a reminder again to Arafat not to get too close to Jordan.[39] In January 1983, Syria gave its blessing to the convening of the Tripoli conference for the PLO rejectionist groups on an anti-Arafat platform. The regime also had allowed its capital to be used as a haven for Arafat's critics. The mutiny against Arafat on May 10, 1983, may also be seen as part of these warnings. The dissident movement was meant to be a sharp reminder to Arafat not to overlook Syria's role and interests.

Arafat, however, did not give in to Syria's pressures, or alternatively he may not have assessed precisely the implications of Syria's political warnings against what was perceived as defiant behavior. As noted earlier, Arafat and his associates continued to assert that Syria was behind the mutiny within Fatah and that the Syrian troops were actually participating in the fighting. In response, the Syrian government, through its media, dismissed such allegations as erroneous and invalid and claimed that from the beginning it had adopted a neutral stand concerning the crisis and had urged both sides to reconcile their differences in a "brotherly fashion" and "democratic manner." It further argued that had the Syrian military intervened directly, the opposition to Arafat's leadership would have assumed a different intensity and magnitude.[40]

With Arafat's repeated charges, the Damascus government terminated its publicly proclaimed neutral stand. Starting on June 21, 1983, the Syrian news agency began to report the military communiqués of Arafat's opponents, and three days later the Syrian government expelled the PLO chairman from Damascus and banned him from returning to Syria and to areas in Lebanon under Syrian control. The government's statement cited Arafat's "continuous lies and slander against Syria" as motivating the expulsion order. This action was followed by an intense media campaign against Arafat, who was described as "irresponsible, arrogant," and determined to liquidate his opponents. He was also held directly responsible for the crises inside the PLO.[41]

In its endeavor to limit the damage to its credibility inside Arab and Palestinian circles that resulted from Arafat's expulsion order, the Syrian government was careful to point out that the move was taken against Arafat personally without any implications concerning the PLO or Syrian support for the Palestinian cause. Despite Syria's statements of reassurance, the expulsion order was alarming to the members of Fatah's Central Committee; Abu Iyad characterized the Syrian move as "more dangerous and serious than Sadat's trip to Jerusalem."[42]

Fatah's leaders were worried that because of Syria's overall military preponderance and its control over the PLO's radical groups the government might try to create an alternative PLO. These concerns prompted some of Fatah's Central Committee members to make conciliatory statements toward the regime despite the humiliation of their chief.[43] Seeking to avoid any further political or military confrontation with Damascus, they called for a meeting between Syrian and Fatah leaders to normalize their relations and to discuss their differences. Arafat himself also proposed an immediate meeting between his group and the Syrians, offered to withdraw his troops from central Lebanon to diffuse the crisis, and called for the imposition of a strict and immediate cease-fire between Fatah's warring factions.

Palestinian Reactions and Mediating Efforts

The outbreak of mutiny within Fatah and the rupture of its relationship with Syria had a profoundly negative impact upon the unity and cohesion of the PLO, as the crisis worked to deepen the already existing divisions inside the Palestinian nationalist movement. Palestinian reaction to these political developments varied significantly, ranging from open support for the rebels and Syria, to attempts for mediation and reconciliation, and to bitter denunciation of the mutineers and their Syrian backers. Initially, the dissidents' demands for reform received some public sympathy from within Fatah's ruling circles. The majority of Fatah's Central Committee members were reportedly prepared to accept some of the opposition's demands as long as they remained within the confines of a "positive protest."[44]

Abu Iyad, Farouq al-Qadoumi, and the PLO's representative in Saudi Arabia, Rafiq al-Natshe, contacted the leaders of the opposition in an attempt to mediate between them and Arafat. They demanded that the channels of communication remain open between leaders of the opposition and Fatah's Central Committee members so as to resolve the dispute peacefully. They were concerned about avoiding the transformation of Fatah's uprising into a larger problem that could be exploited by rival Arab regimes. Abu Iyad even publicly expressed some sympathy for the rebels when he characterized some of their demands as "valid" and called the leaders of the opposition "sincere, honorable men" and "good fighters."[45] He blamed Arafat for the failure to broaden the decision-making apparatus within Fatah and urged him to reconsider his approach. Abu Iyad's statement, however, came short of being an all-out endorsement of the rebellion; he was careful to indicate his disapproval of the rebels' techniques of expressing their demands outside Fatah's political councils. He also softened his criticism of Arafat when he attributed the mistakes of the PLO chairman to his "immense responsibilities" and said that he regarded him as a symbol of the Palestinian revolution.

Arafat reportedly was prepared initially to accept some of the dissidents' demands including the rescinding of some of his military appointments and the removal of those officers charged with military negligence and defeatism during the Israeli invasion of southern Lebanon.[46] On July 19, 1983, Abu Jihad removed from office Haj Isma'il and Abu Hajem—the two controversial figures that sparked the dissident movement. Around the same time, Arafat introduced some cosmetic organizational changes inside Fatah including relinquishing his direct control over the departments of finance and information.

Perhaps because of this propensity for reconciliation in the first few weeks of the rebellion, Fatah's councils did not take severe measures against the dissidents. For instance, Fatah's Revolutionary Council, convened in Damascus on June 21, 1983, did not advocate harsh measures against the rebels but delegated authority to the Central Committee to take appropriate measures to stop the fighting and to preserve the unity of the movement. The council also called for setting up a number of committees to study the demands of the opposition, to introduce organizational reforms, and to work for the convening of Fatah's fifth popular congress.[47]

The desire of some of Fatah's Central Committee members to mediate was impeded by the refusal of the leaders of the opposition to engage in a dialogue. Later, the escalation of the fighting and the deepening of the rift between Arafat and Syria prompted some Fatah leaders to propose that the dissidents separate from Fatah and establish their own independent faction within the PLO.[48] A spokesman for the rebels, however, categorically rejected such an offer and asserted that his followers firmly believed in the "indivisibility and unity" of the movement.[49]

While Fatah's Central Committee officials were trying to bring about a reconciliation with the opposition, mediating efforts by other PLO factions and institutions were made in an attempt to resolve the conflict and avoid a total rupture in Fatah's relationship with Syria. Such efforts were made by the PLO Executive Committee, the Palestine Central Council, and the Popular and Democratic Fronts. Following Arafat's expulsion from Damascus, the Executive Committee in its meeting toward the end of June decided to establish a six-member mediating committee under the chairmanship of Khaled al-Fahum, president of the Palestine National Council. This committee was entrusted with the task of mending Fatah-Syrian relations and of reconciling Arafat with his Palestinian opponents.

The committee was able to arrange a three-week cease-fire, but its work was ultimately impeded by the different priorities of the various actors in the conflict.[50] In the first place, the leaders of the opposition were only interested in mediations that would lead to the attainment of their goals. Second, Arafat himself was more concerned with improving relations with Syria before tackling Fatah's internal crises since in his view his opponents were not operating on their own. Third, the work of the committee was complicated by Syria's repeated insistence that it was not party to the conflict and therefore had nothing to do with these mediating efforts. Finally, the committee's ability to mediate was severely curtailed when it issued a statement denying that Syrian and

Libyan troops were fighting on the side of the opposition and asserted that no evidence existed to sustain Arafat's charges. The statement also urged Arafat's leadership to avoid any inaccuracy in its reporting and to refrain from provoking Syrian troops in Lebanon.[51]

Because of the inconclusive nature of the mediating efforts by the six-member committee, the Palestine Central Council (the intermediary body between the PLO's Executive Committee and the Palestine National Council) met in early August to discuss Fatah's crisis and the status of Palestinian-Syrian relations. In its final communiqué, the council reconfirmed the need to preserve Palestinian national unity and Fatah's cohesion and to resolve its internal crisis through democratic and peaceful means.[52] In addition, the conferees passed resolutions to serve as guidelines for political and organizational reform inside the PLO and recommended that a military committee be formed to arrange for a cease-fire between Fatah's warring factions. They also called for establishment of another political committee to work for the resolution of the conflict inside Fatah and between Arafat and Assad and to coordinate its work with that of the six-member committee. The council also authorized this committee to denounce publicly any party that violated the cease-fire.

In a similar move designed to reduce tension, the participants appealed to all sides to halt all propaganda warfare and media campaigns. With regard to Palestinian-Syrian relations, the council recommended the augmentation of the strategic relationship with Syria and the Lebanese national forces and referred to the significance of Syria's support to the PLO to preserve it as the only representative for the Palestinians. An appeal was made to broaden the participatory role of the political institutions of the PLO and to introduce measures that would ensure collective leadership. Finally, despite the humiliating expulsion of Arafat from Damascus, the conferees only registered their deep regret over the Syrian move.

The fact that the Central Council met against the background of Palestinian fighting, divisions, and Syria's hostility to Arafat signified a number of important points. The convening of the council could be considered a personal victory for Arafat and the legitimacy of his leadership of the PLO. Out of the eighty-one members of the council, seventy-nine attended the session, including the secretary generals of the various PLO factions, despite Libyan pressure upon them to boycott the meeting. The two absent members were the representatives of the Popular Front General Command and the Fatah dissidents. The spokesman for the rebels in central Lebanon denied any significance to the convening of the council and asserted that the council was not an executive agency but a consultative one. Commenting on the convening of the council, Abu Musa pointed out that Fatah's crisis should be resolved within its own institutions and not through the political councils of the PLO or through Arab mediations.[53] Convening the Central Council and holding the subsequent meeting of the PLO's higher military councils a few days later in North Yemen left no doubt that Arafat was trying to press for wider political participation and the engagement of the PLO's institutions in the process of policy formulation. This policy was intended to invalidate his opponents' charges of his autocratic behavior inside the PLO.

Aside from Arafat's personal political gains, the large number of Palestinian leaders of different political persuasions at the conference indicated their desire to preserve the unity and viability of the PLO and maintain their representational role. One could also argue that the high attendance of the rejectionists in the meeting was intended to avoid the endorsement of resolutions that would harshly denounce the Syrians for the expulsion of Arafat, on the one hand, and not allow Arafat a free hand in shaping the Central Council's resolutions and recommendations, on the other.

In line with the recommendation of the council, an eighteen-member conciliation commission was formed to arrange for a cease-fire and mediate between Fatah's two camps. After meeting with both sides, the commission submitted recommendations and proposals on August 21, 1983, to tackle Fatah's political and organizational crises.[54] The commission reiterated the need for a firm cease-fire and cessation of all types of propaganda warfare. It also requested that Fatah's Central Committee issue a declaration reasserting its adherence to the strategy of armed struggle as an effective medium to liberate the occupied territories and stating its opposition to U.S.-sponsored plans.

At the organizational level, the commission pointed out the need to widen political participation inside the movement and adhere to the principle of collective leadership. It further proposed the establishment of a provisional committee of Arafat's supporters and opponents, in coordination with the president of the Palestine National Council, to supervise Fatah's political, military, financial, and organizational affairs. This new body was also entrusted with the task of preparing for Fatah's fifth popular congress.

On October 12, the eighteen-member conciliation committee published a progress report.[55] Although complimenting the dissidents' acceptance of its recommendations of August 21, 1983, and Syria's encouragement of the commission's mediating efforts, the report indirectly criticized Fatah's Central Committee for its reluctance to accept the proposal to form a provisional committee. The report also reiterated the commission's appeal to introduce a system of collective leadership and urged Fatah leaders to halt their media campaigns against Syria.

Three days later Fatah's Central Committee issued a statement refuting the contentions of the report.[56] Contrary to the report's suggestions, the Central Committee asserted that it had studied the commission's recommendations and submitted its counterproposals and further contended that the dissidents and their Syrian backers were the ones who continued to oppose a democratic dialogue and mediating efforts. In addition, the Central Committee's statement proposed the formation of a committee with equal representation from both sides of Fatah to study the requirements and the means needed to carry out the reform demands.

The joint committee was expected to submit its recommendations to Fatah's Central Committee, which would convene with all its members, including Abu Saleh and Qadri, to study such recommendations. The Central Committee rejected the commission's implied reference to the continuation of individual autocracy inside Fatah, contending that the system of collective leadership had always been preserved. With regard to the commission's request to cease propaganda warfare against Damascus, Fatah's leaders expressed their willingness to do so provided the Syrians followed suit. Finally, the Central Committee refused to issue a new policy statement on the grounds that such a statement had been issued earlier by Fatah's Revolutionary Council on June 21, 1983.

The members of the Central Committee believed that the conciliation commission was biased in favor of Syria and the dissidents, which led to a loss of confidence in the commission's mediating efforts. In addition, the work of the commission was rendered irrelevant by developments on the ground: When Arafat returned to northern Lebanon in mid-September, bitter fighting broke out as Syria and its Palestinian clients were determined to end Fatah's military presence in Lebanon.

The Democratic and Popular Fronts maintained a neutral posture toward the split within Fatah and declined to participate in the fighting. Nevertheless, in view of their political differences with Arafat, the two fronts joined the rebels in criticizing some aspects of Arafat's leadership. Like the dissidents, they attributed the uprising inside Fatah to political considerations and authoritarianism in decision-making.[57] In particular, they lamented the absence of collective leadership inside the PLO and the diminishing role of the organization's institutions in decision-making.

Officials from both organizations charged that in his formulation of PLO policy, Arafat had rarely confined himself to the parameters defined by the PLO's charter and had given more weight to tactical considerations than to the organization's long-term strategy. In their opinion, the primacy of tactics over strategy occurred in a number of cardinal areas, including Arafat's entertainment of U.S.-sponsored plans for the resolution of the

Palestinian problem and his deliberate disregard for the fact that Zionism and Palestinian nationalism could not coexist. They further charged that Arafat undermined the need to preserve the PLO as an integral part of the Arab national liberation movement by creating a wedge between the PLO and the progressive Arab regimes and making preferential dealings and consolidating ties with the conservative Arab states.

Criticism of Arafat's style of diplomacy and leadership was not a sufficient reason to compel the Popular and Democratic Fronts to join the rebel ranks. Instead, they advocated the introduction of reform within the movement and urged Arafat and his opponents to resolve their differences in a peaceful and democratic manner. They also called for the infusion of safeguards into the PLO to guard against individual autocracy and the dominance of one group over another. They requested that Arafat adhere strictly to the Palestine National Charter and the various resolutions of the Palestine national councils. In particular, they called upon Arafat to reject the Reagan initiative and the confederation plan with Jordan so as to preserve the organization's unity and autonomy. Likewise, they wanted Arafat to strengthen his ties with Syria and the Lebanese nationalist forces and to abide by the principle that armed struggle was the main vehicle to liberate Palestine. For this reason, they demanded the regrouping of the dispersed PLO troops in Lebanon to resume Palestinian military operations against Israel.

With the outbreak of fighting between Arafat loyalists and opponents, the two fronts requested the imposition of a strict cease-fire and proposed the formation of a military committee to supervise the cease-fire and separate the fighting forces.[58] They also suggested that a resolution to the Fatah crisis should be based on the proposal submitted by the conciliation commission and advocated the opening of a comprehensive dialogue among the PLO's various factions and institutions in an attempt to end the split inside Fatah and to introduce reforms.

With regard to Arafat's rift with Syria, the two fronts sided with the Syrian ruler when they dismissed the PLO chairman's contentions that the mutiny inside the movement was engineered by Damascus. They viewed Arafat's repeated charges of Syrian intervention as a sign of his lack of desire to mend his relationship with the Assad regime. The pro-Syrian posture of the Popular and Democratic Fronts emanated from their political and territorial dependence upon Syria. Both organizations were concerned about preserving their political headquarters in Damascus and retaining their military bases in central Lebanon.

Because of their vulnerability to the Syrian regime Habash and Hawatmeh's response to Arafat's expulsion from Damascus was mild. It was also in line with Syria's wishes that the Popular Front insist that a resolution to the crisis should come from within Fatah itself and not through the convening of an emergency session of the Palestine National Council or through an Arab summit.[59] Both Habash and Hawatmeh justified their strong ties with Damascus on the basis of the Assad regime's anti-United States posture and Syria's declared readiness to check Israel's expansionist drive in the region. Syria's continued support of the PLO was also seen as vital in countering Jordan's ambitions to represent the Palestinian people. For this reason, the Popular and Democratic Fronts advocated the conclusion of a strategic alliance agreement between the PLO and Syria.

The attitudes of the two fronts toward the Fatah crisis generated resentment in both camps. Arafat defenders did not like the sympathies expressed by both organizations toward the rebels' demands or their pro-Syrian posture.[60] They interpreted the two fronts' repeated calls to reassemble the PLO's dispersed forces in Lebanon as a denunciation of Arafat's decision to evacuate PLO troops from Beirut. In their view these calls were exercises in political outbidding since both fronts attempted to project themselves as supportive of the strategy of armed struggle whereas Arafat was running away from it. Arafat loyalists rejected the implications of the call for a strict adherence to the national charter and the Palestine National Council resolutions. In their opinion, this rejection meant that the two organizations were upholding such resolutions whereas Arafat was deviating from them. Moreover, the Popular and Democratic Fronts' opposition to the idea of convening an emergency session for the Palestine National Council was seen as a shift toward the dissidents. Their real aim was to gain the time needed to strengthen the forces of rejectionism within the PLO and pose themselves as an alternative leadership for the commando groups.

Fatah's fears and suspicions were substantiated when on June 26, 1983, joint leadership for the two fronts was proclaimed for the purpose of coordinating their political and military activities. The two fronts denied that their merger was intended to form a separate axis within the PLO; rather they asserted that it came about as a result of the similarities and congruities in their views on Palestinian, Arab, and international issues. They further claimed that their move stemmed from the desire to strengthen the viability and the legitimacy of the PLO institutions.

These assurances were not sufficiently strong to allay the fears of Fatah leaders. Their suspicions were compounded by the fact that the merger came only one day after Arafat's expulsion from Damascus and followed a lengthy meeting between Habash, Hawatmeh, and Syrian President Assad. The newly formed joint leadership also provided evidence of Syria's intention to create an alternative leadership for the PLO. This explained why the unity of the two fronts was seen by Fatah's supporters as a "capitulation to Syria's interests and desires." Such a reaction on the part of Fatah's proponents should not have been surprising, particularly because the political and military position of their leader was weakened in the wake of the mutiny, whereas the charismatic leadership of Arafat's two main rivals, Habash and Hawatmeh, continued to receive relatively widespread support in the Palestinian community.

Like the pro-Arafat forces, Fatah's opposition was not pleased with the political attitudes of the Popular and Democratic Fronts. The two organizations' public sympathy with the dissident movement was insufficient: The rebel leaders wanted a clearer commitment and an open endorsement of their goals. They deplored the invitation by the two fronts for a reconciliation with Arafat's leadership and contended that the call should have been for a comprehensive reform inside Fatah and the PLO. They demanded that both organizations align themselves with the "revolutionaries" to defeat "deviation, corruption and authoritarianism."[61] Fatah dissidents also did not welcome Habash and Hawatmeh's efforts for mediation on the grounds that the political sensitivity of the issues under contention left no room for such an endeavor. In the rebels' opinion, Fatah was an indivisible organization, and Arafat and his followers were no longer part of the movement.

The outbreak of mutiny and its culmination in an all-out war between the PLO's factions generated a deep sense of disappointment, frustration, and anguish among the Palestinians inside the occupied territories. Many Palestinians feared the adverse repercussions of the fighting upon the morale of the population of the West Bank and the Gaza Strip and the prospects for ending the Israeli military occupation. Commenting on this fear, Elias Fraij, the mayor of Bethlehem, stated,

> It is a very horrible and cruel civil war. We call it here "Black November." We call upon all sides to stop this crazy fighting. I am sorry to say that the fighting has reduced the power and influence of the PLO everywhere. We are confused. We are bewildered and we are frustrated. . . . [T]he people are just losing hope about a settlement for the West Bank.[62]

Notwithstanding the feelings of anguish and frustration generated by the fighting, the reaction of the Palestinians inside the occupied territories was undoubtedly crucial to the long-term political outcome of the military battle between Arafat's supporters and the rebels.

The rebellion inside Fatah furnished another opportunity, though a bitter one, for testing Arafat's popularity in the West Bank and the Gaza Strip. Although the reform demands of Fatah's opposition group in the initial phase of the uprising had generated some sympathy inside leftist circles, particularly the student movement, it did not undermine the widespread support for Arafat's leadership. Various political organizations, trade unions, youth movements, professional associations, and municipalities denounced the mutiny against Arafat's leadership and urged the mutineers to preserve the unity of the movement and work to achieve their goals through democratic and peaceful means. They were also critical of the rebels' resort to violence to press for their demands. According to a public opinion poll conducted by *al-Bayader al-Siyassi* in late June and early July, 92 percent of the 1,150 respondents supported Arafat's leadership.

The lack of support for the militants in the occupied territories resulted from the interplay of a number of factors. Despite the initial sympathy generated around their demands in some leftist circles, the leaders of the opposition failed to cultivate such sympathy to keep their cause active. Their uncompromising positions and their quest to achieve their extreme demands diminished the rebels' chances for any real support. Moreover, because of the long relationship between the people of the occupied territories and Arafat and his colleagues, it was extremely difficult to imagine that the majority of the Palestinians inside the occupied territories would drop the mainstream PLO leaders and follow the dissident movement. One could also argue that the radical overtone of the rebels' demands was irritating to many West Bank politicians since in their opinion Arafat's moderation and diplomatic flexibility were more likely to bring an end to the Israeli military occupation of their land. Finally, the linkage of the dissident movement with both Syria and Libya, and Arafat's repeated affirmation of such a connection, reduced the political credibility of the opposition group.

It is no secret that West Bank and Gaza Strip Palestinians harbor bitter feelings against the Syrian regime in view of its anti-PLO stands during the Lebanese civil war in the 1970s. The expulsion of Arafat from Damascus only nine months after he was forced out of Beirut, coupled with Syria's policy of military inaction during the war in summer 1982, only extenuated these hostile sentiments. A large public rally convened in Jerusalem's al-Aqsa Mosque on June 26, 1983, widely condemned the Syrian regime and the rebels. During the meeting, the Shaikh Sa'ad al-Din al-Alami, head of the higher Islamic council, proclaimed, "It is the duty of every Moslem to assassinate the Syrian president for the crimes that he committed against the Palestinian people."

Arab Reaction and Mediating Efforts

As the outbreak of the fighting inside Fatah and the rift between Arafat and Assad generated mixed reactions among the Palestinians, it produced similar responses among the Arab countries. Perhaps with the exception of Syria and Libya, the majority of Arab kings and presidents were not happy to see that Arafat's moderate leadership was undermined and the PLO's viability and autonomy were eroding. With regard to the question of Syria's support to the rebellion, Arab attitudes diverged. Broadly speaking, the reaction in the Arab world can be classified into two main groupings. The first group, led by Iraq and Jordan and to a lesser degree by Egypt, accepted the version alleging Syrian-Libyan intervention in Fatah's internal affairs and maintained that the rebellion itself was engineered by them. The three countries, concerned that the PLO not be transformed into an instrument in the hands of rival Arab regimes, repeatedly appealed for an end to Syrian and Libyan attempts to dominate PLO institutions and leadership and deprive it of its autonomy.[63] Iraq, Jordan, and Egypt sharply denounced Arafat's expulsion from Damascus, claiming that such a move would only serve U.S. and Israeli interests. Egyptian Deputy Prime Minister and Foreign Minister Kamal Hassan Ali contended that the PLO's loss of its ability to make its decisions freely would have a negative impact upon the Palestinian cause.[64]

The concern of the moderate Arab countries for the fate of Arafat and the survival of the PLO was rooted in their traditional hostility and rivalry toward the Syrian regime. Both Jordan and Egypt did not abandon hope for the revitalization of the Jordanian-Palestinian dialogue, and both were certain that a more radical leadership for the PLO would not be interested in the resumption of such talks. They were convinced that if Arafat disappeared it would be difficult to find another moderate leader that would command overall respect and legitimacy among the Palestinians. Another consideration for this group of states was their desire not to assume the responsibility for the recovery of the occupied territories. They were well aware that Palestinian legitimacy and blessings were needed to sanction any territorial concession made in favor of Israel and any political settlement. In the absence of a political settlement, the presence of the PLO would to a large extent absolve the Arab moderates from the task of liberating the occupied territories. Such a task has been the prerogative of the Palestinian resistance movement since the mid-1960s. Finally, King Hussein in particular was concerned about the serious implications to the domestic stability of his regime should Arafat disappear and be replaced by a more radical Palestinian leader.

In contrast to Jordan, Egypt, and Iraq, the second group of Arab states, led by Saudi Arabia, the Gulf countries, Algeria, and South Yemen, tried to mediate Fatah's internal fighting and reconcile Arafat and Assad. In contrast to the first group, these countries projected a neutral posture concerning the charges and countercharges of the various antagonists. Their aim was to end the fighting and to bring about a cease-fire between Fatah's warring factions so as to preserve the autonomy and the unity of the PLO and to attend to more pressing problems, such as the Iran-Iraq War and the resolution of the Arab-Israeli conflict.

Like Palestinian mediating efforts, attempts by these countries failed to realize any of their limited objectives. Despite its colossal economic clout and its enormous leverage with the concerned actors, Saudi Arabia was unable to end Fatah's internal fighting until seven months after the outbreak of the mutiny. Throughout these months, the Saudi Arabian mediating efforts were ineffective and low-keyed. This response resulted partly from its inability to persuade the Syrian regime to adopt a more tolerant and flexible attitude toward the chairman of the PLO and was perhaps a deliberate delaying tactic awaiting better prospects for successful and effective mediation.[65] One cannot dismiss the possibility that Saudi Arabia was angered by Arafat's return to northern Lebanon in September 1983; this step provoked the Syrians and led to rapid escalation in the fighting between the opposing troops. This serious deterioration in Fatah-Syrian relations came at a critical moment during which Saudi Arabia was preparing for the convening of an Arab summit in its capital.

The convening of the Arab summit never came about, however, nor did other mediating efforts succeed. With the exception of Saudi Arabia, none of the Palestinian or Arab mediators possessed sufficient leverage to deal with the complex issues under contention. In addition, none of the parties in the dispute showed enough enthusiasm or cooperation toward the mediators. The Syrians were unyielding in their hostility toward Arafat and consistently refused to meet with any mediating team for the purposes of reconciliation. In contrast, Arafat insisted on implicating the Syrians in the mutiny and refused to accept the demands of his opponents and the recommendations of the Palestinian conciliation commission.

The attitudes of the rebels constituted additional constraints in the path of the mediating efforts. The leaders of the mutiny did not deviate from their maximalist demands and insisted on introducing organizational changes to ensure the implementation of their reforms. In particular, they wanted to introduce drastic changes in the structure of Fatah's leadership, including stripping Arafat of his power, replacing Abu Jihad with Abu Musa, and forming an emergency committee to supervise Fatah's internal affairs.[66] They also refused to accept guarantees offered by the PLO's political councils and factions to ensure the implementation of any agreement that might be reached with Fatah's Central Committee.[67] The dissidents' demand to form an emergency committee to replace Fatah's Central Committee and Revolutionary

Council was unacceptable to Arafat's leadership on the grounds that it would entail the dissolution of the organization's political councils and would violate the rules and procedures that governed the operation of Fatah's movement.[68] Finally, as mentioned earlier, the dissidents opposed the establishment of contacts with those members of Fatah's Central Committee who initially expressed some sympathy toward their demands.

While the mediating efforts continued, though inconclusively, development on the ground began to take a dangerous turn as Syria demanded that the remainder of Arafat's troops withdraw from central Lebanon to positions further north. In early September 1983, Israel decided to redeploy its troops from the Shouf mountains southward to the more defensible line of the Awali River, leading to the outbreak of fierce battles between the Druze militia and the Lebanese army for the control of the Shouf mountains. Amid this political and military confusion, Arafat returned to Lebanon in the middle of September.

The Exodus from Tripoli

Why Arafat chose to return to Lebanon at this critical time continues to be a controversial question. His return to Lebanon may have been dictated by his desire not to be left behind or outbid by his rivals within the PLO. Following the outbreak of fighting between the Lebanese army and the Druze militia, supported by leftist Palestinian groups including those of Abu Musa, the Lebanese nationalist forces and their Palestinian allies seemed to be gaining ground in the Shouf area. Arafat was determined not to stay in the background because the battles in the mountains were making his bitter enemies look like the true revolutionaries and fighters. He may also have calculated that with the Israeli withdrawal from the Shouf mountains, the road to Beirut would be short, and he was certainly determined not to be left behind.

A less convincing argument was presented by Arafat's aides as they stated that by returning to Lebanon, Arafat intended to reactivate the strategy of armed struggle against the Israeli army and fight alongside the Syrian and Lebanese nationalist forces.[69] It is more plausible to argue, however, that by coming back to Lebanon Arafat wanted to dismiss his enemies' charges that he had abandoned the armed struggle and stayed away from his troops. One cannot exclude the possibility that Arafat's return was a sign of defiance toward Damascus, particularly as the Syrian expulsion order banned him from coming back to areas in Lebanon under Syrian hegemony.

It is also possible to stretch this argument farther and point out that Arafat aimed at launching a military offensive against his Palestinian opponents. The regrouping of some of his troops in northern Lebanon and the stockpiling of weapons there were intended to facilitate such a task. Finally, Arafat himself contended that his return to Tripoli was necessitated by the increasing prospects of an all-out attack by the rebels and their Syrian and Libyan backers upon his troops. "I came back to Tripoli when I found my people exposed to a definite massacre. I came to stand by their side in this crisis," Arafat told Radio Monte Carlo on November 18, 1983.

Irrespective of the real motives behind Arafat's return, his presence increased the level of violence and added to the tension sweeping the Palestinian nationalist movement. Spokesmen for Arafat's opponents declared that the real aim behind Arafat's presence in Tripoli was to strike at the opposition group and not to reactivate the strategy of military struggle because no Israeli troops were in the area.[70] Criticism of Arafat's presence in northern Lebanon also came from other Palestinian leaders. The president of the Palestine National Council and representatives of the Democratic and Popular Fronts envisaged that Arafat's return to Lebanon and the stockpiling of weapons were dangerous moves that would lead to further bloodshed and violence.[71] They requested Arafat leave northern Lebanon, arguing that his departure would serve "the Palestinian cause" and salvage the city of Tripoli from destruction.

It also was contended that Arafat's departure was necessitated by the need to reactivate the functioning of the PLO's political councils, particularly the Executive Committee, which could not meet without its chairman. Both the Popular and Democratic Fronts pointed out that Arafat's withdrawal from Tripoli would enable him to meet the leaders of the various PLO factions and members of the mediation teams to discuss the ways and means to preserve the unity of the PLO. They were further convinced that Arafat's withdrawal would arrest the already deteriorating relationship between the Palestinians and the Lebanese nationalist forces and the Syrians. This deterioration came in the wake of the reported support extended by Arafat and his followers to the Islamic Unification Movement in Tripoli. Both fronts regarded Arafat's backing of the movement as "offending to the Palestinian revolution" and its Lebanese nationalist allies.

This shift in the publicly proclaimed neutral stands of the Popular and Democratic Fronts toward Arafat most likely came in response to Syrian pressure upon both organizations to condemn Arafat's return to northern Lebanon. Another request for Arafat's withdrawal came from the prominent pro-Syrian Tripoli politician, Rashid Karameh. Karameh suggested, "If Arafat's departure will constitute a way out of the crisis, that, in my opinion, is not a very high price to pay."[72] He also claimed that his views reflected the opinions and attitudes of the population of Tripoli. Karameh's assertion, however, was contested and dismissed by a rival politician, Shaikh Sa'id Sha'ban, leader of the Islamic Unification movement. Sha'ban stated that he and his supporters and the people of Tripoli in general welcomed the presence of Arafat in their city. "No one has the right to ask Abu Ammar [Arafat] to leave Tripoli. Abu Ammar is a Moslem Arab in a Moslem Arab city. It is the right of Abu Ammar to stay wherever he wants and to go wherever he wishes," Sha'ban told Radio Monte Carlo on November 11, 1983.

Arafat's supporters did not heed the repeated appeals for their leader's departure from Tripoli, however, as they argued that his presence was necessitated by the outbreak of the fighting in northern Lebanon.[73] Concerning the argument that Arafat's stay in Lebanon had impeded the functioning of the PLO's institutions, they contended that this period was not the first time that the work of the PLO's political councils had been disrupted. During the civil war in Lebanon in the mid-1970s and throughout the siege of Beirut in summer 1982, the PLO's institutions could not meet for several months. For their chief to leave Tripoli, Arafat loyalists demanded that the rebels end their siege of Tripoli, stop shelling the Palestinian refugee camps of Nahr al-Bared and al-Baddawi, and withdraw their troops from that region. They argued further that Arafat would withdraw from the city only if he was requested to do so by the inhabitants of Tripoli and only after the imposition of a stable cease-fire under Arab supervision.[74]

While this controversy continued, Arafat's troops lost their last military strongholds in Nahr al-Bared and al-Baddawi on November 6 and 17, respectively. Fatah officials held the Syrian government directly responsible for the outbreak of the fighting and the shelling of Arafat's positions in and around Tripoli. Abu Iyad launched one of his most severe attacks upon the Syrian president when he stated, "In all frankness, the cruelty that Hafez al-Assad has displayed in the last few months is unprecedented and the crimes that he committed against the Palestinian people surpassed those of the Israeli enemy."[75]

With the loss of his last military bases in Lebanon, the heavy casualties inflicted upon Palestinian and Lebanese civilians, and the intense shelling of the remainder of Arafat's troops in Tripoli, the prospects of the physical annihilation of the PLO chairman and his troops were looming on the horizon. To many moderate Arab countries, such an eventuality was extremely discomforting as the departure of Arafat from the political scene could lead to a more radical group gaining the upper hand in the PLO. The Arab rulers could no longer ignore Arafat's repeated appeals for help. In particular, the Saudi Arabian ruling elite concluded that they would have to move fast to salvage Arafat's leadership and avoid the possible carnage of the Moslem city of Tripoli. Their active diplomatic involvement began when King Fahd succeeded in setting up a meeting with the Syrian president for Fatah's Central Committee member, Kahled al-Hassan on October 20, 1983, to discuss ways to end the fighting. Saudi Arabia's next move came almost a month later when Crown Prince Abdallah publicly denounced the rebels during a visit to Kuwait, ending Saudi Arabia's apparent neutrality concerning Fatah's crisis. The prince described the mutiny as a "military coup against Arafat's legitimate leadership" and concluded that the mutineers' military successes in northern Lebanon would not bestow upon them political legitimacy and legality.[76]

This Saudi Arabian verbal declaration of support was accompanied by the dispatch of Saud al-Faisal, the foreign minister to Damascus, to negotiate an agreement with his Syrian counterpart, Abd al-Halim Khaddom, to end the fighting and to provide an honorable departure for Arafat and his troops from Tripoli. This move resulted in the announcement of a Saudi Arabian–Syrian joint agreement on November 25, 1983, which called for the imposition of a firm cease-fire and the disengagement of the fighting troops. The agreement underlined the need to preserve Palestinian national unity and to resolve the PLO's quarrels in a democratic and peaceful manner. It also proposed the formation of a higher coordination committee, headed by the pro-Syrian politician, Rashid Karameh, to make the necessary arrangements for the departure of Arafat and his followers. The agreement reflected Syria's official viewpoint, which maintained that Syria had nothing to do with Fatah's crisis; likewise, it encompassed Syria's insistence that Arafat and his followers should under no condition be allowed to stay in Lebanon. Referring to this issue, Abu Jihad stated that the Syrian government was adamantly opposed to the return of any of Fatah's troops to central Lebanon or the retention of some in the north.[77]

Fatah's leaders announced their acceptance of the agreement in an attempt to avoid further friction but demanded assurances of safety and security for the Palestinian civilians in the refugee camps. For this reason, they requested that the rebels and their supporters withdraw their troops to central Lebanon. A spokesman for the rebels, Mahmoud al-Labidi, declared on November 25, 1983, that his followers accepted the agreement and added that the call for a troop withdrawal was only confined to Arafat's forces.

Following Arafat's acceptance of the Saudi Arabian–Syrian agreement, several European countries, including France, Italy, and Greece, expressed their willingness to assist the PLO chief in his departure from Tripoli. Upon Arafat's request, the UN Security Council agreed to extend its protection to the ships carrying the evacuated PLO troops. Preparation for the evacuation, however, was hampered for some time by Israel's repeated declarations that it intended to sabotage the departure. The

Israeli navy blockaded Lebanon's northern coast for three weeks to prevent the arrival of the Greek ships that were to take Arafat and his troops out of Tripoli. The Israeli government also protested the Security Council's offer to provide a safe conduct for Arafat's troops. Only under pressure from Western European countries and the United States did the Israeli navy withdraw its ships from Lebanese territorial waters, allowing the evacuation to proceed.

On December 21, 1983, five Greek ships transferred more than 4,000 of Arafat's people to their new destinations in Algeria, Tunisia, North Yemen, Iraq, and Sudan. Unlike Arafat's first exodus from Beirut, when his troops were besieged for three months by Israeli forces (the PLO's avowed enemy), his second exodus resulted from the pressure of "the brothers in arms" and by the self-proclaimed guardians of the Palestinian revolution—the pan-Arabist regimes of Syria and Libya. In contrast to the withdrawal from Beirut, which was accompanied by sentiments of heroism and triumph, the new exodus was marred by feelings of defeat and anguish. The military battles in northern Lebanon left Arafat more politically and militarily vulnerable and rendered the PLO more fragmented than ever before.

As Arafat's new journey began, many questions were raised: Would Arafat reconcile with Syria after the bitter lessons of central and northern Lebanon? Would Syria itself admit him back after his humiliation, or would Arafat go back to Jordan to resume his dialogue with the king on the basis of the Reagan initiative? Would he try to form a government in exile as the unity of the PLO appeared to be shattered forever? Would he allow the PLO to go underground and follow the path of revolutionary violence and terrorism, or would he try to bring together his divided organization? Would the rebels and their supporters within the PLO, following their military victory, try to form an alternative PLO?

Notes

1. An interview with Hassan Abd al-Rahman, director of the Palestine Information Center, Washington, D.C., October 28, 1984.
2. In this context see Habash interview in *al-Mustaqbal,* August 13–19, 1983. See also Abu Musa interview in *al-Watan al-'Arabi,* June 24–30, 1983, and Abu Saleh interview in *al-Watan,* June 30, 1983.
3. An interview with Abu Iyad in *al-Watan al-'Arabi,* July 15–21, 1983.
4. Hassan Abd al-Rahman interview.
5. For a brief discussion of the rebellion, see Eric Rouleau, "The Mutiny Against Arafat," *Merip Reports,* November-December 1983, pp. 13–16.
6. For an English translation of parts of his speech, see Mohammed Shuqair, "The Roots of Fatah's Split," *Journal of Palestine Studies* 12 (summer 1983):169–174.

7. An interview with *al-Watan al-'Arabi,* August 12–18, 1983, p. 30.
8. See *al-Ta'mim* (published twice weekly by Fatah's opposition), no. 1, June 6, 1983; no. 2, June 9, 1983; no. 7, June 25, 1983.
9. Interview with *al-Watan al-'Arabi,* June 24–30, 1983.
10. See Abu Musa's speech in Salwa al-Amad, *Shihadet al-Harb* (Beirut: Palestine Research Center, 1983).
11. For more information, see Yazid Sayegh, "The PLO's Military Performance in the 1982 War," *Journal of Palestine Studies* 12, no. 4 (summer 1983):8–23.
12. *Al-Ta'mim,* no. 9, July 2, 1983; no. 7, June 25, 1983; no. 5, June 12, 1983.
13. *Al-Ta'mim,* no. 5, June 12, 1983; no. 11, July 19, 1983; no. 17, July 30, 1983.
14. *Al-Ta'mim,* no. 7, June 25, 1983.
15. *Al-Ta'mim,* no. 11, July 19, 1983.
16. *Al-Ta'mim,* no. 9, July 2, 1983.
17. *Al-Ta'mim,* no. 15, June 18, 1983.
18. For more information, see *al-Watan al-'Arabi,* July 15–21, 1983.
19. Interview with Radio Monte Carlo, July 23, 1983.
20. *Al-Ta'mim,* no. 11, July 19, 1983; no. 13, July 16, 1983; no. 14, July 20, 1983; no. 17, July 30, 1983.
21. *Al-Ta'mim,* no. 8, June 28, 1983.
22. Interview with BBC Arabic service, July 7, 1983.
23. *Al-Ta'mim,* no. 11, July 19, 1983.
24. Interview with Radio Monte Carlo, July 11, 1983.
25. Interview with *al-Safir,* May 26, 1983.
26. Abu Iyad's interview with Radio Monte Carlo, September 2, 1983.
27. *Al-Ta'mim,* no. 30, July 16, 1983; no. 14, July 30, 1983.
28. *Al-Ta'mim,* no. 17, July 30, 1983; no. 14, July 20, 1983.
29. Interview in *al-Watan al-'Arabi,* June 24–30, 1983. Similar views were expressed by Abu Khaled in his interview on Radio Monte Carlo, June 24, 1983.
30. A list of their demands can be found in *al-Ta'mim,* nos. 1–3.
31. Abu al-Za'im interview, Radio Monte Carlo, June 24, 1983. Abu Iyad interview in *al-Khalij* (United Arab Emirates daily), June 1, 1983. Arafat interview in *al-Hawadeth,* July 1, 1983. Arafat interview in *Newsweek,* July 4, 1983.
32. Interview in *al-Watan al-'Arabi,* July 15–22, 1983, p. 37.
33. WAFA News Agency on June 21–23. During his interview on Radio Monte Carlo on July 11, 1983, Arafat presented documents signed by the commander of al-Sa'iqa's military department. The reports spoke of surrounding Arafat's troops in central Lebanon in coordination with the Syrian army. This report was also produced in *al-Watan al-'Arabi,* July 15–21, 1983, pp. 31–32.
34. *Al-Ta'mim,* no. 12, July 12, 1983; no. 8, June 28, 1983; no. 7, June 25, 1983.
35. Interview with Radio Monte Carlo, June 24, 1983.
36. Yazid Sayegh, "The Roots of the Syrian-PLO Differences," *Middle East International,* October 29, 1982, pp. 15–16.

37. Eric Rouleau, "The Future of the PLO," *Foreign Affairs* 62, no. 1 (fall 1983):144–146.
38. Interview with Hassan Abd al-Rahman, October 29, 1984.
39. *Davar,* December 20, 1982.
40. *Al-Thawra,* June 22 and 23; and *Tishrin,* June 23, 1983.
41. See for instance, *Tishrin,* June 25, 1983; *al-Thawra,* June 30, 1983.
42. *Al-Watan al-'Arabi,* July 15–21, 1983.
43. Statements of this sort were made by Abu Jihad, Khaled al-Hassan. Interviews on Radio Monte Carlo, June 24, 1983, and Arafat's interview in *Der Spiegel,* July 17, 1983, and Associated Press, July 7, 1983.
44. See the remarks attributed to Yasir Abd Rabbo in Shuqair, "The Roots of Fatah's Split," pp. 175–176.
45. Interview with *al-Khalij* (United Arab Emirates daily), June 1, 1983.
46. Shuqair, "The Roots of Fatah's Split," p. 183.
47. WAFA News Agency, June 21, 1983.
48. Interview with Abu Iyad in *al-Watan* (Kuwaiti daily), October 19, 1983.
49. Mahmud al-Labadi interview, Radio Monte Carlo, October 21, 1983.
50. *Al-Watan al-'Arabi,* July 8–14, 1983.
51. *Al-Safir,* August 1, 1983.
52. Broadcast by Voice of Palestine (Baghdad), August 6, 1983.
53. *Al-Safir,* August 5, 1983.
54. *Al-Ra'i al-'Am* (Kuwaiti daily), August 27, 1983.
55. Radio Damascus, October 13, 1983.
56. *Filistin al-Thawra,* October 27, 1983.
57. For instance *al-Hadaf,* July 4, 1983, and June 6, 1983; Habash interview in *al-Mustaqbal,* August 13, 1983; Yasir Abd Rabbo in *al-Safir,* June 26, 1983. See also the Popular Front and Democratic Front's joint program for reform inside the PLO in political, organizational, military, and financial fields in *al-Hurriya,* October 23, 1983. Also Bassam Abu Sharif interview with Radio Monte Carlo, June 28, 1983.
58. *Al-Safir,* November 22, 1983.
59. Interview with Habash in *al-Mustaqbal,* August 13, 1983.
60. "The Phenomenon of Mutiny and the Unity of the Two Fronts" (pamphlet in Arabic), 1983.
61. *Al-Ta'mim,* no. 12, July 12, 1983; no. 13, July 16, 1983.
62. Interview on BBC's "The World Today," November 22, 1983. Similar comments were also made by the deported mayor of Halhul, Mohammed Milhem, Radio Monte Carlo, June 24, 1983.
63. *Al-Thawra* (Iraqi daily), June 23–25, 1983; *al-Dustur, al-Ra'i,* and *Sawt al-Sha'ab* (Jordanian dailies), June 23–26, 1983.
64. *Al-Ahram,* November 8, 1983; see also statements of President Mubarak, June 28, 1983, and November 6, 1983.
65. Hassan Abu Taleb, "al-Wasata al-Saudiya fi al-Azamat al-'Arabiya," *al-Siyassa al-Dawliya,* no. 75 (January 1984):173–178.
66. Interview with Abu Saleh in *al-Shira'* (Lebanese weekly), August 6, 1983. See also the interview with Abu Musa as reported by *al-Mith'aq,* October 22, 1983.

The Split Within Fatah and the Rift with Syria 175

67. Interview with Yasir Abd Rabbo in *al-Safir,* June 26, 1983.
68. Interview with Arafat, Radio Monte Carlo, July 11, 1983.
69. Abbas Zaki (member of Fatah's Revolutionary Council and the PLO's representative in South Yemen) interview, Radio Monte Carlo, October 21, 1983, and Abu Iyad's interview in *al-Majalla,* November 26, 1983.
70. Interview with Mahmud al-Labadi, Radio Monte Carlo, October 21, 1983; interview with Abu Musa, Radio Monte Carlo, November 11, 1983.
71. Such statements were made by Bassam Abu Sharif and Abu Laila (member of the Democratic Front's political bureau) in their interview with Radio Monte Carlo, October 21, 1983. Khaled al-Fahum made his statement on Radio Monte Carlo on November 25, 1983.
72. Radio Monte Carlo, November 11, 1983.
73. These views were expressed by Arafat's spokesmen, Ahmed Abd al-Rahman and Abbas Zaki, in their interview with Radio Monte Carlo, October 21, 1983.
74. WAFA News Agency, November 12 and 30, 1983.
75. Interview in *al-Majalla,* November 26, 1983.
76. Kuwait News Agency, November 21, 1983.
77. Radio Monte Carlo, December 9, 1983.

7
The Post-Tripoli Era: Toward a New Political Order

As Arafat's troops were being evacuated from Tripoli, the PLO's chances for political survival were no longer assured. None of the countries—Lebanon, Syria, Egypt, or Jordan—that in the past had provided a haven for the Palestinians was prepared to embrace Arafat and his followers. Not only did Arafat and his troops lose the remainder of their last military sanctuary in Lebanon, but their departure from Tripoli meant that the PLO's relationship with Syria had reached a point of no return. This virtually ended any Syrian backing for the mainstream PLO as long as it was chaired by Arafat. In addition, the fact that Palestinian-Egyptian relations had been dormant since Sadat's trip to Jerusalem in November 1977 further compounded the PLO's uncertain future.

The reconvening of the Jordanian parliament, with 50 percent of its membership drawn from the West Bank, at a time when the Arafat-Hussein dialogue was suspended also seemed to usher in the renewal of the political battle for representation of Palestinian interests. This situation became more dismal in the wake of bitter fighting in northern Lebanon and the military defeat of Arafat's troops, as the grounds for Arafat's leadership of the PLO were becoming increasingly questionable.

Within this setting Arafat's subsequent political moves should not have been surprising. It was imperative for the PLO chief to address this situation and come up with solutions for his organization's misfortunes. His overriding goals were to preserve the PLO at the center of inter-Arab politics and advance his political legitimacy within his organization and the Palestinian community at large. Arafat was determined to bring about a new political order that would ensure the survival of his own brand of the PLO at both Arab and Palestinian levels. First, Arafat's choice of Cairo as his first stop after leaving Tripoli was intended to bring Egypt back into the Arab fold so as to limit the damaging effects of the political disorder that had beset the Arab political

177

system. The forging of a moderate Egyptian-led Arab alliance was also intended to neutralize Syria and Libya's hostility toward his organization. Second, instead of challenging King Hussein's decision to reconvene the Jordanian parliament, Arafat and his colleagues accepted Hussein's move and proceeded to renew the dialogue with him. The net effect of Arafat's pro-Egypt–Jordan policy was to make the Palestinian question an Arab issue, as it had been before 1967.

Third, in an attempt to redress the negative impact of his military defeat in northern Lebanon and the challenge to his leadership from within his organization, Arafat insisted upon convening the seventeenth session of the Palestine National Council as soon as possible. This served to renew his political mandate and obtain the necessary backing for his post-Tripoli era policies. In addition, Arafat initiated a dialogue with the Popular and Democratic Fronts to arrest the deterioration of relations with them following his trip to Egypt. By improving his relationship with both organizations, Arafat wanted to isolate further his Syrian-backed opponents. Finally, Arafat and his followers continued to emphasize the importance of the strategy of armed struggle to free the occupied territories from Israel's control. This emphasis was motivated by Arafat's concern not to be outdone by his rivals within the PLO, who continued to possess front-line bases with Israel. Fatah's political councils and leaders played down the significance of the loss in northern Lebanon, arguing that the Tripoli region was not adjacent to Israel and could not be used as a base from which to launch military operations.

Reconciliation with Egypt

Arafat's trip to Cairo was not simply a sign of frustration and anger over his expulsion from Tripoli; the journey was a well-calculated move that set the PLO on a new course of political alignment in the Arab world. Arafat's welcome in Cairo provided him with the confidence to cope with the uncertainties of the new era. He was convinced that only Egypt's political weight could restrain the Syrians and neutralize their opposition to his leadership. This move would also ensure that the PLO would continue to occupy a pivotal position in inter-Arab politics. By making his trip to Cairo, Arafat also intended to facilitate the process of readmitting the Egyptian regime into the Arab arena. In this context, the chairman of the PLO stated, "My trip sought to unite those Arab countries that were trying to resolve the Palestinian problem through political means. . . . [T]he continued isolation of Egypt was harmful to the Palestinian question."[1] As Arafat was planning to renew his talks with King Hussein, he knew that the backing of the Egyptian government would diminish Jordan's chances of taking advantage of the PLO's weakened position. Cairo's support would be instrumental in preserving a separate Palestinian national identity and ensuring a role for the PLO in any political settlement.

Other incentives were influential in Arafat's decision to reconcile with the Egyptian regime against official Palestinian and Arab consensus. By embarking upon such a controversial diplomatic move, he aimed at demonstrating to his opponents and critics that he was still capable of taking bold initiatives despite his military defeat. The trip could also be seen as a sign of appreciation for the pro-PLO stance adopted by the Egyptian government during the siege of Beirut and Tripoli. He declared that his trip came in response to repeated demands by Egyptian opposition groups to improve relations with President Mubarak. Finally, in making his trip to Egypt Arafat was counting upon the widespread popularity and legitimacy that he enjoyed within the Palestinian community.

Arafat's trip to Cairo did not go against prevailing opinion within Fatah's Central Committee, since many members recognized the need to bring Egypt back into the Arab world and acknowledged the dangers in the continuing efforts to ostracize the Egyptian regime. Despite public assertions by some of Fatah's officials that contacts between Egypt and the PLO had been frozen since Sadat's visit to Jerusalem, such ties had never been severed. According to Egyptian Minister of State for Foreign Affairs Boutros Ghali contacts between the PLO and Egypt had been kept at a low profile between 1977 and 1982, but following the Israeli invasion of Lebanon in summer 1982, they were conducted in the open.[2]

Senior Fatah officials did not rule out the possibility of Palestinian leaders visiting Egypt. In an interview, Abu Iyad declared that he had accepted in principle an invitation to attend a popular rally convened by Egypt's opposition groups. He contended, however, that his visit was contingent upon the consent of Fatah's Central Committee and the various PLO institutions.[3] Fatah's leaders asserted as well that the return of Egypt to the Arab world would dissociate it further from the Camp David accords and its peace treaty with Israel and would reduce Egypt's military and economic dependence upon the United States.[4] They acknowledged that the Egyptian president had taken several measures to distance his country from Israel, including withdrawing the Egyptian ambassador from Tel Aviv and freezing the normalization process with the Jewish state. In their opinion, a reconciliation would ensure that the Egyptian government would continue its efforts in Western Europe, the United States, and Israel to promote and defend Palestinian interests.

Just as Arafat's military and political vulnerability stood mainly behind the PLO's opening toward Cairo, Egypt's political isolation and its desire to be readmitted to the Arab world prompted Mubarak to invite Arafat to visit Cairo. The reconciliation between the PLO and Egypt was expected to arouse the anxieties of the Israeli leaders. For this reason, the Egyptian government indicated that Arafat's reception would not mean the transfer of PLO headquarters to Cairo, nor would it mean the loosening of Egypt's commitment to the peace treaty. In his welcoming remarks, the Egyptian president underlined the moderate nature of Arafat's views within the PLO.

Despite Egypt's assurances, the Likud government denounced Arafat's visit to Cairo, considering it a violation of the peace treaty and a major setback to the "peace process."[5] The Israeli government was worried that reconciliation between Egypt and the PLO and renewal of the dialogue with Jordan would increase the prospect of reactivating the Reagan initiative, which the Israelis had categorically rejected. In addition, Arafat's close ties with Egypt would further advance the PLO's chances of political survival and reinforce the voices of moderation within the organization.

A spokesman for the Egyptian government expressed surprise over Israel's opposition to increasing signs of moderation within the PLO. Usama al-Baz, a political advisor to the Egyptian president, regarded Israel's criticism of Arafat's visit as an encroachment upon Egypt's sovereignty.[6] Following Arafat's visit to Cairo, the Egyptian government issued a statement defining its political position with regard to the Palestinian question and the methods of resolving it. The government urged Arafat to resume talks with King Hussein and reach an agreement with Jordan to settle the Palestinian problem on the basis of the Reagan initiative.[7] Egyptian Deputy Prime Minister Kamal Hassan Ali advised the PLO chairman to break away from the tradition of preserving Palestinian national unity at any cost and to avail himself of the new opportunities for settling the Palestinian problem. He argued that national unity should no longer be the primary goal in view of Israel's continuing settlement activities, Arab countries' interference in Palestinian internal affairs, and the presence of incompatible ideologies and attitudes between moderates and radicals within the PLO.[8]

Although the visit to Cairo allowed Arafat to remain in the mainstream of Arab politics and opened new opportunities for Arab realignment, it nevertheless deepened the cleavage within the PLO. Arafat's reconciliation with Egypt was harshly condemned by the various Palestinian hard-line groups. Critics charged that he went too far in his "deviationist policies, treachery and autocracy" and demanded his removal from the PLO chairmanship. The speaker of the Palestine National Council,

Khaled al-Fahum, regarded Arafat's trip to Cairo as a "flagrant violation" of the various resolutions of the National Council. He contended that the PNC in its last three sessions had unanimously decided not to establish contact with the Egyptian regime unless it abandoned the Camp David accords.[9] Al-Fahum contended that Arafat also violated the rules and regulations that govern the functioning of the PLO's councils and that he failed to consult with his colleagues in the Executive Committee and with other Palestinian leaders before making his trip. He also denied that Mubarak had departed from the policies of his predecessor and argued that the Egyptian leader had inherited and adhered to Sadat's policies, noting that Mubarak had accepted the Reagan initiative and the Israeli-Lebanese troop withdrawal agreement of May 17, 1983. He concluded that Arafat had lost his political legitimacy, therefore could no longer speak in the name of the PLO, and should resign his post.

More criticism came on December 30 from 110 members of the Palestine National Council living in Syria, who denounced Arafat and demanded that he be removed from office. A few days later, a three-member delegation representing the Popular and Democratic Fronts and the Palestine Communist party went to Tunis to meet with Fatah's Central Committee members to convince them to oust Arafat. The anti-Arafat campaign was led by George Habash, leader of the Popular Front. Habash appealed to Fatah leaders to withdraw their vote of confidence. Arafat's leadership of the PLO, after all, derived from the fact that he represented Fatah, the PLO's largest faction.[10] Habash also recommended the formation of a Palestinian national front to bring about the downfall of Arafat.

Attempts were also made to convene the Executive Committee to vote Arafat out of office and to appoint Khaled al-Fahum as temporary chairman. The leaders of the hard-line groups decided to boycott all sessions of the Executive Committee as long as it was chaired by Arafat and refused to accept Arafat's invitation to attend the meeting of the PLO's higher military council, convened in North Yemen in early January 1984. A petition was also sent to the Islamic Conference Organization declaring that Arafat no longer represented the PLO.

Although the various PLO hard-line groups agreed among themselves upon the need to remove Arafat from office, they differed on the method to bring about his downfall. Both the Popular and the Democratic Fronts wanted Arafat's removal to go through the political and legal channels of the PLO. They were also careful to indicate their commitment to the preservation of the PLO's unity and cohesion. Both fronts were keen to point out that their denunciation of Arafat was not directed at Fatah's Central Committee members. They nevertheless objected to

Fatah's characterization of Arafat's visit as "a personal mistake and individual initiative that can be retracted." In contrast, the four pro-Syrian groups (the Popular Front General Command, the Popular Struggle Front, al-Sa'iqa, and Fatah dissidents) demanded the immediate ousting of Arafat without resort to the PLO legal framework. They were equally uncompromising to the members of Fatah's Central Committee, as they held them responsible for Arafat's visit to Cairo. Like the Popular and Democratic Fronts, the four groups called for the formation of a national front to include all those advocating the downfall of Arafat.

Some of the most severe attacks upon Arafat came from government-controlled newspapers in Syria. Articles in *al-Ba'ath* and *Tishrin* remarked that the visit to Egypt amounted to "launching a war against the Palestinian people and a recognition of the Camp David accords." The trip was also viewed as an outright violation of Palestinian and Arab consensus. Syrian newspapers warned that their government would not allow the emergence of "a new Sadat in the region" and would use "nonamicable methods" to frustrate "defeatist and liquidationist solutions." The papers reminded Arafat that the Palestinian problem was not his own preserve but rather "the prerogative of the whole Arab nation and the future Arab generation."[11]

Despite their severe denunciations, Arafat's critics were unable to bring about his downfall because they failed to rally majority support within and outside the PLO. Of the fourteen Executive Committee members, they were able to enlist the support of only six and won over only 160 members of the 382 Palestine National Council delegates. Once Arafat began to express his interest in convening the Palestine National Council, the leaders of the various hard-line groups retreated from their position, fearing that Arafat's policies would be vindicated should the PLO's political councils be convened. Al-Fahum, Habash, and Hawatmeh justified their shift in position on the grounds that if the council were to be convened it could lead to a permanent split within the Palestinian nationalist movement.

Arafat was fully aware of the negative repercussions of his trip to Egypt within leftist circles in Palestinian society and expected the kind of outcry made by the PLO's hard-line groups. He was nevertheless aware that his policies would enlist majority support within and outside the occupied territories. He was also certain that his own organization would not abandon him and that, because of its control of the majority vote within the various PLO councils, Fatah would be able to defeat any motion to oust him from office. As discussed earlier, no apparent differences existed among Fatah leaders over the need to improve Palestinian-Egyptian relations and bring Egypt back to the Arab world. Abu Iyad asserted that no disagreement was present within Fatah's

Central Committee over a reconciliation with the Mubarak regime, except that such a reconciliation should have been sanctioned by the PLO's councils and coordinated with the rest of the Arab countries.[12]

In a move geared to absorb much of the criticism generated by the trip, Fatah's Central Committee issued a statement on December 22, 1983, criticizing Arafat's visit to Cairo. The statement characterized the trip as a procedural violation of Fatah rules and regulations and claimed that it did not conform to the resolutions of the sixteenth session of the PNC. Arafat was blamed for failing to consult with his colleagues before making the trip. The Central Committee held him personally accountable for such a move, pledging that Fatah would not be bound by any outcome of the visit.[13]

Fatah's initial and relatively harsh criticism did not last for long. A second statement by the Central Committee issued on December 24, 1983, noticeably softened its criticism; it asserted that, despite his visit to Cairo, Arafat continued to be the indisputable leader of Fatah, and it dismissed any chances for a split within the organization. Fatah leaders were also critical of public denunciations of Arafat by the PLO's hard-line groups, demanding that they keep their criticism within the institutions and councils of the PLO. Although not mentioning Habash, Hawatmeh, and al-Fahum by name, Fatah leaders pointed out the failure of these three men to denounce the fighting against Arafat's troops in northern Lebanon and rejected their suggestion to remove Arafat from office.[14]

Fatah's Central Committee on January 4 and the Revolutionary Council on January 12 gave their final verdicts on Arafat's visit to Cairo. Both councils avoided any formal denunciation of the trip, considering it an ill-conceived personal initiative and a violation of the regulations that govern Fatah. Both statements listed the reasons that prompted Arafat to travel to Cairo, including the needs to distance Egypt from Israel, to diminish Egypt's reliance upon the United States, and to facilitate the process of Egypt's return to the Arab world. The trip was intended to demonstrate to the Egyptians that the Palestinian people appreciated their sacrifices for the Palestinian cause.

With regard to the reaction in the occupied territories, Arafat's trip pointed to differences between his supporters and opponents. The majority of the West Bank and Gaza Strip politicians, who wanted to see an end to Israel's military occupation through political means, believed that the evolving relationship between Egypt and the PLO would serve such an end. The proponents of this trend expressed their satisfaction with the visit and viewed it as a sign of Arafat's strong leadership. They were further convinced that Arafat's ties with Egypt would advance the PLO's bargaining power. These leaders were also anxious to see the PLO chairman renew his dialogue with King Hussein. Commenting on this issue, Rashad al-Shawa, mayor of Gaza, stated,

> We call upon Arafat to cooperate in our name with both Jordan and Egypt in any effort that will guarantee an end to the Israeli military occupation. . . . [W]e want Arafat to go back to Jordan, we want our views and opinions to be the guiding principles for Arafat's policies. . . . [W]e think that a solution can never come except through Jordan and Egypt working jointly in coordination with the Palestinians.[15]

In contrast to these views, a minority of politicians within the occupied territories denounced Arafat's trip to Cairo, believing it would deepen the divisions within the Palestinian nationalist movement and undermine the viability of the PLO. For these leaders, the preservation of Palestinian national unity was an article of faith and was therefore a far more important goal than rapprochement with Egypt. The trip was further criticized on the grounds that it conflicted with Palestinian and Arab consensus. Bassam al-Shak'a, mayor of Nablus, remarked that the visit was conducted in "an individualistic manner and without prior consultation with the rest of the PLO leadership."[16] He blamed Arafat for acting against Palestinian and Arab resolutions. Al-Shak'a also differed with Arafat and the Fatah Central Committee assessment of the Mubarak government, seeing it as an extension of the Sadat regime. Unlike the PLO's hard-line groups, however, critics of the Cairo visit in the occupied territories did not go to the extent of calling for Arafat's resignation or his ouster. Only a very small minority, mainly the supporters of Fatah dissidents and some Popular Front followers, openly advocated the resignation of Arafat.

In conclusion, despite the mixed reaction that Arafat's visit to Cairo produced within the PLO and the Palestinian community at large, the reconciliation with Egypt helped to keep the PLO in the mainstream of Arab politics and secured Arafat's leadership for the Palestinian nationalist movement. The trip also laid the foundation for a new Arab political order within which Egypt would play a leading role. Two months after his visit to Cairo, Arafat began to direct his attention to the improvement of Jordanian-Palestinian relations.

The Jordanian-PLO Dialogue Revisited

The split within Fatah and the rift between Arafat and Assad accelerated the process of reconciliation between Jordan and the PLO following the breakdown of their talks in early April 1983. Prior to Arafat's departure for Tripoli in September 1983, King Hussein dispatched two of his ministers to Tunis for a meeting with the PLO chairman. In response, Arafat sent two of his senior aides to Amman to communicate his willingness to resume the dialogue. While besieged in Tripoli, Arafat repeatedly declared his intention of going back to Jordan once the fighting was over.

Like his reconciliation with Egypt, Arafat's interest in renewing talks with King Hussein was designed to avoid the transformation of the PLO into a marginal factor in inter-Arab politics and to counterbalance Syria's support to his opponents. His concern about preserving a separate Palestinian national identity and ensuring the PLO's participation in any political settlement could only be alleviated (1) by receiving Jordan's pledge to continue to honor its commitment to the 1974 Rabat resolution and (2) by denying King Hussein the opportunity to exploit PLO political and military weakness. Consequently, the cultivation of Jordan's friendship was intrinsic to Arafat's overall strategy for the post-Tripoli era. Arafat's interest in renewing the dialogue also emanated from his recognition that only a joint Palestinian-Jordanian approach offered reasonable chances for salvaging the occupied territories and countering Israel's policy of creeping annexation.

The resumption of the dialogue was expected to secure a privileged position for Arafat and his followers in Jordan, where a significant portion of the Palestinian people live. It would also enable the PLO to maintain regular contact with the Palestinians inside the occupied territories.[17] Arafat characterized the relationship between the Palestinians and the Jordanians as "strategic"—rooted in strong economic, historic, cultural, and familial ties. The interest in renewing the dialogue came not only from Arafat; the Jordanian monarch was equally anxious to forge a diplomatic venture with the PLO. Hussein was determined to preserve Arafat's moderate line and prevent the PLO from falling under Syrian hegemony. In this regard the king remarked, "Palestinian legitimacy is a target. There are definite efforts by a sister Arab country to extend its control over the PLO, and this is unacceptable and illegal. . . . [T]he PLO should derive its legitimacy, power and reason for existence from the people it represents."[18] Jordan also considered the support given by the Syrian government to Fatah's dissidents as a breach of the 1974 Arab Rabat resolution and pledged that it would only deal with what was described as a "free and legitimate PLO," presumably dominated by Arafat.[19] The Jordanian government also urged Arafat to consider the Palestinians living on the West Bank and the Gaza Strip as his "principal constituency" and demanded that the views of those Palestinians dominate the resolutions of the PLO's political councils.[20]

Earlier, as the battles between Arafat and his opponents in northern Lebanon increased the possibility of the PLO falling under Syrian domination, the Jordanian government began to speak of reconsidering its attitude toward the 1974 Rabat resolution, which designated the PLO as the sole legitimate representative of the Palestinian people. This move was evident in the king's decision to reconvene the Jordanian parliament—half of which was made up of West Bank representatives—which had not met for ten years.

By so doing, the Jordanians intended to reaffirm their claims of sovereignty over the occupied territories and reestablish constitutional links between the East and West Banks. This move also meant that Amman was assuming direct responsibility for the Palestinian question, reminding the Arab world that Jordan offered the best prospects for the recovery of the occupied territories. Similarly, the revival of the parliament furnished another indication of Jordan's resolve not to allow the Syrians and their Palestinian protégés any authority over the future of the occupied territories, should Arafat depart from the political scene.

The restoration of constitutional links between the East and West Banks placed King Hussein in a more advantageous position vis-à-vis the politically and militarily vulnerable PLO chairman. The king was keen on avoiding the frustrating experience that he had had with Arafat during their first round of talks in early 1983. By reconvening the parliament, Hussein made it clear that the Palestinian question concerned Jordan equally as much as it did the PLO. This step was expected to make Arafat more amenable to Jordan's desires and interests. Were the PLO chairman to retreat from any agreement that he had reached with the king or were he to disappear from politics, Hussein, supported by the West Bank representatives in the parliament, could unilaterally move toward settling the Palestinian question.

The return to parliamentary life was also dictated by domestic developments in Jordan. The Jordanian government could no longer ignore the ever growing discrepancy between economic development and low-level political participation by the people. According to the government, the timing for the return to constitutional life was dictated by the concern over losing the two-thirds quorum necessary to convene the parliament, particularly in the wake of the deaths of several deputies since the last parliamentary elections, which were held shortly before the 1967 June War.[21] To avoid what was termed a "constitutional paralysis," the government introduced a constitutional amendment to allow for separate elections to take place on the East Bank. The people of the East Bank would choose their representatives to the parliament, whereas those members representing the West Bank would be elected by the parliament itself, since free and direct elections could not be held in the occupied territories under Israeli military control.

The government officials who promoted this amendment denied that any foreign policy implications were behind Jordan's move and argued that their government was firmly committed to the 1974 Rabat Resolution. Hussein claimed that his government decided to suspend the parliament in 1976 only for a limited duration in order to give the PLO the opportunity to enhance its political credibility and advance its international stature. In return, Arafat and his colleagues accepted Jordan's assurances and explanation for the reconvening of the parliament and called for the strengthening of Jordanian-Palestinian relations.

Jordan also spelled out its position on the future settlement of the Arab-Israeli conflict and the Palestinian problem and its strategy for achieving such a settlement. First, the government was interested in reaching an agreement with the PLO that would end Israel's military occupation of the West Bank and the Gaza Strip. Second, Jordan confirmed its support for UN Security Council Resolution 242—which advocates the exchange of land for peace—as the proper framework for negotiating with the Israelis. Jordan's position arose from the conviction that the resolution, if implemented, would lead to a comprehensive settlement of the Arab-Israeli dispute. It would also involve all interested parties, including Syria, which had persistently opposed any separate agreements with Israel.

Third, in his dialogue with Arafat, Hussein insisted that the future of the relationship between the occupied territories and Jordan would be determined directly by the Palestinians and the Jordanians after the evacuation of Israel's military troops from these territories.[22] Fourth, unlike the 1982–1983 Palestinian-Jordanian talks, which were based on the Reagan initiative, the new dialogue called for the convening of an international peace conference under the supervision of the UN Security Council. This conference would be attended by all permanent members of the Security Council and thus would include the Soviet Union, a move that would avert Soviet obstruction of any political settlement. Both Israel and the PLO would participate in such a conference.

King Hussein's frustration with U.S. Middle Eastern diplomacy, particularly the reluctance of the Reagan administration to push for its own initiative, was the main reason behind his call for the convening of an international peace conference. Jordan was also angered by Washington's refusal to use its considerable leverage with Israel to freeze the construction of additional Jewish settlements in the occupied territories and by its objection to a Jordanian draft resolution to the Security Council calling for a freeze on Israel's settlement activities.[23]

The Jordanian government lost confidence in the Reagan administration's ability to play an objective role in the resolution of the Middle East conflict. Jordan's distrust resulted from the consolidation of U.S.-

Israeli strategic cooperation in early December 1983 following Shamir's visit to Washington. The withdrawal of U.S. troops from Lebanon, without a simultaneous evacuation of Israeli troops, further increased Jordan's lack of respect for U.S. credibility. Jordanian disillusionment grew as Israel's supporters within the U.S. Congress drafted a resolution advocating the transfer of the U.S. Embassy from Tel Aviv to Jerusalem and as opposition developed in Congress against the sale of military equipment to Jordan on the grounds that it would threaten Israel's security. King Hussein was further dismayed by the reluctance of the White House to use its influence with Israel to allow those members of the Palestine National Council in the occupied territories to participate in the council's meeting to enforce the voice of moderation within the PLO.

Both Arafat and Hussein deliberately kept their dialogue on a low key. They did not rush to reach definitive and far-reaching conclusions since prevailing conditions in the Middle East and the United States ruled out chances for serious political initiatives. Both Washington and Tel Aviv were preoccupied with their general elections. The Arab world was still suffering from severe political fragmentation, precluding any possibility for the emergence of an Arab consensus to back the Jordanian-Palestinian joint initiative. In addition, Arafat was unprepared to commit himself to a far-reaching agreement with Hussein at a time when the fallout of his trip to Cairo had not yet settled.

Arafat's own opponents had not abandoned their demand to oust him from office. The PLO chief therefore needed time to attend to his Palestinian constituency: He needed to justify his trip to Egypt and receive a fresh mandate for his political legitimacy. Attaining both these objectives was not possible without convening the seventeenth session of the Palestinian National Council. Arafat also needed to mend his relationships with the other two main partners within the PLO, the Popular and Democratic Fronts, to ensure their presence at the National Council's session. Finally, Arafat needed to clear away the restrictions imposed upon his freedom of action by the sixteenth session of the PNC before he could conclude a meaningful accord with the Jordanians.

In keeping with the low profile of their dialogue dictated by these conditions, the communiqués issued after Arafat's visits to Amman were cast in general terms and concentrated on practical issues, such as strengthening the steadfastness of the Palestinians in the occupied territories and soliciting Arab financial aid to advance their cause. Publicly, it appeared that both the Jordanian monarch and the PLO chairman had set aside the more complex and crucial issues of the nature of a final peace settlement, the future of the relationship between the East and West Banks, and the role of the PLO in any political settlement.

In Search of an Elusive Goal: The Failure of Reconciliation Efforts Within the PLO

After securing the support of both Egypt and Jordan, Arafat's third urgent task was to ensure Palestinian backing for his leadership. The convening of the Palestine National Council was essential for this task, as Arafat needed to get a fresh mandate from council members and obtain their endorsement for his policies. Arafat also wanted the council to pass new guidelines for the PLO's future course of action.

Although Arafat preferred to convene the council as soon as possible, this did not take place until late November 1984. The delay was caused by the vehement opposition of pro-Syrian groups within the PLO and by the hesitation and indecisiveness of the Popular and Democratic Fronts. Moreover, members of Fatah's Central Committee wanted to delay the council session in order to explore the prospects for improving relations with both the Democratic and Popular Fronts, which were the second most important factions within the PLO and which continued to enjoy relatively wide popular support within the Palestinian community. Although both organizations had severely denounced Arafat's visit to Egypt, Fatah leaders were concerned about further alienating the two fronts, particularly since they had not participated in the fighting against Arafat's troops.

By improving relations with the two organizations, Fatah's Central Committee hoped to ensure that the majority of the political forces within the PLO would attend the upcoming sessions of the Palestine National Council.[24] Some of Fatah's leaders were convinced that Habash and Hawatmeh wanted to preserve their own organizations' independence and freedom of action from Syrian control. Reconciliation with them would therefore enhance the chances of maintaining the independence of both organizations. Finally, Fatah's interest in the dialogue with the two fronts came in response to the mediating efforts of Algeria and South Yemen to reconcile the various factions of the PLO and to mediate between Fatah and Syria.

Following the reluctance of Fatah's Central Committee and Revolutionary Council to denounce Arafat's visit to Cairo and to take punitive measures against him, the Popular and Democratic Fronts, in addition to their boycott of the PLO's Executive Committee sessions, decided not to establish direct contact with Fatah's Central Committee. Between March 24 and 27, 1984, representatives of the Democratic Front, the Popular Front, the Palestine Liberation Front, and the Palestine Communist party, which came to be known as the Democratic Alliance, met in Aden, South Yemen, to discuss the deep-seated divisions within the PLO. They endorsed a working paper that would serve as a framework for a dialogue among the various PLO groups.[25] The conferees called for the preservation of the PLO's unity and viability on the basis of strict adherence to the PLO's national charter and the resolutions of the various Palestine National Councils, as well as opposition to Arafat's leadership. The alliance further appealed to Fatah's Central Committee to explicitly denounce Arafat's visit to Cairo.

To ensure against individual autocracy, they advocated a system of collective leadership, including the redistribution of the seats within the Executive Committee among the various PLO factions. They also proposed the formation of a broad Palestinian National Front to include all those forces and figures that opposed Arafat's leadership. The four groups, although viewing their newly formed alliance as a nucleus for the national front, asserted that neither the working paper nor their alliance aimed at creating an alternative PLO or forming institutions parallel to those of the PLO. The working paper pointed out that reconciliation within the PLO was a prerequisite for the convening of the Palestine National Council.

With regard to the crisis within Fatah, members of the Democratic Alliance proposed the formation of two separate factions, both of which would be represented within the PLO's institutions. They dismissed the claims of Fatah's dissidents that they exclusively represented the movement as a whole, insisting that Abu Musa and his followers represented only a trend within the Fatah movement. The Democratic Alliance members invited the four pro-Syrian groups—Fatah dissidents, al-Sa'iqa, the Popular Front General Command, and the Popular Struggle Front, all of which came to be known later as the National Alliance—to start a dialogue for the formation of the Palestine National Front. They rejected, however, the demands by these organizations to form an alternative Palestinian leadership.

The National Alliance and the Fatah Central Committee both rejected the working paper of the Democratic Alliance. The National Alliance favored its own proposal for creating a new Palestinian leadership and removing Arafat and his colleagues from the leadership of the PLO.[26] Similarly, it dismissed the Democratic Alliance's suggestion to form two separate factions within Fatah. The National Alliance considered the working paper of the Democratic Alliance to be too conciliatory toward Fatah leadership. It opposed the call to start a dialogue among the various factions of the PLO on the basis of the sixteenth session of the Palestine National Council. In its opinion, such resolutions reflected Arafat's political preferences and disregarded the opinions of the rest of the PLO factions. Members of the National Alliance further argued that the endorsement of such resolutions enabled Arafat to make his trip to Cairo and forge an accord with Jordan.

In response to the Democratic Alliance working paper, Fatah's Central Committee submitted a plan for PLO reconciliation to South Yemen, which was acting as a go-between. The plan aimed at defining the structure of the PLO and introducing a system of checks and balances to govern the functioning of its institutions. The plan also incorporated a number of principles that would serve as guidelines for the PLO's political actions; these principles included adherence to the resolutions of the sixteenth session of the Palestine National Council and to the Arab peace plan, rejection of the Camp David accords and the Reagan initiative, and consolidation of the PLO's ties with Jordan as well as normalization of relations with Syria.

The refusal of the members of the Democratic Alliance, particularly the Popular Front, to establish a direct dialogue with Fatah's Central Committee and their consistent opposition to the convening of the Palestine National Council prompted Fatah leaders to warn that they would unilaterally convene the council and call for the meeting of a large popular congress of 5,000 Palestinians to review the membership and credentials of the PLO's hard-line groups.[27] The Popular Front position was particularly irritating, since it had been behind the move to boycott Fatah leaders. The remainder of the Democratic Alliance members were not as hostile in their attitude; they continued to acknowledge Arafat's leadership of the PLO.

The Popular Front's opposition to direct dialogue with Fatah's leaders was eventually mitigated by the moderating influence of its partners within the Democratic Alliance, the mediating efforts of South Yemen and Algeria, as well as Fatah's toughened its stance. The change in the Popular Front's attitude also stemmed from the fears of its leaders that their political standing within the Palestinian community and the PLO would erode if Fatah went ahead in its threat to convene a large popular congress. By opening a dialogue with Fatah's Central Committee, the leaders of the Democratic Alliance hoped to postpone indefinitely the meeting of the Palestine National Council, a move that would deny Arafat's followers the opportunity to vindicate his policies and legitimize his leadership. Moreover, they thought that they could perhaps convince the Fatah leadership to remove Arafat from the chairmanship of the PLO; their optimism was based on the fact that various Fatah institutions had criticized Arafat's trip to Cairo.

This combination of factors resulted in a meeting between Fatah's Central Committee and the members of the Democratic Alliance in Algiers on April 20, 1984. The discussion revolved around three main issues: the convening of the PNC, Arafat's trip to Cairo, and relations with Syria. Abu Jihad, head of the Fatah delegation, advocated the convening of the PNC as soon as possible and regarded Arafat's trip to Cairo as a procedural violation of the PLO's regulations, insisting that the PNC was the only political body qualified to judge Arafat's initiative. He was also opposed to Syria's participation in the Palestinian reconciliation talks before it mended its relationship with the PLO. Abu Jihad nevertheless lifted the objection of his movement to the participation of National Alliance members in the proposed Palestinian dialogue but was adamant about the exclusion of Fatah dissidents from any talks.[28]

In contrast, members of the Democratic Alliance insisted upon deferring the council's meeting until after the restoration of PLO unity and the improvement of Fatah-Syrian relations. The Democratic Alliance, although maintaining its demand to remove Arafat from office, requested that Fatah's Central Committee issue a statement denouncing Arafat's trip to Cairo. Democratic Alliance members further expressed the opinion that they would like to see Syria participate in the reconciliation talks alongside South Yemen and Algeria. The alliance further insisted that the organizational privileges of the members of the National Alliance be preserved within the PLO's political councils and that they participate in the proposed Palestinian national dialogue.[29]

Though three extensive meetings were concluded between Fatah's Central Committee and the Democratic Alliance between April 20 and late June 1984, there was no sign of a breakthrough on any of these controversial issues. Only under the pressure of both South Yemen and Algeria, as well as Fatah's threat to walk out of the talks and unilaterally convene the PNC, was an agreement signed on June 27. This document, known as the Aden-Algiers Agreement, was based upon the working paper presented by the Fatah delegation to the talks.[30]

The Aden-Algiers Agreement contained a number of provisions designed to limit Arafat's power and authority, including the appointment of three deputies for the PLO chairman and the formation of a general secretariat for the Executive Committee. It also recommended the broadening of the PLO's Executive Committee membership. The agreement delegated more power to the Central Council, including the right to oversee the functions of the Executive Committee to ensure that its policies were congruent with the resolutions of the PNC. The Central Council was also authorized to suspend up to one-third of the members of the PLO. The agreement stipulated that the Central Council be expanded and that its members be directly elected by the PNC, instead of the previous system in which various PLO factions chose their own representatives.

The agreement urged the various Palestinian organizations and groups to engage in a comprehensive dialogue to preserve the unity of the PLO. This dialogue would be based on the resolutions of the sixteenth session of the PNC, the rejection of the Camp David accords and the Reagan initiative, and the reaffirmation of Palestinian rights, including the right of self-determination, the creation of a Palestinian state, and the PLO's right to represent the Palestinian people. Although characterizing Palestinian-Syrian relations as strategic, the agreement stipulated that improvement of relations with Damascus should be sought within the framework of preserving Palestinian autonomy.

Other provisions of the agreement called for continuation of the Jordanian-Palestinian dialogue and made the normalization of relations with Egypt subject to the resolutions of the PNC. The agreement regarded Arafat's trip to Egypt as a violation of PLO resolutions but left the final verdict on the trip to the PNC. Fatah and the Democratic Alliance agreed to convene the seventeenth session of the PNC before mid-September 1984. To ensure the success of the meeting, the conferees called for a dialogue among the various factions of the PLO.

Soon after the signing of the Aden-Algiers Agreement, hopes were raised that Palestinian national unity would be preserved after all and that the PLO's viability and cohesion would be maintained. Initially, both Fatah's Central Committee and Democratic Alliance members were anxious to implement the agreement and to convene the PNC on the designated date. Leading figures within Fatah spoke of the positive results of the agreement although, if implemented, it would severely curtail Arafat's powers. Fatah's Central Committee members sent a memorandum to the Syrian government expressing their willingness to open a new page in relations between Syria and Fatah. It suggested sending a delegation to Damascus to discuss all points of difference.[31]

Similarly, members of the Democratic Alliance were initially anxious to convene the council at its designated date. They were uncertain whether Arafat would continue to adhere to the Aden-Algiers Agreement in view of the constraints that it would impose upon his authority. Their initial enthusiasm began to wane two weeks after the ratification of the agreement. By early August the convening of the council was no longer a primary issue; promoting Palestinian national reconciliation and improving relations with Syria began to assume primacy.

Various arguments were employed to justify these new stands. Members of the alliance, particularly the Popular Front, argued that more time was needed to mediate between Fatah and Syria and among the various factions of the PLO. They also wanted to ensure the participation of members of the National Alliance in the council's upcoming meeting. They asserted that the convening of the council should come about as a result of mutual consent between themselves and Fatah's Central Committee.

The background for the dialogue and the complex issues under discussion, as well as Syrian pressure, made the participation of the Democratic Alliance very doubtful. First, Syria was not pleased with some provisions of the Aden-Algiers Agreement. In a meeting between Syrian Vice President Abd al-Halim Khaddom and speaker of the PNC Khaled al-Fahum, the Syrian government reportedly demanded the introduction of a number of amendments to the agreement, including a provision for a complete ban on any contact with the Egyptian government unless Egypt abandoned the Camp David accords and the peace treaty with Israel. Damascus also demanded the formation of a transitional leadership consisting of members of the Executive Committee, the president of the PNC, and the leaders of the various PLO factions. This new leadership was expected to supervise the PLO's affairs. Khaddom also ordered the Democratic and National Alliances to issue a joint statement denouncing Arafat's leadership and insisted that both alliances form a delegation to discuss with Fatah's Central Committee the time, place, and agenda for the PNC. In case the talks failed, he requested that the two alliances convene the PNC without Fatah attendance. In response, Habash reportedly promised the Syrian president that his organization would not attend the session of the National Council without Syria's prior consent and without the presence of the members of the National Alliance.[32]

Second, the change in position of the Democratic Alliance may have resulted from threats by members of the National Alliance. The four pro-Syrian groups warned that they would attack and destroy the bases of the Popular and Democratic Fronts in Lebanon should they attend the seventeenth session of the PNC. They urged the Democratic Alliance to renounce the Aden-Algiers Agreement and join their ranks to form a new Palestinian leadership.

Third, the Democratic Alliance's shift was also the by-product of the similarities between both alliances that, according to Habash, surpassed their differences.[33] Fourth, one could argue that Habash's initial agreement to convene the PNC at its designated date in mid-September was made only to please his more moderate partners within the Democratic Alliance. According to this interpretation nothing was new in the attitude of the Popular Front. Despite his signing of the Aden-Algiers Agreement, Habash never abandoned his goal of removing Arafat from office. Similarly, his opposition to the convening of the National Council was consistent with his organization's earlier stand.

Although the position of the Popular Front was unyielding, the attitudes of its other partners within the Democratic alliance were not as rigid.

The Democratic Front, for instance, did not favor an indefinite postponement of the council meeting, but rather insisted upon convening it as soon as possible to endorse the Aden-Algiers Agreement. For this reason, it was unwilling to grant an unlimited period for the mediating efforts. According to Hawatmeh, the National Alliance was not interested in preserving Palestinian national unity or reactivating the PLO's political councils. Hawatmeh made it clear that if attempts for reconciliation within the PLO failed, he would attend the council's meetings without hesitation.[34]

The Democratic Front went along with the Popular Front's demand to postpone the meeting of the National Council in order to give more time for the mediation efforts of Algeria and South Yemen. Like Habash, Hawatmeh did not want the Fatah Central Committee to unilaterally convene the National Council. Also Hawatmeh probably consented eventually to delay the PNC session to deprive Habash of any opportunity to retreat from the Aden-Algiers Agreement and to draw closer to the members of the National Alliance. He hoped that in the meantime the Soviet Union would come out in favor of convening the National Council, a move that would mitigate the opposition of both Syria and the PLO's hard-line groups. Finally, the concentration of the Democratic Front's troops in Lebanese areas under Syrian control undoubtedly limited Hawatmeh's freedom of action. His attendance at the Palestine National Council meeting could have resulted in the harassment of his troops by the National Alliance. He also ran the risk of divisions within his organization.

The growing differences between the Popular and Democratic Fronts over the convening of the PNC caused the Democratic Alliance to meet in Aden from October 19 to 24, to call for a postponement of the National Council for a two-month period to allow the South Yemen and Algerian mediations to continue. Meanwhile, the conferees proposed to convene the Palestine Central Council and reactivate the PLO's Executive Committee by ending their boycott of its sessions. Although the Democratic Front, the Palestine Communist Party, and the Palestine Liberation Front adhered to the terms of the new agreement, the Popular Front made its participation in the Executive Committee contingent upon the consent of its Central Committee, which since January 1984 had boycotted these sessions.

In response to the Popular Front's wavering attitude, Hawatmeh's Central Committee issued a statement deploring what it termed the counterproductive, negative stance of the Popular Front, including its retreat from the Aden-Algiers Agreement, its attempt to delay the National Council, and its failure to uphold the October 24 Aden agreement. For these reasons Hawatmeh suspended the joint leadership between his organization and that of the Popular Front, which had been established after Arafat's expulsion from Damascus in June 1983. The suspension order did not include the Democratic Front's membership in the Democratic Alliance.[35]

The Seventeenth Session of the Palestine National Council in Amman and Beyond

In reaction to demands to postpone the PNC session, Fatah officials insisted upon convening the council at its proper time, arguing that failure to do so would be a retreat from the Aden-Algiers Agreement.[36] Fatah leaders later altered this position upon the request of Algeria and South Yemen. On September 22, 1984, Fatah's Central Committee issued a statement postponing the council meeting for a twenty-day period, giving more time for the mediating efforts. Fatah's move was motivated by its desire to ensure the presence of as many of the various political forces as possible at the session and to avoid a formal split within the ranks of the PLO. The decision also reflected the conviction of some Fatah leaders that members of the Democratic Alliance continued to enjoy some degree of autonomy from Syrian control, which was manifested in their signing of the Aden-Algiers Agreement.[37] Fatah leaders also demonstrated some understanding of the reasons behind the Popular and the Democratic Fronts' reluctance to attend the PNC meeting. Clearly, with their political headquarters and troop concentrations under Syrian control, the two fronts were susceptible to Syrian government pressures.

As the twenty-day period ended without any sign of progress, Fatah's Central Committee decided unilaterally to convene the National Council. Its patience had been stretched thin by the equivocal attitude of the members of the Democratic Alliance. The question of whether to convene the PNC became increasingly a test of Fatah's political power and credibility. Should it fail to convene the council, Fatah probably would lose political ground. Its opponents within the PLO would then perhaps try to convene their own national council. Commenting on this issue Abu Iyad stated,

> If we fail to convene the Palestine National Council, I think the setback will be even more dangerous than the withdrawal from Beirut. Our people will be frustrated, the leadership will be frustrated, and we will lose the initiative, and once we lose the political initiative, we will lose the leadership and we will wait for our decisions to come from Syria and Libya. Palestinian decision-making becomes a joke.[38]

Fatah leaders also refused the suggestions by the members of the Democratic Alliance to convene the Palestine Central Council and reactivate the work of the PLO's Executive Committee as a preparatory step for the convening of the PNC. They feared that such a meeting would be used to postpone the council indefinitely. Fatah's Central Committee was equally opposed to the October 24 meeting of the Democratic Alliance in Aden without a Fatah representative. For these reasons, Fatah leaders saw no point in continuing the dialogue with members of the Democratic Alliance.[39]

On October 12, 1984, Arafat summoned seventy leading Palestinian politicians to his political headquarters in Tunis to discuss the obstacles in the way of the PNC meeting. The conferees agreed to convene the council before the end of November.[40] Finding a place to host the meeting presented a problem for Fatah's Central Committee members. Algeria, which had been designated as the site for the meeting by the Aden-Algiers Agreement, declined to host it on the grounds that such a meeting would lead to formal divisions within the PLO; actually, the Algerians probably abstained in deference to Syria's wishes. Moreover, in the wake of unity talks between Libya and Morocco, Algerian President Chadli Ben Jadid hoped that his Syrian counterpart would persuade Libyan leader Qaddafi not to take Morocco's side in the dispute over the Western Sahara. Similarly, South Yemeni President Ali Nasser Muhammad abstained from hosting the PNC's meeting in Aden. Arafat's efforts to convene the conference at PLO headquarters in Tunis also failed. The Tunisian government declared that it would be unable to provide the elaborate security arrangements needed for the personal safety of the PNC members. Like Algeria, Tunis did not want to provoke the Libyan leader, who was opposed to the convening of the National Council.

The PLO received invitations from Iran, Iraq, and Jordan. The Iranian offer was turned down after the Ayatollah Khomeini regime refused to stop the war with Iraq.[41] Similarly, the PLO decided against Iraq as a meeting place to avoid alienating the Iranians. Toward the end of September Arafat was able to secure King Hussein's consent to host the council in the Jordanian capital, a distinctly advantageous location to Fatah. First, meeting in Amman would reconfirm Arafat's commitment to his talks with King Hussein, particularly after the failure of their first dialogue in early spring 1983. Second, it would strengthen the standing of the PLO among the Palestinians living in Jordan and facilitate contacts with Palestinians in the West Bank and the Gaza Strip. Third, from a Jordanian perspective the hosting of the council would strengthen the voice of moderation within the PLO and diminish the chances of Syria and PLO hard-line groups dominating the organization. King Hussein also hoped that it would lead to the endorsement of moderate resolutions congruent with Jordan's political preferences. A step of this sort would enable him to advance his quest for a resolution of the Palestinian problem. Finally, holding the meeting in Amman was also in line with Hussein and Arafat's efforts to forge a new Arab political alliance among Egypt, Jordan, Iraq, and the PLO.

On November 12, 1984, Arafat requested National Council speaker Khaled al-Fahum to invite the various PNC delegates to the Jordanian capital on November 22. Al-Fahum refused on the grounds that without complete reconciliation within the PLO, this action would cause further divisions. He appealed for more time to reconcile the PLO's rival groups. Al-Fahum contested Arafat's claim that the need to convene the council was urgent, arguing that this was not the first time that the council meeting had been postponed: Sessions had been delayed for periods ranging from nine months to two years.[42] After al-Fahum declined, Arafat himself issued the invitations. According to Fatah sources, 261 of 374 active members attended the council meeting on November 22. The meeting was boycotted by members of the National and Democratic Alliances. Israel and Syria prevented those council members residing in their territories from going to Amman.

The convening of the council was a personal victory for the PLO chief and an opportunity to vindicate his policies. It also meant that Arafat continued to enjoy majority support within the Palestinian community and that his opponents were a small and isolated group. Moreover, convening the council in Jordan undermined the influence of Syria over PLO affairs.

Arafat's departure from the standard practice of preserving Palestinian national unity by endorsing resolutions through consensus allowed the passage of more moderate resolutions than in previous sessions. However, the council's final communiqué fell short of providing a well-defined strategy to cope with the pressing problems confronting the PLO. The communiqué was deliberately worded in broad terms to avoid the further alienation of the PLO's hard-line groups and their Syrian backers. It also reflected the fact that the conferees at the PNC did not hold a unified opinion; some were sympathetic to the views of the hard-line groups. Moreover, the continuing inflexibility of the Israeli government with regard to relinquishing the occupied territories, as well as the indifference of the Reagan administration to the national aspirations of the Palestinians, did not allow the council members to go further in their resolutions. The participants chose not to commit themselves to any specific policy but rather to prescribe broad policy guidelines and give the PLO more authority in formulating the details of the policy at a later date.[43]

Relationships with Jordan, Syria, and Egypt, and with those PLO factions that did not attend the conference, figured prominently in the council's discussion. With regard to the relationship with Jordan, the delegates deliberated upon the proposal that King Hussein outlined in his opening speech. The king reminded the delegates that time was not on the side of the Palestinians and urged them to put aside their internal problems and work jointly with his government to salvage the occupied territories from an otherwise inevitable Israeli annexation. The king also called upon the Palestinians to endorse publicly UN Security Council Resolution 242 and accept the principle of restoring Arab sovereignty over the occupied territories in return for full recognition and peaceful relations with Israel. Such an arrangement would take place through the convening of an international peace conference attended by all concerned parties, including Israel, the PLO, and the five permanent members of the Security Council. The king's plan stipulated that the future relationship between the occupied territories, once liberated, and Jordan would be determined, without external interference, by the Palestinians and the Jordanians on the basis of the right to national self-determination.[44]

Although many PNC members welcomed Hussein's call for a diplomatic alliance between the PLO and Jordan, leading PLO figures, including Abu Iyad and Abu Jihad, did not accept the king's call to endorse UN Security Council Resolution 242. Palestinian opposition to this resolution traditionally arose because the resolution did not address Palestinian national rights but instead treated the Palestinian problem as a refugee question. Although some council members spoke openly of adopting the king's proposal, others preferred to let the PLO decide upon it at a later date in view of its controversial nature. The council's final communiqué tried to reconcile these three trends by advocating the further consolidation of special ties with Jordan and calling for the formation of a joint Palestinian-Jordanian diplomatic approach.

Although the king's proposal contained ideas with serious implications for PLO goals and tactics requiring specific answers by the National Council, the final communiqué neither rejected nor endorsed it. The council preferred to authorize the PLO to decide upon it at a later date. The communiqué pointed out that the Executive Committee's final decision should be guided by the resolutions of the sixteenth session of the National Council, the resolutions of the Arab summit conferences at Rabat and Fez, and those UN resolutions that pertain to the Palestinian problem. Although these guidelines were meant as safeguards to limit Arafat's freedom to maneuver, many of them were vague and open to multiple interpretations. This deliberate obscurity revealed that the council members had voted in favor of quiet diplomacy in dealing with King Hussein's peace proposal: The conferees were careful not to commit themselves to what could turn out to be unpopular decisions leading to further dissent within the PLO.

The council's final communiqué went along with King Hussein's invitation to convene an international peace conference for the resolution of the Palestinian problem but insisted that the PLO participate in such a conference on equal footing. The communiqué added that the PLO would not attend any conference based upon the Reagan initiative, the Camp David accords, or any other plan or UN resolution that did not recognize Palestinian rights of self-determination and statehood.

The council's communiqué did not condemn Arafat's visit to Cairo; on the contrary, it spoke of the need to bring Egypt back into the Arab world and praised the Egyptian government's support for the PLO. Unlike the resolutions of the sixteenth session of the PNC, the new communiqué did not make the improvement of relationships with Egypt contingent upon the regime's abandonment of the Camp David accords. The council authorized the Executive Committee to follow up on the question of normalization with Cairo in coordination with the rest of the Arab countries.

The council eventually adopted a conciliatory resolution toward Syria. During the debates, many delegates had bitterly denounced the Assad regime's expulsion of Arafat from Damascus and its support of Fatah dissidents. These delegates demanded that the council endorse harsh resolutions against Syria. Leading PLO figures, however, cautioned against taking tough stands, reminding the participants of Syria's support of the PLO over the years. They argued that such stands would only serve to provoke the Syrian government and prompt it to place obstacles in the path of any political settlement. The final PNC communiqué spoke of the need to improve Syrian-Palestinian relations on the grounds of equality, noninterference in each other's affairs, and mutual respect for each other's rights and freedom.

The issue of preserving Palestinian national unity also caused some controversy among the participants. Some council members proposed to exclude the hard-line groups from the council and deprive them of their seats within the PLO's Executive Committee. Similarly, they opposed the endorsement of the Aden-Algiers Agreement within the council's final communiqué on the grounds that the Democratic Alliance had violated the terms of that agreement. In contrast, other delegates wanted the Aden-Algiers Agreement to serve as a guideline for the resolutions of the final communiqué. They also expressed strong interest in preserving Palestinian national unity and resuming the dialogue with the Democratic Alliance.

The final communiqué reflected the reconciliationist viewpoint by keeping the seats of the representatives of the Popular and Democratic Fronts and al-Sa'iqa vacant in the Executive Committee. The communiqué also called for the renewal of the dialogue between Fatah's Central Committee and members of the Democratic Alliance on the basis of the Aden-Algiers Agreement. Another call was made to initiate a dialogue among the various PLO factions to preserve the unity and viability of the Palestinian nationalist movement. Furthermore, the communiqué appealed to all factions to adhere to the Palestine National Charter and the resolutions of the various PNCs and to abide by the principle of resolving inter-Palestinian disputes through democratic and peaceful means. The council's communiqué reiterated the PLO's adherence to armed struggle and the need to step up this strategy in the occupied territories. Finally, the National Council authorized the Executive Committee to establish contacts with those anti-Zionist Israelis and Jews who supported the national rights of the Palestinians.

Contrary to the demands of the Democratic and National Alliances that Arafat be removed from office or at a minimum that his powers be curtailed, Arafat's authority was not only kept intact but was even enhanced by the decisions of the PNC meeting. The council authorized Arafat and his colleagues within the Executive Committee to decide upon cardinal issues such as the pursuit of a diplomatic settlement of the Palestinian question in coordination with both Jordan and Egypt. Serious issues like these had previously been determined by the council itself. Arafat's freedom to maneuver was advanced further by the appointment of leading moderate figures to key positions within the PLO. The election to the Executive Committee of Fahd Qawasmi and Muhammad Milhem, the mayors of Hebron and Halhul, and the election of Shaikh Abdul Hamid al-Sayeh, the former head of the Islamic Council in Jerusalem, as the speaker of the PNC were clear indications that the PLO was determined to concentrate on the occupied territories in the coming period. Moreover, the convening of the council's seventeenth session in the Jordanian capital did not only mean an end to the Palestinian-Hashemite enmity, but also entailed that the leadership of the mainstream PLO had conclusively chosen to seek a political solution to the Palestinian question in cooperation with Jordan. By doing so Arafat and Hussein demonstrated a considerable degree of courage and readiness to take risks against Syrian wishes. In addition, while the convening of the council in Amman had formalized the split within the PLO it also marked Arafat's breaking away with the principle of consensus building in favor of majority rule. Finally, the interests and the wishes of the Palestinians in the West Bank and the Gaza Strip, who in the wake of the Lebanon War became Arafat's primary constituency, would serve as a guiding principle for the PLO's future course of action.

Notes

1. Interview in *al-Ahram,* December 23, 1983.
2. Interview on Radio Monte Carlo, January 6, 1984.
3. Interview in *al-Majalla,* no. 217, April 7-13, 1984.
4. Interview with Farouq al-Qadoumi and Radio Monte Carlo, October 5, 1983; interview with Jamal Surani, PLO Executive Committee member, *al-Majalla,* no. 226, June 9-15, 1984. Interview with Arafat in *Rose al-Yusuf,* December 3, 1983.
5. *Jerusalem Post,* December 23, 1983.
6. *Al-Ahram,* December 28, 1983.
7. *Al-Ahram,* December 23, 1983. Interview with Boutros Ghali on Radio Monte Carlo, January 6, 1984.
8. Interview on Voice of America, December 22, 1983, and Radio Monte Carlo, December 30, 1983.
9. Interview on Radio Monte Carlo, December 23, 1983.
10. Ibid.
11. *Al-Ba'ath* and *Tishrin,* December 23 and 24, 1983.
12. Interview with *al-Majalla,* no. 217, April 7-13, 1984.
13. This statement was broadcast by Voice of Palestine (Baghdad), December 22, 1983.
14. Interview with Abu Iyad, Radio Monte Carlo, December 23, 1983.
15. Interview with Rashad al-Shawa, Radio Monte Carlo, December 30, 1983.
16. Ibid.
17. Interview with Khaled al-Hassan, *al-Dustur,* February 25, 1984. See also Arafat's comments in *al-Majalla,* no. 241, September 23-29, 1984.
18. King Hussein's interview on Jordan TV, January 2, 1984.
19. King Hussein's remarks came from his opening address to the parliament, January 16, 1984, *Jordan Times,* January 17, 1984.
20. Crown Prince Hassan interview on Cable News Network, reproduced by Jordan TV, November 18, 1984.
21. Such statements were made by Prime Minister Mudar Baddran on Jordan TV, January 9, 1984, and Laila Sharaf, Jordan's minister of information, Jordan TV, January 12 and 18, 1984, and King Hussein's press conference, January 24, 1984, reported by *Jordan Times,* January 25, 1984.
22. Hussein's interview on Jordan TV, January 2, 1984, and *Jordan Times,* January 25, 1984.
23. King Hussein's interview with the *New York Times,* March 15, 1984, and the king's interview with the BBC Arabic service, March 20, 1984.
24. Interview with Abu Iyad in *al-Majalla,* no. 217, April 7-13, 1984; Farouq al-Qadoumi interview in *al-Majalla,* no. 228, June 23-29, 1984.
25. *Al-Hadaf* (Popular Front weekly publication), April 9, 1984.

26. *Al-'Asifa* (Fatah dissident publication), May 1984.

27. Interview with Abu Iyad in *al-Majalla,* no. 217, April 7–13, 1984.

28. Ibrahim Abu al-Nab, "Arafat Gets Tough," *Middle-East International,* April 20, 1984, pp. 7–8; also interview with Abu Jihad in *Sawt al-Sha'ab* (Jordanian daily), April 7, 1984. Interview with Mahmoud Abbas (commonly known as Abu Mazen) in *al-Tadamon,* reproduced in *al-Sha'ab* (Jerusalem Arabic daily), March 30, 1984.

29. *Al-Zabas* (Kuwait daily), April 22, 1984. See also Saleh Qallab, "al-Mubahathat fi al-Jaza'er," *al-Majalla,* no. 224, May 26–June 1, 1984. See also interview with Jamal Surani (PLO Executive Committee member) in *al-Majalla,* no. 226, June 9–15, 1984.

30. Saleh Qallab, "Sirr al-Lahadat Al-Akhira," *al-Majalla,* no. 230, July 7–13, 1984.

31. Interview with Hani al-Hassan (political advisor to Arafat), *al-Majalla,* no. 236, August 18–24, 1984; and Abu Mazen interview in *al-Majalla,* no. 241, September 22–28, 1984.

32. Reported by *al-Majalla,* August 18–24, 1984.

33. Interview with *al-Hadaf,* October 1, 1984.

34. Interview in *al-Hurriya,* November 11, 1984. Also the statement of the Democratic Front Central Committee in *al-Hurriya,* October 27, 1984.

35. *Al-Hurriya,* November 25, 1984.

36. See the comments of Abu Mazen in *al-Sharq al-Awsat,* August 27, 1984. See also the interview with Hani al-Hassan in *al-Majalla,* no. 236, August 18–24, 1984.

37. Interview with Abu Iyad in *al-Majalla,* no. 241, September 22–28, 1984.

38. *Al-Majalla,* no. 241, September 22–28, 1984.

39. For a detailed account of the developments that led to Fatah's decision to convene the PNC, see the statement by the Central Committee of Fatah, November 1984 (pamphlet).

40. *Al-Sharq al-Awsat,* October 14, 1984.

41. Salim Nasser, "Aina Yana'qed al-Majles al-Watani al-Filistini," *al-Mustaqbal,* October 6, 1984.

42. Al-Fahum's letter appeared in *al-Sharq al-Awsat,* November 14, 1984.

43. The Arabic text of the communiqué can be found in *Filistin al-Thawra,* no. 536, December 8, 1984.

44. For an English text of the king's speech, see *Jordan Times,* November 23, 1984.

8
Epilogue: Arafat-Hussein Agreement for Joint Action

With the rupture of Palestinian-Syrian relations and the departure from the principle of preserving Palestinian national unity, some of the most important constraints upon Arafat's freedom of maneuver were removed. Two months after the termination of the seventeenth session of the Palestine National Council, an agreement was reached between Arafat and Hussein for joint diplomatic action. The agreement was based on the peace proposal outlined by King Hussein before the PNC meeting and on the last two sessions of the Palestine National Council. According to the agreement and to Jordan's interpretation of its provisions, the PLO had accepted all UN resolutions, including those of the Security Council, that dealt with the Palestinian question. Taher Hikmat, Jordan's acting minister of information, announced that Arafat had in effect accepted UN Security Council Resolution 242 when he signed the political accord. The agreement also committed the PLO to seek a political settlement to the Palestinian question through a UN-sponsored international peace conference and called for the formation of a joint Palestinian-Jordanian delegation to represent the interests of the Palestinian people in such a conference. The agreement advocated the implementation of the UN resolutions that dealt with the rights of the Palestinian refugees, such as compensation, return, and repatriation.

One of the most significant provisions of the accord was the PLO's acceptance of the principle of peace in exchange for land, embodied in the UN Resolution 242. The agreement called for complete Israeli withdrawal from the West Bank, Gaza, and East Jerusalem and for full diplomatic recognition and a peaceful relationship with the Jewish state. The agreement also spoke of the Palestinian rights to self-determination and the formation of a Palestinian state in the occupied territories and the association of such a state with Jordan through a confederal arrangement.[1]

Arafat's signing of the agreement for joint action was significant in a variety of ways. First, the PLO's acceptance of those UN resolutions dealing with the Palestinian question and of the principle of exchanging land for peace implied that the PLO chairman had accepted the gist of UN Security Council Resolution 242 and Israel's right to exist.[2] Public endorsement of Resolution 242, the abandonment of the aspiration of the Palestinians to have a state of their own, and the renunciation of the use of military force to achieve the PLO's political goals were unlikely to be adopted for the time being. Should the PLO be associated with the peace process, Arafat might very well compromise his organization's position over these issues.

Second, by agreeing to associate the West Bank and the Gaza Strip with Jordan, Arafat laid to rest the PLO's strategic goal of establishing a secular democratic state in all Palestine as well as the narrower goal of setting up a fully sovereign, independent Palestinian state in the West Bank and the Gaza Strip. By advocating the confederation of the West Bank and Gaza Strip with Jordan, the agreement for joint action went beyond the 1982 Arab peace plan of Fez that called for the formation of a sovereign, independent Palestinian state. In this sense the agreement came more in line with the Reagan initiative than the Arab peace plan. The Palestinian-Jordanian political accord apparently reduced the meaning of sovereignty and the right to self-determination to the notion of a homeland and self-government in a confederation with Jordan.

Third, notwithstanding public rhetoric, the agreement represented another compromise in that Arafat accepted the notion of a joint negotiating team with Jordan. Thus it appeared that the Palestinian leader had compromised the status of his organization as the sole legitimate representative of the Palestinian people. This compromise also went beyond the provisions of the Fez peace plan and the resolutions of the various Palestine national council sessions that insisted upon the PLO's direct participation in any political settlement and its exclusive representation of the interests of the Palestinians. The new political accord formalized the doctrine of shared representation of Palestinian demands and interests between the PLO and Jordan. Arafat's compromise on the PLO's exclusive representative role and on a fully independent sovereign Palestinian state were essential to keeping the PLO relevant to the peace process; such compromises, it was hoped, would lessen U.S. and Israeli opposition to PLO participation in any political settlement. The manner, methods, and composition of the joint Palestinian-Jordanian delegation were left deliberately undefined, leaving the door open for non-PLO, West Bank–Gaza Strip Palestinian participation in the peace talks and avoiding U.S. and Israeli objection to the PLO's direct participation.

Fourth, the PLO had committed itself officially and explicitly to a political settlement of the Palestinian question and the Arab-Israeli conflict, departing from its policy of armed struggle. This political settlement conflicted sharply with the various PNC resolutions that reiterated the PLO strategy of military struggle while simultaneously pursuing diplomacy to resolve the Palestinian question.

Fifth, the compromises were also intended to arrest King Hussein's growing impatience with Arafat's hesitation and equivocation. If some agreement was not reached, both Egypt and Jordan might move toward a political accommodation with Israel, leaving the PLO behind. Arafat and Hussein signed the agreement in response to repeated appeals by Egypt and Saudi Arabia to resolve their differences, thereby facilitating the missions of the Saudi Arabian monarch and the Egyptian president to the U.S. capital. Western European countries and the United States had repeatedly argued that a joint Jordanian-Palestinian diplomatic approach would accelerate the peace process. Finally, by signing the agreement only one week before the commencement of the Geneva talks between the Soviet Union and the United States on February 19, 1985, Arafat and Hussein might have intended to present the superpowers with a joint plan for solving the Palestinian problem.

Despite the far-reaching implications of the Arafat-Hussein agreement, the accord failed to generate sufficient enthusiasm and the needed support among the concerned actors. Its fate will depend upon the degree of commitment of both Hussein and Arafat and their ability to preserve and develop it. It will also depend upon how such a joint initiative is received by the Arab world and whether Arafat and Hussein will give in to the pressures and intimidations of Syria, Libya, and the PLO's hard-line groups. Likewise, the accord's success relies upon the willingness and the readiness of the Reagan administration to alter its present posture of political inaction and to search actively for a settlement to the Arab-Israeli dispute and the Palestinian problem. Finally, if Israel maintains its negative attitude toward the Arafat-Hussein accord, its chances of survival will be nonexistent.

The political concessions to Jordan in the agreement were bound to generate negative reaction within the Palestinian nationalist movement. Criticism of the agreement was not confined to the PLO's hard-line groups (the traditional source of opposition to Arafat's political moves), but Fatah's Central Committee was divided into proponents and critics. Fatah Central Committee members Farouq al-Qadoumi, Abu Iyad, Rafiq al-Natshe, and Abu Mazen criticized the agreement's ambiguous attitude toward Resolution 242, the PLO's exclusive right to represent Palestinian interests and to participate directly in any political settlement, and the formation of an independent Palestinian state in the West Bank and the Gaza Strip. The ambiguity of the agreement's provisions on such cardinal issues accounted for the differences in interpretations between Jordan and the PLO.[3] Some members even openly advocated the cancellation of the agreement should the differences between Jordan and the PLO persist.

Critics of the agreement further asserted that the PLO alone enjoyed the right to represent the interests of the Palestinian people and would not therefore share that representation with anyone or authorize any Arab state to speak in the name of the Palestinians. Similarly, they rejected the suggestions by Jordan's acting minister of information that the PLO in effect had accepted Resolution 242 when it signed the political accord. According to the critics, the creation of an independent Palestinian state and the PLO's direct representation of Palestinian interests in any political settlement were the least that Fatah would accept. After it had survived for two decades, the abandonment by the PLO of "its struggle and sacrifices" in favor of confederating with Jordan and playing a small, indirect role in the resolution of the Palestinian problem was hard to imagine.

Dissatisfaction with the agreement among Fatah Central Committee members was further reinforced by the categorical rejection of it by the PLO's hard-line groups in Syria. The reservations to the accord expressed by some leading politicians in the West Bank and Gaza Strip contributed further to its critics' insistence that several amendments be introduced to the agreement.

A second group of Fatah Central Committee members led by Arafat, Abu Jihad, Hayel Abd al-Hamid, Khaled al-Hassan, and Hani al-Hassan supported the Jordanian-Palestinian political accord, arguing that the differences over the interpretation did not necessitate its abrogation. Their concern was to encourage further diplomatic coordination between the PLO and Jordan; they werre convinced that such coordination was mandatory to finding a settlement for the Palestinian question.[4] They were sure that diplomatic coordination with Jordan would not undermine the status of the PLO as the sole legitimate representative of the Palestinian people and denied that the political accord had compromised this status. On the contrary, they maintained that Jordan remained committed to the concept of the PLO's participation on an equal footing in any settlement. Abu Jihad confirmed to Radio Monte Carlo on February 22, 1985, "Nobody asked to negotiate on our behalf or requested a mandate, or demanded to share our representation of the Palestinian people."

The division of opinion within Fatah's leadership was behind the qualified endorsement given to the agreement by the PLO's Executive Committee and the Fatah Central Committee. On February 19, the

PLO's Executive Committee spelled out its basic understanding of the accord:[5] The agreement aimed at realizing Palestinian national rights to repatriation, self-determination, and the creation of an independent Palestinian state. The committee also reiterated its objection to the Reagan initiative, the Camp David accords, and Resolution 242, which it considered inappropriate and incapable of satisfying the national aspirations of the Palestinians. This statement contrasted sharply with the assertion of Jordan's acting minister of information that the PLO had in effect accepted Resolution 242 when it signed the joint accord with Jordan.

To dissipate the ambiguities concerning the PLO's role in any political settlement the Executive Committee reconfirmed the PLO's status as the sole legitimate representative of the Palestinian people and its unwillingness to authorize or share the representation of Palestinian interests with any Arab party. The statement pointed out that the participation of the PLO in the proposed peace conference would take place through an Arab delegation and not through a Jordanian-Palestinian delegation as the agreement stipulated. To allay the malaise and the suspicions of the Syrians and the PLO's hard-line groups the Executive Committee envisaged the Arafat-Hussein agreement as the nucleus for a more comprehensive Arab political approach. Finally, the Executive Committee underlined the need to enlist full Arab support for the joint agreement (a condition that if fully carried out would keep the accord a dead letter because of the bitter divisions and mutual hostilities prevailing among the Arab countries).

In the context of this understanding the PLO's Executive Committee endorsed the Arafat-Hussein agreement and tried to obtain an understanding with Jordan over its ambiguous clauses. In particular the PLO sought verification of two points: First, the Palestinian people would exercise their right to self-determination soon after Israel terminated its military occupation of the West Bank and the Gaza Strip and prior to the confederation of these territories with Jordan. Second, the PLO leadership wanted to reemphasize the exclusive role of the organization in representing the interests of the Palestinians and asserted that the PLO would attend the proposed peace conference through an Arab delegation rather than through a joint Palestinian-Jordanian delegation.[6] On March 4 a spokesman for the PLO announced that the Jordanian government had accepted the PLO's verifications. King Hussein played down the seriousness of the reservations of leading Fatah figures to the accords by arguing that the agreement was still in effect and that the PLO was seeking only verifications and not changes to the agreement.[7]

Sorting out of differences within the Fatah Central Committee over the provisions of the agreement does not necessarily mean that differences of opinion will not emerge over the composition of the negotiating team. Even if the United States were to reactivate its search for a political settlement to the Arab-Israeli dispute, Arafat's colleagues may not be prepared to facilitate a political settlement on U.S. terms. They will most likely be hesitant to publicly recognize Israel or accept Resolution 242 and abandon their strategy of armed struggle; such concessions are not likely to be given without tangible political rewards in return. Such rewards will be needed to enable Arafat and his colleagues within Fatah to rationalize the PLO's concessions on such cardinal issues. Fatah Central Committee members will try hard to keep Arafat's diplomatic maneuvering within the limits defined by the resolutions of the sixteenth and seventeenth sessions of the Palestine National Council.

Division of opinion over the Arafat-Hussein political accord was also visible among politicians in the West Bank and the Gaza Strip. Supporters of the hard-line PLO groups insisted upon the creation of an independent Palestinian state and were not prepared to compromise the PLO's role as the exclusive representative of Palestinian interests. They also distrusted the Jordanian regime and the United States and were convinced that the U.S. government in particular could never play an objective role in the resolution of the Palestinian problem. The supporters of the PLO's hard-line groups concluded that prevailing local, regional, and international conditions were not favorable to the launching of a political initiative.

Another group of West Bank and Gaza Strip politicians welcomed the Jordanian-Palestinian agreement for joint action. It did not express opposition to the formation of a joint Palestinian-Jordanian delegation or the creation of a Palestinian-Jordanian confederation. In its opinion such steps were essential to avoid U.S. and Israeli objections and to terminate Israeli military control over the occupied territories as soon as possible. Some members of this group, including the mayors of Bethlehem and Gaza, expressed their willingness to join a Jordanian-Palestinian delegation should they be asked by the PLO. They saw no other way to end Israel's military occupation of the territories except through a joint Jordanian-PLO action that would prompt the United States to reactivate its search for a Middle Eastern settlement.

Should the current attempts by King Hussein and Arafat to find a political settlement to the Palestinian question fail, the voice of moderation within the occupied territories might lose further ground in favor of leftist forces and Islamic groups. It might also create pressure from local politicians on the PLO chairman to reconcile with the various Palestinian hard-line groups. A considerable number of politicians in the occupied territories continues to attach great value to the principle of preserving Palestinian national unity. Such a reconciliation with the rejectionist groups is not likely without Arafat abrogating his political accord with King Hussein.

The Arafat-Hussein agreement for joint action generated bitter denunciation within the leftist circles of the Palestinian nationalist movement. The various PLO hard-line groups singularly and jointly rejected the accord, contending that it sharply conflicted with the PLO's political program, the various resolutions of the PNC, and the Palestine National Charter. They opposed the agreement because it conceded the exclusive right to represent Palestinian interests and compromised the rights of the Palestinians to return, self-determination, and the creation of an independent sovereign state. The rejectionists contended that the agreement transformed the Palestinian question into an internal Jordanian matter and reduced it to a question of borders between Israel and Jordan. They warned that the signing of the Arafat-Hussein political accord was a prelude to "further concessions and liquidationist solutions." In this context George Habash, leader of the Popular Front for the Liberation of Palestine (PFLP), characterized the agreement as "a dangerous and qualitative turning point in the path of liquidationist solutions and a serious deviation from the nationalist course of the revolution."[8] The pro-Syria National Alliance contended that signing the agreement amounted to high treason and placed the Palestinian question under Jordanian "tutelage."[9] Abu Musa regarded the conclusion of the agreement as a logical outcome of the convening of the Palestine National Council in Amman.[10]

Although the PLO's hard-line groups were united in their condemnation of the accord and their resolve to foil it, they differed on the means to achieve this objective. For example, the Democratic Front, supported by the Palestine Communist party and the Palestine Liberation Front, believed that the abrogation of the accord could best be achieved by the various PLO factions, nationalist forces, institutions, and personalities applying pressure upon Fatah's Central Committee. The Democratic Front was firmly opposed to the formation of a national front on the grounds that such a political coalition would contribute further to the polarization and the division of the PLO and would ultimately lead to the formation of an alternate, rival institution.[11] The preservation of Palestinian national unity and the viability, political legitimacy, and cohesion of the PLO, as well as its representation of Palestinian interests, were paramount for the Democratic Front.

By contrast, the Popular Front and the members of the National Alliance made demands beyond the abrogation of the Arafat-Hussein accord, requesting the removal of the Arafat leadership and an end to his policies. To achieve such objectives they advocated the formation of a national front comprising all those PLO factions, Palestinian nationalist forces, and political personalities that opposed Arafat's leadership and policies. They wanted to entrust this front with the task of putting the PLO on "a progressive national course."[12] Habash appealed to Fatah leaders and rank and file to reject the accord, resume their military operations against Israel, and work jointly with the PLO's hardline groups to redress the regional balance of power in favor of "the Palestinian revolution."[13] Likewise, Abu Musa wanted the national front to guide the policies of the Palestinian nationalist movement in the coming phase and to safeguard the "nationalist course of the revolution" from deviationism.[14]

The call by these factions for the formation of a national front was not a novel idea; demands of this sort were made shortly after Arafat's visit to Cairo in December 1983. Until March 1985, none of these attempts succeeded in bringing a coalition of this sort into existence. The inability of the rejectionist groups to enlist majority support of the Palestinian political forces for such a coalition, particularly from among the members of the Palestine National Council and West Bank politicians, prompted them to form it from the members of the National Alliance and the Popular Front. It was named the Palestinian National Salvation Front.

This front could have hardly claimed any political credibility or legitimacy in Arab or international circles compared to the widely recognized PLO. Moreover, the reluctance of the Democratic Front to join the coalition discouraged Habash's Popular Front from aggressively pursuing this course. Finally, the sincerity and seriousness of Habash's efforts in forming such a front could be seen as questionable, and it can be argued that Popular Front interest in the idea came mainly as a response to Syrian pressures. Such a front would probably lead to an organization that would serve as an alternative and rival to the PLO, formalizing the split within the Palestinian nationalist movement. Habash's previous hesitation to set up such a front resulted from his reluctance to align the PFLP with a very small extremist minority within the Palestinian nationalist movement. Should Habash continue to commit his organization to this new political alignment, much substance would be given to charges that the Popular Front is under the yoke of Syrian control and domination.

The lack of a positive response by the United States and Israel to the Jordanian-Palestinian diplomatic initiative increases the chances for the PLO's radical groups to bring down the accord and compel Arafat to retreat from his pro-Jordan policy. Other effective devices to derail the Jordanian-Palestinian initiative might be a sustained and coordinated campaign by the extremist groups, intimidation, and the elimination of leading Jordanian and PLO officials. (Only one month after the convening of the PNC in Amman, some Palestinian extremists assassinated Fahd Qawasmi, the deported mayor of Hebron and a newly elected member to the PLO's Executive Committee.) Though such acts of violence may not necessarily deter Jordan or the PLO from pursuing their joint diplomatic initiative, nevertheless they would constantly haunt the thoughts of both Hussein and Arafat. Another factor strengthening the hard-line stance against the advocates of diplomacy is the recent success of the Lebanese resistance movement against Israeli troops in southern Lebanon. In such a setting, one may wonder how long Arafat can sustain his diplomatic venture in the absence of any tangible political gains. Israel's air raid upon the PLO's headquarters in Tunis on October 1, 1985, can only serve to reinforce the political posture of the hard-line groups against the PLO moderates.

The responses from the Arab world to the Arafat-Hussein accord mirrored the Palestinian responses. The reaction of the moderate Arab countries (with the exception of Egypt) was subdued and low-keyed. In contrast the radical Arab countries openly attacked the accords and pledged to void them.

Both Hussein and Arafat are keen on crystallizing a united Arab stand to enhance their bargaining power vis-à-vis the United States and Israel and to increase the political credibility of their initiative. Since the termination of the seventeenth session of the PNC in late November 1984, both men tried to enlist the support of two-thirds of the Arab countries, the quorum needed to convene an Arab summit conference. Their attempts to introduce the principle of majority rule to govern the Arab League proceedings came to an inconclusive ending when the emergency Arab summit conference, which convened in Morocco in early August 1985, refused to endorse the Arafat-Hussein agreement. The Arab rulers present at the conference chose to give deference to the wishes of Syria, Libya, Algeria, and South Yemen, who boycotted the session. The bitter division among Arab countries, mutual hostilities, rivalries over the Iran-Iraq War, the Lebanon crisis, the Syrian military presence in Lebanon, the return of Egypt to the Arab League, the divisions within the PLO, and the differences over the ways and means to bring about a settlement were the reasons behind the inconclusive results of the emergency conference. Even if a regular Arab summit were convened, it is not certain that it would lead to the emergence of a unified Arab position and the adoption of a common strategy allowing Jordan and the PLO to commence negotiations with Israel. Without the support of the majority of Arab countries, Jordan and the PLO can not deal with Israel because of their concern not to replicate the Egyptian experience of concluding a separate peace with the Jewish state, particularly in view of the high risk of failure of any negotiations. In addition, the Palestinian question has been an Arab issue for a long time. The residue of pan-Arabism would serve as a deterrent to any unilateral political moves by Jordan and the PLO.

Saudi Arabia, the host of the thirteenth Arab summit conference (the next regular conference), has not yet been anxious to assemble hastily the politically divided Arab kings and presidents. To ensure the success of the summit, the Saudi Arabians have argued that Arab differences should be resolved in advance. Aside from this official explanation, the Saudi Arabian reluctance to convene a summit perhaps results from the country's displeasure over Arafat's trip to Cairo and the restoration of full diplomatic relations between Egypt and Jordan. King Fahd believes that the return of Egypt to the Arab world should come about as a result of a collective Arab decision, since the severing of relations with Egypt was authorized by the 1978 Arab summit conference in Baghdad. One may also wonder whether the Saudi Arabians are anxious to bring Egypt back to the Arab world, in any case, as Egypt's demographic and political weight will certainly threaten the position of leadership and supremacy that the Saudi Arabian royal family has occupied since the mid-1970s by virtue of its oil wealth.

In line with its attitude toward the first round of talks between Arafat and Hussein, Saudi Arabia is likely to continue to be attentive to the Syrian viewpoint and accordingly would not openly and enthusiastically support the Jordanian-Palestinian agreement. Syria's regional and military preponderance and its close connection with Iran lie behind Saudi Arabia's leaning toward Damascus. Saudi Arabia hopes that Assad will use his special relationship and influence to convince the Khomeini regime not to advance the Islamic revolutionary thrust into the Gulf region and to accept a cease-fire with Iraq.

The reluctance and/or inability of Saudi Arabia to extend effective political support to the Arafat-Hussein agreement for joint action is not confined only to considerations of inter-Arab politics. It is unlikely that Saudi Arabia and the other Gulf states will use their economic leverage and military cooperation with the West as inducements or threats to enlist support for the Jordanian-Palestinian political accord. Indeed, the ability of these states to influence Western Europe and the United States is not what it was a decade ago partly because of the drop in the oil price and the surplus in oil production and partly because of diminished Western dependence upon Gulf oil. Moreover, the limits to Saudi Arabian diplomacy in changing the behavior of the other Arab countries is being increasingly recognized in the West. In addition, these countries need Western protection and military assistance to arrest the threat of communism and Islamic fundamentalism and to guard against Soviet and Iranian encroachment in the Gulf region. The combination of these factors has reduced the political influence and bargaining power of Saudi Arabia and its partners in the Gulf region.

The reluctance of the moderate Arab countries to rally sufficient political backing for the Arafat-Hussein political accord was the result of the opposition of Syria and Libya and, to a lesser degree, South Yemen. These three countries denounced the Jordanian-Palestinian joint accord as a serious impediment in the path of Arab and Palestinian reconciliation. It is not an overstatement to say that without the neutralization of Syria's opposition, the current diplomatic efforts do not stand much chance of success. The Syrian government regarded the conclusion of the agreement for joint action as a political alliance directed against Damascus.[15] The government-controlled press repeatedly warned that the fate of the Jordanian-Palestinian accord would be similar to that of the Israeli-Lebanese agreement of May 17, 1983. Commenting on this issue *Tishrin,* a Syrian government newspaper, pointed out that "this lesson must be fully understood by Arafat who concluded an agreement with King Hussein and fabricated a battle with Syria to save his own skin; that Syria will not let him sell Palestine to Hussein and Perez."[16] *Tishrin* also spoke of the beginning of a new Arab era in which the Assad regime would play a pivotal role in defeating policies of the reactionary Arab regimes, Israel, and the United States.[17]

The convening of the PNC in Amman and Arafat's insistence upon the preservation of the autonomy of his organization and its freedom of maneuver contradicted Damascus's perception of itself as the principal Arab capital qualified to defend the Palestinian cause. In an address to the eighth regional congress of the Ba'ath party, President Assad inquired,

> How does Syria stand in the face of an independent Palestinian decision? Do they want to say that the Palestinian cause is their own preserve and is not our own concern as well? They know the dangers that lie behind such an eventuality. How can the Palestinian question not be of concern to us, particularly as we have mobilized all of the human, economic, political capabilities and resources of this country to defend such a cause? We have been in a state of war for several years for the sake of the Palestinian cause. We have sacrificed so many martyrs and they say that the cause is their own! Those who speak about the independence and the autonomy of the Palestinian decision simply want a liquidationist solution to the Palestinian question and want to empty it from its Arab content.[18]

At this point in time it seems that the Assad regime's hostility to Arafat is irreversible, although one must wait to see if Syria can promote its protégés within the PLO to be the sole legitimate representatives of the

Palestinian people. For the time being, the Syrian government no longer considers Arafat and his associates as spokesmen for the PLO. Assad commented that "we are confident that those 'high bidders' and defeatists cannot represent the Palestinian people and cannot be representatives of the Palestinian cause."[19]

The Syrian government's opposition is not only confined to Arafat's leadership; it is directed equally against the emerging Arab axis of Egypt, Jordan, the PLO, and Iraq. So far Syria has succeeded in blocking the convening of an Arab summit conference that might serve the interests of Iraq against Iran or endorse the Arafat-Hussein joint diplomatic accord or accept the readmission of Egypt to the Arab League. In his speech to the Ba'ath party, the Syrian leader asserted, "Syria will not deal with the agents of imperialism or with Egypt of Camp David. Syria supports Arab consensus and solidarity but on the basis of anti-imperialism and anti-Zionism. Syria supports an Arab consensus which reinforces Arab steadfastness, but will not work for an Arab solidarity that reinforces surrender."[20] Finally, the Syrian government appears to be fearful that Hussein and Arafat may reach an agreement with the United States and Israel to recover the West Bank and the Gaza Strip, leaving Damascus alone in its quest to recover the Golan Heights.

Notwithstanding Syria's present hostility toward Jordan and the PLO, the Syrian objections to the Arafat-Hussein diplomatic approach are not so much doctrinal as a divergence in tactics. Damascus is not opposed to a political settlement of the Arab-Israeli dispute. President Assad, however, is convinced that without building up Arab military might and attaining military parity with Israel, the expansionist drive of the Israeli government will continue unabated. The Syrian government also believes that Arab political concessions, such as the Arafat-Hussein agreement, will only lead to furthering Israel's intransigence and will in no way contribute to the resolution of the Palestinian problem.[21]

For these reasons, Assad believes the negotiations with the Israeli government from the position of military weakness and political disunity will not lead to the recovery of the occupied territories. According to the Syrians the attainment of military parity cannot be expected to take place overnight; the struggle with Israel will be a long one. Thus, Assad's willingness to prolong the Palestinian problem and the Arab-Israeli dispute varies sharply with the views of Hussein and Arafat, who favor reaching a political settlement with Israel as quickly as possible. Syria's recent political successes in Lebanon, including the abrogation of the Israeli-Lebanese troop withdrawal agreement, the U.S. and French troop withdrawal from Beirut in early 1984, and Israel's decision to unilaterally withdraw its troops from southern Lebanon, served only to reinforce the conviction of Syrian policymakers of the correctness of their strategy.

Will Arafat and his colleagues, and perhaps Jordan and Egypt, be convinced of the logic and the pragmatism of the Syrian position, particularly in view of the inconclusiveness of their own diplomatic efforts, or will they try to co-opt the Syrian government into their initiative?

The Syrian president wants the prestige, the military preponderance, and the pan-Arabist role of his country to be fully acknowledged by the Arabs and particularly by the Reagan administration. No doubt Egypt, Jordan, and the PLO are aware of the need to involve Syria in the search for a political settlement of the Palestinian question and the Arab-Israeli dispute. During King Hussein's visit to Cairo in early December 1984, Usama al-Baz, the political advisor to the Egyptian president, pointed out that Syria's interest in recovering the Golan Heights, its pan-Arabist ideology, and its military power should be acknowledged in any political settlement.[22] Will the Syrian government agree to go along with its current adversaries and support the Arafat-Hussein joint accord, or will Syria wait for these moderate Arab countries to come back to it on Syrian terms? In view of Hussein's growing disillusionment with the Reagan administration's reluctance to engage itself actively in the peace process, it seems that the Jordanian monarch has already chosen to move in the direction of full reconciliation with Syria. Under the auspices of Saudi Arabia, a joint Jordanian-Syrian delegation met in the middle of September 1985 for the purpose of improving relations between the two countries.

In any case, the Syrian objection may be mitigated if special attention is given by the United States to Syria's national grievances. In view of recent Soviet advances in the Middle East, including the restoration of full diplomatic relations between Cairo and Moscow and Soviet military sales to both Jordan and Kuwait, the Soviet leaders may possibly attempt to attenuate the position of President Assad toward the Hussein-Arafat agreement, particularly if those leaders continue to insist upon convening an international peace conference with Soviet participation. However, the Soviet capacity to influence the behavior of the Syrian president is limited, and the Soviets are concerned not to strain their relationship with Damascus—their main strategic ally in the Middle East.

With the continuing hostility of Syria and the failure to convene a summit, Arafat and Hussein have concentrated on enlisting the support of the majority of individual Arab states to the agreement. Immediately after signing the joint diplomatic accord, King Hussein went to Algeria to obtain the endorsement of President Ben Jadid. A few weeks later, Arafat followed Hussein's footsteps by visiting the Algerian capital. Algerian support was particularly important for the success of the joint initiative because of Algeria's close ties to Syria and the PLO's hard-line groups. As noted in the preceding chapter, the Algerian government exerted endless efforts to reconcile the various Palestinian factions and the PLO with Syria. Should the Algerians adopt the plan, Arafat and Hussein hope that Ben Jadid will then try to convince Syria and various Palestinian leftist groups of the merits of the agreement and to soften their hostility toward it. Because Algeria is a radical Arab country, its endorsement would also signal the rest of the Arab world to follow suit. In the wake of President Ben Jadid's visit to Washington in April 1985, an early Algerian endorsement of the agreement would reinforce Saudi Arabian and Egyptian requests that the Reagan administration reactivate its search for a political settlement to the Arab-Israeli conflict. On February 13, 1985, the second day of King Hussein's visit to Algeria, the government-controlled newspaper *al-Mujahed* pointed out that Algeria would not accept or reject the Arafat-Hussein agreement but rather would study it carefully. This approach conformed to the traditional Algerian policy that a united Palestinian and Arab position was indispensable for the success of any political initiative.

As Palestinian and Arab cooperation, or the lack of it, will determine the success of the Hussein-Arafat joint diplomatic initiative, the policy that the Reagan administration ultimately endorses will also have considerable impact on its destiny. Despite repeated appeals by Saudi Arabia, Egypt, and Jordan, to the Reagan administration to make use of the Arafat and Hussein agreement, the United States has remained disinclined to engage itself actively in the search for a political settlement. Following the failure of its diplomacy in Lebanon and the death of hundreds of U.S. marines and several U.S. diplomats in Beirut, the U.S. government is not treating the Arab-Israeli dispute with a sense of urgency or immediacy.

The United States is not keen to search actively for a political settlement until the directly concerned actors define their positions and express their readiness to begin direct negotiations. U.S. policymakers believe that a final political settlement will only evolve as a result of direct negotiations between Israel and its Arab neighbors, the Arab recognition of Israel's right to exist, and the renunciation of the use of violence. The Reagan administration is firm in its opposition to the convening of an international peace conference. Both Jordan and the PLO have insisted that talks with Israel should take place under an international umbrella. Despite the formation of a joint Jordanian-Palestinian delegation, the U.S. government has so far declined to meet such a delegation, as it insists that such a meeting should be followed by direct negotiations between the Israelis and the Arabs. The Reagan administration is opposed to the inclusion of the PLO in any political settlement until the latter explicitly recognizes Israel's right to exist, accepts UN Security Council Resolution 242, and abandons the use of violence. In conformity with the Israeli position, the Reagan administration rejected King Hussein's offer to convene a UN-sponsored peace conference to resolve the Palestinian problem and the Arab-Israeli dispute on the basis of UN Security Council Resolution 242.

Indeed, the Reagan administration's Middle Eastern policy was to reject any political initiative not acceptable to the Israelis. This attitude has made the Reagan administration the most pro-Israeli of all U.S. governments since the creation of Israel in 1948. Such an extremely pro-Israel U.S. posture will certainly diminish the incentive of any Israeli government to display diplomatic flexibility over the future of the occupied territories. It will also reduce U.S. political credibility, bargaining power, moral imperative, and ability to mediate effectively. Should the United States decide to reactivate its search for a diplomatic settlement of the Arab-Israeli dispute and the Palestinian question, it remains doubtful that the Reagan administration would use its leverage to compel Israel to make the necessary territorial concessions. With the exception of the firm stand taken by the Dwight D. Eisenhower administration in 1956—demanding that Israel withdraw its troops from Sinai in the wake of the Suez invasion—recent U.S. administrations have abstained from seriously employing the influence resulting from their economic and military assistance to Israel. The few times in which U.S. foreign aid was manipulated to bring about a change in Israeli political behavior were cosmetic and very limited in duration.

Despite these pessimistic remarks, a flicker of hope can be traced to U.S. acceptance of negotiations with a joint Palestinian-Jordanian delegation and the opening of informal talks on the Middle East with the Soviet Union in February 1985. Such moves can be considered positive steps, particularly if they are followed by further dialogue.

However, the United States and Israel continue to oppose the convening of a UN-sponsored peace conference in which the Soviet Union and the PLO could participate. Moreover, the asymmetry in the attitudes of the superpowers toward the Arab-Israeli dispute makes it doubtful that if talks on the Middle East were resumed they would have better chances of success than the discussions in 1968–1969 and October 1977. Moscow and Washington maintain divergent views on how to resolve the Palestinian question. The Soviet Union favors the creation of an independent Palestinian state in the West Bank and the Gaza Strip and the participation of the PLO in any political settlement as well as the convening of an international peace conference; the United States, in contrast, wants Jordan to speak in the name of the Palestinians, to exclude the PLO from any political settlement, and to restore Jordanian sovereignty over the occupied territories.

These differences in their political positions are not irreconcilable, particularly if the United States alters its exclusivist approach toward peace-making in the Middle East. The Soviet Union would like to be involved in the peace process as an equal partner with the United States. To ensure its participation, the new Soviet leadership may be prepared to make some trade-offs to neutralize the Israeli opposition, including the relaxation of immigration rules for Soviet Jewry and possibly the resumption of diplomatic relations with Israel. Over the years, Moscow has not been opposed to a political settlement of the Arab-Israeli dispute and has consistently called for the convening of an international peace conference to bring about a lasting settlement to the conflict. Should the United States, however, decide to reactivate its Middle Eastern policy of being the sole performer in the resolution of the Arab-Israeli dispute, the Soviet Union will try hard to obstruct any political settlement that does not take into account its prestige as a superpower.

Because of their increasing disillusionment with the U.S. position, Egypt, Jordan, and the PLO have directed their attention to Western Europe, trying to engage the Europeans in the peace process and cultivating their sympathies for the convening of an international peace conference. They hope that members of the European Economic Community (EEC) will use their persuasive power to convince the United States of the merits of the Arafat-Hussein political agreement. These efforts were highlighted by the visits of President Mubarak in March 1985 to France, Britain, and Germany, and those of several senior Jordanian officials to numerous European capitals. The ability of Western Europe to alter the behavior of the United States and that of the local participants in the Arab-Israeli dispute is very limited. The EEC countries neither collectively nor individually possess sufficient leverage with both sides of the Arab-Israeli conflict. In addition, U.S. and Soviet regional military preponderance excludes them from any effective role in the peace-making process.

Despite the far-reaching implications of the Jordanian-PLO agreement for a permanent settlement of the Arab-Israeli dispute, the accord was dismissed by Israel's two main parties as insignificant. The leaders of the Labor party criticized the agreement for its failure to recognize Israel's right to exist and even to mention Israel by name. According to Abba Eban, Israel's former minister of foreign affairs, the Arafat-Hussein agreement hardly went beyond the typical articulation of Arab demands for a political settlement. The agreement did not advocate direct negotiations with the Jewish state but rather suggested the convening of an international peace conference as a forum for conducting negotiations. Abba Eban concluded that both the United States and Israel oppose the convening of such a conference.[23]

Although the Labor party did not think that the agreement went too far, its main partner in the national unity government, the Likud, categorically rejected the Jordanian-Palestinian political accord and dismissed as totally insincere Arab moves to find a political settlement to the Palestinian question. Yitzhak Shamir, the leader of the Likud, told an Israeli radio correspondent, "We must admit that this agreement does not offer any important contribution to the prospects of peace in the area. The three main elements of this agreement, the establishment of the Palestinian Arab state, the participation of the PLO in the negotiations, and the international conference about peace in the Middle East with the participation of Soviet Russia, these three elements will not be accepted by us."[24] Earlier he was very skeptical about Arab intentions, arguing that moderate Arab countries began to talk about political settlement only after their failure to defeat Israel on the battlefield. Shamir inquired: "They asked us to give what we have, what we hold. What do the Arabs have to give? Demands to annihilate Israel? Why should peace come about by Israel making serious and dangerous compromises."[25]

Despite the increasing signs of the PLO's political moderation and its acceptance of a political solution to the Palestinian question, Israel remains absolutely opposed to the participation of the PLO in any political settlement. The majority of Israel's body politic categorically rejects inclusion of the PLO in any talks and does not view Arafat's moderation as genuine. They are convinced that Arafat and his followers are bent upon the destruction of the Jewish state. Israel's uncompromising attitude toward the PLO was formalized in the coalition agreement that led to the formation of the national unity government. This agreement prohibited the cabinet from negotiating with the PLO under any circumstances. The Likud, in particular, considered the rapprochement between King Hussein and Arafat and the convening of the seventeenth session of the Palestine National Council in Amman as negative developments, posing direct threats to Israel's national security. Leading Likud figures argued that Arafat's real intention in the dialogue was to reestablish the PLO's military bases in Jordan in order to resume military operations against Israel.[26]

In addition to its vehement opposition to the PLO, the Israeli government is categorical in its refusal to grant the Palestinians their right to self-determination. Whereas the Labor party continues to talk about its readiness to initiate direct negotiations with Jordan on the basis of territorial compromise, the Likud remains firm in its stance never to relinquish the West Bank and the Gaza Strip. It remains to be seen if the leaders of the Labor party are serious about making territorial compromises in favor of Jordan. Or are they just engaged in a public-relations campaign to improve Israel's image abroad and advance the popularity of the party at home? When the Labor party was in power before 1977, it failed to respond positively to King Hussein's peace moves, particularly the 1972 proposal to federate the occupied territories with Jordan, or to his suggestion to disengage the Jordanian and the Israeli troops in the wake of the 1973 October War.

Even if the Labor party was serious about reaching a political accommodation with the Jordanians and the Palestinians, it is uncertain whether the Israeli prime minister could mobilize majority support within his cabinet and the Israeli Knesset behind an agreement with Jordan that would require substantial territorial compromises. The present distribution of power in the Israeli Knesset, manifested in the political weakness of the Labor party, Israel's leftist parties, and peace groups, does not facilitate or encourage the launching of peace talks based upon territorial compromises. Should Shimon Perez declare his intention to engage in such talks, the Likud would almost certainly withdraw from the coalition, bringing down the national unity government. The Likud joined the government with the understanding that no territorial compromises would be made on the West Bank and the Gaza Strip. Since his assumption of power, Prime Minister Perez has been very careful to avoid any crisis that might lead to the collapse of his government. Perez and his colleagues within the Labor party would like to prolong their stay in power and to broaden the party's political base within Israeli society. For this reason, Perez may continue to avoid any policy that would jeopardize the coalition government.

In addition to these considerations, the overriding priority for Israel's coalition government is the country's ailing economy. Israel's policy in the occupied territories is hardly conducive to fostering confidence among the Palestinians or to reaching accommodation with Jordan and the PLO. Despite the optimism evident after the appointment of a Labor minister to the Ministry of Defense, which is in charge of the occupied territories, the Labor-led military practices and policies in the occupied territories did not noticeably depart from those of the preceding Likud administration. For instance, despite Israel's severe economic hardships, the government authorized the construction of six additional settlements in the West Bank in January 1985. Moreover, the Israeli military authority's repressive measures against the population have not been relaxed. No attempt was made by the new Israeli defense minister to reinstate the democratically elected mayors removed from office by the Likud government in 1982 and replaced by Israeli military officers. Nor did the Israeli government allow those members of the Palestine

National Council residing in the occupied territories to attend the seventeenth session of the PNC in Amman—a step that would have added further to the voice of political moderation within the PLO.

Some truth may be found in the argument that increasing signs of Palestinian and Arab moderation, and willingness to recognize Israel's right to exist, may advance the Palestinian cause within Israel and perhaps diminish the political power and influence of Israel's hard-line and rightist parties. The PLO's recognition of Israel may increase the strength of Israel's peace groups and leftist parties to the extent that the support of such parties will be crucial in any government formation. Accordingly, their input to Israel's foreign policy will be more noticeable. The Citizens Rights movement, Israel's Communist party, and the Progressive Party for Peace had all recognized the positive aspects of convening the Palestine National Council in Amman and the signing of the joint agreement for action between the PLO and Jordan. They asked their government to acknowledge such positive changes and demanded that the government should not forgo these opportunities to settle the Arab-Israeli dispute.

Although the Arafat-Hussein political accord represented a major step toward full recognition of Israel, Arafat's explicit recognition of Israel's right to exist, open endorsement of UN Security Council Resolution 242, and outright surrender of the PLO's role to represent the Palestinian interests are unlikely to take place at this point. To embark upon such a hazardous course the PLO chief will need some political gains in return or at a minimum some sincere promises that in the long run Israel will recognize the Palestinian right to national self-determination and that it will relinquish control over the West Bank and the Gaza Strip. Such gains would enable Arafat to prove to his opponents that the PLO's short-term concessions will in the long run produce tangible political rewards. Many of Arafat's followers believe that there is no point in making concessions to the Jewish state in view of its unyielding hostility to Palestinian national aspirations and to the PLO in particular. They regard as too naive the belief that the Israeli government will make any concession to promote Palestinian national rights. After vanquishing the PLO from Lebanon and watching the various divisions within the PLO ranks, the Israeli government will avoid any contribution to strengthening the PLO or enhancing its credibility or prestige.

The Future of the PLO

Despite the opportunities made possible by the Hussein-Arafat agreement, the road bringing these initiatives into full political fruition is hazardous and engulfed with formidable obstacles. What will be the impact upon the future of the PLO if such political initiatives completely fail? Can Arafat continue the march that he began with King Hussein in a climate of political uncertainty, U.S. political inaction, and unyielding Israeli hostility to the PLO and to Palestinian nationalism? Or will he retreat from the diplomatic option and resume the military course? Will Arafat attempt a reconciliation with Syria? Would the Syrians accept him? And, if so, under what conditions? What will be the long-term effects of the Lebanon War on the current divisions within the PLO's ranks and on the political ideological orientation and organizational discipline of the Palestinian nationalist movement? Are the current divisions within the PLO irreversible or is there room for political reconciliation? Can the PLO's dispersed forces be regrouped in Lebanon in the wake of the Israeli withdrawal from the south? How will the PLO's relations with the Arab world evolve?

In the remainder of this chapter, an attempt will be made to sketch several possible scenarios for the future of the PLO. The first scenario assumes that the current divisions will continue and that the split between the moderates and the hard-line groups will be formalized and institutionalized. This dichotomy will be nourished and sustained by inter-Arab politics and rivalries. The PLO's political and military weakness will make the Palestinian question an Arab issue again. In contrast, the second scenario assumes that the various PLO groups will reconcile and Palestinian national unity will be restored. The failure of current Arab political initiatives will compel the various factions of the PLO to regroup to ensure their survival. According to this scenario primary attention will again be given to the preservation of Palestinian national unity. The third scenario may take place as a result of increasing disillusionment with both pan-Arabism and Palestinian nationalism and their inability to check Israeli expansionism and to redress Palestinian national grievances. For these reasons the PLO may have to respond to the growing strength of Islamic groups, and the Palestinian nationalist movement may accordingly take on an Islamic political orientation and coloration. The fourth scenario assumes the takeover of the PLO by radical Marxist and Leninist groups. Disillusionment with Arab and Palestinian nationalism could push the PLO in this direction.

Among these four scenarios, the complete domination of the PLO by Marxist-Leninist groups is a very remote possibility. An extremely radical PLO cannot enjoy a high degree of political legitimacy and recognition by the Palestinian people and the Arab world. The anti-communist nature of the Palestinian and the Arab societies, because of the influence of Islam, deprives the Marxist PLO of any widespread political support.

Despite the appeal of Marxism-Leninism to some middle-class Palestinian intellectuals, the prevailing socioeconomic conditions within Palestinian society do not favor communism. Many of the Palestinians live in urban areas, work in the service sector, and are upwardly mobile, with middle-class aspirations and national rather than class political orientation. In addition, a large industrial working class or a radicalized peasantry is absent. The unlikelihood of a Marxist takeover of the PLO may be attested to by the fact that, despite their existence since the late 1960s, the two Marxist organizations—the Popular and Democratic Fronts—have remained marginal within the PLO and Palestinian politics and society. A radicalized PLO is also unlikely to gain Arab diplomatic recognition. The overwhelming majority of the Arab countries will oppose the transformation of the PLO into a Marxist-Leninist organization that might advocate the destabilization of their own regimes and societies.

The outlined scenarios relate to the PLO's future in the intermediate term. None of them envisions that the PLO will disappear from the political scene. For this reason an independent West Bank Palestinian option is ruled out for the period under consideration. Palestinians in the occupied territories will continue to recognize the PLO as their sole legitimate representative and view it as a symbol of Palestinian nationalism. An independent role for the Palestinians in the occupied territories is also ruled out by the fact that since 1967 Israel has worked persistently to prevent the emergence of an all West Bank–Gaza Strip Palestinian leadership.

Similarly, a unilateral Jordanian option supported by the majority of West Bank politicians is unlikely to occur in the immediate future. The Jordanian government will agree to speak on behalf of the Palestinians only if a new Arab accord is mandated that would reverse the 1974 Rabat Resolution. The Arab countries are unlikely to abandon the PLO in favor of Jordan partly because of the traditional significance that the Palestinian question and the PLO have assumed in inter-Arab politics. More important, the continued survival of the PLO will absolve these Arab regimes from assuming direct responsibility for the Palestinian question. Finally, a change in the West Bank political orientation from a pro-PLO to a pro-Jordanian posture is also needed to enable Jordan to assume an independent course of action. None of these conditions is likely to take place in the foreseeable future. Should Arafat disappear from the political scene and should the transfer of power to a new leadership that will command overall respectability and allegiance within the Palestinian community not be smoothly effected and should more splits occur within Fatah, the situation might change and more preeminence might be given to the political attitudes of the Palestinians in the occupied territories and to the Jordanian option.

A Divided PLO

According to the first scenario not only will the current divisions within the PLO endure, but they may become more profound, particularly if the present bitter divisions within the Arab world continue. Should the current diplomatic initiatives meet with some success, the struggle within the PLO will intensify. The formation of the Palestinian National Salvation Front on March 25, 1985, formalized and consolidated the split within the Palestinian nationalist movement, dividing the PLO between the majority of Palestinian moderates and a minority of hardline groups, with a group of independents in between. Within this scenario it is still possible that temporary, tactical alliances may emerge, such as that between Arafat supporters and opponents in defense of the Palestinian refugee camps near Beirut.

The mainstream PLO, led by Arafat and his colleagues within the Fatah Central Committee, will continue its efforts to resolve the Palestinian question through diplomacy and will go on deriving its political support from Egypt, Jordan, and Iraq, while its financial backing will come from Saudi Arabia and the Gulf states. A combination of local and regional factors will continue to reinforce Fatah's efforts toward political coordination with both Egypt and Jordan and in turn deepen the divisions within the PLO. The resolutions of the sixteenth and the seventeenth sessions of the Palestine National Council will provide Arafat and his associates with a green light for continued political coordination with Jordan to recover the occupied territories. Arafat and his Executive Committee recognize that coordination with Jordan and the rest of the moderate Arab countries will bring about certain political advantages; in particular a joint Palestinian-Jordanian approach offers better prospects for the recovery of the occupied territories. Jordan's centrality to any political settlement is recognized by the United States and a considerable portion of Israeli society, including the Labor party; in contrast, neither the United States nor Israel is willing to talk to the PLO. Moreover, Arafat is concerned to reach an agreement quickly with Israel as he fears the return to power of the Likud led by Ariel Sharon.

Arafat's breaking away from the tradition of preserving Palestinian national unity and consensus building among the ideologically diverse PLO factions, with their varying external Arab political allegiances, will also enhance his diplomatic contacts with the moderate Arab states. Because of these contacts the PLO chairman will no longer have to contend with the demands of the PLO hard-line groups or the pressures of Libya and Syria. Second, the PLO's loss of its "state within a state" status in Lebanon will push Arafat and Fatah toward a political settlement and accommodation with Israel. The dispersal of Arafat's troops to the various corners of the Arab world reconfirmed the illusiveness and the irrelevance of the strategy of armed struggle, since after two decades this strategy—like the Arab conventional armies—they failed to liberate Palestine. Third, the pressure upon Arafat and Fatah to follow a moderate line will continue to come from the Palestinians living in the West Bank and the Gaza Strip. Those Palestinians are most concerned to end the Israeli military occupation of their territories as soon as possible.

In contrast, the pro-Syrian National Salvation Front will continue to undermine Arafat's diplomatic maneuvering and stress instead the inevitability of armed struggle to free the occupied territories from Israel's military control. The engagement in military action is extremely significant in the process of depicting the hard-line groups as "the true fighters and revolutionaries." The resort to armed struggle over the years has been the main yardstick for gaining political legitimacy within the Palestinian community. The survival of the Palestinian National Salvation Front will depend upon support from Syria and some backing from the leftist circles of Palestinian society. However, its economic, political, and military dependence upon Syria will severely curtail its freedom of maneuver and action and its political credibility and legitimacy.

One overriding goal for the National Salvation Front in the coming period is to topple Arafat's leadership and end his "deviationist policies." This goal includes the cancellation of the Jordanian-Palestinian agreement for joint action. The members of the National Salvation Front will try to use every opportunity to present themselves as genuine alternative leadership for the Palestinian people who would assure the pursuit of a "progressive and revolutionary course of action." These groups will also demand to democratize the PLO and to introduce a system of collective leadership and checks and balances to the PLO's political councils. Under Syrian tutelage further coordination between these hard-line groups and Lebanese Moslem groups can be expected.

To force the PLO to retract its pro-Western political orientation and to dissociate itself from both Jordan and Egypt, the members of the National Alliance will probably continue their policy of intimidation against leading Palestinian and Arab moderates. The formation of a joint command for Fatah dissidents and the Abu Nidal group would enhance their capacity to carry out intimidation tactics against the PLO's leaders.[27] If any progress toward resolving the Palestinian question takes place through the association of the occupied territories with Jordan, members of the National Alliance probably will step up their attacks upon PLO and Jordanian officials. They may also engage in what is termed "revolutionary violence and terror," including bombing civilian targets, sabotage activities, and taking hostages. The aims of such activities will not be to liberate the occupied territories but rather to gain international visibility and recognition, boost the morale of their followers, intimidate and discredit their adversaries, cause confusion in enemy ranks, and force the PLO to retract from a "liquidationist policy." Obvious targets for such a policy would be Palestinian and Arab moderates as well as Western and Israeli interests. One cannot exclude the possibility that this group will align itself with the existing fundamentalist groups in the region who share the PLO hard-line groups' anti-Western, anti-Israeli attitude and oppose Arab and Palestinian moderation.

Somewhere between the moderates and the radicals, the Democratic Front, the Palestine Communist party, the Palestine Liberation Front, and, from time to time, the Popular Front (the four groups that constituted the Democratic Alliance) will continue to occupy an independent middle position. As noted the Democratic Front and the Palestine Communist party refused to join the Palestinian National Salvation Front on the grounds that such a political coalition would intensify the polarization within the PLO and deepen the split within its ranks. Democratic Alliance members remain committed to the preservation of the PLO's unity and viability. They were also opposed to the signing of the Arafat-Hussein political accord for joint action and continued to demand the convening of a new Palestine National Council.

One of the areas of competition between the PLO's moderates and radicals will be control over the Palestinian refugee camps in Lebanon where Arafat enjoys majority support. Leading Fatah officials warned that the members of the National Alliance are planning to fight Arafat's followers in the camps.[28] In response Abu Musa denied these charges and argued that Arafat had no military troops in Lebanon. At any rate should fighting break out between these groups it probably would not be of the same intensity and magnitude as the battles that took place in northern Lebanon in late fall 1983 because the bulk of Arafat's troops were compelled to leave Lebanon in August 1982 and December 1983.

In the wake of Israel's decision to withdraw its army from southern Lebanon, Arafat may try to regroup his dispersed forces there. Their return may also be dictated by continuing attacks against the Palestinian refugee camps by the Lebanese Christian militia and the Shi'ite Amal. In the last quarter of 1984, reports spoke of the return of several hundred PLO members to the refugee camps in Beirut. In his efforts to bring Fatah troops to Lebanon, Arafat is likely to seek the assistance of his traditional ally, the Islamic Unification movement in Tripoli and the Sunni militia in Beirut. Because of the political and military weakness of the Sunni community within the Lebanese political system, its leaders may very well assist Arafat in bringing his troops back into Lebanon, in order to strengthen the community's shaky position. However, the establishment of an elaborate Palestinian military presence in Lebanon, like the one the PLO possessed prior to the outbreak of the war, is unlikely.

Opposition to the regrouping of Fatah's troops in Lebanon will come from several quarters. As long as the present animosity between Arafat and Assad persists and the Syria-Fatah rift remains unbridged, Damascus will vehemently resist the return of any of Arafat's followers to areas in Lebanon under its hegemony. The Shi'a attacks against Palestinians in the camps in May and June 1985 are evidence of this. Likewise, the Israeli government will oppose the return of the PLO troops to Lebanon: Several Israeli government leaders have repeatedly warned that the army will not tolerate the reestablishment of Palestinian military bases in southern Lebanon and will act swiftly to dismantle such bases. A third source of opposition will come from the PLO's hard-line groups. The Lebanese militia groups, including those of the Shi'ite, Druze, and Christian forces, will also resist the return of Fatah's fighters to any area in Lebanon under their jurisdiction. Finally, under pressure from Syria and because of the desire of the central government in Beirut to spread its authority over the entire country, President Amin Gemayal's government will object to the return of the PLO's troops to Lebanon. For these reasons it is difficult to imagine that Arafat will be able to establish a military presence resembling the one that existed prior to summer 1982.

Engagement in military operations against the Jewish state may continue to be a main area of competition between PLO moderates and radicals. Despite their interests in finding a political settlement to the Palestinian question, Arafat and Fatah's Central Committee may feel compelled to step up their strategy of military struggle, particularly in the West Bank and the Gaza Strip, so as not to be outmaneuvered by their rivals. In addition, the momentum generated by the military successes of the resistance in southern Lebanon may induce Arafat and his followers to intensify their military operations in the occupied territories. Although Fatah's engagement in armed struggle when it is seeking a diplomatic settlement to the Palestinian problem and trying to appropriate a role for itself in the peace process may prove to be counterproductive, the continuation of the PLO as a "national liberation organization" is contingent upon the pursuit of the "revolutionary armed struggle." This situation may be significant if a diplomatic settlement is not in the making. Moreover, Arafat and his colleagues within Fatah have never fully abandoned the strategy of military force to back up their political moves.

Fatah and the Palestinian National Salvation Front will also compete to win the sympathy and the backing of the members of the Democratic Alliance, particularly the Democratic Front. The Fatah Central Committee has expressed its desire to resume the dialogue with the Democratic Front on the basis of the Aden-Algiers Agreement.[29] Indeed, the contacts between Fatah and the Democratic Front and the Palestine Communist party have not been interrupted despite the presence of a multitude of differences between them.[30] Fatah leaders acknowledged the right of the Democratic Alliance to criticize the policy that the PLO was pursuing and to express its concern about the future direction of the Palestinian problem.

A complete reconciliation between Fatah and the Democratic Alliance at this point is unlikely. Two obstacles presently stand in the path of full normalization. First, Fatah's Central Committee opposes the convening of a new session of the Palestine National Council. The resolutions of the seventeenth session were after all in line with the political statement of the sixteenth session, which was unanimously endorsed by the various PLO factions and Palestinian national forces at Algiers in February 1983. The Democratic Front, in contrast, feels that a council meeting attended by all PLO factions would help restore Palestinian national unity and preserve the PLO's viability and cohesion. The second sticking point between Fatah and the Democratic Alliance results from the Democratic Front's opposition to the Arafat-Hussein political accord. Nayef Hawatmeh, leader of the Democratic Front, insists that the agreement should be cancelled as it violates Palestinian national rights and aspirations. Fatah leaders, while recognizing the Democratic Alliance's right to criticize the agreement, oppose the abrogation of the agreement particularly since the ambiguity that initially surrounded some provisions has been clarified and amendments to that effect have been introduced.

The political weakness and the military vulnerability of both Fatah and the Palestinian National Salvation Front; the damaging effect of the Lebanon War upon the bargaining power and political influence of the PLO; the dispersal of PLO forces to several Arab countries; and the dismantling of its military infrastructure in southern Lebanon and Beirut—all will increase the reliance of the various PLO groups on their respective Arab patrons and accordingly will diminish their organizational autonomy and freedom of action. The end result of the PLO's vulnerability and increased dependency upon the Arab countries since the exodus from Beirut in 1982 was that it made the Palestinian question an Arab issue again.

The Arabization of the Palestinian problem, if it continues, will end the 1967–1982 phase during which the PLO was invested with the primary responsibility of promoting and defending Palestinian national interests. During this phase the PLO was designated as the sole, legitimate representative of the Palestinian people, and the role of the Arab countries was secondary. They accepted the PLO's political ascendancy and respected its newly acquired political rights and privileges. The re-Arabization process in the post-1982 era will necessitate the transformation of the PLO into a relatively marginal force whereas the pro-Western, moderate Arab countries—Egypt and Jordan as well as radical Syria and Libya—will assume larger roles in promoting the interests of their respective Palestinian protégés. The re-Arabization of the Palestinian problem will not, however, recreate the same pattern that prevailed prior to the 1967 June War. In the pre-1967 era the Arab regimes and their conventional armies were entrusted with liberating Palestine and the Palestinian question was considered the core of Arab nationalism and a major source of legitimacy for Arab kings and presidents. In the post-1982 era, notwithstanding the rhetoric of the radical Arab regimes, diplomacy has replaced the military option as the only viable means to resolve the Palestinian question. Arab interests in resolving the Palestinian question and Arab-Israeli dispute do not revolve around a pan-Arabist obligation to settle the Palestinian question but rather emanate from a desire to find a solution as quickly as possible to be able to focus on other pressing problems.

Significantly, in the re-Arabization of the Palestinian problem the principle of the PLO's exclusive representation of Palestinian interests is no longer invested with the same degree of sanctity and inviolability. The doctrine has been officially subsumed by the principle of shared representation and the recognition that the PLO alone is incapable of producing any political settlement. The re-Arabization of the Palestinian problem has also altered another Palestinian political objective: The concept of an independent Palestinian state in the West Bank and the Gaza Strip has been replaced by the notion of confederating the occupied territories with Jordan. Arafat and his associates are fully aware of the waning of their political influence and bargaining power in the wake of the Lebanon War and the divisions within the organization; for this reason they can be expected to accept less ambitious political objectives during this phase.

Reconciliation Within the PLO

In contrast to the first scenario, which envisages the continuation of the current divisions within the PLO and the increasing Arabization of the Palestinian question, the second scenario assumes that the diverse factions of the PLO will be reconciled, and preservation of Palestinian national unity and separate Palestinian identity will receive primary attention. Political accommodation between Syria and Fatah, on one hand, and between Syria and the moderate Arab countries, on the other, will hold the key for a broader normalization of relations among the PLO's rival groups. In particular, an improvement in the relationship between Jordan and Syria and the coordination of their positions concerning a political settlement of the Palestine question would reconcile the various Palestinian groups. Any opposition to such a reconciliation from within the PLO's hard-line circles would likely be discouraged by Damascus. Although Jordanian and Syrian rapprochement would advance the chances of restoring some of the occupied territories and the restoration of Palestinian national unity, nevertheless the PLO's autonomy and freedom to maneuver would be more restricted as the organization will be more subservient to Jordanian and Syrian interests.

An alternate avenue for reconciliation within the PLO may result from the failure of the current diplomatic efforts: The initiative to reunite the PLO's groups may come from within Fatah itself. Being a shrewd politician and a master of the tactics and the politics of survival, Arafat may choose to resolve his differences with his opponents inside the PLO and in Syria. The continued inconclusiveness of Arafat's diplomatic efforts will most certainly force Fatah toward reconciliation with the PLO's rejectionist front. The disinclination of the United States to search actively for a resolution to the Palestinian question, U.S. refusal to recognize Palestinian national rights and deal directly with the PLO, unyielding Israeli opposition to the PLO and Palestinian national aspirations, the inability of Israel's Labor party to rally majority support in the Knesset for territorial compromise in the West Bank and the Gaza Strip, or the return of the Likud to power—any of these could tip the balance within Fatah's Central Committee in favor of the militants and the advocates of reconciliation with the hard-line groups and Syria. Similarly, the indifference with which the United States and Israel treated the PLO's demonstrable acceptance of political moderation and pragmatism could compel the Fatah leadership to acknowledge the validity of the Syrian position and the PLO's hard-line groups that advocate building up Arab military strength and Arab solidarity to back the Palestinian cause. It should be recalled also that Arafat and his colleagues have never denied the significance of Syrian support to the PLO; they have frequently described the Syrian regime as a "strategic ally for the Palestinian revolution."

The restoration of PLO unity may also result from Arab mediation. Since the outbreak of the mutiny within Fatah in spring 1983, both

South Yemen and Algeria have exerted considerable effort to restore Palestinian national unity and mend the differences between Assad and Arafat. In addition, the moderate Arab countries including Saudi Arabia, the Gulf states, Jordan, and Egypt have a vested interest in the continued political survival of the PLO as well as its organizational cohesion and viability. Arab backing for the PLO's reconciliation would not mean that the organization would become a free and autonomous institution in formulating its policies and recruiting and training Palestinians in host Arab states. Nor would such backing entail granting a haven for the PLO from which to conduct military operations against Israel. As pointed out, the Arab countries are determined not to deploy their military and economic power to resolve the Palestinian problem. By preserving the PLO's viability and unity and reconfirming its status as the sole legitimate representative of the Palestinian people, these Arab countries will ensure that the burden of liberating the occupied territories and of carrying the Palestinian banner will fall upon the PLO and not them. Moreover, by supporting the PLO's organizational viability these countries will be trying to avoid the radicalization of the Palestinians and their transformation into a destabilizing factor in the region.

For these reasons, Arab political, economic, and military assistance to the PLO will continue, PLO membership in Arab political councils will be preserved, and its chairman will continue to be treated as a head of state. The Arab regimes will thus ensure the preservation of the PLO as a status quo power and guarantee its support for the concept of *raison d'état* and the doctrine of noninterference in internal Arab affairs. Finally, the interest of the Arab nations in the political survival and organizational cohesion of the PLO can be considered part of a wider Arab effort to arrive at Arab solidarity and to crystallize a united Arab stance in an attempt to end the political disarray that has characterized the Arab world in the last few years.

The restoration of Palestinian national unity will find strong support among the politicians in the West Bank and the Gaza Strip. Despite their denunciations of Arafat's policies, the members of the Democratic Alliance will not oppose a reconciliation with Fatah, provided Arafat abandons his pro-Jordan policy and stops flirting with the West. The Democratic Alliance members indeed never denied Arafat's political importance to the Palestinian question and his efforts in promoting Palestinian interests on the international scene. Out of concern to preserve the unity of the PLO, the Democratic Front, the Palestine Communist party, and the Palestine Liberation Front did not join the Palestinian National Salvation Front. Even after the convening of the Palestine National Council in Amman and the signing of the Arafat-Hussein political accord, the Democratic Front expressed its interest in resuming dialogue with Fatah's Central Committee. The Popular Front—the most vocal in its opposition to Arafat's policies—hinted that it will reconcile with Fatah's Central Committee provided Arafat retreats from his "deviationist policy."[31] The prospects for reconciliation between Fatah and the National Alliance will be governed by the kind of relationship that develops between Syria and Fatah. Should the Assad regime embrace Arafat, National Alliance obstructionism to Palestinian reconciliation and to the restoration of PLO unity will be muted.

Should the failure of the diplomatic option result in reconciliation among the various PLO factions, it probably would be based upon the principles of the Aden-Algiers Agreement. This would require that the PLO strictly adhere to the various resolutions of the Palestine national councils. Most certainly Arafat's powers and freedom of maneuver and action would be severely curtailed whereas the influence of his main rivals, Habash and Hawatmeh, would be significantly enhanced within the PLO. The Democratic Alliance, together with Fatah hard-line figures, will play a more influential role in the PLO's policymaking process. They will also demand the introduction of a system of collective leadership, checks and balances, and broadening of political participation by the various PLO groups in the decision-making process. Demands will also be placed upon the PLO leadership to slow down its reconciliation with the Mubarak regime (so long as Egypt continues to abide by the Camp David accords), to minimize its diplomatic coordination with Jordan, and to abandon its dealings with the West. The PLO would complete its reversal by consolidating its ties with Syria and reactivating the friendship and cooperation of the socialist camp and countries of the Third World.

The expected increasing influence of the PLO's hard-line groups does not mean that the organization will be taken over by the leftist Marxist factions. As mentioned, a step of this sort would deprive the PLO of its legitimacy, its popularity, and its representative character within Palestinian society. More likely, because of their concern for consensus politics and the preservation of Palestinian national unity, the PLO leaders will cast their policies and political statements with the same ambiguity as in the past. No doubt the political option will be deemphasized, although it will not be abandoned outright.

The strategy of armed struggle will continue to occupy a pivotal position in the PLO's ideology, particularly after a failure of its diplomatic initiative. Demands from within the PLO will mount to step up military operations against Israeli troops in the occupied territories. The success of military resistance in southern Lebanon will certainly recommend itself to the PLO's leaders who will seek similar successes in the West Bank and the Gaza Strip. However, formidable obstacles stand in the way of any attempt to replicate the Lebanese experience in the West Bank and the Gaza Strip. These obstacles stem from the dissimilarities between the West Bank and southern Lebanon. First, the West Bank and the Gaza Strip lack the difficult terrain and topography of southern Lebanon, which provided the commando groups with an appropriate environment for their guerrilla warfare. Second, the storage of large numbers of arms over the years in southern Lebanon enabled the commando groups to engage in sustained guerrilla warfare against the Israeli army; the unavailability of weapons in the West Bank and the Gaza Strip constitutes the foremost problem inhibiting a successful guerrilla movement. Israel's tight military control over the occupied territories since 1967 and the policy adopted by Jordan, Syria, and Egypt of not permitting the flow of arms or the infiltration of commando groups into the occupied territories compound the problem. Also noteworthy is that government policy during Jordan's rule over the West Bank between 1950 and 1967 did not allow the free circulation of arms, their storage, or the military training of Palestinians. Third, unlike southern Lebanon, the West Bank and the Gaza Strip lack a tradition of guerrilla warfare as well as the presence of commando groups, military bases, and civilian cadres cooperating with the resistance. Moreover, the fighters in southern Lebanon are highly organized and have a long tradition of engaging in paramilitary activities. None of these conditions exists in the West Bank and the Gaza Strip: The PLO failed to create an underground network to resist Israel's military occupation.

These limitations do not mean that military operations by the PLO cannot take place in the West Bank and the Gaza Strip or be intensified. Nevertheless, they cannot reach the intensity, magnitude, and scope of the military operations in southern Lebanon. Attempts also will be made by the PLO to launch its military operations from contiguous Arab countries. However, Israel's Arab neighbors, including Jordan and Syria, will continue to observe their past policy of not allowing any Palestinian military infiltration from their territories into Israel for fear of Israeli retaliatory and punitive strikes. Any Palestinian military operation from Egyptian territory is also ruled out for the time being because of the Israeli-Egyptian peace treaty. Finally, although southern Lebanon may provide an arena for the waging of military operations, the determination of the Israeli government not to allow the rebuilding of any PLO military infrastructure in the south and the opposition by the various Lebanese militias and of the central government to the return of the Palestinian military presence in Lebanon will make the launching of military attacks from Lebanese territory an exceedingly difficult task.

An Islamic PLO

The third scenario assumes that Islam may in the future compete more effectively with pan-Arabism, Palestinian nationalism, and the leftist ideologies of Marxism and Leninism as the rallying point for the Palestinian people. Though a complete Islamic takeover of the PLO remains only a remote possibility, the continuation of current divisions within the PLO and Arab political fragmentation may provide fertile ground for the flourishing of an Islamic movement. From an Islamic perspective attempts by the advocates of these three ideologies over the years to check Israeli expansionism and to undo the injustice inflicted upon the Palestinians have failed. According to the proponents of Islamic revivalism, the incompetence and the unsuitability of such ideologies in terms of guidance, leadership, and inspiration for the Palestinian people make it mandatory to return to Islam, which alone, in their view, is capable of providing answers to the Palestinian question. Indeed, the increasing frustration of the Palestinians with such ideologies, as with Western or Soviet-sponsored political settlement plans, is behind the Islamic resurgence within the Palestinian community, particularly in the West Bank and the Gaza Strip. This increasing disillusionment may allow in the future substantial political gains by the Islamic movement within Palestinian society, perhaps eventually culminating in control of the PLO.

A brief survey of the poor performance of both Arab and Palestinian nationalism in addressing Palestinian national grievances is enlightening in explaining why Islam may attract an ever-widening segment of Palestinian society. Pan-Arabism at both the military and the diplomatic levels has failed to secure Palestinian national rights. As early as 1948 the dispatch of the Arab salvation armies to Palestine did not succeed in preventing the advent of the state of Israel. Twenty years later the conventional Arab armies of Syria, Egypt, and Jordan, which were entrusted with the task of liberating Palestine, were not only defeated in the 1967 June War but lost considerable territory to Israel. The 1973 October War was not intended to free the West Bank and the Gaza Strip but to address the Egyptian and Syrian grievances and to compel the reluctant United States and Western Europe to find a settlement to the Arab-Israeli conflict. At any rate, the military outcome of the war, in final analysis, was inconclusive, once again highlighting the ineffectiveness of the pan-Arabist military approach.

The record of Arab nationalism at the diplomatic political level is equally unimpressive. Though following the 1973 October War the Arab regimes promised the PLO leaders a share in the political settlement if they would give up military force as an instrument to realize Palestinian national rights and urged them to lower their political expectations by accepting an independent Palestinian state in the West Bank and the Gaza Strip, the Palestinians after more than a decade are no closer to achieving their political goals than they were in 1973.

Not only did pan-Arabism fail to liberate Palestine, but leading pan-Arabist regimes dealt the PLO its heaviest blows. In 1976 Syria intervened in the Lebanese civil war on behalf of the Christian rightist forces against the PLO and its leftist Lebanese allies. Two years later Egypt, the other leading pan-Arabist state, concluded a separate agreement with Israel leaving out the Palestinians altogether. The signing of the second part of the Camp David accords for Palestinian self-autonomy was little more than window dressing to legitimize the implementation of the first part of the Camp David accords, which called for the return of Sinai to Egyptian sovereignty. In summer 1982 another sign of the incompetence and failure of pan-Arabism became evident. For three months Israel was pounding an Arab capital and the PLO was subjected to an all-out war; neither radical nor moderate allies among the Arab countries came to the aid of the embattled Palestinians and Lebanese. The collapse of pan-Arabism was further signalled in summer and fall 1983 when, with Syrian encouragement and complicity, a mutiny took place inside Fatah and the remainder of Arafat's troops were expelled from northern Lebanon.

Though the achievements in the narrower cause of Palestinian nationalism are more impressive than those of pan-Arabism, nevertheless after two decades the PLO has not succeeded in securing Palestinian national rights. No doubt the PLO has reawakened Palestinian national consciousness, fostered a separate Palestinian national identity, and directed the world's attention to the Palestinian problem. The pursuit by the PLO's commanding groups of the strategy of armed struggle, following the Arab defeat in the 1967 June War, also gave preeminence to the PLO and advanced the hope that if Arab conventional armies failed to liberate Palestine, the PLO would be able to carry on.

The PLO, like its Arab predecessors, has been unable to free the occupied territories from Israeli military control. The PLO's ability to engage effectively in military activities against Israel has been severely curtailed by civil wars in Jordan (in 1970) and in Lebanon (since 1975). The ability to engage in military struggle was further shattered when the PLO's military infrastructure in southern Lebanon and Beirut was dismantled during summer 1982. A year later most PLO forces were expelled from Lebanon at the hands of fellow Palestinians and Syrians.

While militarily paralyzed, the PLO has flirted inconclusively with the diplomatic option. More significantly, as a result of the fissures within the PLO, Palestinian national unity has been lost. Disillusioned with both Arab and Palestinian nationalism, more Palestinians may be convinced that the answers to their problems are to be found in Islam; indeed, since the late 1970s the Islamic movement in the West Bank and the Gaza Strip has been gaining ground. The coming to power of the Likud Coalition in Israel in 1977, its claim that the West Bank and the Gaza Strip were integral parts of Israel, and its intensification of settlement activities were among the main reasons for the emergence of a Palestinian Islamic movement. The Islamic revolution in Iran and the rise of several Islamic revivalist groups elsewhere in the Middle East served as added impetuses for the resurgence of Islam within the occupied territories.

The Israeli invasion of Lebanon in 1982 and U.S. tolerance of Israel's war objectives further aroused Islamic sentiments in the occupied territories. The war was depicted as a joint Christian and Jewish attack upon the Palestinian and Lebanese Moslems. More recently, the success of the Shi'ite resistance to Israel's military occupation in southern Lebanon must have left a positive image of Islam among the Palestinians within the occupied territories and inside the refugee camps in Lebanon. Likewise, the continuing attacks by the Christian forces in southern Lebanon upon the Palestinian refugees are likely to promote Islamic sentiments among the camp dwellers. Finally, the inconclusive nature of current Arab diplomatic efforts, including the Arafat-Hussein agreement, the Mubarak initiative, and the Saudi Arabian mediating efforts with the United States, discrediting the pan-Arabist and the Palestinian routes, may reinforce the conviction among increasing numbers of Palestinians of Islam's potential to defeat Israel.

Will this rising Islamic movement in the West Bank and the Gaza Strip and perhaps among the Palestinians in Lebanese refugee camps be a prelude for an Islamic takeover of the PLO? Although Fatah had some Islamic tradition within its ranks and leadership, its Central Committee has so far refused to give its movement an Islamic orientation or political coloration. The PLO leaders have also ruled out the Islamic option on the basis of its implications to Palestinian national unity, particularly as Palestinian society is composed of both Christians and Muslims.

Indeed, Fatah has indirectly been working to check the growth and popularity of the Islamic movement within the occupied territories by promoting the concept of national unity among the PLO followers in these areas. But the open split within the PLO and the shattering of the notion of Palestinian national unity sharply reduced the ability of the PLO's followers in the occupied territories to arrest the Islamic movement. Should this trend continue to grow until it becomes the most powerful single trend among the Palestinians, the PLO will have to reflect Islamic tenets within its ideology if it wishes to represent accurately Palestinian society.

In the meantime, Fatah, or somewhat less likely the PLO's leftist groups, may possibly choose to cooperate with the Islamic movement to check the influence and the power of the other. Fatah moderates may align themselves with the Islamic groups against the Left if the current bitter struggle between the moderates and the radicals within the PLO deteriorates further. Such a political coalition has occurred in local universities and student-council elections. Indeed, the Islamic movement within the occupied territories supported Arafat following the outbreak of the mutiny within Fatah and held the communists, the Arab Left, Syria, and Libya responsible for the rebellion. Undoubtedly, Islamic support for Arafat was linked to hostility toward the Assad regime in Syria and to communism. The alliance between Fatah and the Islamic group will provide opportunities for the Islamic movement to work from within Fatah's institutions and to increase its influence over the PLO and its direction; however, an alliance between Fatah and the Islamic movement is not likely to be an easy one.

Advocates of the Islamic movement are opposed to the secular orientation of the PLO and do not agree with its endeavor to create a secular national state in the West Bank and the Gaza Strip. Instead, they propose the formation of an Islamic state in all Palestine and firmly believe that only through Jihad or holy war can such a state be established. In the opinion of advocates of the Palestinian Islamic movement, no room exists for any political compromise with Israel. The proponents of the Islamic movement are critical of the PLO's narrow focus on Palestinian nationalism and its exclusion of the "Islamic masses" and the capabilities of the Moslem world in the struggle against Israel. In their view Arab and Palestinian nationalism is incapable of defeating the Western countries and Israel, and only an Islamic state can check Christian-Jewish encroachment upon the domain of Islam in Palestine.

Despite the zeal of its proponents no guarantee can be given that an Islamic PLO would be more successful than a PLO based upon Palestinian and Arab nationalism. Furthermore, the leaders of the PLO are fully aware of the adverse effects generated by a strong Islamic revivalist movement. The resurgence of Islam within the Palestinian community will deflect attention from Palestinian nationalism, the PLO, and the formation of a nationalist independent state in the West Bank and the Gaza Strip. An Islamic movement will replace such political objectives with the formation of an Islamic state that may be centered somewhere outside Palestine. Perhaps this broader focus of the Islamic trend beyond Palestine and its opposition to the secular orientation of the PLO explain Israeli tolerance for the activities of the Islamic groups within the occupied territories. Under normal conditions of Palestinian national unity the PLO's leadership would resist the Islamization of the Palestinian question and the widening of Islamic revivalist influence among the Palestinians. With the erosion of Palestinian national unity and the bitter divisions within the PLO, it is doubtful that the organization can arrest the growth of the Islamic trend or safeguard itself against Islamic infiltration.

Concluding Remarks

At the time of this writing, three years have elapsed since Israel waged its war against the PLO in summer 1982. Except for the dismantling of the PLO's military infrastructure in southern Lebanon and political headquarters in Beirut and the dispersal of Palestinian troops, Israel's military venture in Lebanon failed to accomplish many of its political objectives. First, Israel's northern borders are not necessarily more secure than they were before 1982; on the contrary, the prospects of instability on these borders are far more serious today. Despite its occasional shelling of towns and settlements in northern Israel, the PLO's military threat to Israel was not uncontrolled: Arafat demonstrated considerable willingness to restrain his followers and to respect international agreements for a cease-fire. But with the eviction of Arafat's troops from Lebanon and the split within the PLO's ranks, Arafat's ability to restrain the hard-line groups' military operations has been undercut.

Second and more significant, by occupying southern Lebanon, the Israelis succeeded to provoking Shi'a elements in the south; the same Shi'a elements that in summer 1982 welcomed the invading Israeli army have inflicted heavy casualties upon the Israelis through guerrilla warfare and suicide missions. Third, instead of consolidating the influence of Israel's Christian allies in southern Lebanon, the war led to an increase in the power of the Shi'ite element within Lebanon's political system. As a result of the war, the traditional Christian hegemony in Lebanon has eroded, giving way to Muslim ascendancy. In view of Israel's severe crackdown on the Muslim resistance groups in the south, coupled with the support the resistance receives from Iran, Syria, and PLO hard-line groups, it is unlikely that the population will normalize relations with Israel or maintain tranquility following the withdrawal of the Israeli army. The pro-Israel Christian militia, known as the south Lebanese army, was significantly weakened after the death of its founder, Sa'ad Haddad. Mounting military operations against its members forced many soldiers to desert. The viability of the Christian militias may stand on even shakier ground now that the Israeli army has completed its withdrawal from the south.

Finally, not only did Israel fail to install in Beirut a Maronite Christian government of its liking—ready to sign a peace treaty with the Jewish state—but Israel's invasion of Lebanon left Syria as the dominant crisis manager of Lebanese internal affairs. This situation, contrary to Israel's hopes, rendered the Lebanese central government totally dependent upon Syria and unresponsive to Israeli demands, as demonstrated by the cancellation of the Israeli-Lebanese troop withdrawal agreement of May 17, 1983.

The Lebanon War no doubt has diminished the PLO's political influence, shattered its military potential, and deepened its divisions. Nevertheless, the PLO has managed to survive. Its wide base of political legitimacy within the Palestinian community, the Arab countries' continued adherence to the 1974 Rabat resolution, its recognition by the majority of states in the international community, and the skillfulness of its leaders and their politics of alignment within the Arab world— all are factors that contributed to the PLO's political survival and its continued centrality to any political settlement. The war failed to break the linkage between the PLO and the Palestinians within the occupied territories, to dissipate Palestinian nationalism, or to subdue Palestinian local resistance to Israel's military control.

The overwhelming majority of the Palestinians in the West Bank and the Gaza Strip continue to see the PLO as a living embodiment of their national aspirations and the only political actor in the Arab world genuinely trying to advance their interests. Despite the PLO military defeat in Lebanon and its weakened political position, no West Bank or Gaza Strip politician expressed any interest in cooperating with Israel to resolve the Palestinian question. Even the Israeli-sponsored Village Council Leagues lost any credibility they may have enjoyed among their followers when the Israeli military closed down their newspaper, dissolved their union, and significantly reduced their financial support.

The PLO's increasing political moderation and flexibility after the Beirut exodus have enhanced its chances of being included in any political settlement, to a greater extent than at any time before the 1982 war. The support that the PLO derives from the overwhelming majority of Palestinians within and outside the occupied territories invests it with the political legitimacy needed to keep it pertinent to any political settlement. It is a gross mistake to think that Jordan or Egypt can singularly or jointly negotiate on behalf of the Palestinians without PLO participation; indeed, both countries have made it very clear that they would not do so without PLO authorization. Moreover, despite Jordan's new role of shared representation, the Jordanian government cannot alone represent Palestinian interests; it enjoys the right to share in the representation of such interests only so long as the PLO accepts that principle. It is therefore unlikely that Jordan will enter any negotiations with Israel without full and active Palestinian participation. The Jordanians are fully aware that in the event of a final political settlement with Israel that would entail territorial concessions, only the Palestinians, and for the time being the PLO, can put the stamp of legitimacy to such a political settlement. Similarly, the moderate politicians in the West Bank and the Gaza Strip declared that they are prepared to join a Palestinian-Jordanian delegation only if so requested by the PLO.

A long-term solution to the Palestinian question and the Arab-Israeli dispute is unlikely to be found by the exclusion of the PLO from the peace process. Under the chairmanship of Arafat the PLO has evolved into a moderate voice within the Palestinian community and has attracted the support of the overwhelming majority of Palestinians within and outside the occupied territories. Since the 1973 October War the PLO has also been progressively (though slowly) moving toward a political solution to the Palestinian question. The PLO's political efforts culminated in the signing of the Arafat-Hussein agreement, which formally committed the PLO to a political settlement through negotiations and peaceful means and away from the exploitation of military force. By so committing itself the PLO had already accepted the principles of peaceful coexistence with Israel and exchanging peace for land, as called for in UN Security Council Resolution 242. The PLO has also adjusted its position concerning the formation of an independent, sovereign, Palestinian state: It accepts the notion of a confederation of the West Bank and the Gaza Strip with Jordan and concedes that the Palestinian right for national self-determination should be exercised within the context of a confederal state.

Both King Hussein and PLO Chairman Arafat have taken serious personal and political risks by concluding their joint political accord against the wishes of the PLO's hard-line groups, Syria, and Libya. The Israeli government has not made reciprocal moves to advance the prospects of a political settlement. The moderate and conciliatory statements of Israeli Prime Minister Perez have been offset by those of his rival partners in the Likud who oppose any territorial concessions.

Israel's experience after the 1973 October War and the Lebanon War fiasco point to one outstanding lesson—that the equation of territoriality with security and the overconfidence placed in the efficacy of military force are meretricious and cannot provide long-term security, peace, or stability for Israel. Such objectives can best be achieved by promoting peaceful relations between Israel and its Arab neighbors. Israel's refusal to relinquish the occupied territories and its invocation of religious justifications to legitimize permanent control of the West Bank and the Gaza Strip cannot bring the country the security and the peace it desires. On the contrary, they will only serve to strengthen the forces of extremism and fanaticism in the region and encourage the outbreak of violence.

Arafat, Hussein, and the moderate Arab countries are not likely to make any further political concessions without reciprocation from Israel and the United States. Indeed, both the Jordanians and the Palestinians will continue to be restrained by the lack of receptiveness on the part of the Reagan administration to their diplomatic moves and its insensitivity to their demands and limitations. Needless to say, without the active participation of the United States and its involvement in the search for peace, little can be achieved. The conclusion of the Israeli-Egyptian peace treaty in 1979 would not have been possible without the full engagement of the Carter administration. The Reagan administration has a moral obligation to reconcile the opposing views of both the Israelis and the Palestinians and help them overcome their long-held mutual suspicions and hostilities.

Despite the political preferences of both Israel and the United States for direct bilateral talks between Israel and Jordan, such an approach is not likely to ensure a durable long-term settlement. A more comprehensive solution to the Arab-Israeli conflict—that in addition to Jordan, the Palestinians, and Israel engages the Syrians—offers a better chance for a stable peace. One should draw the appropriate lessons from the conclusion of the separate Israeli-Egyptian peace treaty. Despite the signing of such a treaty, peace between the two countries has hardly gone beyond the stage of nonbelligerency. Palestinian and Arab readiness to discuss a long-term comprehensive resolution to the Palestinian problem and the Arab-Israeli dispute in all its dimensions is a sign of Arab seriousness and political maturity. Should this opportunity be missed, a long time will pass and more suffering will take place before a new initiative emerges, if ever. There is no room for vacillation or for a policy of "wait-and-see": Extremists on both sides of the Arab-Israeli dispute share common interests in dissipating any hope for a political settlement and are determined to silence the voice of moderation and reason.

Notes

1. Such a political arrangement came in line with the resolutions of the Palestine National Council's sixteenth session, which endorsed the concept of confederation between the occupied territories and Jordan.

244   *Epilogue*

2. The PLO's reluctance to accept explicitly and publicly Resolution 242 was not so much that it would entail the PLO's recognition of the state of Israel as that the resolution treated the Palestinians as mere refugees without any national rights or aspirations.

3. Farouq al-Qadoumi interview, Radio Monte Carlo, February 13, 1985; Abu Iyad interview, Radio Monte Carlo, February 22, 1985; Abu Mazen interview, *Filistin al-Thawra,* no. 544, February 9–15, 1985; and Rafiq al-Natshe interview, *al-Sharq al-Awsat,* February 26, 1985.

4. Arafat interview, *al-Hawadeth,* February 21, 1985; Abu Jihad interview, Radio Monte Carlo, February 22, 1985.

5. *Al-Dustur,* February 20, 1985.

6. Interview with Ahmed Abd al-Rahman, spokesman for the PLO, in *al-Siyassa* (Kuwait daily), February 27, 1985.

7. *Al-Ahram,* March 7, 1985.

8. George Habash interview, BBC (Arabic service), February 14, 1985.

9. Damascus Radio, February 13, 1985.

10. Abu Musa interview, Radio Monte Carlo, February 22, 1985.

11. Nayef Hawatmeh interview, Radio Monte Carlo, February 22, 1985.

12. George Habash interview, Radio Monte Carlo, February 22, 1985.

13. Ibid.

14. Abu Musa, Radio Monte Carlo, February 22, 1985.

15. Farouq al-Shara interview, *al-Nahar al-Arabi wa al-Dawli,* February 25, 1985.

16. *Tishrin,* February 25, 1985; quoted in FBIS Daily Report: Middle East and Africa, February 27, 1985.

17. Ibid.

18. Damascus Radio (Arabic service), January 5, 1985.

19. Ibid.

20. Ibid.

21. *Al-Nahar al-Arabi wa al-Dawli,* February 25, 1985.

22. *Al-Ahram,* December 2, 1984.

23. Abba Eban interview, BBC, "The World Today," March 3, 1985.

24. Israel Radio (English service), February 25, 1985.

25. Israel Radio (English service), December 2, 1984.

26. *Ma'ariv, Davar, Jerusalem Post,* November 23–25, 1984.

27. The joint command between Fatah dissidents and Abu Nidal was announced by Abu Musa, Radio Monte Carlo, February 22, 1985.

28. Arafat interview in *al-Hawadeth,* February 21, 1985; Abu Jihad interview, Radio Monte Carlo, February 22, 1985.

29. Abu Iyad interview, Radio Monte Carlo, February 22, 1985.

30. Abu Mazen interview, *Filistin al-Thawra,* no. 544, February 9–15, 1985.

31. *Al-Hadaf,* December 17, 1984.

Afterword

The political developments that took place in the early fall of 1985 may prove to be crucial to the PLO's credibility and diplomatic flexibility. On October 1, 1985, six Israeli war planes attacked the PLO's political headquarters in Tunis, presumably in retaliation for the PLO's alleged instigation of acts of violence within and outside the occupied territories. A week later, four Palestinians from the Palestine Liberation Front (a small pro-Arafat PLO faction) hijacked the *Achille Lauro,* a luxurious Italian tourist ship. Before surrendering to the Egyptian authorities, the hijackers killed an American passenger on board. On October 9 some U.S. war planes from the Sixth Fleet intercepted an Egyptian airliner carrying the four hijackers to Tunis. The plane was forced to land at a NATO airbase in Sicily, where the Italian police arrested the hijackers.

More damaging to the PLO's diplomatic standing was its indecisiveness in the face of a real opportunity to further its cause. On October 14, the foreign minister of Britain canceled his scheduled meeting with the Palestinian members of the joint Jordanian-PLO delegation because of the refusal of the Palestinians to sign a document recognizing Israel's right to exist. Around the same time, diplomatic efforts to bring Arafat to the United Nations were called off and the foreign minister of Luxembourg (as the head of the European Economic Community Council of Foreign Ministers) postponed his meeting with the joint delegation.

These developments were preceded by an upsurge in the cycle of violence between the Palestinians and the Israelis. They also took place amid Israeli attempts to discredit the PLO and to cast doubt upon the seriousness of its political moves and political moderation. Undoubtedly, the unfolding of these events constituted serious diplomatic setbacks for the PLO's ten-year-old drive to gain international recognition, respectability, and legitimacy. In particular, the recent wave of violence adversely affected its status in the West and undermined Arab diplomatic efforts to depict it as a force of political moderation that was genuinely interested in finding a negotiated political settlement to the Palestinian question.

With the failure of the PLO's delegation to meet with the British foreign minister, the PLO missed an opportunity that would have provided it with British and West European diplomatic backing, which was urgently needed to neutralize Israel's relentless efforts to discredit the organization. Moreover, irrespective of the original intentions of the hijackers, the seizure of the *Achille Lauro* by Palestinians loyal to Arafat damaged the PLO's relationship with Italy (one of the PLO's closest friends in Europe).

In addition to complicating U.S.-Egyptian relations and perhaps Egyptian-Palestinian relations, such recent incidents have also strained Palestinian-Jordanian relations, and may even usher in the end of the Jordanian-PLO joint diplomatic approach. The PLO's diplomatic vacillation was embarrassing to King Hussein personally, who, since early 1985, had made sustained efforts in the West to promote his diplomatic accord with Arafat and to enlist Western support for the inclusion of the PLO in the peace process. For this reason, Jordan was critical of the PLO's inability to compromise and held it accountable for the failure of the planned meeting to take place. Jordan's dilemma, nevertheless, remains that without credible and legitimate Palestinian representation, it is unable to enter any diplomatic discussions with Israel. The PLO leadership also continues to recognize the instrumentality of Jordan in any political settlement to the Palestinian question. For these two reasons, both the Jordanians and the Palestinians would find it in their best interest, as they have in the past, to overcome the strain in their relationship. Should the joint Jordanian-PLO approach head toward a dead-end, King Hussein may move in the direction of full reconciliation with the Syrian government. President Assad does not seem to be opposed to the normalization of relations with his counterpart in Jordan, but he would most likely insist that the rapprochement between the two states be made without Arafat.

Although it is too early at the time of this writing to delineate any definite conclusions from these developments upon the future of the PLO, nevertheless one could say that the PLO's leadership displayed a considerable degree of incompetency and short-sightedness in letting the hijacking of the Italian liner take place and in not fully cultivating European support and sympathy for the Palestinians. Similarly, these developments indicated Arafat's growing inability to control the behavior of those factions that are still loyal to his leadership. Moreover, the frequent recourse to violence within and outside the occupied territories by hard-line Palestinians is an indication of their growing impatience and frustration with the inconclusive outcomes of Arafat's diplomatic approach. These developments may prove to be not only relevant to the PLO's international prestige, but they could also have real repercussions on the degree of centralization of the Palestinian nationalist movement.

The PLO's diplomatic setbacks are likely to influence the political attitudes of the Palestinians inside the West Bank and the Gaza Strip. These developments are likely to reinforce the growing disillusionment of the younger Palestinian generation with the inefficacy of diplomacy and strengthen the growing tendency among them to take into their own hands the task of resisting Israel's military occupation without waiting for the PLO's help. One could also argue that more West Bank Palestinians may look toward Islam as an alternative avenue for addressing their grievances and extricating them from Israel's control.

In conclusion, there is no doubt that the regrettable recourse by some PLO factions to acts of violence, the periodic hesitation of the PLO's leadership to make difficult diplomatic choices, and Israel's intense anti-PLO campaign adversely affect the PLO's political standing, particularly in the West. This does not mean, however, that the PLO is reaching its end. As long as the Palestinian question remains unresolved, the PLO in one form or another will continue to exist. Despite its diplomatic setbacks, the presence or the absence of the PLO will be determined first and foremost by the Palestinian people themselves, who overwhelmingly continue to regard the organization as their sole legitimate representative. In addition, the Palestinian question for a long time has been an Arab issue, and the Arab countries are still committed to the 1974 Rabat resolution, which empowered the PLO with the exclusive right of representing Palestinian interests. It is only through the passage of a similar resolution that the Arab countries can divest the PLO of its status.

Aside from these ideological considerations, the pertinence of the PLO will continue to be governed by two compelling factors. First, in the advent of a final political settlement with Israel, territorial concessions would certainly have to be made, particularly over East Jerusalem and perhaps other areas in the West Bank. Without Palestinian legitimation, none of the Arab countries would embark upon such a hazardous course. The PLO alone can put the stamp of legitimacy on any political settlement of this sort. Second, in the absence of any political settlement, the presence of the PLO would absolve the Arab states from assuming primary responsibility for the resolution of the Palestinian problem.

The U.S. and Israeli determination to exclude the PLO will only serve to isolate the moderate forces within the Palestinian community and reinforce the position of the hard-line groups and the extremists. The majority of the Palestinians want to live in peace alongside Israel and want to have their rights respected. It is only through an active and unbiased U.S. involvement in the search for political solutions to the Arab-Israeli conflict that the incentives to engage in violence and counterviolence will be reduced and the spread of religious fundamentalism and extremism among both the Israelis and the Palestinians will be checked.

Selected Bibliography

Abd al-Majid, Wahid. "The Egyptian Attitude Toward the Israeli Invasion of Lebanon." *Al-Siyassa al-Dawliya*, no. 70 (October 1982):160-162.
_____. "The Palestinians and Jordan: Confrontation or Dialogue." *al-Siyassa al-Dawliya*, no. 57 (July 1979):78-81.
Abu-Lughod, Ibrahim. "Flexible Militancy: Report on the Sixteenth Palestine National Council." *Journal of Palestine Studies* 12, no. 4 (summer 1983):25-40.
_____. "The Meaning of Beirut, 1982." *Race & Class* 24, no. 4 (spring 1983):345-360.
Abdul Jawad, Jamal. "European Policy Toward the Israeli Invasion of Lebanon." *al-Siyassa al-Dawliya*, no. 70 (October 1982):154-159.
Abu Taleb, Hassan. "The Evolution of the American Role and the Lebanon Invasion." *al-Siyassa al-Dawliya*, no. 70 (October 1982).
_____. "The Evolution of the Jordanian-Palestinian Dialog." *al-Siyassa al-Dawliya*, no. 70 (January 1983):55-58.
_____. "The Jordanian-Palestinian Dialog: Continuity or Discontinuity." *al-Siyassa al-Dawliya*, no. 75 (January 1974):116-118.
_____. "Issues for Palestinian Actions." *al-Siyassa al-Dawliya*, no. 74 (October 1983):5-25.
_____. "Saudi Mediation and Arab Crisis." *al-Siyassa al-Dawliya*, no. 75 (January 1984):173-178.
Adams, Michael. "Israel's Treatment of the Arabs in the Occupied Territories." *Journal of Palestine Studies* 7, no. 2 (winter 1977):19-41.
Ajami, Fuad. *The Arab Predicament*. Cambridge: Cambridge University Press, 1981.
_____. "The Crusade in Lebanon, Shadows of Hell." *Foreign Policy*, no. 48 (fall 1982):93-115.
Allon, Yigal. "Israel, the Case for Defensible Borders." *Foreign Affairs* 55, no. 1 (October 1976):38-53.
Amos, John W., II. *Palestinian Resistance: Organization of a Nationalist Movement*. New York: Pergamon Press, 1980.
Aronson, Geoffrey. "Israel's Policy of Military Occupation." *Journal of Palestine Studies* 7, no. 4 (summer 1978):79-99.
Artner, Stephen J. "The Middle East: A Chance for Europe?" *International Affairs* (London) 56, no. 3 (summer 1980):420-442.

Avineri, Shlomo. "Beyond Camp David." *Foreign Policy,* no. 46 (spring 1982): 19–37.

Awad, Mubarak. "Non-Violent Resistance: A Strategy for the Occupied Territories." *Journal of Palestine Studies* 13, no. 4 (summer 1984):22–36.

Bailey, Clinton. *Jordan's Palestinian Challenge, 1948–1953: A Political History.* Boulder, Co.: Westview Press, 1984.

Ball, George. "The Coming Crisis in Israeli-American Relations." *Foreign Affairs* 58, no. 2 (winter 1979-1980):231–256.

Bar-on, Mordechai. "The Palestinian Aspect of the War in Lebanon." *New Outlook* 25, no. 7 (October 1972):28–34, 49.

Batatu, Hanna. "Syria's Muslim Brethren." *Merip Reports* 12, no. 9 (November-December 1982).

Beit-Halachmi, Benjamin. "The Home Front: Reflections on the Consensus that Never Was." *New Outlook* 25, no. 7 (October 1982):35–38, 49.

Ben-Yishai, Ron. "Israel's Move." *Foreign Policy,* no. 42 (spring 1982):43–58.

Berge, Steinar, and Oyvind Moller, "Israeli Captivity." *Journal of Palestine Studies* 11, no. 4/13, no. 1 (summer/fall 1982):85–93.

Bolling, Landrum R. "A Realistic Middle East Policy." *Orbis* 26, no. 1 (spring 1982):5–10.

Boutros-Ghali, Boutros. "The Foreign Policy of Egypt in the Post-Sadat Era." *Foreign Affairs* 60, no. 4 (spring 1982):769–788.

Campbell, John C. "The Middle East: A House of Containment Built on Shifting Sands." *Foreign Affairs* 60, no. 3 (winter 1982).

Cobban, Helena. "The PLO in the mid-1980's: Between the Gun and the Olive Branch." *International Journal* 38, no. 4 (1983):635–651.

———. *The PLO: People, Power and Politics.* Cambridge: Cambridge University Press, 1984.

Cooley, John. "Iran, the Palestinians and the Gulf." *Foreign Affairs* 57, no. 5 (summer 1979).

Danaher, Kevin. "Israel's Use of Cluster Bombs in Lebanon." *Journal of Palestine Studies* 11, no. 4/12, no. 1 (summer/fall 1982):48–57.

Davidson, Larry. "Lebanon and the Jewish Conscience." *Journal of Palestine Studies* 12, no. 2 (winter 1983).

Dawisha, Karen. "The U.S.S.R. and the Middle East: A Superpower in Eclipse." *Foreign Affairs* 61, no. 2 (winter 1982-1983):438–452.

Demant, Peter. "Israeli Settlement Policy Today." *Merip Reports* 13, no. 6 (July-August 1983):3–18.

Disney, June. "U.S. and Israeli Weapons in the Lebanon War." *Merip Reports* 12, nos. 6–7 (1982):51–54.

Disney, Nigel. "Why Syria Invaded Lebanon." *Merip Reports* 51, no. 6–8 (October 1976):3–10.

Drysdale, Alasdair. "The Asad Regime and its Troubles." *Merip Reports* 12, no. 9 (November-December 1982).

Fabian, Larry L. "Red Light, West Bank?" *Foreign Policy,* no. 50 (spring 1983):53–72.

Farjoun, Emanuel. "A Dier Yassin Policy for the 80's." *Merip Reports* 12, nos. 6–7 (September-October 1982).

Feldman, Shai. "Peacemaking in the Middle East." *Foreign Affairs* 59, nos. 3–4 (1980-1981):765–781.
Freedman, Robert O. *Soviet Policy Toward the Middle East Since 1970.* New York: Praeger, 1975.
Fukuyama, Francis. "Nuclear Shadowboxing: Soviet Intervention in the Middle East." *Orbis* 25, no. 3 (fall 1981):579–606.
Garfinkle, Adam M. "U.S.-Israeli Relations: The Wolf This Time?" *Orbis* 26, no. 1 (spring 1982):11–18.
Giannou, Chris. "The Battle for South Lebanon." *Journal of Palestine Studies* 11, no. 4/12, no. 1 (summer/fall 1982):69–84.
Golan, Galia. "The Soviet Union and the Israeli Action in Lebanon." *International Affairs* (London) 59, no. 1 (winter 1982-1983).
———. *The Soviet Union and the Palestine Liberation Organization: An Uneasy Alliance.* New York: Praeger, 1980.
Goldberg, John. "Israel Reacts to the Massacre." *New Outlook* 25, no. 7 (October 1982):17–18.
Haley, P. Edward, and Lewis W. Snider, eds. *Lebanon in Crisis.* Syracuse, N.Y.: Syracuse University Press, 1979.
Halliday, Fred. "The Arc of Crisis and the New Cold War." *Merip Reports* 11, nos. 8–9 (October-December 1981):1435.
Hamid, Rashid. "What is the PLO?" *Journal of Palestine Studies* 2, no. 4 (summer 1973).
Harb, Usamah al-Ghazali. "Toward the Future of the Palestinian Resistance After the Sixth War." *al-Siyassa al-Dawliya,* no. 70 (October 1982):131–136.
Hays, Stephen D. "Joint Economic Commissions of U.S. Foreign Policy in the M.E." *Middle East Journal* 31, no. 1 (winter 1977).
Hudson, Michael C. *The Precarious Republic: Political Modernization in Lebanon.* New York: Random House, 1968.
———. "The U.S. Decline in the Middle East." *Orbis* 26, no. 1 (spring 1982):19–25.
Hurewitz, J. C. "The Middle East: A Year of Turmoil." *Foreign Affairs* 59, nos. 3–4 (summer 1980-1981).
Ibn Talal, HRH Hassan. "Jordan's Quest for Peace." *Foreign Affairs* 60, no. 4 (spring 1982):802–813.
Ibrahim, Ahmad Ibrahim. "Israel's Greed for the Waters of Southern Lebanon." *al-Siyassa al-Dawliya,* no. 70 (October 1982):167–169.
Ibrahim, Sa'ad al-Din. "The Initiative of Reagan." *al-Siyassa al-Dawliya,* no. 70 (October 1982):146–150.
Jansen, Michael. *The Battle of Beirut.* London: Zed Press, 1982.
Jiryis, Sabri. "Israeli Rejectionism." *Journal of Palestine Studies* 7, no. 1 (autumn 1978):61–85.
Kalb, Marvin, and Bernard Kalb. *Kissinger.* New York: Dell Press, 1974.
Khadouri, Walid, ed. *International Documents on Palestine: 1969.* Beirut: Institute of Palestine Studies, 1972.
Khalidi, Walid. *Conflict and Violence in Lebanon.* Cambridge: Harvard University Press, 1979.

———. "Regiopolitic: Toward a U.S. Policy on the Palestine Problem." *Foreign Affairs* 59, no. 5 (summer 1981).

Kol, Moshe. "A Dissident Rabbi—An Interview Interim Summary of the Lebanese War." *New Outlook* 25, no. 7 (October 1982):23-27.

Korany, Bahgat. "The Cold Peace, the Sixth Arab-Israeli War, and Egypt's Public." *International Journal,* summer 1983.

Kreczko, Alan J. "Support Reagan's Initiative." *Foreign Policy,* no. 49 (winter 1982-1983):140-153.

Lawson, Fred. "Social Bases for the Hamah Revolt." *Merip Reports* 12, no. 9 (November-December 1982).

Lesch, Ann. *Political Perceptions of the People in the Occupied Territories.* Washington, D.C.: Middle East Institute, 1980.

Lockman, Zachary. "The Israeli Opposition." *Merip Reports* 12, nos. 6-7 (September-October 1982):25-32.

Lustick, Ian S. "Israeli Politics and American Foreign Policy." *Foreign Affairs* 61, no. 2 (winter 1982-1983):379-399.

MacBride, Sean S. C., et al. *Israel in Lebanon: The Report of the International Commission.* London: Ithaca Press, 1982.

Mallison, Sally V., and Thomas Mallison. "The United States and Israel's Violations of Law." *Journal of Palestine Studies* 11, no. 4/12, no. 1 (summer/fall 1982):58-61.

Mandell, Joan, and Salim Tamari. "The 100 Year War: Report from the West Bank and Gaza." *Merip Reports* 12, nos. 6-7 (September-October 1982):42-44.

Ma'oz, Moshe. *Palestinian Leadership on the West Bank.* London: Frank Cass, 1984.

Miller, Aaron David. *The PLO: The Politics of Survival.* New York: Praeger, 1983.

———. "The PLO: What Next?" *Washington Quarterly* 6, no. 1 (winter 1983):116-125.

Milson, Menachem. "How to Make Peace with the Palestinians." *Commentary,* May 1981.

Mishal, Shaul. *West Bank/East Bank: The Palestinians in Jordan, 1949-1967.* New Haven, Conn.: Yale University Press, 1978.

Moisi, Dominique. "Mitterrand's Foreign Policy: The Limits of Continuity." *Foreign Affairs* 60, no. 2 (winter 1981-1982).

Muslih, Muhammad Y. "Moderates and Rejectionists Within the Palestine Liberation Organization." *Middle East Journal* 30, no. 2 (spring 1976):127-140.

Mustapha, Hala. "The Israeli Invasion of Lebanon in the United Nations." *Al-Siyassa al-Dawliya,* no. 70 (October 1982):137-140.

Nakhleh, Khalil. "The Lebanon War and the Occupied Territories." *Merip Reports* 13, no. 5 (June 1983):22-23, 38.

Nakhleh, Khalil, and Clifford Wright. *After the Palestine-Israel War, Limits to U.S. and Israeli Policy.* Belmont, Mass.: Institute of Arab Studies, 1983, pp. 43-51.

Neuman, Robert G. "Toward a Reagan Middle East Policy?" *Orbis* 25, no. 3 (fall 1981):491-495.

Oren, Michael. "A Horse Shoe in the Glove: Milson's Year on the West Bank." *Middle East Review* 16, no. 4 (fall 1983).
Oye, Kenneth A., Robert Lieber, and Donald Rothchild, eds. *Eagle Defiant: U.S. Foreign Policy in the 1980's.* Boston: Little, Brown and Co., 1983.
Perez, Shimon. "A Strategy of Peace in the Middle East." *Foreign Affairs* 58, no. 4 (spring 1980):887-901.
Perlmutter, Amos. "Begin's Rhetoric and Sharon's Tactics." *Foreign Affairs* 61, no. 1 (fall 1982):67-83.
_____. "Begin's Strategy and Dayan's Tactics: The Conduct of Israeli Foreign Policy." *Foreign Affairs* 56, no. 2 (January 1978):357-372.
_____. "Reagan's Middle East Policy." *Orbis* 26, no. 1 (spring 1982):26-29.
Pipes, Daniel. "How Important is the PLO?" *Commentary* 75, no. 4 (1983):17-25.
Quandt, William B. *Decade of Decisions: American Policy Toward the Arab-Israeli Conflict, 1967-1976.* Berkeley: University of California Press, 1979.
_____. "The Middle East Crisis." *Foreign Affairs* 58, nos. 3-5 (1979-1980): 540-563.
_____. "Riyadh Between the Super Powers." *Foreign Policy,* no. 44 (fall 1981):37-57.
_____. "Soviet Policy in the October Middle East War I." *International Affairs* 53, no. 3 (July 1977):377-390.
_____. "Soviet Policy in the October Middle East War II." *International Affairs* 53, no. 4 (October 1977):587-604.
Quandt, William B., Fuad Jabber, and Ann Mosely Lesch. *The Politics of Palestinian Nationalism.* Berkeley: University of California Press, 1973.
Rasa'il min Qalb al-Hsar. Jerusalem: Abu Arafa Agency for Publication and Press, July 1983, p. 161.
Rashwan, Dia. "The Impact of the Issues of a Political Settlement on the Internal Cohesion of the Palestine Liberation Organization." *al-Siyassa al-Dawliya,* no. 71 (January 1983):59-63.
Reilly, James A. "Israel in Lebanon, 1975-1982." *Merip Reports* 12, nos. 6-7 (September-October 1982):14-20.
Rosenbaum, Aaron D. "Discard Conventional Wisdom." *Foreign Policy,* no. 49 (winter 1982-1983):154-167.
Rouleau, Eric. "The Future of the PLO." *Foreign Affairs* 62, no. 1 (fall 1983).
_____. "The Mutiny Against Arafat." *Merip Reports* 62, no. 1 (November-December 1983):13-16.
Rubenberg, Cheryl A. "The PLO Response to the Reagan Initiative: The PNC at Algiers." *American-Arab Affairs,* no. 4 (February 1983):53-69.
_____. "Beirut Under Fire." *Journal of Palestine Studies* 11, no. 4/12, no. 1 (summer/fall 1982):62-68.
Ryan, Sheila. "Israel's Invasion of Lebanon: Background to the Crisis." *Journal of Palestine Studies* 11, no. 4/12, no. 1 (summer/fall 1982):22-35.
Said, Abd al-Mun'am. "The Future of Arab-American Relations." *al-Siyassa al-Dawliya,* no. 75 (January 1984):105-111.
Salibi, Kamal S. *The Modern History of Lebanon.* London: Weidenfeld and Nicolson, 1965.

Salim, Muhammad al-Said. "Possible Alternatives for the Arab-Israeli Conflict." *al-Siyassa al-Dawliya*, no. 75 (January 1984):112–128.

———. "The Soviet Union and the Palestinian-Israeli War." *al-Siyassa al-Dawliya*, no. 70 (October 1982):151–153.

Saunders, Harold. "An Israeli-Palestinian Peace." *Foreign Affairs* 61, no. 1 (fall 1982):100–121.

Sayegh, Fayez A. "The Camp David Agreement and the Palestine Problem." *Journal of Palestine Studies* 8, no. 2 (winter 1979):3–40.

Sayegh, Yazid. "The PLO's Military Performance in the 1982 War." *Journal of Palestine Studies* 12, no. 4 (summer 1983):8–23.

———. "The Roots of the Syrian-PLO Difference." *Middle East International*, October 29, 1982, pp. 15–16.

Schenker, Hillel. "1977–1981: A Comparision." *New Outlook*, July-August 1981, pp. 22–23.

Schiff, Ze'ev. "Green Light Lebanon." *Foreign Policy*, no. 50 (spring 1983):73–85.

———. "Who Decided, Who Informed." *New Outlook* 25, no. 7 (October 1982):19–22.

Schiff, Ze'ev, and Ehud Ya'ari. *Israel's Lebanon War*. New York: Simon and Schuster, 1984.

Schueftan, Dan. "The PLO After Lebanon." *Jerusalem Quarterly*, no. 28 (summer 1983):3–24.

Seale, Patrick. "PLO Strategies: Algiers and After." *World Today* 39, no. 4 (April 1983):137–143.

Shaham, David. "An Uneasy Coalition." *New Outlook*, July-August 1981, pp. 23–24.

Shamir, Yitzhak. "Israel's Role in a Changing Middle East." *Foreign Affairs* 60, no. 4 (spring 1982):789–801.

Shlaim, Avi, and Avner Yaniv. "Domestic Politics and Foreign Policy in Israel." *International Affairs* 56, no. 2 (winter 1980):242–261.

Shuquair, Mohammed. "The Roots of Fatah's Split." *Journal of Palestine Studies* 12, no. 4 (summer 1983):161–181.

Sicherman, Harvey. "Politics of Dependence: Western Europe and the Arab-Israeli Conflict." *Orbis* 23, no. 4 (winter 1980).

Sigler, John H. "United States Policy in the Aftermath of Lebanon: The Perils of Unilateralism." *International Journal* 38, no. 4 (1983).

Smith, Pamela Ann. "The European Reaction to Israel's Invasion." *Journal of Palestine Studies* 11, no. 4/12, no. 1 (summer/fall 1982):38–47.

Spagnolo, John P. *France and Ottoman Lebanon, 1861–1914*. London: Ithaca Press for the Middle East Center, St. Anthony's College, Oxford, 1977.

Stein, Kenneth. "The PLO After Beirut." *Middle East Review* 15, nos. 3–4 (spring/summer 1983):11–17.

Stevans, Georgiana G. "America's Moment in Middle East." *Middle East Journal* 31, no. 1 (winter 1977):1–16.

Stork, Joe. "Israel as a Strategic Asset." *Merip Reports* 12, no. 4 (May 1982):3–13.

Stork, Joe, and Jim Paul. "The War in Lebanon." *Merip Reports* 12, nos. 6–7 (September-October 1982):3–7, 58–60.

Taylor, Allen. *The Arab Balance of Power.* Syracuse, N.Y.: Syracuse University Press, 1982.

———. "The Euro-Arab Dialogue: A Quest for Inter-Regional Partnership." *Middle East Journal* 32, no. 4 (fall 1978).

———. "The PLO and Inter-Arab Politics." *Journal of Palestine Studies* 11, no. 2 (winter 1982).

Tillman, Seth P. *The United States in the Middle East: Interests and Obstacles.* Bloomington: Indiana University Press, 1982.

Tueni, Ghassan. "Lebanon: A New Republic?" *Foreign Affairs* 61, no. 1 (fall 1982):84–99.

Van Hollen, Christopher. "Don't Engulf the Gulf." *Foreign Affairs* 59, no. 5 (summer 1981):1064–1078.

Weitzman, Bruce Matti. "The Fragmentation of Arab Politics: Inter-Arab Affairs Since the Afganistan Invasion." *Orbis* 25, no. 2 (summer 1981).

Wright, Claudia. "The Implications of the Iraq-Iran War." *Foreign Affairs* 59, no. 2 (winter 1980-1981):275–303.

———. "Iraq—New Power in the Middle East." *Foreign Affairs* 58, no. 2 (winter 1979-1980).

———. "The Turn of the Screw—The Lebanon War and American Policy." *Journal of Palestine Studies* 11, no. 4/12, no. 1 (summer/fall 1982):3–22.

Yaari, Arieh. "The Lebanese War and the Diaspora." *New Outlook* 25, no. 7 (October 1982):39–40, 49.

Zagorin, Adam. "A House Divided." *Foreign Policy,* no. 48 (fall 1982):111–121.

Zahra, al-Said. "Israeli Opposition to the Lebanon Invasion." *al-Siyassa al-Dawliya,* no. 709 (October 1982):173–177.

Index

Abdallah, Crown Prince (Saudi Arabia), 171
Aden-Algiers Agreement, 192–93, 196, 200, 201
  possible future use of, 230, 234
Afghanistan, 9, 58
Algeria
  and the Arafat-Hussein accord, 213, 217–18
  efforts to unify PLO, 166–67, 189, 191, 192, 196, 197, 233
  reaction to Lebanon War, 41
  and the rejectionists, 106
Ali, Kamal Hassan, 166, 180
Allon plan, 77
Allush, Naji, 142
Amleh, Khaled al- (Abu Khaled)
  and the Fatah rebellion, 143, 145, 173(n29)
  and PLO divisions, 141, 142
Arab countries
  and the Arafat-Hussein accord, 207, 213–14, 215
  and the Baghdad resolution, 119
  conflicts within, 3, 7–9, 27, 36, 38–39, 46–47, 55, 188, 209, 213, 226
  and France, 61–62
  and the Israeli invasion of Lebanon, 34–35, 36–41, 47
  on the Jordanian-PLO dialogue, 133–35
  military capabilities of the, 57, 236–37

  and the PLO, 39–40, 81, 89, 92, 111, 140, 177, 230–31, 235
  and the PLO rejectionists, 106–7
  and PLO unity, 166–67, 232–33
  and the PLO withdrawal from Beirut, 41–43
  and the Rabat Resolution, 117, 118, 119, 225
  and the Reagan initiative, 78–80, 82–83
  and the Soviet Union, 57
  and the United States, 19–21
  See also Arab peace plan of Fez; *individual countries*
Arab Liberation Front, 142
Arab peace plan of Fez, 19, 71, 80–82, 120–21, 206
  PLO reaction to the, 90, 91, 94–95, 100, 131, 148–49
  and the PNC communiqué, 109
  and the rejectionists, 103–4
Arafat-Hussein accord, 205–7, 242
  Arab reaction to the, 213–18
  Israeli reaction to the, 220–23
  Palestinian reaction to the, 207–13, 228, 230, 244(n2)
  United States reaction to the, 218–20
  Western Europe and the, 220
Arafat, Yasir, 38
  and the Arab peace plan, 94–95
  diplomacy of, 45, 67(n83), 71–72, 89, 96–97, 100, 121, 130–31, 143, 146, 155, 208, 223, 226–27, 242, 243. *See also*

257

Index

Arafat-Hussein accord;
Jordanian-PLO dialogue
and Egyptian reconciliation,
178–84
erosion of support for, 105,
142–52, 161–62, 177–78,
180–82
and Hussein, 126–27, 185–89,
205–7
and the 1984 PNC meeting,
197–98, 201–2
and PLO divisions, 87, 91, 142,
232, 240
reaction to the Fatah rebellion,
152–54, 156–58, 167
return to Lebanon of, 167,
168–72
and the Soviet Union, 55
support for, 92, 127–28, 139–40,
159, 165, 179, 182–84, 198,
239
and Syria, 98, 99, 100, 154–55
See also Fatah; Palestine
Liberation Organization
Arens, Moshe, 13
Assad, Hafez al-
and Arafat, 98, 99, 154–55,
215–16
and the Palestinian cause, 215,
216–17
reaction to Lebanon War, 37, 42
See also Syria
Awdeh, Adnan Abu, 123

Baddawi, al-, 170
Baz, Usama al-, 180, 217
Begin, Menachem, 5, 32
and Israeli-United States
relations, 11, 48, 53
and the Lebanon War, 13, 14, 15,
16
policy of, 3, 7, 12
reaction to Reagan initiative, 76,
77
See also Israel
Ben Alisar, Eliahu, 77

Berri, Nabih, 150
Brezhnev, Leonid, 55, 58, 109
Brzezinski, Zbigniew, 75

Cairo Agreement, 4
Camp David accords
and Arab division, 8, 119
and Egypt, 44, 95, 96, 104
and Israel, 7, 17, 76
and the Palestinians, 109, 237
Carter, Jimmy, 7, 73, 243
Chamoun, Camille, 5
Christian Maronites, 4–5, 6
Christian Phalange party
Israeli support for, 4–5, 16,
24–25(n51)
Citizens Rights movement, 223
Clark, William, 53
Committee for the Defense of Arab
Land, 30
Committee of Solidarity with
Birzeit University, 28

Dayan, Moshe, 7
Democratic Alliance
and the Arafat-Hussein accord,
228
and the 1984 PNC meeting, 198,
200, 201
and PLO reconciliation efforts,
190, 191–97, 228, 233
possible future of, 234
Democratic Front for the
Liberation of Palestine, 102,
117, 225
and the Arab peace plan, 91
and Arafat, 169, 178, 181–82, 188
efforts to unify the PLO, 189,
195–96, 201, 230, 233–34
and the Fatah rebellion, 161–64
the future of the, 228
and Israeli peace groups, 105
and the Jordanian-PLO dialogue,
129, 211, 230
and the Reagan initiative, 102–3
and rejectionism, 101, 212

Druckman, Rabbi Chaim, 77
Druze militia, 168, 229

Eban, Abba, 30, 220–21
Economic sanctions, 38, 58, 62
Egypt, 113(n33)
 Arafat's reconciliation with, 178–84
 Egyptian-French peace plan, 46, 62, 121
 future role in Palestinian problem, 231
 and Jordan, 214
 on the Jordanian-PLO dialogue, 133, 207
 and the Lebanon War, 13, 40, 44–46
 and the PLO, 45, 95–96, 100, 104, 106, 149, 154, 177–78, 198, 226, 235, 237
 and the PNC, 109, 199, 200
 separation from Arab world, 7–8, 20, 36, 43–44, 178, 179, 184, 214
 and the Soviet Union, 57
 and Syria, 166, 216, 217
 and Western Europe, 220
 See also Mubarak, Husni
Egyptian-Israeli peace treaty, 36, 44, 243
 Arab reaction to, 8, 119
 and the Palestinians, 45, 95, 104
Eitan, Rafael
 foreign policy of, 12, 13, 15, 18
European Economic Community (EEC), 58–61, 220

Fahd, Crown Prince (Saudi Arabia), 170–71
 peace plan of, 9, 19, 39, 81
Fahum, Khaled al-, 158, 194, 198
 Arafat's reconciliation with Egypt and, 181, 182, 183
Faisal, Saud al-, 38, 171
Falkland Islands, 9
Fatah, 54, 116
 influence in PLO, 91–92, 139–40
 internal divisions in the, 87, 89, 91, 95, 102, 111, 136, 140–42, 182. *See also* Fatah rebellion
 and the Islamic movement, 238–40
 moderation in the, 117
 and the rejectionists, 102
 and Syria, 193, 232
 See also Arafat, Yasir; Fatah Central Committee; Palestine Liberation Organization
Fatah Central Committee
 and Arafat's reconciliation with Egypt, 179, 181, 182–83
 and the Fatah rebellion, 157–58, 160–61, 163–64
 future diplomatic efforts of, 226
 and militarism, 229–30
 and PLO unity efforts, 189, 190, 191–93, 196–97, 201, 230, 234
 reaction to Arafat-Hussein accord, 207–8, 209–10
Fatah rebellion, 139, 152–54, 155–57
 and Arabian mediation efforts, 166–68
 and Arafat's return to Lebanon, 168–72
 causes of the, 142, 143–52
 and Palestinian mediation efforts, 157–65
 and pan-Arabism, 237
Fraij, Elias, 164
France
 and Arafat's departure from Tripoli, 171
 Egyptian-French peace plan, 46, 62, 121
 Middle East policy of, 9–10, 61–62
 reactions to the Lebanon War, 60–63
Franjieh, Sulaiman, 150
Front for Democracy and Equality, 28

Front of Steadfastness and
   Confrontation States, 9, 110
   establishment of, 7, 8, 22(n15)
   Palestinian criticisms of the, 34,
     98

Galilee region, 7, 30–31
Gaza Strip, 5, 7, 11, 17–18, 19–20
   and the Arab peace plan, 80
   and the Arafat-Hussein accord,
     208, 210
   and Arafat's reconciliation with
     Egypt, 183–84
   the Islamic movement within the,
     236, 238–40
   Israeli settlement in the, 76, 108,
     111, 123, 132, 187, 238
   and the Jordanian-PLO dialogue,
     127–28
   militarism in the, 101, 106,
     234–35
   and the PLO, 110, 117–18, 126,
     201–2, 225, 227, 233, 241, 242
   reaction to the Fatah rebellion,
     164–65
   reaction to the Lebanon War, 27,
     33–35, 64(n26), 65(n34)
   and the Reagan initiative, 75, 78
   and Syria, 165
   See also Palestinian nationalism;
     Palestinian state
Gemayal, Amin, 25(n51), 149, 229
Gemayal, Bashir, 25(n51), 82
Gemayal, Pierre, 5
Geva, Eli, 29
Ghali, Boutros, 47, 179
Golan Heights
   and the Arab peace plan, 80, 81
   Israeli annexation of the, 9, 11,
     12
   Syria and the, 79, 134, 155, 216,
     217
Goshe, Samir Abu, 129
Greece
   and Arafat, 71, 171, 172
   reaction to the Lebanon War,
     60–61

Gromyko, André, 54
Gulf Cooperation Council, 40,
   66(n47)

Habash, George, 102, 103, 107, 234
   and Arafat's reconciliation with
     Egypt, 181, 182, 183
   and the Fatah rebellion, 162–63,
     164
   and the Jordanian-PLO dialogue,
     128, 211, 212
   and PLO reconciliation efforts,
     189, 190
   See also Popular Front for the
     Liberation of Palestine
Habib, Philip, 7, 13, 37, 42, 49
Haddad, Sa'ad, 6
Haig, Alexander, 13, 47, 48
   and U.S. foreign policy, 11, 53
Hajem, Abu, 143, 157
Hamid, Hayel Abd al-, 208
Hassan, Crown Prince (Jordan),
   122
Hassan, Hani al-, 208
Hassan, Khaled al-, 97, 171,
   174(n43), 208
Hassan, King (Morocco), 80, 136
Hawatmeh, Nayef, 102, 105–6, 234
   and Arafat, 182, 183
   and the Arafat-Hussein accord,
     230
   and the Fatah rebellion, 162–63,
     164
   and the Jordanian-PLO dialogue,
     129
   and PLO reconciliation efforts,
     189, 195
   and the Soviet Union, 54–55
   on Syria, 107
   See also Democratic Front for
     the Liberation of Palestine
Hikmat, Taher, 205
Holland, 60
Hussein, King (Jordan), 243
   and the Arab peace plan, 80, 81
   as leader of the Palestinians, 115,
     117, 122, 124

and negotiations with
Palestinians, 103, 126–27, 130,
184–89, 205–7, 209, 242
and the 1982 PNC communiqué,
111
peace proposal of, 199–200, 201,
205, 219
reaction to the Lebanon War, 36,
42
and the Reagan initiative, 78,
88–89, 121
See also Arafat-Hussein accord;
Jordan; Jordanian-PLO
dialogue
Hussein, Saddam, 8

Iran
Islamic revolution in, 8, 238
and the PLO, 134, 197
and Syria, 214, 216
See also Iraq-Iran War
Iraq
acceptance of PLO evacuees, 41,
43
and the 1970 Jordanian civil war,
141
and other Arab countries, 39, 216
and the PLO, 142, 197, 198, 226
and Syria, 7, 166
See also Iraq-Iran War
Iraq-Iran War, 133
Arab reaction to the, 9, 36, 38,
39, 213, 214
the PLO and the, 154
Islamic movement
and Iran, 8, 214
and the National Alliance, 228
and the PLO, 224, 236, 238–40
Islamic Unification Movement, 169,
170, 228
Isma'il, Haj, 143–44, 157
Israel
and the Arafat-Hussein accord,
220–23
and Arafat's departure from
Tripoli, 171–72

and Arafat's reconciliation with
Egypt, 180
domestic considerations of,
27–35, 222, 240
and the Hussein peace proposal,
219
and the Jordanian-PLO dialogue,
132, 206, 207, 212
and the Lebanese Christians,
4–5, 6, 12, 13, 16, 24–25(n51)
and the Lebanon War, 3, 8,
11–22, 25(n53), 28, 240–41
militarism of, 6, 7, 12, 57, 60,
213
and the 1978 invasion of
Lebanon, 5–6, 7, 22(n10), 142
and the PLO, 4–5, 6–7, 18–19,
93, 96–97, 221, 223, 226, 229,
230
policy on occupied territories,
132, 198, 221–23, 242–43
and the Reagan initiative, 76–78,
132
and Syria, 6, 7, 51
and the United States, 11–12,
20–21, 23(n27), 49–50, 219
Israeli Communist party, 28, 223
Israeli peace groups, 223
and the 1982 PNC communiqué,
109–10
the PLO and, 96, 100, 105, 147,
201
Italy, 71, 171
Iyad, Abu. *See* Khalaf, Salah

Jadid, Chadli Ben, 197, 217, 218
Jibril, Ahmed, 154
Jihad, Abu. *See* Wazir, Khalil al-
John Paul II, 71–72
Jordan
and Egypt, 214
and the Lebanon War, 36, 39, 40
national security of, 122–24, 133,
166
1970 civil war in, 3, 23(n27),
116, 141, 154, 237

as the Palestinian representative, 115–21, 126, 129, 177, 186, 206, 225–26, 231, 241–42
and the PLO, 90, 103, 106, 178, 226
and PLO evacuees from Beirut, 41, 42, 43, 124
PLO military presence in, 4, 116, 119, 120, 126, 141
and the PNC, 108–9, 197–98, 199, 201
and the Reagan initiative, 72, 74, 75, 78–79, 88–89, 123
and reconvening the Jordanian parliament, 186–87
and Syria, 166, 217, 232
and Western Europe, 220
See also Arafat-Hussein accord; Hussein, King; Jordanian-PLO dialogue
Jordanian-PLO dialogue, 121, 126–27, 166, 184–89
the Arab world on the, 133–35
breakdown in the, 127–36
Israel on the, 132
Jordanian motives for a, 121–25, 185
and the 1984 PNC meeting, 199–200
PLO motives for a, 63, 89, 100, 115, 120, 125–26, 185
role of Reagan initiative in the, 82–83, 94, 131
the Soviet Union and the, 135–36
the United States and the, 135
Jumblatt, Walid, 150

Karameh, Rashid, 169, 171
Khaddom, Abd al-Halim, 171, 194
Khalaf, Salah (Abu Iyad), 54, 199, 207–8
on Arafat's reconciliation with Egypt, 179, 182–83
and PLO internal divisions, 91, 142, 157, 196

and Syria, 98, 100, 153, 156, 170
Khaled, Abu. See Amleh, Khaled al-
Kirkpatrick, Jeane, 53
Kissinger, Henry, 117
Knesset, 30, 222

Labidi, Mahmoud al-, 171
Labor Alignment party, 30, 32, 77, 220–23
League of Heads of Arab Town Councils, 30
Lebanese Christian militia, 228, 229, 240–41
Lebanese National Salvation Front, 150
Lebanon
civil war in, 4, 237
government of, 16, 25(nn51 & 53), 39
and the PLO, 3–4, 87–88, 97, 105, 149–50, 152, 228–29, 235, 237
removal of foreign troops from, 104–5, 213
Shouf mountain fighting in, 168–72
societal divisions in, 4, 88, 240
and Syria, 241
See also Lebanon War
Lebanon War
causes of and preparations for the, 3, 8, 12–14
impact of the, xi, 120–21, 230–31, 240–41
international reaction to the, 27–33, 237
and the Islamic movement, 238
Israeli objectives in the, 14–22, 25(n53)
Levy, David, 29
Libya
and Algeria, 197
and the Arafat-Hussein accord, 213, 215
future role of, 231

and the Jordanian-PLO dialogue, 134
and the PLO, 92, 106, 150, 153–54, 159
reaction to the Lebanon War, 37–38, 39, 41, 120
Likud Coalition, 5, 29–30, 76–77, 221–23, 238, 242
Linowitz, Saul, 76
Litani River, 21

Mapam party, 77
Marxist-Leninist groups, 224–25, 234
Mazen, Abu, 207–8
Media
　Algerian, 218
　Arab, 41
　Israeli, 77–78
　Palestinian, in Israel, 34
　Soviet, 55
　Syrian, 156, 159, 182, 215
　United States, 52
Meir, Yahuda Ben, 76–77
Memorandum of Strategic Understanding and Cooperation, 10, 11, 21
Milhem, Muhammad, 201
Military struggle
　and Arab countries, 134
　and the Fatah dissidents, 145, 146, 150, 151
　Israel and, 12
　in the occupied territories, 101, 106, 234–35
　and the PLO, 3, 5, 88, 99, 110, 125, 126, 178, 201, 227, 229–30, 234–35, 237
　and the rejectionists, 97, 101, 106, 107
Milson, Menachem, 17
Mitterrand, François, 10, 62–63
Morocco, 197
Mubarak, Husni, 7–8, 44–46, 220
　and the PLO, 95, 109, 180, 181, 184

See also Egypt
Muhammad, Ali Nasser, 197
Musa, Abu, 95, 142, 151–52, 168, 228
　on the Arafat-Hussein accord, 211, 212
　and the Fatah rebellion, 143, 144, 145, 147, 155, 160, 167, 190

Nahr al-Bared, 170
National Alliance
　and the Arafat-Hussein accord, 211–12
　and intimidation, 227–28
　and the 1984 PNC meeting, 198, 201
　and PLO unity, 190–91, 194, 234
　See also Rejectionists
National Liberals, 5
Natshe, Rafiq al-, 157, 207–8
Nidal, Abu, 141, 155
　and the assassination of Sartawi, 96, 143
　and intimidation, 227
Ni'man Eval, 21
1973 October War, the, 20, 117, 141, 236
1967 June War, the, 3, 23(n27), 116, 236
North Yemen, 41

Occupied territories. *See* Gaza Strip; West Bank
Oil
　as a political weapon, 38, 214
Organization of Petroleum Exporting Countries (OPEC), 38

Palestine
　an Islamic state in all, 239
　the liberation of all, 3, 147, 152, 206
Palestine Central Council (PCC), 90, 91, 112(n6)
　and the Arab peace plan, 95

efforts to unify PLO, 159–61, 167, 195, 197
and the Jordanian-PLO dialogue, 129
Palestine Communist party, 181, 211, 228
and PLO unity efforts, 189–90, 195, 230, 233
Palestine Liberation Front, 211, 228
and PLO unity efforts, 189, 195, 233
Palestine Liberation Organization (PLO)
in Arab countries, 3–4, 87–88, 177, 233
and the Arab peace plan, 94–95
consequences of the Lebanon War for, xi, 34–35, 63, 71–72, 87–91, 101, 108, 139, 230–31, 241
economics of the, 119, 140
efforts to unify the, 189–96, 232–34. See also Fatah Central Committee
and Egyptian diplomacy, 95–96, 177–78
evacuation from Beirut of the, 40, 41–43, 45, 146
internal divisions in the, 82, 87, 89–91, 108, 111, 119, 128–31, 157, 180–83, 200–201, 226, 237. See also Fatah rebellion
and Islamic groups, 224
and Israel, 96–97, 110, 223
and Jordan, 178. See also Arafat-Hussein accord; Jordanian-PLO dialogue
and the Lebanon War, 13–14, 145
and Marxist-Leninist groups, 224–25
moderation in the, 18–19, 33, 67(n83), 91–101, 117, 207, 242–43
and the Reagan initiative, 74, 90, 93–94, 125
relationship with Arab countries, 39–40, 44–46, 81, 89, 92, 230–31
and the Soviet Union, 54–55, 57–58, 99
support for and recognition of the, 3, 19, 24(n37), 92, 116–18, 121–22, 140, 146, 206, 225, 241–42
and Syria, 97–100, 129, 134, 150–51, 154–55, 159, 177, 205, 217
and the United States, 93, 94, 111, 130
and Western Europe, 59, 62, 63, 220
See also Arafat, Yasir; Military struggle; *PLO factions and political organizations*; Rejectionists
Palestine Liberation Organization Executive Committee, 91, 169
and the Arafat-Hussein accord, 208–9
committee to mediate the Fatah rebellion, 158–59
and the 1984 PNC meeting, 201
pressure on, to oust Arafat, 181, 182
Palestine National Council (PNC), 87, 90, 91, 102, 117, 118
and the Arab peace plan, 95
and Arafat, 169, 178, 181, 182, 188, 189, 210
and Jordan, 119–20, 129
1982 communiqué of the, 108–11
and the 1984 meeting of the, 193–95, 196, 197–202
Palestine National Front, 106, 114(n37), 118
Palestine Popular Struggle Front (Popular Struggle Front), 101, 102
and the Arab peace plan, 104
and Fatah, 153, 154, 182
and the Jordanian-PLO dialogue, 129

and a Palestine National Front, 190
and the Reagan initiative, 102–3
Palestinian-Israeli 1981 cease-fire agreement, 7, 13–14, 19, 142
Palestinian nationalism, 3, 71, 110–11, 117–18, 129, 130, 141
  Israel and, 17–18, 22, 33–34, 65(n28)
  in Jordan, 36
  success of, 237–38
  See also Palestine; Palestinian state
Palestinian National Salvation Front, 212, 226
  possible tactics of the, 227–28
Palestinian refugees
  and the Arafat-Hussein accord, 205
  in Jordan, 116
  in Lebanon, 4, 30, 88, 97, 145, 149, 150, 171, 228, 238
  and the rejectionists, 102
Palestinian state
  confederation with Jordan, 205, 206, 208, 231, 242, 243(n1)
  Israeli support for, 28, 30–31, 32
  provisional government for a, 148
  support for, in occupied territories, 147, 148, 237
Pan-Arabism
  effectiveness of, 236–37
  future role in the Palestinian problem, 231
  rejectionists and, 105, 106
Peace Now movement, 28, 31–32
Perez, Shimon, 30, 77
  policies of, 222, 242
Poland, 9, 58
Popular Front for the Liberation of Palestine, 101, 225
  and the Arab peace plan, 91, 95
  and Arafat, 169, 178, 181–82, 188
  and Fatah divisions, 141, 161–64
  the future of the, 228
  and the Jordanian-PLO dialogue, 128, 211–12

and PLO reconciliation efforts, 189, 191, 193–94, 195–96, 201, 234
and Syria, 212
Popular Front for the Liberation of Palestine General Command, 101
  and the Arab peace plan, 95, 104
  and Fatah divisions, 141, 153, 154, 182, 190
  and the Jordanian-PLO dialogue, 128–29
Progressive Party for Peace, 223

Qaddafi, Mu'ammar al-, 37, 197
Qadoumi, Farouq al-, 54, 93, 157, 207–8
Qawasmi, Fahd, 201, 213
Quayk, Samih (Qadri), 143, 161

Rabat Resolution
  Jordan on the, 130, 185, 186, 187, 225
  and the PLO, 129
Rabin, Yitzhak, 32
Reagan initiative, 46, 71, 72–73, 74–75, 121
  Arab reaction to the, 78–83, 121, 123, 180
  Israeli reaction to the, 76–78, 132, 180
  Palestinian reaction to the, 78, 88–89, 90, 93–94, 100, 125, 128
  and the PNC communiqué, 109
  and the rejectionists, 102–3
  role in the Jordanian-PLO dialogue, 82–83, 94, 131, 206
  United States backing of the, 135
  United States domestic reaction to the, 75–76
Reagan, Ronald
  and the Lebanon War, 40, 47, 48, 49, 50, 51
  Middle East policy of, 8, 10–11, 53

responsiveness to the Israeli-PLO conflict, 7, 135, 243
See also Reagan initiative; United States, the
Rejectionist Front, 141
Rejectionists
on the Arab peace plan, 103-4
and the Arab world, 106-7, 119
and Fatah, 160, 229
on Fatah's diplomatic efforts, 103, 104, 128, 134, 208, 211-13
on Israeli peace groups, 105
militarism of the, 97, 101, 106, 107
in the postwar era, 101-8
on the Reagan initiative, 102-3
and Syria, 107-8, 155
See also PLO rejectionist organizations

Sabra massacre, 33, 82
PLO reactions to the, 90, 94, 97, 143
Sadat, Anwar al-, 7
Saguy, Yehoshua, 13
Sa'iqa, al-, 101
and Fatah, 105, 153, 154, 173(n33), 182, 190, 201
moderation in the, 117
Saleh, Abu. *See* Saleh, Nimr
Saleh, Nimr (Abu Saleh)
and the Arab peace plan, 95, 143, 149
and the Fatah rebellion, 161
and PLO internal divisions, 91, 142
Sartawi, Issam, 96, 130, 143
Saudi Arabia
on Egypt, 214
influence of, 20, 214-15
on the Jordanian-PLO dialogue, 133, 207
and the PLO, 89, 106, 149, 166-67, 170-71, 226
response to the Lebanon War, 38, 39, 40, 43

and Syria, 133-34, 214
Sayeh, Shaikh Abdul Hamid al-, 201
Schultz, George
and the Reagan initiative, 73, 74
and United States Middle East policy, 48-49, 54, 67(n80)
Seelye, Talcott, 75-76
Sha'ban, Shaikh Sa'id, 170
Shak'a, Bassam al-, 184
Shamir, Yitzhak, 12, 19
on the Arafat-Hussein accord, 221
on Jordan, 122-23
and the United States, 53, 73-74
Sharon, Ariel, 17, 47, 76, 226
on Jordan, 122-23
and the Lebanon War, 12, 13, 15, 16, 20, 24(n41)
popularity of, 29, 32
Shatilla massacre, 33, 82
PLO reactions to the, 90, 94, 97, 143
Shawa, Rashad al-, 127-28, 184
Sheli party, 28
Shi'a, the, 240
Shi'ite Amal, 6, 150, 228, 229, 238, 240
Shintov, Victor, 77
Shouf mountains, 168-72
Skandar, Ahmad, 134
South Yemen
and the Arafat-Hussein accord, 213, 215
efforts to unify PLO, 166-67, 189, 191, 192, 196, 197, 233
reaction to the Lebanon War, 41
and the rejectionists, 106
Soviet Union, the
and the Arab peace plan, 81
Arab reactions to, 9, 10, 57, 214
and the Hussein peace proposal, 187
Middle East policy of, 27, 43, 54-55, 56-57, 68(n100), 217, 219-20

Index   267

and military assistance to Syria
  and the PLO, 15, 135–36, 155
and the PLO, 54–55, 57–58, 99,
  195
and the United States, 55–56,
  135, 219–20
Strategic consensus, 10–11, 72
Sudan, 41
Sunni militia, 229
Syria
  acceptance of PLO evacuees, 41,
    42–43, 56, 151
  on the Aden-Algiers Agreement,
    194
  and the Arab peace plan, 81
  and the Arafat-Hussein accord,
    213, 215–17
  and Arafat's return to Lebanon,
    168–72, 229
  future role of, 231, 243
  and Iraq, 7
  and Israel, 6, 7, 51
  and Jordan, 118, 134–35, 232
  and Lebanon, 4, 5, 6, 141, 154,
    237, 241
  and the Lebanon War, 15, 37,
    40, 41, 65(n38), 98, 120
  and the PLO, 92, 97–100, 116,
    129, 134, 143, 150–51, 154–55,
    159, 177, 193, 232
  the PLO within, 4, 107, 151
  and the PNC, 110, 196, 198, 199,
    200
  reaction to the Reagan initiative,
    79
  and the rejectionists, 106, 107–8,
    162–64, 227
  role in the Fatah rebellion,
    152–54, 155–56, 158–59, 167
  and Saudi Arabia, 133–34, 214
  and the Soviet Union, 135–36

Terrorism, 11, 227–28
Tripoli, 169–72
Tunisia, 41, 42, 197
Tzwpuri, Mordichai, 29–30

United Arab Kingdom, 117
United Nations (UN)
  and the Arab peace plan, 81
  and the Arafat-Hussein accord,
    205
  and Arafat's departure from
    Tripoli, 171, 172
  and Hussein peace proposal, 187,
    199
  and the Lebanon War, 5–6, 7,
    40–41
  and the PLO, 92, 140
  United States vetoes in the, 48,
    67(n75)
United States, the
  commitment to Middle East
    peace, 135, 198, 243
  diplomatic ineffectiveness of, 132,
    135, 187–88
  and Egypt, 44–45, 46
  foreign policy of, 10–12, 20–21,
    50–52, 218–20, 243
  foreknowledge of the Lebanon
    War, 13, 24(n43), 47–48
  and Israel, 3, 20–21, 23(n27),
    49–50, 132, 219
  and Jordan, 123, 219
  on the Jordanian-PLO dialogue,
    207, 212, 218
  marines in Lebanon, 49, 51,
    55–56, 188
  and Middle East peace
    initiatives, 7, 8, 57, 210, 226.
    See also Reagan initiative
  and the PLO, 49, 67(n82), 93,
    94, 111, 130, 146, 151, 206,
    232
  reaction to the Lebanon War, 27,
    32, 48–54, 67(n75)
  and Saudi Arabia, 214
  and the Soviet Union, 219–20
  and Syria, 217
  See also Reagan, Ronald

Village Council Leagues, 17, 241

Walid, Abu al-, 155

Wazir, Khalil al- (Abu Jihad), 130, 145, 167, 174(n43)
  and the Arafat-Hussein accord, 208
  and the Hussein peace proposal, 199
  and Palestinians in Lebanon, 97, 149
  and PLO reconciliation efforts, 192
  on a provisional government for a Palestinian state, 148
  and Syria, 97–98, 100, 171
Weinberger, Caspar, 53–54, 73
Weizman, Ezer, 5, 7
West Bank, 5, 7, 11, 17–18, 19–20
  and the Arab peace plan, 80
  and the Arafat-Hussein accord, 208, 210
  and Arafat's reconciliation with Egypt, 183–84
  Islamic movement within, 236, 238–40
  Israeli settlement in the, 76, 108, 111, 123, 132, 187, 222, 238
  and Jordan, 116, 121, 122, 133, 147, 186, 225, 235
  and the Jordanian-PLO dialogue, 127–28
  militarism in the, 101, 106, 234–35
  and the PLO, 110, 117–18, 126, 201–2, 225, 227, 233, 241, 242
  reaction to the Fatah rebellion, 164–65
  reaction to the Lebanon War, 27, 33–35, 64(n26), 65(n34)
  and the Reagan initiative, 75, 78
  and Syria, 165
  See also Palestinian nationalism; Palestinian state
Western Europe
  and Egypt, 46
  and the PLO, 71, 146
  reaction to the Lebanon War, 27, 58–63
  role in a Middle East peace, 207, 220
  and Saudi Arabia, 214
  See also European Economic Community
West Germany, 60

Yadin, Yigael, 7

Zionism, 147